Love and Fury: the Extraordinary Life, Death and Legacy of

joe Meek

Having hosted the Radio 2 documentary Holloway Dreams back in 2007, I thought I knew the Joe Meek story pretty well. Yet this sensitively researched new biography is packed with fresh twists and surprises. Best of all was the fascinating final chapter detailing the human and musical fallout from Joe's catastrophic implosion in February 1967 – and the way its consequences have continued to spread in unexpected ways across the five following decades. Tragic and uplifting by turns – *Love and Fury* is a wonderful read.

Tom Robinson

A searching, in-depth portrayal of Joe Meek, the tempestuous pop genius who, with his electronic effects and echo units, single-handedly changed the independent pop landscape in the UK. Drawing from detailed research, fresh interviews and eye-witness accounts, Bullock's book presents Meek as a tortured, troubled yet gifted soul. It also investigates fifties and sixties gay culture in the music industry, at a time when homosexuality was illegal, and the impact such legislation had on so many lives. A tragic story, vividly told."

Lucy O'Brien, music journalist,
author of *Lead Sister: The Story of Karen Carpenter*

The definitive biography of one of the leading lights of the 1960s music scene, this splendidly written book dispels many rumours and myths to unravel the mystery of the man and his music.

John Pickford, producer of *The Joe Meek Story*

Love and Fury is an incredibly well-crafted biography. I struggled to put it down... the attention to detail is staggering. Despite being a Meek Freak for thirty years, I've still learnt plenty of new information.

Craig Newton, the Joe Meek Society

Love and Fury: the Extraordinary Life, Death and Legacy of

Joe Meek

⬅ **DARRYL W BULLOCK** ➡

OMNIBUS PRESS
London / New York / Paris / Sydney / Copenhagen / Berlin / Madrid / Tokyo

For everyone whose lives were shattered by the events of
3 February 1967.

Copyright © 2025 Omnibus Press
(A division of the Wise Music Group
14–15 Berners Street, London, W1T 3LJ)

Cover designed by Fabrice Couillerot

ISBN 978-1-915841-24-7

Darryl W Bullock hereby asserts his right to be identified as the author of this work in accordance with Sections 77 to 78 of the Copyright, Designs and Patents Act 1988.

All rights reserved. No part of this book may be reproduced in any form or by any electronic or mechanical means, including information storage or retrieval systems, without permission in writing from the publisher, except by a reviewer who may quote brief passages.

Every effort has been made to trace the copyright holders of the photographs in this book but one or two were unreachable. We would be grateful if the photographers concerned would contact us.

Typeset by Evolution Design & Digital Ltd (Kent)
Printed in the Czech Republic.

A catalogue record for this book is available from the British Library.

Contents

Introduction		vii
Chapter 1	Country Boy	1
Chapter 2	Hobbies	11
Chapter 3	Keep Moving	21
Chapter 4	Please Let It Happen to Me	34
Chapter 5	You've Got to Have a Gimmick Today	45
Chapter 6	I Hear a New World	59
Chapter 7	I'm Waiting For Tomorrow	73
Chapter 8	Dreams Do Come True	85
Chapter 9	Time Will Tell	96
Chapter 10	Johnny Remember Me	109
Chapter 11	Can't You Hear the Beat	120
Chapter 12	Something Better Beginning	136
Chapter 13	Telstar	148
Chapter 14	There's Lots More Where This Came From	159
Chapter 15	Globetrotter	171
Chapter 16	Chills and Fever	185
Chapter 17	Just Like Eddie	198
Chapter 18	Boy Trouble	213
Chapter 19	Have I the Right?	229
Chapter 20	Questions I Can't Answer	242
Chapter 21	Nice While It Lasted	258
Chapter 22	Wipe Out	272
Chapter 23	Please Stay	287
Chapter 24	It's Hard to Believe It	302

Chapter 25	Nobody Waved Goodbye	318
Chapter 26	Guess That's the Way It Goes	330
Chapter 27	Don't You Know	338

Bibliography   351

Acknowledgements   353

Notes   355

Index   375

Introduction

In recent years there has been a flood of interest in the career of the British record producer, songwriter and recording engineer Joe Meek. A hit 2005 stage play, *Telstar*, spawned a successful film of the same name, and since then there have been boxed sets of previously unheard Meek-produced sessions, documentary films and a number of radio productions looking at different aspects of Meek's life and legacy. This upsurge shows no sign of abating. In October 2023 musician Jasper Marsalis (aka Slauson Malone 1) covered the title track from Meek's 1960 space opera, *I Hear a New World*, on his critically acclaimed album *Excelsior*, and the following month Micko & the Mellotronics issued their second album, *Le Vice Anglais*, featuring a tribute to Meek, 'Holloway Road'. In December, singer Ella Raphael released 'All In', a single which she described as being 'inspired by many greats such as Joe Meek',[1] and in the first half of 2024 there were more than half a dozen highly praised releases from the legendary Tea Chest tapes, the treasure trove of material that Meek left behind following the shocking events of 3 February 1967.

Meek was one of the pioneers of independent production in Britain, establishing one of Britain's earliest independent labels (the first to aim its output entirely at a brand new demographic: teenagers) and helping to create the blueprint for what would become the independent music industry. His output was phenomenal: between 1960 and 1967, he was involved in the production, engineering and/or composition of more than 250 singles, including forty UK Top 50 hits. That feat is even more incredible when you consider that he achieved it all working from a rundown flat above a leather goods shop on Holloway Road. Life for this perennial outsider was

Love and Fury: The Life, Death and Legacy of Joe Meek

fraught with problems: his first business partner was jailed for fraud, and at the height of his career he was taken to court and accused of plagiarism over his two biggest hits. He almost certainly suffered from undiagnosed mental health issues and was constantly beleaguered by financial pressure, yet somehow he still managed to engineer dozens of UK chart hits in the last half of the 1950s and write and produce the first US number 1 by a British band, more than a year before the Beatles began to dominate the stateside charts.

As a producer, Meek scored three number 1 singles in Britain and also had four chart toppers in Sweden, three in New Zealand and number 1 hits in America, Australia, Canada, France and several other territories. Today, artists and producers are still awestruck by his ability to conjure otherworldly sounds from his equipment fashioned, legend would have it, from a collection of rusty gate springs and broken radios. It's little wonder then that in 2012, the readers of the *New Musical Express* named Meek 'The Greatest Producer of All Time', beating the Beatles' musical maestro George Martin for the accolade and leaving the man he is most often compared to, Phil Spector, trailing in fifth position. As filmmaker Russell Caligari puts it, 'When you scratch below the surface of Joe Meek, you open up a universe.'[2] You can understand why, almost sixty years after his death, the maverick engineer, songwriter, artist manager and record producer still commands a loyal cult following.

Joe Meek was a man directed by his passions and obsessions. He held an ardent belief in life after death, to the point of being convinced that he was able to communicate with those who had passed on. His fascination with outer space and life on other planets is hardly surprising when you consider that his sexuality meant that he *was* an alien, and he would have grown up feeling as if, as far as polite British society and the law was concerned anyway, he was of an entirely different species to his family, his friends and most of the people he knew. 'It's true that a lot of what Joe did was about escapism from the real world,' Tornados' drummer Clem Cattini would later reflect. 'I think a lot of it was to do with his sexual you-know-what's... It was taboo then, you were drummed out of the world for that.'[3] He was fully aware that he was not like other people: in the 1950s and sixties, at a time when being gay could see you jailed (or worse: many homosexual men were institutionalised and forced to undergo shock 'therapy' or to

Introduction

take court-prescribed chemicals to lessen their libido), Meek lived openly as a gay man, unashamed and without compromise, until his arrest for cottaging and subsequent blackmail demands saw him thrust back into the closet, a move that would have a disastrous effect on his already fragile psyche.

Towards the end of his life, at a time when he became increasingly reliant on pep pills to get through the day, Meek was involved with shady characters from the criminal underworld; he was convinced that enemies inside the recording industry were after his production secrets, and he was worried that he would become implicated in the grisly murder of a young man he is alleged to have known. Mystery still surrounds his death. Although the official line is that he committed suicide after shooting dead Violet Shenton, his landlady, possibly while suffering from paranoid, drug-induced delusions, some who knew him are convinced to this day that he was the victim of a gangland hit.

There were two very different sides of Joe Meek: one was the pioneering genius who wrote and recorded some of the most influential pop music of all time, a man who – far from being thought of as an odd eccentric – was one of the most sought after writers, producers and engineers of the day, with recording artists, managers and record companies eager to benefit from his magic touch. The other was the man with the mercurial temper, who was finally brought down by his health issues and his constant financial battles. It is well documented that he often flew into blind rages which saw him hurl the nearest throwable article at his artists (and, it has been claimed, threaten more than one of them with a loaded gun *à la* Spector), but others attest to his gentle nature and his kindness: 'He was a great guy,' says his close friend Tony Grinham. 'It was a pleasure to know him.'[4] He was paranoid about people stealing his ideas, yet freely shared his experience and knowledge with those he trusted. He was serious, obsessed and laser-focused on his work, yet he could also be great fun to be around, cracking jokes and camping it up in the studio to break the tension. When he died, along with his released output he left a legacy of more than 1,860 reels of tape – the legendary Tea Chest tapes – long rumoured to include unreleased recordings by David Bowie, Marc Bolan, Ray Davies of the Kinks and others.

'Joe's been gone for almost sixty years now,' says filmmaker Howard S. Berger, 'so all we can do is listen to the ones who can relate their unique and

Love and Fury: The Life, Death and Legacy of Joe Meek

privileged and differing vantage points and try to get as complete a picture as we can. There will always be mysteries surrounding Joe, his work, his life and his death... But despite the highs and lows, we can piece together a somewhat celebratory mosaic that people who have both adored his music or those who have never heard of him can hopefully relate to and appreciate – and learn from.'[5]

Pioneer, genius, maniac, naïf. Meek was all of these things... and more.

CHAPTER 1

Country Boy

On the south side of the Gloucestershire market town of Newent lies a housing estate, Oak Park, made up of smart, brick-built houses overlooking the fields that the children of George and Biddy Meek played in almost a century ago. One cannot help but wonder what the family would have thought about the main residential street on that estate being called Meek Road, in tribute to the couple's middle son. No doubt they would have been amazed to hear that it was officially opened by broadcaster and radio DJ Mike Read and Joe's niece, Sandra, on the same day that a blue plaque marking Joe's place of birth was unveiled, just shy of his 82nd birthday.

Robert George Meek, known since birth by his family as Joe, was born on 5 April 1929, not in a hospital, as might be expected today, but at 1 Market Square in Newent, Gloucestershire, in the centuries-old Forest of Dean, a former hunting ground of kings and princes on the border between England and Wales. At the time of Joe's birth the population was less than 3,000, and everybody knew everybody. Settled since Roman times and mentioned in the Domesday Book, the ancient town had been the site of an important market since the 13th century and, like much of the Forest, has a past steeped in folklore, superstition and local ghost tales. Stories abound of grey ladies, ghostly publicans, deceased mill workers and spirits wandering the roads leading to the town; in adulthood Meek would enjoy telling these same tales to the friends he brought to visit the area. Heinz Burt, who would find fame first as a member of Meek's big hit act the Tornados and then as a star in his own right, would later recall one such incident: 'We were coming back [to London, via Gloucester] and the fog come down.

1

Love and Fury: The Life, Death and Legacy of Joe Meek

He said, "I love all this," and he started telling us these stories. He was on about a dog that had one leg cut off, somebody murdered somebody and [the dog] limped all the way to capture him... and about the ghost he'd seen on this road where a certain amount of accidents [had occurred] and he reckoned that people who had been in hospital had seen a woman who had walked out of the hedge... It felt really eerie, you know? You get these cold sweats... I literally went cold when he was telling these stories.'[6]

Joe was the second son of the four children of Alfred George Henry Meek (who from a child had been known as George) and Evelyn Mary 'Biddy' Birt. George was born, in 1896, in the nearby village of Aston Ingham, just over the county border in Herefordshire. Biddy – the nickname awarded because she was small and birdlike – was born in Westbury-on-Severn in 1901; a former school teacher, she had already given up her job when she and George wed, in Huntley (5 miles south of Newent), on 3 April 1927. Biddy's father, James, died that same year; her mother, Matilda, predeceased him by two years. Joe's eldest brother Arthur had been born in the same house in Market Square in 1928: the couple's third son, Eric, came along in 1932.

Standing proud behind the town's Tudor market hall, the house young Joe was born in – less than a ten-minute walk from what is now Meek Road – was rented from a local farmer, George Freeman, at the cost of £14 a year by his paternal grandparents, Charles and Lydia Meek. It was his grandmother who bestowed his familial nickname upon him, taken from his father's older brother, who had been killed at Ypres in October 1914 while serving in the Royal Engineers, an early British casualty of World War One. The war scarred the family deeply: another of Lydia's sons, Arthur (whose name would be handed down to George and Biddy's firstborn), would die in Flanders in 1917. Like his brothers, George Meek also saw action; he enlisted in September 1914 – within a month of England declaring war on Germany – alongside his brother Arthur. Serving as a driver in the Royal Field Artillery, in 1916 George was hospitalised with scabies, a painful parasitic infestation caused by mites that burrow into the skin and lay eggs, which was usually treated by the liberal application of a sulphurous ointment to the open sores. Two years later he was in hospital again, this time suffering from trench fever, another disease that was rife during the conflict, spread by lice. Having already lost two of her

Country Boy

children, George's mother petitioned his commanding officer to have her only remaining son repatriated. His distressing experiences during the war would inevitably affect him for the rest of his life: today we would recognise George Meek as suffering with post-traumatic stress disorder, or PTSD.

Following his discharge he dabbled in a number of different professions, but did not stick at one job for very long – bouts of illness and a quick temper meant that few were willing to take a risk in employing him. Short and stocky, at just five feet six inches tall, George Meek was often in trouble and not afraid to use his fists. His Napoleon complex saw him hauled into magistrates' court in 1930 following a violent altercation with Sid Matthews, the secretary of the Newent Pigeon Club: George had been in possession of a clock belonging to the club which had gone missing, and following an argument about who was liable for the cost of the timepiece, Meek struck Matthews, splitting his lip and knocking him to the ground. The Meek temper was infamous, and all three of his boys inherited their father's incendiary traits, but while Arthur and Eric vented their anger and frustrations in the fields and streams around the family home and used up any excess energy playing football and cricket with their friends, Joe did not enjoy those rough games. He was an indoor boy, who preferred the company of his mother or, better still, to be left alone to do his own thing. While Arthur and Eric were always out in the fields, climbing trees and playing with their friends, Joe was tied to his mother's apron strings, so much so that his brothers picked on him and called him 'sissy'.

It has often been said that Biddy Meek wanted a girl and for the first few years of Joe's life she brought him up as one, allowing his hair to grow long and keeping him in dresses. Years later, Joe would tell people that his upbringing had in some way influenced his homosexuality; however, in the early years of the 20th century it was not that unusual to see a boy of pre-school age wearing what appeared to be a frock: their practicality made nappy changing and toilet training easier, although once a boy started to play outside he would almost exclusively be seen in shorts and a shirt.

For a while George Meek ran a fish and chip shop at number 7 Church Street, delivered fresh fish from a van to his neighbours (he is listed as a 'fish merchant' on Joe's birth certificate) and when in season sold pints of elvers, a local delicacy. It was while they were in Church Street that Joe's youngest brother, Eric, was born. Sometime around 1933, George, Biddy

Love and Fury: The Life, Death and Legacy of Joe Meek

and their three boys moved to Churchdown in Gloucester, some 14 miles away from Newent. George had given up the fish business and had taken a job at a garage on Parton Road, and the family quickly became part of the local community. Biddy insisted that the children attend Sunday School (Arthur and Joe sang in the church choir), and on 31 May 1934 Joe appeared in his first concert, at the Mission Room in Churchdown. The two eldest Meek boys, alongside four other children, danced in costume to a song called 'Daffodils and Pixies', written and performed by a Miss E. Leach. The song was the hit of the show, and Miss Leach and the children were invited to perform it again a few weeks later, to help raise funds for the Mission Room's upkeep, at the nearby United Services Club.

Typically, George did not stay in Churchdown for long; he was not earning enough to keep his family (after being fined £1 for driving his car without a licence in October 1933, he had been unable to pay the full amount due and six months later was fined a further £1 for non-payment) and needed to rectify that. Ever on the lookout for the next opportunity, in the second half of 1934 he moved the family back to Newent, setting up home in Broad Street. For a while he worked as a light haulage contractor and made some extra money breeding greyhounds and racing pigeons: decades later youngest son Eric would become a highly respected breeder of champion greyhounds. George Meek had not been back in Newent long when he fell victim to an insurance fraudster, Henry William Pilgrim, who conned him out of £3 for a worthless policy for the haulage firm he and Biddy were running. At least this time there was no report of George having used his fists to exact revenge on the crooked Mr Pilgrim, who would be sent to prison for nine months' hard labour as a result of his fraud.

If Biddy had insisted that her blue-eyed boy be dressed as a girl, that finished with the birth of the only Meek girl, Pamela, whose arrival in 1934 completed the family. Luckily for him, this coincided with Joe starting at the Newent Public Elementary School, known as Picklenash, some ten minutes' walk from his grandmother's house in Market Square. Picklenash took local children from 4 years old and up, many of whom would go on – assuming that they passed the dreaded 11 Plus – to the local co-educational grammar school. School would encourage him to make friends with other local children, and although he was not much of a scholar, he was popular and his social circle expanded rapidly. The school was very community-

Country Boy

minded, and Joe and his new friends were encouraged to participate in the annual school show (which took place at the Newent Picture House each July) and in April's daffodil harvest, when thousands of the wild-growing blooms would be gathered by the town's children before being packed up and sent off to hospitals in London as a gift from the townsfolk.

Sometime late in 1935, the 6-year-old Joe saw a colourful toy record player in a local shop and begged his parents to buy it for him. On 25 December he was duly presented with a selection of fragile 78s and the coveted item, fashioned from brightly painted tin plate, which he later described as 'a toy gramophone with a celluloid sound box and a key to wind it up. I remember I had seen it in a shop window and asked for it for Christmas, and as quite often happened my wish came true and I got this with some children's records. I used to play this all the time and it was quite obvious to my parents that this fascinated me, and when I was 7 years old they bought me a proper gramophone.' This new acquisition, a portable, second-hand 78 player with a winding handle awakened something in the formerly quiet and introverted youngster, and he would spend hours in his own world, accompanied by his very own grown-up record player. 'I used to try and experiment with my gramophone,' he later revealed. 'I discovered that if you played a record at the end, the run out groove, and shout down the sound chamber then the sound would be imprinted in the grooves. I thought that I had discovered something marvellous, of course I was really just doing what Edison had discovered years before.'[7] Now, to the delight of his school friends, as well as playing with sound he began to make his own toys, crafting puppet theatres from shoe boxes, and would put on shows for the local kids, charging them a ha'penny to come and see his magic lantern slides, or to watch him perform in his one-man, self-written pantomimes.

The following year, George satiated his middle son's growing fascination with sound by paying for a subscription to *Practical Wireless* magazine for his birthday: 'After that,' his brother Eric recalled, 'he never did anything else bar fiddle with wirelesses, records or music in general.'[8] The purchase paid dividends: one of the first things Joe built was a small crystal radio receiver, a simple device cobbled together from bits and pieces hanging around the home but that could only be listened to through an earpiece. This was soon followed by a valve-driven radio, complete with its own amplifier and speaker, something that the whole family could enjoy.

Love and Fury: The Life, Death and Legacy of Joe Meek

As well as his haulage business, George Meek was also dealing in fruit and vegetables, buying up crops from local producers and selling them on at Gloucester market and making and selling his own cider. This new business soon became all-consuming, and it would be as a greengrocer, wholesale fruiterer and manager of several acres of farmland he would prove most successful, although even then he still found time to get into trouble with the law, and in July 1937 – while still living in Church Street – both of Joe's parents appeared in court. Biddy was fined £1, plus £3/11 costs (which she paid off at five shillings a month), after she had been caught driving their van without the proper licence. George was charged with the same offence six weeks later.

The move back to Newent, and George's subsequent success in the fruit and veg business, was prescient. Joe was just 10 years old when, in September 1939, Britain declared war on Germany following Hitler's invasion of Poland, and by the start of the following year rationing was introduced, meaning that most of the families in the country had to contend with strict rules that governed how much food they could buy and share each week. The Meek family, with their land, fruit, vegetables and poultry, thrived: although farming was soon declared a reserved occupation, the Meek boys were too young to be called up anyway, and George was precluded from active service because of his health. Over the next few years Meek Senior was able to increase the amount of land he and his family worked, and he expanded his business from dealing in fruit and veg to buying and selling horses, livestock and timber, and even dealing in property: Joe would later describe his father as 'an estate agent'. All in all, the Meek family had a pretty good, typically bucolic life.

When Joe did venture outside, it was usually in the company of his friends Gerald Beachus, whose father ran the local garage, and Eric Freeman, whose family owned the house he was born in and whose father sold his annual crop of cherries to George Meek. The boys called themselves the Market Square Gang, just kids hanging around, playing Cowboys and Indians, their games influenced by the movies and film serials they saw at the Plaza Talkie Theatre on Culver Street, formerly known as the Newent Picture House. Occasionally Joe would bring his magic lantern to Gerald's home – a flat above the garage – and put on a show: Eric, whose father ran

Country Boy

a small dairy farm and used to deliver milk around the town by horse and cart, remembered that the first time he saw Mickey Mouse was at one of Joe's magic lantern shows in the flat over the Beachuses' business when the boys were around 12 years old. From there Joe progressed into playing with cine film and was soon the proud owner of his own 8 mm camera.

With another friend, Pete Constable, he would spend hours in the woods around Newent trying to capture the sound of wildlife on his portable reel-to-reel tape recorder, sending Pete up into the trees armed with a microphone in an attempt to record birdsong. Eric Meek remembered that 'he'd always been interested in weird sounds. He had us doing all sorts to get weird sounds on tracks for him. He used to get up at three o'clock in the morning and put microphones out on the wall so that he could record early morning birds singing; he'd have me spinning round the corners [on my bike] and ripping on the brakes and that, and smashing glass to make the smash of a car, and things like this.' 'He was very gimmicky,' the usually taciturn Arthur Meek added. 'A lot of his records were gimmicky... they had a funny start to them, or a funny finish.' 'He was always drawn to weirdness, you know,' Eric added. 'Like in Dracula films... he was always interested in the weird noises.'[9]

One day, playing outside with the rest of the Market Square Gang, Joe found an incendiary grenade in a cattle pen at the town's livestock market, which had been left behind by the local Home Guard, the volunteer force who held training exercises there. Joe decided to try and dismantle the phosphorus-filled weapon by hitting it against the iron bars of a cattle pen and badly burned his hands as a result. Rushed to his grandmother's house, a local doctor suggested that the badly shaken boy should bathe his hands in a bowl of milk: the lactic acid would gently remove the dead skin from the top of the burns and antioxidants in the milk would help reduce inflammation. Following a similar incident in May 1945, ten youngsters (with an average age of 10) from the Forest of Dean were brought up in front of magistrates at the Littledean Juvenile Court, charged with stealing detonators, grenades and other devices from an American depot, and one of the boys 'suffered injuries to his hand when one of the fuses exploded and he had to be taken to Gloucester Infirmary'. Said the chairman of the magistrate's bench, 'The results of this may have been terrible. These boys had no business picking up things that did not belong to them. We have been told not to handle things like these which may have been connected with the war.'[10] If only Joe had heeded the warning. 'He was very, very fortunate,' Eric added. 'The doctor said he would never use his hands again; he burned both his hands right down to the bones. Doctor Johnson treated him for two years... he couldn't move his fingers at all for about nine months, but after that he used to make him do it, the doctor did make him work his hands... He was very fortunate and I think we've only got Doctor Johnson to thank for that.'[11]

This fascination with taking things to bits became an obsession: while recovering Joe would stay in his room or, later, in one of the outhouses in his grandmother's backyard, where he would play endlessly with his records and tinker with any odd bits of electrical equipment he could get hold of. He made his own microphone, using an old bicycle lamp for the housing and conduit pipe to hold the wiring in place. As his father's business flourished the family took on a small shop in the town, 1 High Street, on the corner of Watery Lane and next door to the busy Street's Garage, and the family moved into the accommodation above the store. Primarily selling fruit and vegetables, 'the shop was full of everything under the sun,' Eric Meek recalled. Joe loved to spend time there, playing with whatever he could put his hands on and recording the sounds he made on his tape recorder. 'He was never happier than when he could get somebody in to make a noise, in there, that he could record.'[12]

Intense and secretive, when Joe got an idea into his head there was no shaking it. A fleeting interest in something would quickly turn into a passion, and those passions soon became obsessions. 'I thought he was a nutter,' his brother Eric candidly revealed, 'because he used to do weird things.' Joe would hide microphones around the house and record his family, and visitors, going about their daily routine, and he took great delight in playing embarrassing or funny snippets to them later. 'He'd play it back to us and you would hear us swearing away,' Eric laughed. 'We had some wonderful moments with him.'[13] His niece Sandra, Pamela's daughter, relayed a story she had been told about Joe's secret recordings: 'Nan had a friend that used to come round who used to moan about her husband, and when the husband [came] to pick his wife up Joe would play it back!'[14] It was a habit he would continue throughout his life, and on later visits to the family he would often be caught fiddling around in his pocket, where he had secreted a hand-held tape recorder to capture conversations and embarrass those present.

His family might have thought him weird, but his rapidly-expanding personal sound effects library came in useful when he was called on to produce soundscapes for local theatre productions. Joe recalled that '[when] I was about 16, I used to provide music for local amateur dramatic societies; I remember plays like *The Ghost Train* [written in 1923 by the actor Arnold Ridley, who would find fame in his later years as Private Godfrey in the situation comedy *Dad's Army*], and *The Poltergeist* [by Frank Harvey, written in 1946 and adapted the following year for the film *Things Happen at* Night] and lots of plays, and I used to go out of my way to provide the right sort of music for them and the right sound effects.' The town was home to both the Newent Amateur Dramatic Society and the Newent Amateur Operatic Society, and both produced their performances on stage at the Plaza cinema.

Many in the local community would call on him to help them out, and if a local good cause or charity organisation needed help with a project, young Joe Meek was usually first in line to lend a hand – an act of largesse he would continue for the rest of his life. On family trips to Gloucester he would search out shops that sold second-hand records, spending all of his money on his expanding collection: 'I regularly toured junk shops for old 78s,' he explained. 'At 12, I was a serious collector, specialising in records by dance bands. This was during the war, and they were pretty scarce.'[15] Trying to find a way to get more volume out of his equipment, he made his first valve-driven amplifier, but finding that too primitive he sold his treasured cine camera to raise the funds for a shop-bought version, spending a massive £7/10 on this coveted piece of hardware. This extravagance allowed Joe to build his own PA system, and he was soon organising dances at the village hall, charging people a few pennies to come and listen to his discs, easily the most comprehensive record collection in the area. 'The war was on at that time,' he recalled. 'I used to play records for dancing to, mainly [dance band leader] Victor Silvester and different records that were very popular then. I think that this was when I began to get an ear for the type of music the public liked. Something with a good, solid rhythm and with a tune forced home... I soon found that my entertaining with gramophone records became very popular around Gloucestershire, and I was in pretty big demand.'[16]

Love and Fury: The Life, Death and Legacy of Joe Meek

Although the villages of the Forest of Dean were not an obvious target during World War Two, several German planes crashed and a few bombs fell from above, much of that excess ammunition dumped by the Nazis fleeing the skies above blitz-besieged Bristol, Gloucester and Cheltenham. Many sites in Gloucestershire had been earmarked by German reconnaissance as potential targets, including aircraft factories, engine manufacturers and the city's historic docks, and 250 people were killed (and more than three times as many injured) in attacks from the air. The Forest itself was devastated, with hundreds of acres of trees felled, the timber desperately needed for the war effort. During the 1930s around half of the male population of the Forest of Dean had been employed in coal mining, but with many of the Meek family's friends and relatives called up, local women were taking over their roles both above and below ground, and the population of Newent swelled with the arrival of evacuees from cities including Birmingham and London.

While the war raged on, the family threw themselves into village life. The weekly livestock market was suspended, as was the annual Onion Fayre, which had taken place in the Market Square over a weekend each September, with fun fair rides, attractions and live music from a great steam organ. But other, smaller events continued: the children took part in fêtes and fancy dress competitions, and Arthur and Eric were typical country lads, out with their guns looking for rabbits for the family pot. The two boys would happily go into their father's orchards and take shots at the birds trying to eat their profits, but Joe refused to pick up a gun. Instead he put his interest in sound to good use, placing speakers in the cherry trees to scare the birds away and, at the same time, provide entertainment for fruit pickers. 'He wouldn't shoot a bird,' Arthur Meek recalled. 'This is why, at the end, it just didn't add up…'[17] Eric added wistfully.

Although his father wanted Joe to work with him and his brothers in the expanding family business, as he himself described it, his 'head was always in radio books and audio books,' and so his parents allowed Joe to take a part-time job repairing radios for a local electrical shop, Lester Nicholls on Newent's Broad Street. All in all, Joe enjoyed a good childhood and would stay close to his family, and as an adult when opportunity allowed he would bring his city-dwelling friends to the verdant Forest, where he would spin yarns about his childhood and bask in his family's affection.

CHAPTER 2

Hobbies

The war had been good to George Meek; by the end of it he was no longer the local fish merchant with a sideline in fruit and veg, but a successful fruiter and landowner, and over the post-war period he continued to do rather well for himself. In April 1945, just a few weeks before hostilities in Europe ceased, he bought a 92-acre farm, Berrow Court, near Upton-upon-Severn in Worcestershire, and over the next year he oversaw the sale of several local smallholdings and houses. His fortune had increased so much that, in 1947, he was able to invest £10,000 in the purchase of the Hafod estate in West Wales, with 530 acres of land, a farm and six cottages. George considered taking up residence, but instead the family remained close to their Gloucestershire roots. He continued to expand his business interests in Wales, though, and the following year was trading in timber in Monmouth. Soon he and his family would be seen driving around Newent in a Buick; the whole family would pile into the fancy American car for day trips to Bristol Zoo or to the seaside at Weston-super-Mare. His property deals saw the family moving around constantly, and every time George took on a farm he would encourage his boys to muck in: Arthur and Eric were happy to take on the responsibility of looking after livestock, but although Joe feigned an interest his heart was never in the management of pigs, chickens or cows. The one thing he did enjoy was cooking, having learned the basics at his mother's side. Arthur Meek would recall that his brother was particularly adept at cooking sausages, and for the rest of his life Joe's go-to snack would be a fried egg sandwich.

While his father concentrated on expanding the family business, taking over a local dairy adjacent to the High Street shop (which now included an office for George Meek's expanding property empire) and installing Arthur and Eric to run it, Joe preferred to tinker away with wires and valves in his bedroom, celebrating the end of the war by building the town's first working television. Television broadcasts had been suspended for the duration, recommencing on 7 June 1946, and the teenager could not wait. He assembled two televisions from scratch, the first with a 9-inch screen and a second larger version housed in an orange crate. The family's neighbours would come to their house every evening and marvel at this wonder of modern technology, built and operated by the strange Meek boy. 'He bought the cathode tube and built everything... We had the first television in Newent, before even the radio shops in Newent had a television, we had one,' Eric Meek explained. Meek's television was 'a little 12-inch screen... They used to think that everyone should sit in the dark and watch it, you know? It used to come on about half-past seven at night and we'd all get in there, in the dark, pull all the curtains and sit there until the Epilogue at about twelve o'clock, and when we put the lights on the house was full! It was chock-a-block full of people; they used to sneak through the door, shut the door and nobody said a word. They used to be glued to this box!'[18] June Davies, whose mother worked for the Meek family dairy, would recall watching the Queen's Coronation (in 1953) on that same television: 'I remember that the ceremony seemed very long. My mum would pop in from the dairy every now and then to see what was happening, in between her milk duties... As far as I know, none of my friends actually saw the Coronation until it came to Newent Picture House on Pathé news. I still feel very proud that I saw it as it happened on the TV built by Joe Meek.'[19] That homemade television remained in Meek's possession and was only disposed of by his family after his death.

The biggest consequence of the war, as far as the Meek family were concerned, was the arrival of a mandatory National Service, a compulsory conscription (introduced in January 1949) which saw all physically fit men between the ages of 17 and 21 serve in one of the armed forces for a two-year period. The 19-year-old Joe Meek was soon called up, immediately putting an end to his father's plans to have Joe follow him into the property business. Joe joined the RAF and became a radar operator, while the rest of the family were living at Underhill farm, about 7 miles north of Newent in the village of Pendock. Hardly the most invested scholar, Meek had left

Hobbies

Picklenash school before his fifteenth birthday and had kept himself busy with his various hobbies and passions, but he had not yet figured out how he could turn his obsession for wires and valves into a full-time occupation. The RAF would change that.

The war was over, but relations with the Soviet Union were tense. The recent blockade of Berlin, when British and American planes were used to drop supplies to the residents of West Berlin after the Soviets denied the Allies access to the transport network, kept the RAF busy, and this was quickly followed by the Soviets testing their first nuclear bomb. Meek and his fellow trainee technicians would have been put to work on the Chain Home Low air defence system, an early warning system that had been devised during World War Two to detect incoming hostile aeroplanes and was now being updated to cope with advances in air transportation. Typically, conscripts would spend the first six weeks of their training – which Meek spent in Yatesbury, a tiny village near to the Avebury stone circle in Wiltshire* – being taught everything about the radar system and its electronics, then there would have been written and practical tests for Meek to sit before being posted to his camp: Arthur Meek would proudly boast that 'there were two thousand that sat the exam and only two of them passed. And one was Joe.'[20]

Meek enjoyed his time as a radar operator, later admitting that 'it was helping me increase my knowledge of electronics'.[21] He recalled that his 'two years in the RAF were taken up by learning as much as possible about radar, and also I was pretty handy around the camp repairing radios and record players'.[22] Conscription was not kind to homosexual men, but many saw it as a chance to 'straighten' themselves out, some believing that living in close proximity to other testosterone-fuelled teens would only help them become more manly. But homosexuality was rife in Britain's armed forces, and for some this would have been their first taste of freedom from the constraints of family life. Sleeping in barracks, the daily inspections and strict regime taught the perpetually untidy young man to smarten himself

---

* Also stationed at Yatesbury was Brian Hodgson, who went on to run the BBC's famous Radiophonic Workshop. Hodgson created the sound made by Dr Who's Tardis and later was a member of White Noise with Delia Derbyshire and David Vorhaus, the trio that produced the 1968 album *An Electric Storm*.

up, and in later life he would rarely be seen without a suit, shirt and tie on. Most Britons were still dealing with the scourge of food rationing, but the RAF looked after his meals, his laundry, his accommodation, and provided him with a tight circle of friends.

It was the perfect training ground, teaching him much more about the repair and maintenance of electrical equipment than he already knew, and it allowed him full rein to explore his other great passion, outer space. Spurred on by cinema's obsession with flying saucers, ray guns and rockets, Meek's interest in science fiction and the possibilities of interplanetary communication convinced him that there were life forms on other planets, and he became fixated on contacting them. At around the same time he also developed an interest in spiritualism and began to conduct experiments into capturing the voices of the dead in recordings. Meek would have had no idea that he was walking in the footsteps of giants: recording pioneer Thomas Edison began investigating the possibility of recording voices from the afterlife during the 1870s, following earlier interest from both Guglielmo Marconi and Nikola Tesla, and throughout the 1940s and 1950s similar experiments were being conducted in America and Scandinavia.

George Meek, the family patriarch, died in hospital in Gloucester on 28 January 1950, while his middle son was still serving in the RAF. His estate, then valued at £7,189 (worth approximately £308,700 in 2024) went to his widow, Biddy. The property deals ceased immediately, but the family held on to the dairy and their home next door. The dairy was sold in 1964, but the Meek's eldest boy, Arthur, took over the shop and was still running it with his sister Pamela as a greengrocers at the time of Joe's death. After two years in uniform, Meek left the RAF and went back to Newent, to the house at 1 High Street which he now shared with Arthur and their mother, who was now supplementing their income by taking in laundry for the garage next door.

Back home, and keen to keep his hand in, Joe would happily repair his neighbours' radios and television sets for free. He returned too to the local amateur dramatic society and continued to produce ever more elaborate sound effects for their shows. At weekends he would lug his huge, homemade speaker and his radiogram around to provide music for dances in the local villages. He could not have known that some 170 miles away, in the Lincolnshire market town of Boston, a radio engineer called Ron

Hobbies

Diggins had recently started something similar. Unaware of each other, Meek, Diggins and Bert Thorpe, who had been playing amplified music from a 78 gramophone since the early 1940s, were pioneers of a new form of entertainment, with Diggins, who was taking a pair of 78 rpm players to village hall dances, single-handedly inventing the concept of the twin-deck mobile disco.

Meek's first appearance, following his return to civvy street, was at the annual Newent British Legion fête, held in the grounds of Newent's Old Court House, just yards away from the house he was born in, where 'music during the afternoon was provided by Mr Joe Meek, with his radio-gram'.[23] He later recalled this period as his 'supplying music to the masses with my wind up gram[ophone] and my amplifier',[24] which his friend Derek Davis remembers 'was quite a lump of equipment; it took several people to lift it'.[25] Meek's cottage industry soon took off: employing his friends, and his extensive record collection, at one point Joe was so in-demand at dances and events that he ran three similar set-ups around the area. 'We had dances at May Hill [an area just south of Newent] – he used to do the music there; also, above the bank at Newent there was a large room, and he used to do it there, and in the George Hotel, where there was a big entertainments room... Joe used to do all the sound effects and lighting effects for the amateur dramatics in May Hill. They wanted flashing lights so Joe got a big round tin and cut slots in it, and put a bulb inside, and rotated it slowly with a motor to give the flashing effect.' Davis would remember that 'all the pretty girls, the nice young ladies always had an eye for Joe but he took no notice at all'.[26]

Like the rest of his family, he involved himself in the annual horticultural show and village fête, but Newent was too small and parochial for a man with such grand visions, and in a place where everyone knew everyone else, it was impossible for Joe to enjoy any kind of private life. He hankered after a life in the big city, and the biggest city he knew of was just a little over 10 miles away. In 1952 Joe began working in Gloucester, where he moved about from employer to employer rapidly. Eric Meek later recalled that Joe first worked for electrical retailers Currys, on Eastgate Street (where his boss, Mr North, noted that Meek 'was ambitious, and made known his interests in advanced electronics and noises'), before he moved to Clydesdale, a shop on Westgate Street (the four main shopping streets in

Love and Fury: The Life, Death and Legacy of Joe Meek

Gloucester, which converged on the Cross in the city centre, were Eastgate, Westgate, Northgate and Southgate Streets, all named after the city's original entrance gates) that specialised in bicycles and prams, but also sold radios and televisions. His brothers also remembered Joe attending 'Tech', the Gloucester Technical College, which was on Brunswick Road, just a short walk from Eastgate Street, where Joe studied electrical engineering, either at night school or on day release from work.

Shortly afterwards he took a job with another electrical retail company the Broadmead Wireless Co. Ltd, which had three branches in Gloucester. Broadmead Wireless (a company set up by Herbert William Smith in Bristol in the 1920s and named after Smith's first store, in the city's Broadmead shopping district) advertised themselves as 'England's Largest Radio and Television Specialists', with branches in London, the Midlands, Manchester and elsewhere. As well as radios, they also sold gramophones, records, accessories and had a television rental business, sold expensive equipment on hire purchase and offered a television repair service, with technicians visiting you at your home or repairs done in their in-store workshops. Interest in owning or renting a television was at an all-time high, with the upcoming broadcast of the Coronation of Queen Elizabeth II, and for someone like Joe, who loved to tinker with electrical equipment, it was a job made in heaven. Broadmead Wireless was the perfect place for him to hone his skills and get a grounding in all types of electrical repair work.

From there he moved on to the Midlands Electricity Board (MEB), which had offices on London Road and Commercial Road. The company had formed in 1947, immediately after the nationalisation of Great Britain's electricity supply, and were responsible for supplying and maintaining power to homes and businesses in Gloucestershire, Herefordshire, Worcestershire and into the heart of the Midlands. Soon the company would open a smart new showroom in King's Square, which at that time also housed the city's main bus terminus, and there it would operate a dedicated television repair service. Joe would travel from Newent to Gloucester on the bus with his friend Derek Davis, a fellow MEB employee who lived in the village of Dymock 4 miles north of Newent. Davis would cycle to Newent each day, and the two young men would catch the bus to Gloucester together. 'He was a very good-looking chap,' Davis recalled, 'And very quiet. Joe was

Hobbies

already a qualified radio and television engineer, and I was an apprentice electrician in the contracts department.'

But even with the MEB's plans for expansion locally it soon became obvious to Joe that Gloucester was not big enough for him. He wanted to continue his experiments with sound recording, and he was never going to do that in a city as insular and backwards-looking. Life there was stagnant: the city's biggest industries were match making (the Bryant & May factory, known as Moreland's after its founders, which dominated Bristol Road and manufactured the famous England's Glory match brand) or train carriage making (the Gloucester Railway Carriage and Wagon Company, situated almost opposite Moreland's factory, specialised in coal wagons and in carriages for the London Underground). No one was interested in making records: just about the only studio of any kind locally was a 'make your own recording' booth in the toy department of Cheltenham department store Cavendish House. There had been a similar set-up, coincidentally, in King's Square: during the late 1940s you could make your own record at Photosound Ltd. In the early 1950s, before Joe arrived in town, that business had been taken over by local photographer Gerald Pates and renamed Two Arts Studios, but Pates seems to have moved out of the recording industry by late 1952 to concentrate on his expanding photography business. Life back in Newent offered even less. His few close friends had either married or moved away – or both. Outside his immediate family there was nothing to tie him down.

With little access to suitable equipment, in 1954, shortly before Meek left Gloucestershire, he drew on his experiments with disc cutting while in the RAF to build his own primitive record-cutting lathe, proudly showing the results of his endeavours off to Derek Davis. Housed in the case of a portable gramophone player, with a cutting arm made from a piece of copper pipe, he cut his first recordings in his room in the family home in Newent. 'It was quite a small room, really, but it was full of Joe's radio equipment [and] television equipment,' Davis told BBC Radio Gloucestershire presenter Pete Wilson. 'He had quite a mountain of stuff of his own. He asked me in there one night to read a passage out of a book. He wanted to try out his new recording equipment which he'd just built. So I read this passage out, very nervously, and Joe recorded it and then played it back... He was a very intelligent man, Joe; he was always on about recording and stuff like that.'[27]

17

Love and Fury: The Life, Death and Legacy of Joe Meek

That summer, following his experiments with Davis, he cut his first pop record, an acetate disc featuring the voice of Marlene Williams, his brother Eric's girlfriend and, later, wife; the year before, Marlene had won a beauty contest at one of Joe's dances held in the games room above the George Hotel. The one-sided disc featured Marlene singing the Doris Day hit 'Secret Love', which had reached number 1 in the UK charts in April. On the disc Marlene appeared to be fronting a full orchestra, Joe having already recorded an instrumental version of the song by local act the Melody Dance Band. Joe, being Joe, could not resist tweaking with the sound, adding echo to his soon-to-be sister-in-law's voice, the Meek trademark in place from the very beginning. Eric Meek fondly remembered hearing Marlene's disc being played over the public address system at the Newent fête that summer. The couple would have three children, one of whom they christened Robert in honour of his uncle. The disc cutter was given by his family to the local primary school, along with most of Joe's early, amateur equipment – including his bicycle lamp microphone – in the early 1970s.

Joe left the MEB and went to work for electrical retailer J. & M. Stone, at 18 Northgate Street. But not only was he stymied by the lack of local recording facilities at his previous employers, he was also frustrated by the fact that there were zero opportunities for homosexual men – or any LGBTQ people, for that matter – to meet like-minded souls in the city. One of the reasons for working there had been to improve his social life, but the homosexual 'scene' in Gloucester was a clandestine affair: to be 'queer' (the pejorative most used) in Britain at that time was to break the law, and anyone caught even attempting to make contact with another gay man faced a court appearance and a fine, or possibly imprisonment or worse. Joe Meek would spend his entire life knowing that his sexuality made him a criminal.

A series of recent scandals involving homosexual or bisexual men had kept Britain's tabloids busy, including the much-reported trial and imprisonment of bisexual peer of the realm Lord Montagu of Beaulieu and the suicide of top scientist Alan Turing following his conviction for gross indecency, an ill-defined term that covered any sexual activity between two or more men, but which usually related to trying to procure sex with a stranger in a public place. Turing had been subjected to court-

Hobbies

ordained chemical castration: injections of synthetic oestrogen meant to lower his libido that rendered him impotent. These cases would eventually lead to the founding of the Wolfenden committee, but both national and provincial newspapers were having a field day reporting on the still-illegal sexual activities of homosexual and bisexual men (sex acts between two women have never been legislated against, although lesbian and bisexual women in relationships with other women have been arrested and charged with fraud for impersonating men).

Meek – like all homosexual men – would have been well aware of the consequences should his secret come out. Gloucester's courts regularly passed judgment on men accused of 'importuning for an immoral purpose', for committing 'indecent assault on male persons' or for 'gross indecency', all variations on the same theme, and it was not unusual for men to be imprisoned for these so-called crimes: in September 1950, 50-year-old William Haslam was sent to prison for two years after pleading guilty to two charges of indecent assault on male persons; the following month a canteen manager from Gloucester, Leslie Willman, was given a year's probation for gross indecency – sex with another man. In May 1951 a married man with two children, George Turner, was jailed for eighteen months after being found guilty of gross indecency by a court in Gloucester, and similar sentences would be handed out for years to come. By the end of 1954, there were 1,069 gay men in prison in England and Wales, and life for LGBTQ people in Gloucestershire would remain perilous for decades. Trans pioneer Denise Burrell (assigned male at birth in 1930) lived openly as a woman with her male partner from the late-1940s onwards. Known throughout the city as Chummy, many treated her as a figure of fun, openly jeering at her in the street. She put up with the barracking until her mother passed away and, in the early 1970s, underwent sexual reassignment surgery, spending her last two decades (Denise passed away in 1993) as the woman she was always meant to be.

The only place in the country where a gay man stood any chance of having anything like a normal life was London. Less than a decade after the end of the war, the capital was buzzing, and after a sharp spike in inflation and unemployment at the beginning of the 1950s, things were improving rapidly. Rationing was over, there was a new, young and glamorous queen on the throne, and the air was filled with promise. Money was being spent on rebuilding the bomb-damaged city, and London was filled with exciting and exotic scents and sounds as migrants from Commonwealth countries arrived to help rebuild the motherland. Not everyone was happy with the rapid rate of change, though; many parts of the city were little better than slums, and racial tensions were high. Crime was endemic, and homosexual men were often the targets of blackmailers and police entrapment and under constant threat of losing their jobs and homes should the truth about them come to light.

But for Joe the lure of London was too much, and he began to scour the situations vacant sections of newspapers for suitable work. Eric Meek recalled that Joe's employer did not want him to leave his steady, secure job in Gloucester: 'When he said he was going to go to London, they said that at any future date if you want to come back there's always an opening here. He was pretty good at his job.' Their elder brother, Arthur, agreed. 'He was a wizard with a television or a radio,' he added. Meek, however, knew that he had no option but to keep moving.

CHAPTER 3

Keep Moving

Joe was offered a job working in the studio of a film dubbing company in Soho and moved into a small flat in Cricklewood. He lasted a week, admitting that he 'disliked' the job because 'it wasn't creative'.[28] Never one to let the grass grow under his feet, he soon found a position at J. & F. Stone, a television, radio and record store, at 237 Edgware Road.* He would not remain there long, either: it was a 7-mile round journey between home and work, and besides, he had no intention of continuing to work as a television repair man. He had been at Stone's less than two months when he saw an advertisement for a job as a television engineer for the International Broadcasting Company (IBC). Before 1954 was out, Joe had landed a position 'operating a closed-circuit television set-up',[29] as he described it, with IBC.

Established in 1931 as a commercial rival to the BBC by former RAF officer Captain Leonard Plugge, IBC began by producing radio programmes, and although the war almost put him out of business, Plugge built up a good relationship with European stations, providing them with English language content. When Meek joined, IBC was primarily involved in producing shows for Radio Luxembourg, although they were slowly becoming more and more involved in music production, as IBC also boasted the largest privately-owned recording studio in the country. Meek would be working out of their premises at 35 Portland Place; this was even further away from his new home but it was worth the daily trek, and it did not take long for Meek to establish himself at IBC. The years he had spent in TV and radio

---

* A different company to the J. & M. Stone that Joe had worked for in Gloucester. J. & M. Stone would later become Civic.

Love and Fury: The Life, Death and Legacy of Joe Meek

repair meant that he could fix any broken equipment quickly and without fuss, but not only was he a brilliant and hardworking engineer, he had an ear for the unusual at a time when novelty hits dominated the sales charts. As singer Joy Adams puts it, 'Joe had a very unique mind. He wasn't the usual thinker. Some of those sounds that he was trying to make, the work he did in the studio… What he came up with was some really corny stuff, but in a way no one had thought to do it before.'[30]

IBC was run by Allen Stagg, a Welsh-born former army officer who had previously worked for Radio Luxembourg. Stagg and Meek did not get on; Stagg believed in moulding staff in his own image, insisted that his engineers wore white lab coats and claimed that Meek could be 'a monster if he didn't get his own way'.[31] Meek certainly knew what he wanted and could be incredibly demanding, but for the most part he kept his head down, just happy to be there and to be working in sound.

Shortly after moving to London, Meek met the young man who would become his first real boyfriend. Lional Howard – the dyslexic Meek misspelled the more traditional 'Lionel' and it stuck – was a chef and amateur bodybuilder, who had been photographed for male physique magazines and had entered the Mister Universe competition, held annually in London. The pair met one night in a private club for gay men, the Arts and Battledress Club, otherwise known as the A&B, on Wardour Street,* a thoroughfare with close connections to Britain's film and music industries. Unlike most homosexual haunts in the capital, you had to climb a set of open, rickety stairs which led up from the pavement of Rupert Court, above a Chinese restaurant to gain entrance to the members-only A&B. Once there, you would be greeted by a locked door with a small hatch in it; upon knocking the hatch would slide open and a pair of eyes would examine your membership card before you would be allowed inside. Meek was not much of a drinker, at least not at that point in his life; instead he went in search of company: another favourite haunt was the City of Quebec, a pub that had catered for the LGBTQ community since the mid-1940s. Affectionately known as the Elephants' Graveyard (due to the fact that it was frequented by older homosexual men), the Quebec is still open for business today. The

---

* The Arts and Battledress Club originally opened in 1941 in Orange Street; the club moved to Wardour Street in 1952. By the 1980s it had moved again to Dean Street.

concept of being 'out' did not exist then, but Meek was unashamed of his sexuality, even though he was very much aware that being homosexual carried with it the ever-present threat of arrest, imprisonment or barbaric 'medical' treatment. He was immediately attracted to the taller, slimmer, well-muscled Howard, who in turn was fascinated with Joe's tales of the stars he crossed paths with. 'Lional Howard was a very nice person, a gentle soul,' Roy Phillips, guitarist with the Saints, recalls. 'I believe he worked at Regent's Park Zoo in catering. It never bothered me that Joe was queer.'[32]

Before long, Joe and Lional moved in together to a large bedsit at 15 Leinster Terrace, near Hyde Park, in Bayswater, and Lional soon found himself a new job, working in the kitchen of a café near to the IBC studios. Their one-room apartment was cheap, around £4/10 a month, and with the extra freedom he could enjoy in the capital, Meek began to build himself a social life. Meek had a high sex drive, and although he now had a boyfriend he enjoyed regular dalliances when out on the road with his work. Gay men knew where to go to find sex, and Joe often felt drawn to the clandestine world of the city's cottages. Certain public conveniences, known as 'cottages', were singled out as the best places to meet someone for a casual encounter, and any man wandering in a quiet park in the evening would recognise a knowing look and a request for a light of a cigarette from a like-minded soul. This side of Joe's personality was anathema to Lional, who simply could not understand why his partner seemed to enjoy the thrill of illicit sex in public places, with the twin dangers of possible arrest or becoming a victim to blackmailers or violent 'queer-rollers'.

Although Meek rarely talked about his life before London, he did not attempt to keep his family a secret from his friends in the capital. He wrote home regularly although, as Arthur Meek would later recall, 'he'd only write home when he had something good to write about!', and Lional would often accompany Joe on his return visits to Newent, where the two men were accepted as nothing more than close friends by the Meek family. 'I never put two and two together,' his brother Eric would later confess. 'I never thought that Joe was queer, so I never registered that Lional was his partner. I thought that Lional was a friend, and they had a flat together and that to me was just normal policy. I was being a bit naive... In my opinion he was a gentleman, and Lional would always be welcome in my house.'[33]

Love and Fury: The Life, Death and Legacy of Joe Meek

Despite the childhood accusations of being a 'cissy', Meek's family turned a blind eye to the fact that Joe and Lional were in a relationship. 'He was very, very close to his mother,' Lional recalled. 'I used to go with him and we'd stay there for the weekend.' The trips home were manic affairs, and although Joe loved to be seen in a smart, fast or sporty car, he was a nervous driver who suffered from dreadful road rage and would often drive straight through a red light without noticing it. Lional regularly witnessed how quickly his frustrations with the car or annoyance with other road users would boil over into full-blown temper tantrums. Arthur Meek would later recall that 'they lived together when Joe first went to London… He always spent Christmas with us. We liked Lional very much; he was good for Joe, in my opinion, because Joe was fairly difficult to live with because he wanted his own way, and Lional was a slow sort of lad who used to let Joe have his head. They used to get on very, very well.' When Eric and Marlene married, Joe took Lional to the wedding ceremony and reception as his guest.

At IBC – often with junior engineer Adrian Kerridge assisting – Meek was involved with a number of different radio, television and cinema projects. Referred to as a 'balance engineer', he worked on early episodes of the practical joke game show *People Are Funny* before it made its transition from radio to television in September 1955. Based on an American format and sponsored by Pye radios and televisions, *People Are Funny* was broadcast every Wednesday at 8 p.m. The programme – one of the most popular on Radio Luxembourg at the time – kickstarted a whole genre of hidden camera, practical joke shows, including *Game For a Laugh* and *People Do the Funniest Things*. In 1956 Joe engineered the similar production *Candid Microphone*; a spin-off album, *Candid Mike*, was issued on LP by Pye that year, a couple of years before the show transferred to television as *Candid Camera*.

Making his debut at a recording in Bradford just a fortnight or so after joining IBC, Meek began as a lowly junior in the *People Are Funny* team, running the film projector (the shows would include a 'vox pop' section filmed earlier in the day which would then be screened for the live audience), but within weeks he had proved himself invaluable and had risen to chief recording engineer, a position which was awarded an on-air credit. In an autobiographical recording made at home sometime around 1957, Meek

Keep Moving

described his experience working on *People Are Funny* in some detail. By his own reckoning, he worked on more than 110 episodes of the show (something of an exaggeration), travelling all over the country with Adrian Kerridge. The scenario was much the same, week in, week out: 'We caught the train... usually it was raining or miserable and we'd just raced away from the studio. There were two of us, usually myself and Adrian... on our way to somewhere in England... We used to get some darn good meals on some of the trains,' he recalled, 'especially in the west country.'[34] The work day, which began at 10 a.m., involved a lot of hanging around in theatres as guests came and went, presenters sorted themselves out, musicians rehearsed and equipment was set up before the live audience was allowed in and recording began. This gave Meek ample opportunity to focus on his songwriting, scribbling in notebooks and picking out rudimentary tunes on a piano; in a theatre or village hall there was always a piano nearby, and although it has often been said that Joe could not play an instrument, he was able to pick out the bare bones of an idea, usually on the black notes, while someone else vamped a tune: his friend Bob Kingston, of publishers Southern Music, recalled that Meek certainly knew enough to be able to play a few chords.

Meek and Kerridge also worked on the Radio Luxembourg show *Strike It Rich*, presented by Eamonn Andrews, *Ladder to Fame*, a variety show produced for the Australian market starring the Ted Heath Orchestra, the schmaltzy, faith-inspired human interest story series *This I Believe,* and *When You're Smiling*, an on-air talent show recorded at weekends from a different holiday camp around the UK. Meek loved the work and he enjoyed travelling: most large towns and cities had bars and private clubs where gay men could meet more discreetly, and train stations were ideal places for casual homosexual encounters. Meek took full advantage of life on the road. Usually quiet and shy, Meek could be surprisingly cavalier when it came to his sex life, especially when in the company of a trusted friend like Kerridge. Naturally, word of his antics soon got back to the rest of the team at IBC, and he was often the brunt of a vicious joke or homophobic put-down, which Kerridge thought grossly unfair: 'His personal life never ever interfered with his professional life, or with his creative life. He was always absolutely focused on the project in hand.'[35]

Meek was in Belfast to record a show for Radio Luxembourg when he turned up after one drinking session with a young man he introduced to Kerridge as his 'friend'.[36] After dinner, he would usually go off on his own, and he was seldom without a companion for the evening, someone he had encountered on the train and had arranged to meet up with, or someone he had met in a bar near to the hotel he and Kerridge were staying in, so it was no surprise to Kerridge when he appeared at the studio or theatre the following morning accompanied by yet another new 'friend'. He enjoyed giving these young men the impression that he was a man of some importance, but Kerridge believed that his homosexuality – and the reaction to it from work colleagues – caused Meek to become more isolated. 'I never had any problems with his lifestyle,' Kerridge told writer John McCreedy, 'but it's hard to imagine now just what a taboo subject his homosexuality was back then. People judged him because of it and he reacted by hating them. It was hard for him to fit in.'[37] Meek took to referring to many of his IBC colleagues as 'rotten pigs', but with Kerridge he could let his guard down, and Meek would delight in embarrassing his friend with jokey comments about what certain members of railway staff were hiding in their trousers.

Under Stagg's leadership, IBC was slowly moving from radio and into music production. Like Stagg, Meek was predominantly a classical music enthusiast (although his brothers recall him being a fan of forces sweetheart Vera Lynn), although he was overjoyed when he was asked – just four months after he started at the company – to act as assistant engineer on his first professional recording session, for a disc being made for the US and Canadian market by classical pianist Daniel Abrams, which Meek later called 'the first recording of any importance that I made'.[38] Meek was so happy to be employed by a recording studio that he did not mind who he worked with and what he was asked to do: shortly after the Abrams session he was put to work on the debut session for a new company, Bell Accordions, whose output was made up exclusively of accordion and country dancing music sold through their own specialist accordion shop in Surbiton, Surrey, and advertised through their regular Radio Luxembourg programme. His own rudimentary experience of disc cutting (using his homemade lathe) was put to great use in IBC's own cutting room, where Meek oversaw the cutting of acetates – aluminium discs with a thin coat of lacquer on which would be used to give artists and musicians an idea of how their work would sound once it was released to the public.

Keep Moving

IBC had two recording studios, with one capable of housing a 40-piece orchestra. Dressed in a sober suit and tie (he had yet to develop his Teddy Boy quiff or his habit of combing his hair back dozens of times a day), in 1955 Joe was given the opportunity to work on something more commercially viable than classical piano or accordion music courtesy of Denis Preston, whose company, Record Supervision Ltd, often booked time at IBC to make recordings which were then sold on to major companies. Stagg understood the value of regular customers like Preston and was keen to make sure that the best talent they could offer was available for his sessions. It was not long before Preston began insisting that Meek be assigned to his recordings, but although he recognised Joe's brilliance, Preston and Meek rarely saw eye to eye: Adrian Kerridge remembered that 'Joe and Denis didn't always hit it off, but they believed in each other's talent'.[39] Like Allen Stagg before him, Preston was often frustrated by Meek's way of working: no matter how many times studio staff would tell him that his recordings would sound distorted if he positioned instruments too close to the microphones, or if he forced IBC's delicate equipment into the red, he would simply insist that was what he wanted. 'Everybody said, "Joe, you can't do this. It won't work,"' Kerridge recalled. 'And he said, "But that's what I want. For me, distortion is commercial"... And the sounds were fantastic!'[40] When engineers at EMI refused to master his recordings because they were too compressed, distorted and loud, an angry Meek would insist that they did as he ask and not question his methods. Still, Preston became an important mentor, and Meek would take a lot of his ideas with him when he eventually set out on his own.

Born Sidney Denis Prechner in Stoke Newington in 1916, Preston played violin as a teenager and first began to make a name for himself on radio, presenting shows for the BBC's Home Service from 1940 onward. He championed Black music, especially from the United States and the Caribbean (Preston was instrumental in helping to establish Lord Kitchener – real name Aldwyn Roberts – in the early 1950s, kickstarting a short craze for calypso music)*, and soon became a major player in the booming British jazz scene. His set-up was, for the time, unheralded. He would make

---

* Born in Trinidad and Tobago in 1922, Lord Kitchener came to England on the *Empire Windrush* in 1948.

recordings with different artists and then sell his masters to whichever label offered the best deal. He had little interest in management or in the pressing and distribution of the eventual records, but as Britain's first independent producer he was able to negotiate the best possible deal for himself and his team, and his small but successful operation led to him being referred to as 'the one man record company'[41] and feted as 'probably the most important figure to emerge from the British jazz business'.[42] Preston coined the word 'trad', which first appeared in 1958 on a Lansdowne-produced EP (issued by Columbia) by Terry Lightfoot and his Jazzmen.

In April 1955 Meek was offered the chance to engineer a recording session for Canadian actor and singer Edmund Hockridge, his first job on a pop music release. Hockridge had recently scored a big hit as Sky Masterson in the London production of *Guys and Dolls*, and although he had recorded for several labels he had yet to have any chart success. His association with Preston and Meek would change that: in March 1956 he would enjoy his only Top 10 hit with the Meek-engineered 'Young and Foolish'. Other early sessions that Meek engineered for Preston included 'Georgia's Got a Moon' by singer Betty Miller, issued in the UK on Pye's pop imprint Nixa (the same label that Hockridge was now signed to) in October that year, plus sessions for orchestra leader Alyn Ainsworth (issued in the US under the pseudonym Mark Andrews and His Orchestra), and for singer Gary Miller, who had just been signed to Nixa after several years with Philips. Miller's September 1955 release 'The Yellow Rose of Texas' entered the *NME* singles chart[*] on 21 October at number 19: Meek's first chart entry.

In the same month that Miller's disc charted, Meek was one of the two engineers credited on a couple of sessions by American blues legend Big Bill Broonzy. Engineers and producers (then more usually referred to as A&R men: the artistes and repertoire managers were charged with discovering and nurturing new talent and finding suitable material) were rarely, if ever, credited in those days, but Preston insisted that the work that he – and his team – did was attributed. Eight of the songs captured were issued by

---

[*]   Before February 1969 there was no 'official' national sales chart in the UK. The music industry trade paper *Record Retailer* began publishing a Top 50 in March 1960; prior to that the most widely-circulated sales chart was published by the *New Musical Express*, which printed its first chart on 14 November 1952.

Keep Moving

Nixa on two EPs, or extended plays, the sleeves of which carry the legend 'Recording: Balance Eric Tomlinson and Joe Meek. Supervision: Denis Preston', Meek's first official credit on a record sleeve. The young man from Newent had a lot to thank Preston for. 'I still find it quite interesting, the breadth of work that Joe did in his early years,' says Big Bill Broonzy fan Steve Howe today. The guitar legend, who would find worldwide fame as a member of Yes and Asia, recorded with Meek in the mid-1960s while still a teenager. 'Seeing that Joe Meek, the producer I was working with, was the engineer on that record was astounding.'[43]

Preston was in charge of the recording career of a young guitar-playing singer named Lonnie Donegan, who at that time was well on the way to becoming known as the King of Skiffle, and whose releases were also handled by Nixa. Preston signed Donegan to an exclusive recording contract, a fortuitous move as the singer was on the cusp of major stardom, and Meek quickly saw how he could not only follow Preston's example but build on it.

With so many different artists and such a diverse range of shows to put together, Meek's taste in music widened dramatically, and his ability to think on his feet and cobble together something to emulate a particular sound or effect that the producer was after kept him in demand. Gary Miller's discs were full of special effects – the twang of the arrow at the start of 'Robin Hood' or the storm that introduces 'Moby Dick' which Meek would later reuse for the Moontrekkers' 'Night of the Vampire' – and Meek quickly built a reputation as someone who would not be fazed by an outlandish request. He was much in demand, and the amount of work coming in was relentless, but 1956 was to be the year that producers, record companies, critics, artists and the public really started to take notice of his talents. The previous year or so had been an important training ground, but Meek was a fast learner, and his innovations began to break new ground. Before the year was out he would have his first number 1 on the British charts, engineer the first hit single for a major jazz artist, help design the country's most advanced recording studio and lay the foundations for his own empire.

In February Meek acted as engineer on the first release from a sensational new singer from Cardiff, Shirley Bassey. 'Burn My Candle' and 'Stormy

Love and Fury: The Life, Death and Legacy of Joe Meek

Weather' were issued (on 10-inch only) in Britain that month by Philips, the same company that, a few months later, issued some of the last discs Meek worked on for IBC, including Anne Shelton's number 1 'Lay Down Your Arms' and actor Harry Secombe's version of the Welsh standard 'We'll Keep A Welcome'. He worked as an engineer for sides issued on Polydor by Geraldo and his Orchestra, and by husband and wife team (and early Eurovision hitmakers) Pearl Carr and Teddy Johnson (the couple would later move to Nixa, where Meek would continue to act as their engineer), and on several sides for French label Vega, including a number of tracks by Boulogne-born chanteuse Marjane. For Donegan – who, like Meek, had once worked for electrical retailers J. & F. Stone – he engineered the number 1 album *Lonnie Donegan Showcase*,* and he came up with the distinctive bottle-clinking percussion on his cover of the Mickey and Sylvia hit 'Love Is Strange', the B-side to Donegan's first UK number 1 hit 'Cumberland Gap': another Meek-engineered chart topper.**

Meek's ideas were audacious and original: on 20 April 1956 he engineered a session at IBC by jazz trumpeter Humphrey Lyttelton and his band for a new Parlophone single, 'Close Your Eyes', backed with a Lyttelton original, 'Bad Penny Blues'. Although Meek was, as was the custom, credited as 'engineer' (or 'balance engineer' on the majority of Nixa releases) and Preston 'supervised' the session, the sound of the disc was entirely down to Meek. Recorded using his close-mic technique and heavy equalisation (via a piece of IBC equipment Meek referred to as 'the cooker'), once the session was over Meek – aided by Adrian Kerridge – went back to the control room to mix the recording, boosting the bass, compressing Lyttelton's horn work, bringing drummer Stan Greig's snare drum brushes to the fore and adding distortion to the piano. Lyttelton was no fan of the result, saying that he would never have released the recording had he heard Meek's treatment first: 'Had I not gone on holiday, and had it been a set-up like we have now when we all gather around to hear the playback, I would have had a fit, I would have said

---

*   Early copies had IBC engineer Eric Tomlinson credited by mistake.

**   In 1966 Sylvia Robinson (nee Vanderpool) and her husband set up New Jersey soul label All Platinum; in 1979 the pair would co-found the pioneering hip hop company Sugar Hill Records.

Keep Moving

"That's dreadful", and I would have thrown Joe into one of his sulks.'[44] At first, EMI's technicians (once again) refused to cut masters from Meek's tapes, as they felt it was too distorted.

The public and the critics disagreed with Lyttelton and EMI: 'Bad Penny Blues', with its muted trumpet solo, and rumbling piano and percussion obligato has the kind of beat foot tappers find irresistible',[45] was the typical view. Sir Tom Jones, who would record with Meek in 1963, remembers Meek telling him that the reason he mixed the disc in that way was because half of Lyttelton's band failed to show up for the recording session, and Meek had to find a way to compensate: 'He said, "There were only a few musicians there and I had to make it sound big." That's why the piano was so loud.'[46] Issued in June 1956, 'Bad Penny Blues' became the first British jazz record to make the UK Top 20 singles chart, and almost singlehandedly started a jazz fad that ran alongside Britain's burgeoning interest in a new music coming from the United States, rock 'n' roll.

Following the single's success – 'Bad Penny Blues' was the UK's bestselling jazz record in 1956 – Lyttelton reappraised the work Meek had done, and a sound-alike follow-up, 'Echoing the Blues', was released less than a month after 'Bad Penny Blues' finished its chart run. 'Bad Penny Blues' would heavily influence a generation of British musicians. One of the many thousands of people who bought a copy was a Liverpudlian cotton salesman and part-time jazz band leader Jim McCartney: twelve years later his son would recall the tune and it – alongside Fats Domino's 'Blue Monday', also issued in 1956 – would act as inspiration for the Beatles' international hit 'Lady Madonna'.

To date, Preston – or rather his assistant, Barbara Bray – had simply hired a studio whenever he wanted to record someone and then sold his masters to any record company that wanted them. However, Pye, soon to launch their first 45 rpm titles (the British singles market was still dominated by the sales of 10-inch 78 rpm records; the 45 rpm 7-inch single would become the pop buyers' format of choice during 1958), was keen to expand the range of titles offered by its Nixa label and seemed to be happy to take anything Preston could give them. With other companies jostling to get in on the jazz boom, now seemed like the right time for Preston to establish a more permanent base. Meek was, he reasoned, the ideal person to help him launch his new, independent production company.

Love and Fury: The Life, Death and Legacy of Joe Meek

Impressed with the work he had been doing over the previous eighteen months, Denis Preston decided to poach Meek from IBC. Whenever Preston booked time at IBC he usually asked that Meek be assigned to him, but because of his antipathy towards Meek, Allen Stagg would often assign another engineer instead. Stagg detested the way Meek worked: besides his being secretive, refusing to discuss his methods and using his own equipment, he was also incredibly untidy. Cables ran all over the studio, the editing suite floor was festooned in discarded tape, and half-empty spools were abandoned everywhere. Meek pushed everything to the limits, while Stagg went by the book. Other engineers would complain about Meek's sloppiness and the state he left IBC's equipment in, but he got results. Meek was the first British recording engineer to use distortion on purpose – infuriating IBC colleagues with his demands for more bass, more volume, more feel – and, according to his colleague Arthur Frewin, he was also the first to successfully use phasing: 'During a "live" take he'd play back the previous take into the studio with a microphone by the speaker, and blend the two.'[47] 'He was always getting into rows with people who told him he couldn't do such and such because it wasn't in the manual,' says singer Mike Berry. 'His attitude was always "Stuff the manual".'[48] Preston became frustrated with Stagg's refusal to guarantee Meek's availability, and this frustration boiled over in a showdown between the independent producer and the studio manager.

In the basement of a building in Holland Park, Lansdowne House, Meek found a former squash court that had been used as a classical studio and set about converting it to something more suitable for recording the jazz, pop and novelty records that Preston was intent on making. Meek had the engineers at EMI construct a mixing desk exclusively for Lansdowne, making it one of the most advanced studios anywhere in Europe at the time. Inspired by the studio Meek helped build for him, Preston's company became Lansdowne Productions. The company opened for business in June 1958, and in the first week of July Preston signed Meek to his own exclusive contract. Lansdowne started with just three employees, Preston, Meek and Barbara Bray, but in January 1959 the trio were joined by another former IBC employee, Meek's ex-assistant Adrian Kerridge.

Meek's brilliance – and his years of playing with and recording sound back home in Newent – led him to use such innovative techniques as

Keep Moving

filling a tin box with a handful of gravel (a task he assigned to Kerridge) to replicate the sound of marching feet on 'Lay Down Your Arms', the only number 1 hit for singer Anne Shelton, and to create the sound of an arrow hitting a tree for the opening credits of the hit TV series *The Adventures of Robin Hood* by capturing the sound of a wooden ruler reverberating on a desk; this was the same effect that Meek had used on Gary Miller's version of the theme song, a Top 10 hit in February 1956. Shelton would later say that shaking the tin of gravel left her 'covered in grey dust from her Raymond hairdo to her peep-toed feet. "If it's a hit," she said, "the first thing it owes me is a hairdo."'[49] Meek's experience of making sound effects for the Newent players paid off: he thought differently and came up with solutions to problems that no one else would have seen. He worked like a Foley artist (named after American sound-effects pioneer Jack Foley), utilising everyday items and bits of broken household equipment to create sounds and effects. When a fan heater broke he stripped it down, took out the springs and built his own reverb unit.

Meek was also beginning to see how the industry outside the studio worked to promote its artists. To gain extra publicity for 'Lay Down Your Arms', Ann Shelton's management tried to employ a handful of real soldiers to accompany her on promotional appearances. The government's War Office harrumphed that its conscripts were 'not there to help a singer with her publicity'[50] and denied the request, but that did not stop her agents using every opportunity they could to photograph the singer in close proximity to men in uniform. It was an early example of the lengths that managers would go to simply to get their artists' names in the daily newspapers, and Meek made a mental note. In the future he would often pull similar stunts to get his acts noticed.

CHAPTER 4

Please Let It Happen to Me

Outside of Adrian Kerridge, the staff at IBC did not think much of Joe as a person, but they could hardly argue with his work ethic. The word 'workaholic' could have been invented for him: weekends spent on the road recording for Radio Luxembourg were followed by time in the studio editing the programme for broadcast, and the rest of the week was filled with sessions for clients including Denis Preston. Moving permanently to Lansdowne only saw him increase his workload. Pye's Nixa imprint was putting more and more work their way and Meek would boast that, following Betty Miller's 'Georgia's Got a Moon', 'from that moment on, I recorded all of Nixa's records'.[51] When not in the studio he was at home, sending Lional and their neighbours mad creating strange noises and recording anyone who would step over the threshold. He slept very little, and it would not be unusual for him to leap out of bed in the middle of the night to jot down an idea or capture something fleeting on tape before it vanished. He needed something to help keep him going.

Arriving in Britain in 1956, Preludin was readily available over the counter in any chemist's shop; no prescription was needed for anyone to purchase this popular slimming aid. However, most of those taking the tablets were not doing so to lose weight; they were known amongst medical professionals to have only 'a limited value in [the] treatment of obesity'.[52] London's underground gay bars were full of people gulping down handfuls of 'prellies' (and snapping the necks of glass ampules of amyl nitrite, the distinctive sound giving the over-the-counter heart medicine its popular nickname, poppers) to enhance their buzz, and doctors were well aware that 'one reason for its popularity seems to be that in some

Please Let It Happen to Me

patients it induces euphoria and a desire for physical activity', reporting that 'patients tend to become nervous and sleepless... yet they continue to take it'. Meek – keen to stay awake so that he could continue to work on his own projects at home – happily consumed packet after packet of the little white pills. Adrian Kerridge noted that, while working for Preston, Meek was 'becoming more and more dependent on Preludin, and would flare up at the slightest thing and go into a sulk'.[53] He was not alone: Elvis Presley, John F. Kennedy, Frank Sinatra and Marilyn Monroe all took prellies, and in 1960 a then-unknown band from Liverpool called the Beatles would be introduced to them in the clubs of Hamburg.

Their Leinster Terrace bedsit soon became too small for Joe and Lional, overrun as it was with Meek's ever-increasing collection of electrical gadgets, and Lional was sick of constantly tripping over what seemed to be endless miles of wires which trailed over the floor. It was too cramped, and Meek's increasing temper tantrums, worsened by his use of pep pills, were becoming too much to take in such a confined space. Lional had his own interests, and as well as his bodybuilding equipment he was a keen amateur filmmaker, capturing the sights (if not the sounds) of the city on reels of silent 8 mm film. After eighteen months at Leinster Terrace the pair moved into a flat at 20 Arundel Gardens, Notting Hill, with enough space for Meek to set up a whole room as his makeshift studio.

The ground-floor flat was in a grand terrace of four-storey Victorian houses backing onto an elegant communal garden, although by the time Meek and Howard moved in the area had become a little run down. Their apartment, while rather shabby, retained an aura of elegance from an earlier time, with high ceilings and ornate plasterwork. 'It was a very old property,' Howard revealed, 'but it did us for [at] the time, you know? It was quite near to Portobello Market which was handy.' Meek loved searching out cheap electrical equipment at the market: 'He always used to stop at the radios.' His most treasured possession was a professional-grade, battery-operated, portable, reel-to-reel tape recorder, an EMI L2, which used 5-inch tape reels. 'I used to borrow it from time to time,' Howard added. 'And it was very good quality, with a microphone built into the side. It was the sort of tape recorder that if anything should happen, like a crash, it would survive. Like a Black Box, you know? It was so well made... He'd go [a]round and get different sounds and mess about with them'.[54]

Love and Fury: The Life, Death and Legacy of Joe Meek

One day, Howard took Meek's treasured tape recorder to work, hiding it near the cash desk at the restaurant where he recorded the customers and waitresses without their knowledge, just as Meek himself had done with his family and neighbours back in Newent. The relationship with Lional seemed to give Meek extra confidence; Lional would occasionally join Joe on work trips, and now that they had more space at home, Meek would often host parties for musicians, artists and the friends he had made, including Adrian Kerridge and Denis Preston. Howard would, naturally, end up looking after the catering.

Meek had already proved that he could build just about any piece of electronic equipment he wanted, and when he was after a specific sound or feel that he could not quite realise through his own knowledge of electronics, he was more than capable of 'fiddling about' with another piece of equipment to achieve the desired effect. He discovered that using the direct input method of recording – feeding an instrument directly into the mixing desk or tape machine rather than having to use an amplifier with a microphone in front of it – gave him a different, cleaner and more immediate sound. It would also enable him to balance the sound of the individual instruments: using separate microphones for each of the amplified instruments in the studio would allow sound to 'bleed' and made it impossible to isolate one instrument or performance. Direct input (also known as 'direct injection') was revolutionary: within a few years almost every recording studio would work in the same way. 'His methods were well before their time,'[55] reflected musician Chas Hodges, of 1980s hitmakers Chas and Dave who, in 1960, became a member of Meek's in-house band the Outlaws. He perfected a way of 'close miking' each instrument and singer, allowing him more control when it came to mixing and editing the track. Most of the cavernous studios still tended to record a group 'as live', having them perform together, facing each other, in one room. If a string or brass section was called for, or a full orchestra, the room was usually big enough to have them in there too. With the majority of recordings being made in mono, there was little need or interest from companies to highlight individual players or performances – but Joe was able to isolate different instruments and create the sounds he heard in his head. He would take the front skin (or head) off a bass drum and put microphones inside the shell – unheard of before then. As Hodges would later put it, 'He really

Please Let It Happen to Me

had faith in himself having a "commercial ear". I wasn't quite sure what he meant at the time, but he said, "I know I've got a really commercial ear," which I think he did... He would hear something in his head. What he produced was what he felt inside his brain.'[56]

Meek went to electronics supplier Racal Ltd* and asked them to produce some equipment to his own specification. Vic Keary, who began work for Lansdowne the day after Joe left and who followed his career closely, later owned one of Joe's legendary 'black boxes': 'He basically gave them the design for an Altec compressor, which they copied for him, and also an equaliser which was based around a Pultec but with extra flexibility. Only one of these equalisers was ever made... it's an excellent and quite unique piece of gear. [It had] a very characteristic sound which is especially good on vocals.'[57] Meek took the black box from Lansdowne when he left and used it throughout his career. It eventually ended up in Keary's hands (who himself had used Joe's designs to produce his own equipment), although he sold it in the 1990s.

Whenever he wasn't working for Preston, Meek would be in his Arundel Gardens flat, preoccupied with his own recordings. As much as he enjoyed engineering hits for other people, he wanted to make his own records, the kind that teenagers would respond to when they heard them on the radio, or when they played them on jukeboxes in coffee bars. Most of the kids he saw as his potential customers listened to music on cheap transistor radios, which made everything sound tinny and weedy. Meek pushed bass levels to the limits, to give his records more depth and power: he compressed the sound coming from his instruments as much as possible, again to add extra drive when they were played over the air. Invariably, this extra bass and depth would cause problems for record pressing plants, with needles jumping out of the grooves when the discs were played at home, as he later explained to *Cash Box* magazine: 'Beat is terribly important, and I concentrate on the rhythm tracks first. I go after a colourful sound and try to create a picture with material originality.'[58]

---

*   Then a small British company that specialised in electronic equipment for the military; by the 1980s they had grown and would become the parent company of mobile phone giant Vodafone.

Denis Preston knew he had someone special in Meek and came to rely on him more and more.

In July 1957 Meek acted as engineer on the sessions for the *Moondog and Suncat Suites*, an album by tenor sax player Kenny Graham. Preston, Graham and Meek had already produced one album together, *Presenting Kenny Graham*, but this was something altogether different. A percussion-based exotica opus, one side of *Moondog And Suncat Suites* was based around material written and performed by legendary New York outsider musician Moondog (Louis Thomas Hardin), complimented by a collection composed by Graham himself. As well as a number of A-listers from the British jazz scene, the album featured haunting female vocals from a singer known only as Yolanda, who Meek would work with again a few years later. Alongside his success in the jazz field, more and more pop vocals came his way.

Issued in October 1956, 'The Green Door' was a number 2 hit in the UK for entertainer Frankie Vaughan, engineered by Meek and issued by Philips. Meek's hand in the production was so influential that it has even been suggested that one line in the lyrics – 'When I said, "Joe sent me," someone laughed out loud' – is a knowing reference to the engineer himself visiting well-known underground homosexual haunt the Gateways Club, in Chelsea. Although it would later become famous for its predominantly lesbian clientele, at that time the Gateways was popular with both gay men and lesbians, as well as the local arts crowd and the capital's growing Black community. However, in spite of the legend, that line appears in the original version, recorded by Jim Lowe and issued in the States two months before Frankie Vaughan's version hit British stores. The song's authors, Marvin Moore and Bob Davie, were referencing an earlier song, 'Hernando's Hideaway' and the line 'Just knock three times and whisper low / That you and I were sent by Joe'. The pair had no knowledge of the Gateways, and the idea that 'The Green Door' has anything to do with Britain's best known post-war LGBTQ club is, unfortunately, no more than an urban myth. Still, the huge success with Frankie Vaughan gave Meek the opportunity to work at Philips' own studios, in Stanhope Street near Marble Arch: Meek recorded his first session there before the studio had officially opened, capturing four sides for singer Billy Daniels.

Preston's accomplishments were unheralded: never before had an independent taken on Britain's major record companies, and every one of

Please Let It Happen to Me

them watched with envy as he scored hit after hit on the pop charts. Skiffle was all the rage, and Preston's biggest act, Lonnie Donegan, had gone from playing banjo with Chris Barber's Jazz Band to being a star in his own right following the international success of his single 'Rock Island Line'. Meek had already engineered a number of Donegan sides for Preston (all issued by Nixa) and in 1957 would also work on sessions for American singer and guitar player Johnny Duncan (like Donegan, another Chris Barber alumnus), issued on the Columbia album *Johnny Duncan's Tennessee Song Bag*. He engineered sessions for Barber himself (with Donegan on banjo) for Pye's *Jazz Today* series and for skiffle band the Worried Men, who featured a young man named Terry Nelhams. Nelhams, who at that time was working as a film cutter in the offices of Columbia Pictures in Soho's Wardour Street, would later find fame as chart topper Adam Faith.

Meek might have been a backroom boy, but Preston was all too aware of how important he was to his success: 'With multi-track recordings and other modern methods, seventy per cent of the credit for a hit record belongs to the manager and his engineers,' he told the readers of *Picturegoer* magazine. 'Many of the stars coming up these days have just a basic raw quality. The recording manager's job is to groom this into hit material.'[59] Meek was helping Lansdowne produce hit after hit, and having Preston tip his hat to him in print occasionally was all well and good, but he wanted people to recognise his own brilliance. His greatest successes to date – including 'Bad Penny Blues', 'Green Door' and 'Lay Down Your Arms' – had profited other people, but he had seen very little financial reward. Meek, regularly sending money home to help his widowed mother, wanted to make his own fortune, and he quickly became fed up working with temperamental artists who did their own thing and were always making demands. 'I've heard him cuss about artists and how idle they were,' Eric Meek revealed. 'They wouldn't turn up in the morning…' 'They had to be waited on hand and foot,'[60] his brother Arthur added.

Preston was happy to make the recordings and then sell them on to the highest bidder, but Meek had a better idea: what if he could keep the copyright to his recordings and simply license them to the major companies? What about, instead of working with established stars who came with their own managers, press agents, A&R people and the like, Meek could find and mould his own teen heartthrobs? Larry Parnes, then the biggest and most influential artist manager in Britain, had taken a handful of unknowns from the coffee shops of Soho and turned them into lamé-bedecked, headline-grabbing, audience-seizing stars: why couldn't Meek do the same? Rather than simply recording these performers for other companies, what about taking over their management, which would give Meek total control over the artists, their recordings and the direction of their careers?

Although he has a reputation for missing big opportunities (such as signing Rod Stewart, the Beatles or Tom Jones) and being bull-headed and ignoring shifting fashions, Meek recognised a trend when he saw one and was usually quick to act, often trying to find a sound-alike act or moulding a singer in the vein of another hit artist (Mike Berry as Buddy Holly, Heinz as Eddie Cochran or the Cameos as the Springfields, for example). In the summer of 1957 Meek came across a skiffle group performing in a local club, five teenagers from the West Kensington Congregational Church Youth Club who, because they had been busking in the West Kensington underground station, called themselves the Station Skiffle Group. The group had been performing since the beginning of the year, and by the time Meek 'discovered' them they had already been seen on live TV (on an episode of Carroll Levis's talent show *Discoveries*) and had released their first recordings, as part of their prize for coming first out of sixty-three similar acts at a 'Battle of the Skiffle Groups' which took place at the Metropole Theatre in Edgware at the end of March. Having already engineered several hits for Lonnie Donegan, surely he could work his magic on another skiffle act?

After seeing them perform, Meek took the teenagers for a drink at a nearby coffee bar. Looking around for inspiration, someone noticed the word 'barbecue' on the menu, and Meek and the band settled on Jimmy Miller and the Barbecues, after the group's 18-year-old singer, for the act's new name. Although he had no previous experience, he made it clear that he wanted to manage the act, and shortly afterwards he presented them with a fast, bouncy skiffle tune he had co-written with 17-year-old musician and aspiring musical arranger Charles Blackwell, who Meek had recently encountered working in the offices of Essex Music. 'Sizzlin' Hot' would be the first British single that Meek produced, engineered and had a hand in writing and, as Lional recalled, 'Joe worked very hard on that'.[61] The band demoed the song (and its flip side, 'Free Wheelin' Baby') on Meek's

Please Let It Happen to Me

primitive equipment, including a domestic, two-track, mono reel-to-reel tape recorder, the Grundig TK 820 (which Lional described as 'a valve set that weighed about a hundredweight!'[62]) and a professional, two-speed mono tape deck, the EMI TR50, a chunky piece of metal that weighed almost 30 kilos (Meek would later purchase a TR51 and use both decks side by side). Following a professional recording session at IBC, Joe got to work adding the effects that would soon become his trademark, including a reverb-drenched explosion – created by hitting a tuning fork against one of his home-built 'black box' echo units – at the start of 'Sizzlin' Hot'. Reviewer Neal Arden called the disc 'a masterpiece of orchestrated noise'.[63] With encouragement from Preston, Meek sold the tracks to Norrie Paramor, Columbia's A&R man, where they were issued on both 78 and 45 rpm on 27 September, a week after the group won first prize in a national skiffle contest held at Butlin's Holiday Camp in the seaside town of Skegness.

At the end of September, making the best use of the communal garden he shared with his neighbours, Joe held a barbecue (naturally), catered by Lional with a 'huge roast sizzling on a spit',[64] celebrating the launch of the record with a ceremonial smashing of a copy of the 10-inch. Meek enjoyed throwing parties: Lional would continue to organise the food for his gatherings long after they stopped living together, and he would arrange the catering for launch events after Meek moved to 304 Holloway Road. This particular evening, which was attended by up to 150 people including Paramor, Denis Preston, jazz singer Rosemary Squires, radio presenter Gerry Wilmott (co-presenter of Radio Luxembourg's *Shilling a Second*, which Joe had worked on), Nixa's head of A&R Alan Freeman (not the better-known radio DJ), actor Janette Scott, *Record Mirror* columnist Merry Nolan and Battersea-based nightclub singer Jackie Davies brought on the wrath of his neighbours, their heads already thumping from the bizarre electronic noises that had been pouring out of the flat for the last few months. Nolan was suitably impressed, calling Meek 'Denis Preston's star recording engineer', and boldly stated that he was 'a boy to watch. He's got enterprise, know-how, and the gratitude of a lot of artistes whom he has brought to the attention of the astute Mr Preston.'[65] Unfortunately, the building's owner was less impressed, and Joe and Lional were threatened with eviction. 'The old man in the basement was a bit of a menace,' Lional explained. 'Joe would be recording something and he would shout up and

Love and Fury: The Life, Death and Legacy of Joe Meek

say, "Stop that noise!" and things like that. Very often Joe would put a hose pipe down the stairs and turn the tap on! He had two big Alsatian dogs, this chap did, and he'd say, "I'll set them on to you," and things like that. It was a bit frightening... If those dogs had come up the stairs they would have torn us to pieces.'[66]

Meek thought he had a star in teenage screen-printer Jimmy Miller: he signed the band up to appear in a cinema advertisement for cigarettes and had Miller promote the record by making solo appearances at local record shops where he would strum a couple of numbers and sign copies of the disc. As a result, 'Sizzlin' Hot' sold respectably and was almost a hit, but apart from his misspelled surname as co-writer (Meek is credited on the disc as 'Meekel'), there's no credit for Joe on the label. Columbia was suitably impressed with Meek's production, however, and gave him and the Barbecues a three-month contract, enough time for them to issue their debut and record and release a follow-up, 'Jelly Baby' – the first song released written by 'Robert Duke' – backed with 'Cry, Baby Cry'. The name that appeared on the label beneath the title of the song was a pseudonym for Robert George Meek, inspired by a family friend who told him, shortly before he moved to London, that he would return home to Newent as a Duke. Many have noted that Meek used the name Duke in an attempt to avoid having to share royalties with his later business associates, but he began using the *nom de plume* two years before entering into any such financial arrangements.

'Jelly Baby' was credited to Jimmy Miller and the New Barbecues. The five-piece had grown to seven members with the addition of two young women, 17-year-old Jean Smith and 18-year-old Susan Holloway: 'I thought it would be a good idea to have girls in the group,' Miller explained. 'If we can attract girls as an all-male group, then presumably we can attract the boys if we have some glamorous girls in the group.'[67] Within weeks Miller and Smith were engaged, but with some of the band being called up to do their National Service, and others none too happy with his suggested changes in line-up and equipment, Meek opted to build a studio group around Miller for this recording. Meek wanted to change their sound and replace their traditional skiffle kit with something more contemporary, something he would also later attempt to do for jazz band Chris and the Students. A Jimmy Miller and the Barbecues EP planned for Columbia,

Please Let It Happen to Me

featuring new songs 'My Lord', 'Finding the Way' and 'Jeannie' was shelved, as was a live album – Meek set up a single mic on stage to capture one of the act's lively performances, but the sound was drowned out by the over-enthusiastic audience – but they would appear in the Alec Guinness comedy film *Barnacle Bill* (aka *All at Sea*). Despite the failure of the band to break through into the mainstream (partly as a result of Miller being hospitalised for several weeks in 1958, which meant that the Barbecues missed the chance of a six-month engagement in Spain), Meek and Miller would remain close friends, and the singer was a regular visitor to Meek's home, where both would take part in séances and Ouija board sessions.

Meek had a burning desire to be famous, but how would the world know how brilliant he was if his name was not on the disc? He craved recognition: fame was validation, proof that he, the lifelong outsider, was right and that his critics were wrong. It was also opportunity for him to show his family that the little boy they had accused of being 'soft in the head' was, in fact, a creative artist respected by his peers and in demand by the public, but it would be a while yet before people outside the music industry would know his name.

At the beginning of October 1957 the Russians launched the world's first artificial satellite, the first man-made object placed into the Earth's orbit: *Sputnik 1*. To people still reeling from the aftermath of World War Two, now living in fear of nuclear bombs and the increasingly hostile Cold War between the United States and the Soviet Union, the launch – and Russia claiming the lead in the Space Race – was a cause for concern. Yet for Meek, already fascinated with space travel and exploration, who had spent two years in the RAF monitoring the Russian threat, this seemed like a tremendous leap forward: new technology helping to make the world a smaller place. He voraciously devoured information about *Sputnik 1* and began planning a musical suite about the wonders of space travel and the possibilities of life on other planets. It would take him two and a half years to realise his dream, his 1960 masterwork *I Hear a New World*.

In the meantime, Preston kept Meek furiously busy; Britain was experiencing a jazz boom fuelled by the interest in skiffle and stoked by the country's music papers, who continually insisted that rock 'n' roll was no more than a fad and that trad jazz was 'the next big thing'. In the last half of the year he engineered sessions from Peggy Seeger, the Don Rendell Jazz

Love and Fury: The Life, Death and Legacy of Joe Meek

Six, the Allan Ganley Quartet, the Don Savage Seven, the Melody Maker All Stars and clarinettist Art Ellefson, all for Nixa's 'Jazz Today' series, plus the EP *Frank Holder Sings Calypso* for Decca and many others.

With barely a minute to himself, he somehow still made time for his own work. In December 1957 Meek and Charles Blackwell penned, and Meek engineered and produced, the sole single by Jackie Davies – one of the guests at his 'Sizzlin' Hot' launch party – a Nat King Cole-style ballad 'Land of Make Believe', issued by Nixa. Recorded at Olympic Studios (then in Fulham: the studio would move to Carlton Street, near Piccadilly Circus in 1958 before moving to Barnes in 1966), during which Davies also ran through standards including 'Nice Work If You Can Get It', 'Take the "A" Train' and 'Is You Is or Is You Ain't My Baby?'. The disc got good reviews, with Meek's songwriting skills singled out for praise by Neal Arden of national Sunday newspaper *The People*, who noted that 'Joe is plainly a potential hit writer',[68] but the single failed to chart and multi-instrumentalist Davies turned to teaching, becoming a vocal coach before reinventing himself as Latin dance band leader Chico Arnéz.

CHAPTER 5

You've Got to Have a Gimmick Today

In late 1957 Meek met siblings Dave and Marion (who was known by her middle name, Joy) Adams. Born on Jersey but brought up in Ruislip, although Dave was only 18 and Joy one year older, both teenagers were gifted musically: Dave played keyboards, violin and accordion, and his sister played guitar, saxophone and clarinet. Both could sing, and both had been involved in the family act, a country and western-style pub band (a Triumph Records press release called their sound 'Hilly-Billy')[69] dubbed Big Fred Adams and his Fowl House Pests. 'I come from a very musical family,' Joy reveals. 'There was always singing in my house. Every holiday, every Christmas, every time we'd get together there was always music. It was like second nature.' Joy worked days as a switchboard operator for a large furniture store, Hamptons in Kensington, and young Dave was studying carpentry – a skill that would guarantee him plenty of work with Meek over the next decade.

With their older brother, Brian, and a couple of neighbours, the teenagers had been part of a rock and skiffle act, but were now performing as a duo. 'I would not call myself accomplished,' says Joy modestly. 'I played guitar, but I was busy with other things too. I always wanted to be an artist and always wanted to go to art school, but ever since we were very small children – during World War Two – we sang. We grew up with music, and then of course when rock 'n' roll happened everything broke loose.'[70] Joy gave her first public performance at a street party in 1945. 'I didn't have a shy bone in my body. I was ready to get up and show off for anybody! Dave on the other hand was very withdrawn, quiet, but he also had this desire for recognition and so he sang too. Dave was a man of few words. I was the one with the loud mouth! Dave was a very thoughtful kind of person.

'I remember Joe vividly, and our days with him, the peculiarities and idiosyncrasies he had, like nobody I've ever known before or since. We were already singing as a duo in London nightclubs. We met several acquaintances of Joe's, who recommended us to him. Then we received a call directly from him at our family home. We were both very young and naive at the time.'[71] Meek invited the pair to audition for him at Arundel Gardens. Joy, now a successful wildlife painter in upstate New York, recalls that Meek was 'soft spoken, kind and very interested in us. His recording studio was packed with equipment and dozens of dusty connecting wires running all over it.'[72] In his unpublished autobiography, Dave Adams remembered that first encounter: 'A smiling, well-dressed man stepped into the room carrying a microphone on a stand which he placed next to the piano. Slightly portly, with slicked back brown hair and a carefully combed quiff, long feminine hands and a manner which held the quality of an excited child. Not at all what I had expected, but then I had no idea *what* to expect. "Hello," he said. His blue eyes met mine and in them I saw something that instantly made me at one with him.'[73]

What Dave recognised in Joe was a kindred spirit. 'In those days being gay was a secret you didn't tell anybody,' says Joy. 'Homosexuality was unacceptable in those days and Joe tried to keep it a secret. Well, it was an open secret. Dave was gay too; it was all a huge secret, even in my own family.' Dave would later marry and have two daughters. 'Marriage was a way of hiding what he really was naturally,' Joy admits. 'In our day gay relationships were totally and completely unacceptable, and for that reason Dave kept it to himself, but I think that Joe and he had a thing.'[74] In his unpublished memoir, *After All These Bloody Years*, Dave revealed that he and Joe first slept together around a fortnight later.

That night Dave and Joy cut a demo (under the name The Kids), with Dave bashing out Meek's own song 'The Old Red Lion' at the upright piano in the front room, to Meek's foot-tapping accompaniment. The Red Lion is one of the most common names for a British pub, and Meek was well acquainted with several, including one in Market Square back in Newent and the one he used to walk past on his way to work at Stones on Edgware Road. IBC rented a studio and editing suite in Conway Hall, in Red Lion Square, so the source of inspiration could have come from any number of different places, or perhaps all of them. The Kids' demo of 'The Old Red

You've Got to Have a Gimmick Today

Lion', complete with overdubbed sound effects to create the atmosphere of a pub lounge, went unissued for decades (another Meek composition from the same period, 'Down in the Jungle' remains missing), but the recording was good enough to secure the duo a recording test at Parlophone, which took place on 12 December 1957. The Adams siblings would issue several records engineered, produced and occasionally written by Meek, and Dave Adams would continue to work with him for the rest of Meek's life: one of the first jobs he secured through Meek was working as a carpenter at Lansdowne, where Dave and Joe would use any free time to make demo recordings of their songs.

Work for Preston, and for Pye-Nixa, continued unabated: the jazz boom was keeping Lansdowne busy, and in January 1958 Meek worked on sessions for the Bruce Turner Jump Band and west country jazz superstar Acker Bilk. But even Meek had to have some downtime. Between sessions for Turner and Bilk, during one of his regular table-tapping sessions with Jimmy Miller and another friend (of Middle Eastern descent, Miller later identified him as a Mr Faud),* Meek claimed to have been contacted by a spirit who warned them that the singer with US rock 'n' roll act the Crickets, Buddy Holly, was not long for this world. The three men were sat around a table holding hands: Miller was dealing tarot cards with his one free hand, while the other was holding onto Meek, at one point gripping it so firmly that his fingernails dug into the palm of Meek's hand and drew blood. Meek, in turn, was holding one of Faud's hands, while Faud's free hand held a pen which scribbled the phrase 'February 3rd, Buddy Holly dies'. 'The whole affair was amazing,' Miller, who had not used tarot cards before, recalled. 'The message was written in what looked very much like my own handwriting.'[75]

Holly had only recently become known to British audiences; his band's breakthrough hit, 'That'll Be the Day', had made the UK number 1 spot the previous November, and he was currently riding high with his first solo release, 'Peggy Sue'. The first week of February came and went: Holly not only survived but celebrated two entries in the British Top 10, 'Oh Boy' at number 5 and 'Peggy Sue' two spots below that.

Less than four weeks later the singer and his band embarked on their first (and only) UK tour, a gruelling twenty-five one-night stands (with

---

* Faud is an Arabic given name (male Christian name), meaning 'heart'.

Love and Fury: The Life, Death and Legacy of Joe Meek

two shows each day) throughout March, supported by Gary Miller, the singer whose singles Meek had engineered. Convinced that he had to get word to Holly about the message he and his friends had received, Meek tried to contact him, getting in touch with tour promoter Arthur Howes to insist that someone make Holly aware of his certain fate. Legend has it that Meek went to one of the first dates (Holly and the Crickets opened at the Trocadero, Elephant and Castle, on 1 March, around 5 miles from Arundel Gardens; their second night was in Kilburn, less than half that distance away) to warn Holly of the message from beyond. Somehow word of his impending doom got through to Holly, but the singer laughed it off. Eleven months later Holly, singers Ritchie Valens and the Big Bopper, J. P. Richardson, and their pilot Roger Peterson, would perish when the plane they were travelling on crashed during a snowstorm. The date: 3 February.

Meek held Holly in high regard; he was the first rock 'n' roll singer who had struck a chord with him, and he would continue to see him as a benchmark. He once had a row with Bobby Graham, drummer with his house band the Outlaws, after Graham had disparaged the quality of Holly's recordings, and years later, when reviewing 1965's posthumous collection *Holly in the Hills*, Meek wrote that 'the untimely passing of Buddy Holly robbed the pop music world of one of its finest young talents... His songs never seem to date, and via his unique voice he creates a happy, easy-going form of beat music. So many singers have tried to copy Buddy but none has ever reached his high standard. I rate him next to Presley in importance and influence. His music will never fade.'[76]

Meek was keen to pursue his songwriting, but his boss had other plans for his top engineer, including a trip, on 23 May 1958, to Germany to record Chris Barber and his band in concert for a forthcoming release, *Barber in Berlin*. Recording live always presented problems, but Denis Preston knew how much experience Meek had gained touring the country working for Radio Luxembourg, and he needed him on his team. Setting up their equipment in the stalls of the 12,000-seat Deutschlandhalle, Meek, assisted by Danish engineer Peter Willemoës, had no opportunity to soundcheck with Barber's crew before tapes started rolling, but the results were remarkable, and Meek gained valuable experience recording in stereo in a live setting.

You've Got to Have a Gimmick Today

Preston had been reasonably accommodating when it came to Meek's songwriting, but with most of his current workload dictated by jazz there was little he could do to help place his latest offering, and after months of badgering Preston to no avail, in May 1958 Meek submitted one of his own compositions to the young head of A&R at Parlophone, George Martin, whose acquaintance he had made through Joy and Dave. Former coal miner Eddie Silver (born Edward Sivell, in Newcastle upon Tyne in 1935) had been in London since April, having come down south with his band the Railroaders to take part in a skiffle competition. The band came third. Half of the members elected to stay in London and try their luck, the others returned home: two members, Hank Marvin and Bruce Welch, would join a new group, the Drifters, which the following year would be renamed the Shadows. Silver went solo, and on Sunday 4 May found himself at Meek's Arundel Gardens home.

As Meek wrote in a letter to his mother, 'The day he was at my place I recorded one of my songs, 'Put a Ring on Her Finger'. Well he played this to Parlophone chief George Martin and he said that's perfect for you…'[77] 'Put a Ring on Her Finger', issued in June 1958, was Meek's fourth A-side as a songwriter, and it impressed reviewer Neal Arden, who told his readers that it 'made him stand up and dance', and that he rated the song as 'a potential best seller of the long-lasting sort.'[78] In spite of Arden's ardour the disc (again credited to Robert Duke) was not a hit, although Martin was impressed enough to have Silver cut further demos of Meek's compositions for a potential follow-up. Silver's second release would not include any Meek originals; however, 'Put a Ring on Her Finger' was covered by a number of other acts, from Danish singer Lis Bjørnholt to US stars Les Paul and Mary Ford. Their success – the disc sold 800,000 copies in its first ten days on sale and provided the duo with their last Top 40 hit – helped persuade the Larry Parnes-managed British rock 'n' roller Tommy Steele to cover the song as the B-side to his October 1958 single, 'Come On, Let's Go'. Meek made over £3,000 from 'Put a Ring on Her Finger' (equivalent to more than £87,000 in 2024), money that would eventually help fund his own company.

Written on the train while heading to Blackpool to record an episode of *People Are Funny*, Silver's version of 'Put a Ring On Her Finger' may not have hit the mark, but the continued contact with George Martin would

Love and Fury: The Life, Death and Legacy of Joe Meek

prove useful. Meek recalled a song that the Adams siblings had performed for him at their audition, and he felt that it would be ideal for their debut release. The song, 'Whoopee!', had begun life after Dave Adams had suffered a minor accident at work. While waiting to have a hand injury seen to, he had been scribbling ideas for a song on the back of a cigarette packet. Once home he continued working on the idea until he thought they had something interesting. 'Dave wrote 'Whoopee!' from home,' Joy recalls. 'He was writing music from a very young age, and we had already added it to our song list before we met Joe. It was influenced by the well-known [1928 Eddie Cantor] song 'Makin' Whoopee'.'* The pair took it to Meek who, in turn, offered it to his boss Denis Preston, although the initial recording took place at EMI's studios in Abbey Road, not at Lansdowne, supervised by Martin. Meek, however, could not resist tinkering with the tapes, taking them and adding his own effects before passing them back to Martin for his approval: 'That was just like Joe,' Joy Adams laughs. In September 1958 Parlophone issued 'Whoopee!' (with the pair credited as Joy and David), backed with 'My Oh My!', mistakenly credited to Robert Luke, instead of Meek's preferred songwriting pseudonym Robert Duke. All of the early Meek trademarks are present, including the heavy echo and reverb on the handclaps, and a number of sound effects: the verses of 'Whoopee!' are punctuated with pops (inspired by the Chordettes' recent hit, 'Lollipop') and 'the juiciest kissing sounds ever heard on record';[79] the frantic 'My Oh My!' features percussive 'boing's which burst through the clattering drums to punctuate the choruses.

'The thing about Joe is that he was incredibly corny,' Joy Adams sighs. 'His music was really cornball. And we were all so very, very young and so whatever he said was what we went along with. When I look back on that music now I think about how much better we could have been if he hadn't been such an influence on us. But it was Joe's way or the highway, so you did what he said and went along with it. We were very naive about showbusiness, we were just young kids. Joe, in my opinion, was a very bad songwriter, but we sang his songs. Dave was quite good at it; he wrote some good songs, but Joe wouldn't listen. He had a mind of his own when

---

* The original release credits Joy and Dave as co-writers but, according to Joy, 'I had nothing to do with it.'

You've Got to Have a Gimmick Today

it came to what it should sound like, and it fitted the time period perfectly well.'[80]

Once again, the flat that Joe and Lional shared would be the venue for the duo's official launch party. Meek invited the media around to introduce the pair to the public, where the dutiful Lional provided nibbles, and an EMI publicity agent revealed that he had wanted to call the act 'Adams and Eve', 'a gimmick name you boys can get your teeth into'.[81] The pair gave an impromptu performance for the gentlemen of the press, which led to the disc being reviewed nationally and issued in both the US and Canada. After a hair-raising debut concert in front of the inmates of Wormwood Scrubs, dates on a package tour over the Christmas/New Year period followed, headlined by the fast-rising young star Cliff Richard and his band the Drifters, but sadly the disc failed to register in Britain, despite an appearance to plug the song on BBC radio's popular *Saturday Club*. 'Whoopee!' fared no better elsewhere, selling a miserable eighty-five copies in the United States. The pair's next release, the March 1959 single 'Rocking Away the Blues' (a track co-written by Dave and Joe, backed with Robert Duke's 'If You Pass Me By'), was turned down by Parlophone and instead appeared on Decca. In April Decca advertised the disc in the *New Musical Express*, flipping the sides to favour 'If You Pass Me By', but none of the Joy and Dave singles would chart.*

That summer, at a lavish reception at the Cora Hotel near Russell Square (now the Hilton London Euston), Pye-Nixa introduced the press and their dealers to the wonders of stereo sound, launching their own small range of stereo record players and a selection of gimmick discs. The company had already issued Britain's first stereophonic EP, *Pops Go Stereo*, featuring acts Preston and Meek had worked with, and with such close ties to the company, the pair would have been amongst the industry invitees checking out what stereo could offer. Lansdowne was quick to get in on the act, and following Meek's live work with Chris Barber in Berlin, Lansdowne

---

* The Adams siblings' older brother, Brian, would cut a one-off single for Meek in 1960; the Robert Duke song 'Early in the Morning', backed with 'Cool Water', would end up credited to Chick, Ted Cameron Group and the DJs... the DJs being Dave and Joy. Originally intended for release by Triumph, the disc was eventually issued by Pye. A second Triumph single by Chick would remain in the vaults.

began producing their own stereophonic jazz recordings in London that July. Meek fell in love with the potential of stereo to immerse the listener in the aural experience, and he would continue to play with this new medium whenever he had opportunity. His own experiments, both during work hours and after the rest of the team had gone home, would be put to great use for his magnum opus, *I Hear a New World*.

Following the success of 'Put a Ring on Her Finger', Meek naturally assumed that Preston would be more inclined to let him offer his compositions to the artists recording at Lansdowne. But this was not the case, and their last few months together were marked by furious rows, as Meek tried to persuade Preston to consider his songs for commercial release. Meek's ire would have increased when a 1956 Preston/Meek production, 'Petite Fleur' by the Chris Barber Jazz Band, was resurrected by Pye-Nixa in January 1959 and became a Top 5 hit on both sides of the Atlantic; the disc's sound was heavily influenced by Meek's studio work, yet his name did not appear anywhere on the label. That same month, during the sessions for *This Is Chico*, by Latin band leader Chico Arnéz (real name the much less exotic John Claude Davies, who had already recorded for Meek as Jackie Davies), the band recorded a Meek instrumental, a vaguely Eastern pastiche which Meek had dubbed 'Yashmak'. The track was well liked by the powers that be at Nixa, and it was also issued as the top side of a single. Yet in spite of Preston's acknowledgement of Meek's burgeoning talent – he told the *Daily Mirror* that Meek was an essential member of his small team, the man who looked after 'the technical side of the business' and who made sure that 'the recorded sound is impeccable'[82] – the two men endured a difficult relationship. Arnéz would remember the recordings as fraught, with several major rows between Preston and Meek about the direction the sessions were taking.

This situation was exacerbated by the fact that Meek was unpredictable and would fly into uncontrollable rages when upset. Partly these tantrums were born of frustration: not being a musician he often found it difficult to express his ideas in a way that the artists he worked with would understand, but some of these sudden outbursts seem to have been aggravated by an undiagnosed mental health condition and further exacerbated by his daily intake of pep pills. Preston, for the most part, was more even-tempered, although he liked a drink and could become unpleasant when he'd had a

You've Got to Have a Gimmick Today

few, something that would occasionally vex the virtually teetotal Meek. When the red mist began to descend, Meek would stamp his foot like a petulant child; he would grind his teeth, his face would become flushed, and veins in his face would start throbbing. People knew what to expect and soon scattered.

Tamsin Embleton, psychotherapist, writer and clinical lead of the Music Industry Therapist Collective explains that 'in general, stigma against mental illness was high. People were afraid of mental illness and had a lack of understanding around what possible causes might be and what could help someone recover... I would be tempted to assume that, provided Joe was productive and broadly able to collaborate and communicate, his problems would have been overlooked. Some symptoms might have been framed as personality quirks, eccentricity or a facet of his creative genius: "That's just Joe". Anger may not have been seen as problematic, particularly as he was male, though erratic outbursts would have put people on edge. They might have learnt how to tiptoe around him.'[83]

Although reluctant, Preston still offered Meek the occasional opportunity to showcase his songwriting, such as when he was given the chance (as Robert Duke) to provide the B-side to a novelty single by Terry White, a columnist on *Valentine*, a magazine for teenage girls, and his fictional band the Terriers. White edited the letters page of the picture story weekly, and his single 'Rock Around the Mailbag' reflected this, but Decca preferred Meek's composition, the frantic, echo- and effects-drenched 'Blackout', and promoted this as the plug side.

But it was for his work as an engineer that Meek was getting noticed. In September, Nixa issued the latest single from Scottish actor John Fraser. 'Bye Bye Baby Goodbye' was a stilted ballad, lushly orchestrated by Wally Stott (who Meek first worked with at IBC), who would transition in the mid-1970s and change her name to Julia Morley, but Meek slathered its B-side, 'Golden Cage' (co-written by Dave Adams), 'with so much echo that it sounds like a Stan Freberg burlesque... If you can sort out Fraser's voice from his reverberations, you may think it has hardly been worth the trouble.'[84] Meek claimed to have produced the October 1959 release from Emile Ford and the Checkmates, 'What Do You Want to Make Those Eyes at Me For?', although Ford would counterclaim that he had produced the disc himself. If Meek was involved with the recording, then 'What Do You

Want to Make Those Eyes at Me For?' would have been his first number 1 hit as a producer, rather than as a more lowly engineer: the record hit the top spot the week before Christmas 1959 and stayed there until the last week of January 1960.

One of the last projects Meek worked on for Preston, again with Morley, was the debut album from British actress Diana Dors, *Swingin' Dors*. These sessions seemed to go without too much upset, but Meek's days at Lansdowne were numbered. Preston had become aware that Meek was working at the studio at night, behind his back, on his own productions. He was also finding Meek's secretive way of working and his jealous guarding of the artists he considered to be his acts more difficult to brush off as simple eccentricity. The tension that had been building up was reaching breaking point, and at the beginning of November 1959, during a recording session for Kenny Graham, Meek and Preston had yet another face-off. Meek wanted Graham to record some of his own songs, and Preston was having none of it. After a heated row Joe walked out of Lansdowne, no doubt cursing his former boss as a 'rotten pig' as he slammed the door behind him. The next day Adrian Kerridge was called into the office and given Meek's job.

Much to everyone's embarrassment, Meek turned up for work the following morning as if nothing had happened. 'No surprise there, the pills had worn off,'[85] Kerridge commented. Preston fired him on the spot. Meek would later confess that the strain of working for Lansdowne had been getting too much and that 'he was so physically shattered... that his nose bled and he had to go home and rest'. After being fired he admitted that he 'cried all night and had nightmares about people with holes in their heads'.[86] Luckily, Meek had a bulging address book full of the industry contacts he had made over the last few years. He had recently become reacquainted with Charles Blackwell, the brilliant young musical arranger and orchestra leader he had first worked with two years earlier on the singles from Jimmy Miller and the Barbecues, and Jackie Davies. Blackwell was now working with another young musician, John Barry (under the alias Johnny Prendy), and had been brought in to work on the first single for Lance Fortune, a singer co-managed by Larry Parnes.

Parnes was the biggest name in the entertainment industry at that time, a manager with a 'stable' of stars, many of whom had adopted stage names bequeathed to them by the great impresario: Vince Eager, Marty Wilde,

You've Got to Have a Gimmick Today

Johnny Gentle and the like. Parnes, like Meek, was homosexual and not above exploiting his position to gain sexual favours, something which several young stars of the day knew all too well. Things were not going too well for his second-biggest turn, Marty Wilde, then signed to Philips. Several attempts had been made to record a new single at Philips' own studios, but despite a fast-looming release date none were satisfactory. When Parnes wanted to take Wilde back and try again, he was unable to secure any studio time. Wilde suggested to a frustrated Parnes that they take a look at Lansdowne instead, and the pop Svengali – whose biggest star, Tommy Steele, had already covered Meek's song 'Put a Ring on Her Finger' – was impressed when Meek managed to get the definitive performance of the classic 'Sea of Love' from the singer after just two takes. Parnes recalled that Meek 'seemed to be very innovative. He had ideas that we'd never seen with other engineers,'[87] and his and Wilde's trust in him paid off when Meek's 'commercial ear' presented them with a Top 3 hit. It made perfect sense to Blackwell and Barry to recommend Meek to helm the Lance Fortune sessions. The resulting single, 'Be Mine', was Joe's first fully independent production... and another Top 5 hit.

However, even though he had a track record as an established hit maker, very few of Meek's industry friends came calling. There was the occasional small freelance job – Heinz Burt would later claim that Meek recorded singer Alma Cogan, and her early 1960 B-side 'O Dio Mio' has enough echo on it to suggest that Meek had a hand in it – but the record business of the late 1950s was a virtual closed shop. Preston and Lansdowne had proven that there was room for the independent producer, but his records (outside the Lonnie Donegan hits, anyway) were treated as novelties or, in the case of his jazz output, as part of a passing fad that Britain's biggest companies were not keen to invest in. Larry Parnes had tried to establish his own independent record label, Elempi (from the initials L.M.P, Laurence Maurice Parnes), and had immediately found the majors closing him out, refusing to press his records and threatening to boycott his artists. If Meek was to follow the independent path, he would need someone to back him who was not involved with – or was not afraid to take on – Britain's all-powerful record companies.

Businessman and financier Wilfred Alonzo Banks was able to offer Meek the lifeline for which he was clutching. Born in September 1913, Banks had served in the Royal Army Service Corps during World War Two, where he had reached the rank of major. On leaving the service he became a postmaster before moving into his own business, selling greetings cards, comics and gifts. He began importing and distributing toys and soon moved into the highly lucrative (but obviously seasonal) Christmas market, selling ornaments and setting up the first company in Britain to manufacture and sell artificial Christmas trees.

In 1958 Major Banks had been called in to help pianist Leonard Cassini, the owner of Saga Films. The company was in severe financial straits, but despite having a reputation as someone able to turn failing businesses around, Banks was unable to find anyone interested in taking on the Saga Films catalogue, which consisted almost entirely of documentaries about classical composers and musicians. There was some interest, however, in the recordings the company had made for the soundtracks to their films, and Banks was able to pull the financial backing together to help Cassini establish Saga Records, Britain's first budget record label. Saga, whose albums sold for a modest 25 shillings – significantly cheaper than the average list price of 32 shillings – soon diversified from their classical catalogue into jazz and easy listening music, instructional records (including EPs of guitar lessons and foreign language courses) and sound-alike re-recordings of stage and screen hits. Banks struck a deal with one of the then-popular home shopping catalogues to sell Saga records direct to consumers via mail order, and soon Saga were shifting huge numbers of their titles. When the UK's manufacturers could not provide him with discs at a price he was willing to pay, Banks simply switched to Pathé's pressing plant in France; EMI's Sir Joseph Lockwood discovered just how much business Banks was giving to Pathé (an EMI subsidiary) and offered to press Saga's albums at EMI's own plant in Hayes, Middlesex.

Banks had overseen a turnaround in Saga's financial affairs, but feeling that Cassini's dedication to classical music was holding the company back from further expansion, he unceremoniously ousted Saga's founder. Banks himself had no prior knowledge of the music industry, so he took on William Barrington-Coupe, who had previously run the short-lived classical label the Concert Artist Record Company, to act as Saga's managing director. Keen to move into the lucrative pop market, the company signed British singer Larry Page (later to manage the Kinks and the Troggs) and a young US actor and dancer named George Chakiris, who had recently been receiving rave reviews for his performance in *West Side Story* in London's West End.

Both Banks and Barrington-Coupe could smell money, and neither of them were averse to bending a few rules in the pursuit of profit. Both were constantly on the lookout for a way to make a quick buck, and although Meek was now out of work he had a fat royalty cheque from 'Put a Ring on Her Finger' burning a hole in his pocket. Impressed with Meek's work at Lansdowne, Saga brought him in to produce a session for Chakiris with the view to issuing a single, and although that would remain unreleased for now, the session would prove fortuitous for all concerned because it would lead to Meek striking a deal with Saga to help the company establish their own pop label, Triumph. Banks declined to get involved personally in this new project: his mother had recently passed away and he was embroiled in sorting out his late parents' estate (his father had been a farmer and the owner of several country grocery stores), and that, coupled with his other business interests, meant that he simply did not have the time for another distraction. However, he did provide Barrington-Coupe with the financial backing and, with an initial investment of £1,500 each, at the end of January 1960 Meek and Barrington-Coupe set up as equal partners in a new company, Triumph (Superfi) Sound Ltd* with an office provided by Banks in Empire Yard, Holloway, built on the site of the old Holloway Empire variety theatre. 'It was a tremendous gamble,' Meek later admitted. 'And maybe I was over-ambitious, but that's the way I am.'[88]

The first Triumph recording session took place in the first week of February 1960, while Barrington-Coupe was in discussions with Roulette in the US, a record company notorious for its connections to the criminal underground, about a licensing deal for Triumph masters. That first session featured Sri Lankan-born singer and actor Yolanda (real name Yolande Bavan), who Meek had first worked with when he engineered Kenny Graham's *Moondog and Suncat Suites*. Yolanda, who had recently made a number of appearances on television in Britain, cut two numbers for the

---

*   Although the company was not registered until 31 March 1960, the first mention of Triumph in the national press came in the 29 January edition of the *New Musical Express*. They began promoting their new company on 18 February, with a marketing mailout to potential stockists.

company, the Robert Duke-penned 'With This Kiss' and 'Don't Tell Me Not to Love You', but Meek needed something more peppy for the label's initial release and the disc would not appear until April.*

Britain's major record companies did not much care who pressed their records for them when the company was putting out cheap classical product, but now that Saga was moving into the pop music field the knives were out. EMI, Decca and the likes were not going to allow some upstart to spoil their game, and Pye immediately responded by launching their own budget album series, Golden Guinea. Meek, naturally, was gleefully unaware of the problems looming on the horizon. He had no interest in pressing plants and distribution deals and very little interest in where the money came from to facilitate such things. He just wanted to make records. Someone else could deal with the business side, as long as they left him alone to do his work.

---

* Yolande Bavan would become better known as an actress and jazz singer: she released three albums with the group Lambert, Hendricks & Bavan, and has a string of stage and television credits to her name.

CHAPTER 6

I Hear a New World

Joe came to Triumph with the words of Denis Preston ringing in his ears. 'We don't bid for established people like Vera Lynn,' Preston had told the *Daily Mirror*, 'but work exclusively with what we call "off-beat" talent. We are responsible for the conception, ideas and production of a record.'[89] It was a mantra that Meek would hold dear for the rest of his life. One of Preston's 'off-beat' recordings – probably the last major project that Meek was involved with at Lansdowne – was issued by Columbia in early 1960, while Meek was trying to get Triumph off the ground. An album of songs from the American Civil War, entitled *The Blue and the Grey* and performed by the George Mitchell Singers (better known as the Black and White Minstrels), the material could not have been further removed from what Meek was now investing his time and expertise in.

The birth of the new label was heralded with plenty of press coverage, with the company's representatives taking every opportunity they had to ram home Triumph's chief objective: to make records for the kids. 'A new disc company, Triumph Records, was launched in London this week — which aims to make records for teenagers ONLY. One of the men behind the project knows how to make a noise. He is recording engineer Joe Meek, 28, from Gloucester. He has recorded big hits by Frankie Vaughan, Lonnie Donegan, Emile Ford and Marty Wilde among others.'[90] Meek, who had for so long sought acclaim for his work was more than happy to be the public face of the business. 'A bold 28-years-old businessman named Joe Meek has set up his own record company — Triumph Records – with the stated intention of producing platters designed solely for teenagers who sip coffee or coke around juke boxes. "Let us be clear," says Joe. "The juke box is one

Love and Fury: The Life, Death and Legacy of Joe Meek

of the most important factors in the exploitation of records today. Why make records for those who don't buy them?"' Among the first Triumph records are these singles: Peter Jay singing 'Just Too Late', The Cavaliers and "Magic Wheel", Joy and David Adams with "Believe Me."[91] Meek was not 28, he was almost 31, but for the rest of his life he would shave a few years off his age, aware that anyone over 30 would be considered 'square' by the audience he was aiming for.

One of the first people Meek brought into Triumph was Charles Blackwell, the brilliant young arranger he had first met three years earlier. Blackwell's first project for Triumph, his first session as both musical director and arranger for anyone, was Joy and Dave's peppy 'Let's Go See Gran'ma'. 'He was very distant,' Joy recalls, and despite their ages being similar, she says that 'he appeared to be older than us and we were a bit intimidated by him'.[92] Blackwell, still just 19 at the time, had initially been unsure about getting involved with Triumph: 'I wasn't very confident because I felt that I hadn't the ability, but it was too good an opportunity to turn down.'[93]

The first brace of discs from the new label arrived on 19 February: 'Just Too Late', by singer Peter Jay, and 'Magic Wheel', credited to the rather oddly named Rodd-Ken The Cavaliers. Peter Jay (real name Peter Lynch, and not the same Peter Jay who led the Jaywalkers) was one of the first singers to be signed to Triumph, and the single saw him accompanied by the Blue Men, Meek's alternative name for the Cavaliers. The youngster had, apparently, been discovered by 'a passing stranger' at 'two o'clock one morning on Hampstead Heath, strumming a guitar in the back of a car'.[94] The same stranger is supposed to have signed the guitar picker to a contract on the spot. Strangers did not tend to go to Hampstead Heath at two in the morning looking to sign singers; most went to the notorious gay cruising ground for one thing only. Meek was a regular visitor to the Heath, making use of the men-only swimming pond, a popular pick-up spot now and then. The inference is that the stranger – identified as Meek in *Cash Box* magazine the following week – first spotted the young man when he was looking for something other than guitar players, but however it happened, the young hopeful was given a contract as well as a new name. 'Just Too Late', Triumph's official debut, was written by Meek under his preferred songwriting pseudonym Robert Duke (Meek would use at least half a dozen other names), with the flip composed by Jay himself.

I Hear a New World

Radio personality Keith Fordyce, writing for the *New Musical Express*, felt that 'Just Too Late', with its 'nippy beat and bright rock sound' had the makings of a hit and that it 'could be a big seller if it gets enough exposure'.[95] Meek wanted the public to know that Triumph was different, and that far from simply copying current US hits or taking on established stars, the engineer-turned-A&R man was intent on establishing his own roster of big sellers: 'I've built stars before for other record companies', he boasted, 'And I can do it again. I've been looking out for suitable material for the last six months with this company in mind. Because we're young we know what the pop fans like. I'm a pop fan myself so I should be able to tell. I don't think the big companies know what the youngsters want. It's more a case of hit and miss with them.'[96] Promising a pair of 45s a month, the next release would be 'Let's Go See Gran'ma', which *Disc* magazine thought 'a cute ballad' that was 'tuneful enough to catch on quickly'.[97]

For the single originally scheduled as the fourth release on the label, Meek brought trad jazz outfit Chris Williams and His Monsters into the Triumph fold, an act he had previously worked with after Denis Preston had seen them perform at Humphrey Lyttleton's jazz club, 100 Oxford Street, and had signed them to a one-disc deal. The tune chosen for their debut, issued by Columbia in November 1959, had been one of Meek's own compositions, 'The Monster', but it failed to sell and the album's worth of material that was recorded by the band, under Meek's aegis, at Lansdowne was canned. The two tracks 16-year-old clarinet prodigy Williams and his band would record for Triumph, 'Kicking Around' and 'Midnight Rocker', were slated to be issued alongside 'Let's Go See Gran'ma', but the disc would not make it to the shops, despite white label copies being pressed. Meek obviously liked the tune though, as 'Kicking Around' would later be recorded by the Outlaws (as 'The Outlaws', on their album *Dream of the West*) and by the space suit-wearing Spotnicks as 'Spaceship Rendezvous'.

Triumph, which officially launched with a party in the first week of March, was keen to procure even more new talent for their books, although it often seemed that the label had given little thought about what to do with the acts once they were under contract. South London instrumental quintet the Lee Alan Combo were signed by Meek to a deal that guaranteed the company a minimum of four discs per year, yet no release would emerge from the group in the company's lifetime. Another of Meek's personal signings was Owen Finnigan, a singing bartender from Northern Ireland, discovered in London in 1959 by US actor Broderick Crawford, who was then living and working in Europe. Crawford introduced him to Meek, who had the perfect song, 'A Girl Called Bonnie', co-written by Paul Williams of Chris Williams and His Monsters. However, neither it nor the B-side, Finnigan's own composition 'My Antrim Hills', would be recorded or issued until 1963, when they appeared on the tiny Carlton label credited to Gary Delamere, with the singer accompanied by the Tornados.

In April 1960, Radio Luxembourg began a weekly, 15-minute show, *It's a Triumph*, paid for by the company to showcase their latest releases. The show was presented by Meek, under the alias Johnny Watts, or by other Triumph artists, including 18-year-old Ricky Wayne (real name Learie Carasco), a bodybuilding friend of Lional's from St Lucia, whose career Meek took an interest in. Meek, who described Wayne as 'energetic and dynamic... one of the finest artists I have ever come across – full of vitality with a striking personality',[98] attempted to build a stage show around Wayne that would have culminated in a partial striptease. (According to Meek's assistant, Tony Kent, the producer kept a private stash of nude photographs of the future Mr Universe in a drawer in his office.) Wayne recorded the Meek-composed song 'Muscles' for the show, but the song would gather dust until 1988.

Saga's small marketing team did its best to promote the company and its releases and to find a replacement presenter for the reluctant Meek, who hated the way his Gloucestershire accent sounded on *It's a Triumph*. Triumph and Saga sponsored a competition, through *Disc* magazine, to find a new DJ. With a top prize of £100, a 13-week contract with Luxembourg plus a Saga-branded tape recorder, entrants were asked to send in recordings of themselves hosting a 15-minute show featuring at least two Triumph recordings. The six finalists selected by Meek would be invited to London where they would be judged at a teenage fair, taking place at Park Lane House in late June. Ricky Wayne, Michael Cox and new signing John Leyton appeared at the event, performing live vocals to Meek's backing tapes.

The radio show was quickly followed by real signs of success. In the same month that *It's a Triumph* made its debut, the company issued the Yolanda single, which critic Neal Arden chastised for Meek's 'banging and clattering'[99] production, and the first single from instrumental group the Fabulous Flee-Rakkers (later known as the Flee-Rekkers*), 'Green Jeans', a rocking rewrite of the traditional air 'Greensleeves'. Singer Teddy Johnson, who Meek had recorded at IBC for Polydor, questioned whether this update would find favour with eminent composer and conductor (and Master of the Queen's Music) Sir Arthur Bliss, and Triumph's representative testily fired back that 'we make records exclusively for the teenage market – and in consequence the juke boxes. We do not suppose that Sir Arthur has ever spent an evening dropping sixpences into a coffee bar coin machine.'[100] 'It's true that Triumph is a label primarily for the teenagers,' Meek expanded. 'But that doesn't mean we're recording nothing except rock 'n' roll. Teenage tastes cover all kinds of music just like those of any other age groups, and we will reflect that fact in our releases... It's a fallacy that the kids dislike everything except rock 'n' roll.'[101] In his regular *Disc* column, TV producer Jack Good called Meek a 'near-genius' as both a sound engineer and A&R man and reckoned that the first batch of Triumph releases were 'masterpieces in the art of pop record production... A man can't go on churning out records of this fantastically high calibre without breaking through to the charts fairly soon.'[102]

Good was almost immediately proved right. On 25 May 'Green Jeans' entered the Top 30. Originally known as the Ramblers, and led by Brentford-born saxophonist Peter Fleerackers (whose unusual surname came from his Dutch heritage), the band was heavily influenced by US group Johnny and the Hurricanes, another sax-led combo who specialised in playing rocked-up versions of classic songs, and they scored their first hit at a time when instrumental groups were all the rage. The success of 'Green Jeans' was quickly followed by George Chakiris, whose sole Triumph disc, 'Heart of a Teenage Girl', was rated by the often hyperbolic Good as 'probably the most imaginative pop record I have ever heard',[103] but although it sold respectably it charted for one solitary week.

There can be little doubt that both 'Heart of a Teenage Girl' and 'Green Jeans' would have fared better had Triumph been able to supply stores with copies. Saga's distribution network concentrated on getting their stock

---

* Although they did not officially change their name until the following year, the band were advertised by Triumph as the Flee-Rekkers in March 1960.

Love and Fury: The Life, Death and Legacy of Joe Meek

into department stores and electrical appliance shops, rather than record retailers, and their reliance on European pressing plants meant that stock – if it were ever manufactured – took a long time to arrive at the warehouse. The Chakiris release was further stymied by being in direct competition with another version of the song by singer Craig Douglas, which made the Top 10 in June. Said Good: 'If [Chakiris] had the spins that Craig Douglas had, Craig would have had a tough battle on his hands.'

More than anything, Triumph would offer Meek the opportunity to release his pet project, a series of recordings he had been working on at home in Arundel Gardens for months now, a stereophonic outer space fantasy called *I Hear a New World*. Work on *I Hear a New World* had been all-consuming, so much so that Joe barely noticed when Lional, exasperated with the noise and the chaos, and by Joe's habit of springing out of bed in the middle of the night when he had an idea he needed to get down on tape, moved out and found his own place, a basement flat in Clifton Gardens on the edge of Maida Vale. 'He used to get up at all hours of the morning, all hours of the night if he had an idea in his head and used to hum to it... he used to "la la la la"; it never used to mean nothing to me, you know, but he'd say, "I've got to get up"... he had tapes all over the place.'[104]

His involvement with Triumph was seen by Meek as a means to an end: the 'EP and LP of 'Space Music'' had been discussed in the press before the first Triumph titles were in the stores, and test pressings of the collection were being distributed to reviewers before Triumph had even been incorporated. Meek's aural feast was intended to stretch across both sides of an LP, but the public were first introduced to *I Hear a New World* via a four-track EP. At the end of February, John Rolls of the *Daily Mirror* reviewed the contents of that EP as 'bug eyed monsters from Outer Space on a gramophone record'.[105] Neal Arden, writing in the *Sunday People*, was just as impressed with the man making the record as the disc itself: 'From his name, you might expect Joe Meek to be a quiet little fellow afraid to say a word or answer back. Instead, he is one of the liveliest characters around. A top electronics engineer, he got tired of sitting still while other people produced records and told him what to do. So Joe revolted. He installed recording equipment in his living-room and started making records on his own.' Arden raved about the record, calling it 'a topical fantasy in music'

I Hear a New World

and praising the production: 'He's made it all in stereo so as to give the greatest effect to his sound pictures of what it's like out there. With 'I Hear a New World' Joe Meek has set a high standard of writing and record production.'[106]

Although test pressings had been sent to select members of the press in February, and mention of the disc was made in US trade magazine *Cash Box* in March, the first official release from Meek's masterwork took place in June, when the EP, *I Hear a New World, Part 1: A Stereo Fantasy* finally made it to the stores. In the intervening four months, much of the excitement about Meek's new record had fizzled out, but Ken Graham, reviewing for *Disc*, wrote that 'this is the brain child of recording engineer-producer Joe Meek and I applaud him for a brave try at bringing something new to the world of recording'. Graham likened the tracks included as akin to *musique concrète*: 'a series of mechanical sounds made by such things as mattress springs, spinning tops, taps dripping etc., all blended into a sort of "science fiction" of music'.[107] The EP was something that 'Aldous Huxley would be proud of', according to another reviewer: 'I recommend any readers with futuristic minds to listen to Mr Meek's 'I Hear A New World'. For Mr Meek regards musicians as superfluous when making music. They are things of the past who merely clutter up his recording studio. For Mr Meek, a talented recording engineer, has brought science in to take their place. Instead of using trumpets and saxophones, drums and pianos, violins and tubas, Mr Meek uses mechanical sounds which are harmonised by electronics into "new" music. Stranger ideas have succeeded in the record world. Who knows, Mr Meek may soon be sitting at the top of an electronic hit-parade?'[108]

'I wanted to create a picture in music of what could be up there in outer space,' Meek told the press. 'At first I was going to record with music that was completely out of this world, but realised that it would have very little entertainment value so I kept the construction of the music down to earth.'[109] In another interview he explained how he 'tried, and I had to do it rather carefully, to create an impression of space. Of things moving in front of you... a picture of parts of the moon. At the same time I didn't want music that was impossible to understand, and I wanted it to appeal to the younger generation... after all, they are the people who will be concerned very much with interplanetary exploration.'[110]

Love and Fury: The Life, Death and Legacy of Joe Meek

The initial recording sessions for *I Hear a New World* had taken place in Joe and Lional's flat, although the bassist on the session, Doug Collins, revealed that some of the recording took place 'in a Queensway studio that was used after hours, and all traces of use were wiped after the sessions had finished' (Queensway is minutes away from Holland Park, the home of Lansdowne studios). The flat was small: a front room, kitchen, bathroom and bedroom. The kitchen and bathroom doubled as the control room, and housed Joe's recording equipment, while the front room of the flat became the recording studio, with Meek's usual tangle of tapes and trailing wires all over the floor. In December 1953 Parlophone had issued a 10-inch 78, aimed principally at the children's market, called 'Jakka and the Flying Saucers'. Produced by George Martin and narrated by Peter Sellers, the disc employed many of the same tricks and effects that Meek now sought to exploit, although where Martin's electronic blips and sped-up voices had been used for purely comic effect, Meek made them an integral part of the overall experience. Musician Ken Harvey distinctly recalled the way in which Meek recorded the multitracked vocal of the title song, 'I Hear a New World': 'The first line of the song was a nightmare. It had to be sung at normal speed, half speed then twice the speed, in the same key and all in tune... Joe wanted to keep the actual key constant and if he changed the speed mechanically it changed the key tone.' Harvey's abiding memory of playing on the sessions was one of 'banging, scratching, thumping, shaking, twanging, crashing, tweaking, playing, singing and blowing water... Running around the room and giggling was a valuable contribution to some of the tracks.' Goodness knows what the other musicians, or their neighbours, must have thought of all the madness, but Meek knew exactly what he was after.

Credited as the Blue Men, the group who performed on *I Hear a New World* were the same group that had performed on the first two singles released by Triumph, a skiffle group from Ealing, West London, originally known as the West Five. Meek rated the band, telling the press that he saw them enjoying 'a big future as juke box idols'.[111] The West Five had recorded for Meek at Lansdowne, covering rock 'n' roll standards including 'Please Don't Touch', a recent hit for Johnny Kidd and the Pirates (then featuring future Tornado Alan Caddy on guitar), 'Be Bop A Lula' and 'Sea Cruise', but these recordings were never intended for commercial release.

I Hear a New World

Leader Rod Freeman became the 'Rodd' in 'Rodd – Ken the Cavaliers': 'Ken' was Ken Harvey, who often performed Everly Brothers-style duets with Freeman. The rest of the band consisted of guitarist Roger Fiola (who can be heard playing Hawaiian guitar on *I Hear a New World*), rhythm guitarist Chris White, bass player Doug Collins and drummer Dave Golding, who would later play with The Who for a short period before his position on the drum stool was taken by a teenager with dyed ginger hair called Keith Moon.

Meek wrote extensive sleeve notes for the proposed album, including descriptions of the individual tracks, of the landscapes and the lifeforms one might encounter on the moon: the 'happy, jolly little beings [with] their cheeky, blue-coloured faces', and their modes of transport. Not only did Meek hear a new world, he saw it too. Order forms – listing both the vinyl and reel-to-reel tape versions of the album – were sent out to dealers, and a release date for the complete album was set, but for decades it was believed that only ninety-nine copies of the first EP made it out of the door. It is also widely believed that less than twenty copies of the album test pressing ever existed and that although covers for the second EP (featuring four further tracks from the collection) were designed very few were manufactured and no discs were ever included. However, Saga and Triumph promoted the EP extensively, and it is highly unlikely that the company would have put so much effort into a recording that had been pressed in such small quantities.

With the benefit of hindsight it is easy to dismiss some of Meek's more ridiculous-sounding productions – the sped-up voice of actress Gunilla Thorn on the Geoff Goddard composition 'Merry Go Round', or Goddard's own over-processed and sped up vocal on 'Sky Men' for example – as naive, but at that time novelty was king: porcine puppet act Pinky and Perky were huge television stars with their own recording career, David Seville and the Chipmunks were an international phenomenon, and there are plenty of other instances of recordings that modern listeners would dismiss as unsophisticated that were, at the time, huge hits. *I Hear a New World* is rightly recognised as a masterpiece of early electronica, and when the full album finally saw release in the early 1990s some reviewers, desperately searching for a suitable phrase, described it as 'the first concept album'. It's not: Frank Sinatra's 1955 melancholic opus *In the Wee Small Hours* predated it by half a decade, and Woody Guthrie's *Dust Bowl Ballads* was issued two full decades before *I Hear a New World* saw its initial, limited release.

Sales were dire: Saga's team, in a determined attempt to keep Meek happy, suggested that electrical retailers use the EP to demonstrate their latest stereo equipment. Meek would repurpose several of the tunes for later releases: 'Valley of the Saroos' was re-recorded by the Outlaws in 1961 and issued under the title 'Spring Is Near', with the plinky-plonk keyboard line replaced by a much more attractive lead guitar played by Bill Kuy; 'Entry of the Globbots' and 'Orbit Around the Moon' would be renamed 'Tune for Short Cowboys' and 'Husky Team' respectively, also recorded by the Outlaws for Meek's second concept album *Dream of the West*. 'Husky Team' was re-recorded by the Saints in 1963. But the writing was on the wall: with no sales, poor distribution and major problems with getting their product pressed, Meek was beginning to see that if he wanted to make it as an independent producer he would have little option but to leave Triumph behind.

The issues around distribution and availability would also affect the company's next chart placing, 'Angela Jones'. Liverpool-born singer Michael Cox had already issued two singles when he was introduced to Meek by Jack Good. His first, 'Boy Meets Girl', penned by Good, was issued by Decca in October 1959 and was followed a few weeks later by 'Serious' backed with 'Too Hot to Handle', a pair of songs from hitmakers Doc Pomus and Mort Shuman. Good had attempted to launch Cox, a 19-year-old civil engineer, as a solo singer after his four younger sisters had written to him, telling the producer that he 'sings just like Ricky Nelson'[112] and asking if he would audition their brother for his show, *Oh Boy!* Good had Cox perform on the show in April, was suitably impressed and took him with him when he left *Oh Boy!* for his new show, the Marty Wilde-fronted *Boy Meets Girls*. Good believed that Cox could be a successful recording artist, but after his two Decca singles flopped the company released him from his contract. Good persuaded Triumph to take the singer on instead, feeling that Meek's new, teenager-focused label would prove a good fit. In May, Cox recorded his first (and only) single for Triumph, a pleasant ballad, 'Don't Want to Know', written by Len Praverman. Meek was just as impressed with Cox as Jack Good had been, proclaiming that 'Michael

I Hear a New World

has the makings of a star. In the recording studios he is charming, relaxed and easy to work with. He has an excellent recording voice and needs very little rehearsal before taping.'[113] Meek boasted that 'Don't Want to Know' was 'done in one take', but it was the B-side, John D. Loudermilk's 'Angela Jones', with an arrangement and backing from Charles Blackwell, that gave the label, and Cox, a bone fide hit.

Cox's friend Marty Wilde had suggested that he record the song, having heard the US version by Johnny Ferguson: Wilde would also pen Cox's third Meek-produced single, 'Teenage Love'. Recorded at Olympic Studios, Cox, according to Good, was 'a boy who is all set for a record hit' with 'Angela Jones'. 'He sings well, performs well – and, most important, the fans like him... My feeling is that the success he so richly deserves may come with his very first recording for Triumph. It is the best thing he has done by far, an appealing performance of a catchy song.'[114] Meek was just as effusive, and he was soon talking about follow-up singles and an LP from the singer. 'Michael has the makings of a star,' he said. 'In the recording studios he is charming, relaxed and easy to work with. He has an excellent recording voice and needs very little rehearsal before taping.'[115] Cox would exhibit just as much trust in Meek's ability to look after his recording career, saying that 'I do as he advises. If I had to make a record without him I'd be lost. Whenever he makes a record he always says, "Let's try something different", and I think this gives me confidence... I think I can leave everything to Joe.'[116] The two men would become good friends and continue to work together for several years.

Plugged via Good's latest TV show, *Wham*, 'Angela Jones' debuted on the UK singles chart on 15 June, the same week that a young, Australian-born entrepreneur named Robert Stigwood brought one of his charges to see Meek. Stigwood had a small talent agency that supplied acts to stage and television, and he was now acting as personal manager to a young actor named John Leyton. Stigwood was also friendly with Charles Blackwell, and it was Blackwell who effected their introduction, with Stigwood taking Leyton to Meek's flat in Arundel Gardens one Saturday afternoon to audition in front of Meek and Blackwell. Aware of how the press might represent this innocent trial, Stigwood put it about that Meek had actually met Leyton at a private audition at the Blue Angel club, in

Love and Fury: The Life, Death and Legacy of Joe Meek

Mayfair's Berkeley Street, where the actor had been performing in cabaret, knocking out passable impersonations of Frankie Laine and Johnnie Ray.

Like Meek, Stigwood was homosexual; unlike Meek, the Australian often used his position to his advantage. Most of the men who have mentioned Meek making a pass at them have also admitted that once you said no to Joe, that was the end of it. He would never broach the subject again. Stigwood, on the other hand, was persistent, and there are several tales of his acts threatening him with violence after the drunken entrepreneur refused to take no for an answer. Stephen Komlosy, Stigwood's business partner at that time, recalled how Meek came into their orbit: 'We were looking for ways of getting our artists recorded, because we'd been turned down by Decca, EMI, Pye and everybody else… so we went in to see if we could record our artists with him, which we did. He looked like a Teddy Boy with his quiff; he was scruffy and wore drainpipe trousers and crepe soled shoes and everything, but in the end he was such a likeable character and he taught us how to record artists.'[117] Komlosy's remarks are revealing: most people who met Meek talk about his being immaculately turned out, almost always in a suit and tie and forever combing his Brylcreem-slicked hair.*

Leyton came from a showbiz background: his mother had been an actor and his father had run several theatres and cinemas. Although his parents had warned him against a life on the stage, after a few uncredited bit-parts in TV shows including *The Invisible Man*, he had proved himself the breakout star of Granada Television's serialisation of the *Biggles* books (first broadcast in April 1960), playing the title character's best friend, Ginger. A huge fan club had formed following his success in the role, and many of those who had signed up for a glossy photo and printed autograph of their new favourite TV star wanted to know if he could sing as well. Unknown to any of them, Leyton had auditioned for EMI's Norman Newell (performing the Nat King Cole song '(I Love You) For Sentimental Reasons') before signing with Stigwood. Newell passed, but not long after Stigwood secured a second audition with Pye, which he had also failed. Not that it bothered

---

* Joe was in the habit of using product to slick back his hair from a very early age. When just a teenager, unable to afford tubs of Brylcreem, he made his own substitute, using lard and liquid paraffin, plus scent to mask the smell.

I Hear a New World

him that much, as Leyton had no aspirations to be a singing star, telling *The Stage* that 'I don't particularly want to be a singer, but I do want to be a good all-round performer. Anything I try, I naturally want to do well, but this new venture won't upset my acting career. With me that comes first and foremost.'[118]

Robert Stigwood felt differently. He was obsessed with turning Leyton into a star, and who better to take him to than Joe Meek and his new, teenager-friendly record label? 'I had a recording test with one major record company but they weren't interested. Then I met Joe Meek, who was very interested.'[119] Suddenly, everyone was interested in Leyton: he was charming, good-looking, well-educated and clearly talented, and Stigwood knew how to make the most of his assets. '[Stigwood and I] went into this beautiful flat,' Leyton would later recall. 'In the living room there was this piano, and a mic, and various bits of recording equipment that Joe had there. It was all very relaxed, and then finally Joe said, "Right, let's see what you can do." So I got up and sang, and when he played it back I didn't recognise myself. Joe was a wizard at making you sound good, but nobody had ever heard of Joe Meek then; he was just starting out.'[120] Leyton sang two Nat King Cole numbers for Meek and Blackwell and, following the playback, Meek held out his hand to the young actor and simply said, 'Welcome to Triumph.'

Leyton's debut – a song called 'Three Cute Chicks' (an answer record to the Coasters 'Three Cool Cats') – was recorded at sessions at Lansdowne and Olympic Studios, but although it was announced in the press that he was recording for Triumph, no disc from Leyton would appear on the label, for by the time that he recorded the song the company was already in trouble. The struggle to keep up with demand for 'Green Jeans' was multiplied tenfold by the company's inability to get copies of 'Angela Jones' to stores. Michael Cox was promoting the single on television, it was getting plenty of airplay, and he was about to undertake a series of appearances around London with the Fabulous Flee-Rakkers, yet no one could buy it. Seventy thousand copies of 'Angela Jones' were sold in its first few weeks on sale, not enough to make it a serious contender for the top of the charts, but an impressive figure for an independent label, and the pressing plant that Saga used could not keep up with demand. Even if they could have done, they wanted payment up front, and Barrington-Coupe was either unwilling or

Love and Fury: The Life, Death and Legacy of Joe Meek

unable to release any extra financing to have more copies of either 'Angela Jones' or 'Green Jeans' pressed. UK companies continued to put pressure on other pressing plants to refuse work from the independent company, as Meek later told the television documentary series *World in Action*: 'The major record companies decided that they did not want small operators, and so they did their best to squash us out of the shops.'[121]

CHAPTER 7

I'm Waiting For Tomorrow

Triumph's finances were put under extra strain by the Mechanical Copyright Protection Society (MCPS), the industry body that collected royalties on behalf of songwriters, composers and publishers. The MCPS insisted that Triumph stump up publishing royalties upfront (in the form of stamps which had to be affixed individually to discs), tying up thousands of pounds of the company's cash. Desperate to get his record into the shops, Joe took the masters for both sides of Michael Cox's hit single to Jeff Kruger, owner of the Flamingo Club and Ember Records, to have copies pressed. 'We were all friends, the independents,' Kruger revealed. 'They all came down to the club. It was like a little circle and Joe said to me "I've got this new recording of 'Angela Jones'… Will you put it out on Ember and pay me the royalties?"' [122] The Ember pressings were ostensibly for export, but many 'leaked' – not entirely accidentally – into British stores. However, by the time they reached them it was too late: 'Angela Jones' had peaked at a respectable number 7 but was already tumbling down the charts.

These problems with finance and distribution had put a kink in Meek's plans to expand Triumph's artist roster and nixed his grandiose idea to have Yolanda record an album of jazz standards with members of Quincy Jones's big band in Paris. As well as handling John Leyton, Robert Stigwood had another handsome young actor on his books, Iain Gregory, and Meek had already recorded his intended debut, 'The Night You Told a Lie', but the continuing difficulties at the company meant that it – like many other discs slated for release by Triumph – would not see the light of day: it would appear in November 1960 on Pye. William Barrington-Coupe was keen to expand, but decided to use Meek's chart success as the launchpad for a

Love and Fury: The Life, Death and Legacy of Joe Meek

Triumph-brand home tape recorder, rather than invest in some real talent or improve their reliance on foreign pressing plants. It would not be long before Meek's frustrations would boil over. A projected release from South African singer Eve Boswell, whose sole UK hit was the 1956 Top 10 success 'Pickin' a Chicken', should have done respectable business, but although she recorded 'On the Bridge of Avignon' and 'Around the Corner' for Triumph, neither would be issued in the UK. They would eventually turn up on a single in Italy in 1961.

Meek had had enough of the mess and made up his mind to leave the company that his money had helped found. He laid the blame for Triumph's failure with Barrington-Coupe, and Major Banks seemed to agree, as he decided to withdraw his support for the enterprise too. At the beginning of July, a Meekless Triumph moved out of the Major's offices in Empire Yard, Holloway, and set up at 231 Balls Pond Road. Barrington-Coupe tried to stave off any bad press by delaying the announcement of Meek's departure and forging ahead with the label's scheduled releases. John Leyton's 'Three Cute Chicks' was scrapped, but in the same week as the press learned of Meek quitting his own company, the actor was appearing on television promoting what the media had been assured would be his Triumph debut, the Meek-produced cover of the US hit 'Tell Laura I Love Her'.* It was also revealed that the Flee-Rakkers were about to cut another disc for the label, with one already in the can and ready to go.

'Tell Laura I Love Her' would not appear on Triumph. Neither would its planned follow-up, 'The Girl on the Floor Above', nor any new recordings from the Flee-Rakkers either. Meek's sudden departure killed any hopes Triumph had of capitalising on the success of the Flee-Rakkers hit and put a stop to plans for a package tour featuring the majority of Triumph's roster, including Michael Cox, Ricky Wayne, Peter Jay, the Flee-Rakkers and two new signings, Carol Jones and the Edison Brothers. A projected second single and album from Michael Cox would not be recorded, let alone released, by Triumph. Although Meek's departure was no secret

---

*   Leyton first performed the song on the ATV music programme *The Tin Pan Alley Show* on 30 July, two weeks before the disc was issued. The press release that was sent to newspapers to announce his appearance erroneously listed his song as 'Tell Her I Love Her'.

to Barrington-Coupe or Major Banks, the company believed that it could carry on much as before, overlooking or unaware of the fact that Meek was taking pretty much all of the company's talent with him, including his arranger, Charles Blackwell, and most of the label's acts.

Meek had been canny: his artists had signed exclusive deals with him, rather than Triumph, leaving him able to take them wherever he wished. It was virtually unheard of for a recording artist to sign a contract with an A&R man rather than the company, but then pretty much everything that Meek did was unprecedented. The idea of signing artists to himself was something Meek had picked up from Denis Preston, who had done the same thing with Lonnie Donegan and had been repaid handsomely when, in 1958, Preston sold Donegan's contract to Pye for £10,000. It was a policy that Barrington-Coupe immediately overturned, telling *Cash Box* that 'new artists will in future be signed to the label and not to the A&R manager as previously'.[123] Talk about closing the stable door after the horse has bolted.

When Meek left Triumph he took, as part of his agreed severance, most of the masters he had worked on, including all of the planned Leyton discs and a clutch of other unissued tapes, such as a full-length album from the Charles Blackwell Orchestra, *Those Plucking Strings* (eventually issued in 2006; two tracks had been slated for single release by Triumph before Meek left), and an EP by Smiley, the family nickname for Joy Adams' infant son, Gary.* The rights to all of these recordings were handed over to Meek on 25 July 1960 and were again transferred to his new company, RGM Sound, in 1962.

Within days of his departure, trade magazine *Billboard* was reporting that 'Top Rank has signed Joe Meek as an independent producer. They will have first call on his products but the deal is not completely exclusive.' Top Rank's manager, Bob Roberts, had big plans for expansion, boasting that Meek 'takes [Michael] Cox and other artists to Rank under the deal and in fact two of his discs will be released by Top Rank on August 15'.[124] Three titles in all were slated for release (on 12, not 15, August): John Leyton's

---

*   It has been suggested that Bryan Taylor, who issued a Christmas single 'The Donkey's Tale' on Piccadilly in November 1961, and Smiley are the same person. Bryan was, in fact, the son of singer Neville Taylor, of rock 'n' roll act Neville Taylor and the Cutters.

Love and Fury: The Life, Death and Legacy of Joe Meek

'Tell Laura I Love Her', plus reissues of the Flee-Rakkers' 'Green Jeans' and Ricky Wayne's 'Chicka'roo'. Top Rank boasted that they had secured the rights to all of Meek's Triumph productions bar one, 'Angela Jones', although the George Chakiris single 'Heart of a Teenage Girl' was also excluded from the deal as the actor was signed to Saga, not Meek.

Top Rank had recently released the first single by the Larry Parnes-managed rocker Danny Rivers, a moody cover of the Bill Haley track 'Hawk'. Meek had already encountered the singer (real name David Lee Baker; he took his stage name from two characters Elvis had portrayed in his movies) when he accompanied Parnes to a show at the Top Rank theatre in Kilburn. Both men were attracted to the handsome 17-year-old, and both wanted to manage him, but they needed the consent of Rivers' father, and he refused to allow his son to sign any contract. A short time later, when Rivers was performing in Manchester, Parnes approached him again. This time, television producer Jack Good was also on hand to size up the singer's potential, and with the promise of tours, a record deal and television appearances (Good immediately put him to work on his latest project, the ITV pop show *Wham!*), Rivers and his father agreed to sign with Parnes. The choice was understandable: Parnes had enjoyed a phenomenal rise to fame, and his artists were always working, either in the studio, on radio and television, or out on the package tours he promoted. In spite of his reputation for being stingy, everyone wanted to be signed by Parnes; it seemed like a guarantee to fame and fortune. 'Larry Parnes was the man to be with,' says actor and singer Jess Conrad, another artist favoured by Jack Good. 'I knew he was a gay man, and I knew that if I could get to him and talk to him he would probably sign me, because I was a good looking fellow, you know? I needed to get to know Larry because he had this stable of singers that I wasn't part of. I went to meet him at a steak house, opposite the Hippodrome, and he had dandruff on his shoulder, and his fingers were black because he was a chain smoker, and I didn't like either of those things, so I didn't sign with him!'[125] It was a decision that Conrad would regret. Rivers' version of 'Hawk' was not a hit, but his second single, the Meek-produced 'Can't You Hear My Heart' (issued in November 1960 and recorded at Philips Studio in Marble Arch) would crack the Top 40.

Triumph struggled on, but without Meek that was impossible. Barrington-Coupe hired musician and arranger Johnny Keating, whose first move was

I'm Waiting For Tomorrow

to sign instrumental act Rex Morris and the Minors, a saxophone-led band in the Flee-Rakkers vein. Triumph signed other new acts, including the improbably named Disc Discoveries, and 17-year-old singer Pat Reader, advertised as 'Britain's Princess of Song', from Cowes in the Isle of Wight. On 1 September the company issued three new singles, the Keating-composed 'Chicken Sax' from Rex and the Minors (someone missed a marketing opportunity by not labelling the act Morris and the Minors), Pat Reader's 'Ricky' (backed with 'Dear Daddy', a song Meek had recorded with Petula Clark a year earlier) and 'It Ain't What You Do' from Don Fox. The label already had Carol Jones, a 21-year-old singing hairdresser from Brixton, on the books (she had been scheduled to join the Triumph seaside package tour), and in a somewhat audacious move guaranteed to annoy Meek, her first and only release for the company, 'The Boy with the Eyes of Blue', was a Robert Duke composition. Spotted singing with the Flee-Rakkers at the Majestic ballroom in Finsbury Park, Meek had her record for him while he was still at the helm of Triumph, singing the Jerry Lordan number 'Cinderella Jones' and an early version of 'The Boy with the Eyes of Blue', but he had yet to get her signature on a contract when he left. That particular coupling – slated for an August release – went unissued when Meek left the company (although he retained the masters when he hotfooted it). Barrington-Coupe and Keating had Jones record a copycat version of 'The Boy with the Eyes of Blue', which the company issued in September, after Meek had moved on. Meek retaliated by recording a version with female vocal duo the Lindys, released by Decca that same month.

Although he was not involved in her Triumph release, Pat Reader's management took her to Meek the following year. She waxed a single for him in April 1961 (the IBC-cut acetate is dated 5 April, Joe's 32nd birthday), although that would not see release for more than a year: a fun, effects-laden song very much in the style of Alma Cogan, 'Cha-Cha on the Moon'.* Backed with 'May Your Heart Stay Young Forever', 'Cha-Cha on the Moon' – whose distinctive 'wobble' effect was achieved by shaking a piece of sheet metal – would finally be issued by Piccadilly in September 1962. A third

---

* Reader herself would recall that this session took place for Triumph; however, the sides were not among the tapes that Meek took with him when he left the company.

77

number recorded at 304 Holloway Road, 'My Kind of Love', would remain in the vaults (or, rather, the tea chests) until March 2024, when it was issued (along with the original Meek-produced version of 'The Boy With the Eyes of Blue') on the compilation *Do the Strum!*

Half a dozen singles appeared on Triumph after Meek exited, none of which would chart. Barrington-Coupe, knowing nothing about the pop market, went back to his roots and made plans for Triumph to issue a series of popular classics, including a four-LP set of Handel's *Messiah* from the London Philharmonic Orchestra. Keating, eager to produce pop hits and get in on the jazz trend, announced ambitious plans for Triumph to issue five albums from John Dankworth (whose wife, Cleo Laine, had recorded for Meek at Lansdowne), accompanied by the Royal Philharmonic Orchestra. The Dankworth albums would not appear (although one would be issued by Saga in 1962), but the company did undertake to sponsor a package tour-cum-talent show, the *Big Disc Show of 1960*, and signed another new singer, Ricky Bowden. In September Triumph held another talent search, this time looking for 'The "Golden Boy (or) Girl" or "Golden Group" of 1960'.[126] Winner Graham Hughes, a member of the Denver Rhythm Group, was immediately signed to a management contract by Les Bristow (co-owner of Soho's 2i's coffee bar), offered a recording contract worth £1,000 with Triumph and promised a year of careful grooming to turn him into a star, but like so many others involved in the Triumph saga, he would soon fall by the wayside. Directionless, and without the support of Major Banks or Saga, Triumph would sign no further acts. The company's last release was Laura Lee's 'Tell Tommy I Miss Him' (a cover of the US hit by Marilyn Michaels), issued in mid-October 1960, an answer record to 'Tell Laura I Love Her', the song that had recently been issued as John Leyton's debut on Top Rank. It did not stand a chance, as by the end of October the company was done. A planned single from Ricky Bowden, 'Can't Forget', and the Buddy Holly-styled song 'All Night Crying' would remain unissued, and the company went into liquidation the following year.

The demise of Triumph saw *Disc* magazine step in to save the live final of the DJ competition, which, after months of delay, was eventually held in Finsbury Park in November. Although none of the many hopefuls who sent in tapes would become a star one, drama school student Tony Kent, would find a job in the industry – ironically working for Joe Meek. Kent

I'm Waiting For Tomorrow

took on the role as Meek's assistant and was employed by him for around a year from the summer of 1961 after phoning Meek and asking him for a job. Kent described the position as 'essentially, making tea for the artists and trying to get some sort of semblance of order in the office as far as contracts were concerned. I even had to type contracts out on a standard form... The whole thing was totally disorganised.'[127]

Sadly, Leyton's version of 'Tell Laura I Love Her', issued in August 1960 as part of Meek's deal with Top Rank, was not given the promotion it needed: wary, perhaps, of a potential ban on the grounds of bad taste, the flip side 'Goodbye to Teenage Love' was promoted to the BBC instead, and sales were further stymied by Top Rank being taken over by EMI just a fortnight after Meek joined the company. This was a doubly bitter blow for Meek personally, as it was an EMI-distributed label, MGM, that had issued a competing version of 'Angela Jones' after Michael Cox charted, mopping up some of the sales that would have gone to Triumph had they been able to get their record into stores. No money changed hands, but EMI agreed to take on all of the Top Rank label's debts in exchange for their assets, namely its roster of hit artists and its back catalogue. This deal saw Dick Rowe, head of A&R at Top Rank, return to his former employer, Decca, and EMI subsume the label completely. This was a bitter blow to Meek, as he got on well with Dick Rowe, one of the few people to champion Meek's John Leyton recordings at Top Rank. With no warning, Meek was once again out on his ear, and to make matters worse EMI binned the planned reissue of Ricky Wayne's 'Chicka'roo'; Top Rank had already advertised the single, as 'Hot Chick-A-Roo' (and assigned it the catalogue number JAR 432),* but no copies were pressed. Wayne, and several of Meek's other acts lost in the confusion, would eventually find a home at Pye.

'Tell Laura I Love Her' was a scandalous record for its time. One of a spate of so-called 'death discs' or 'splatter platters', the song told the tale of a young man, Tommy, who lost his life at a speedway track after entering a race to try and win enough money to buy his girl, the eponymous Laura, a wedding ring. It had already been a sizeable hit in the US for Ray Peterson, but Decca, who held the rights to release the disc in the UK, prevaricated for so long over issuing it there that two competing versions – one by

---

*   JAR: J. Arthur Rank.

Leyton and the other by Welsh singer Ricky Valance (born David Spencer) beat them to market.

The controversy over the song's subject matter was not lost on its production team nor its singer, who declared in the press that it was a lot of fuss over nothing. 'I regard it as a ballad telling a contemporary story,' Leyton said. 'At least the words make sense, which is more than you can say for most songs on the pop parade these days.'[128] Leyton recorded the song in both French and Italian for a planned assault on the European continent, but despite the demand (regular exposure on television meant that advance sales for his version were greater than for Valance's) his recording was not a hit. The Ricky Valance version was on EMI's prestigious Columbia label, and EMI actively supressed Leyton's recording in favour of their own. Meek was aware of this and threatened to take the single to Pye, who had coincidentally taken over Top Rank's Sunday night programme on Radio Luxembourg. That did not happen: aware that he had other irons in the fire with EMI, an angry but prudent Meek decided it was best not to upset the powers that be, although it is possible that the decision was made for him by Leyton's manager, Robert Stigwood, who was involved in a personal relationship with the chairman of the company, Sir Joseph Lockwood. By the beginning of October Valance was at number 1 with the song: Leyton's version would not chart.

Meek's productions would appear on many different labels over the next seven years: the deal with Top Rank had brought him in to EMI, but they paid a maximum of 5 per cent of the gross price, and out of that 'musician's fees for the session must be deducted, hire of studios etcetera must also come off and other heavy overheads must be taken into account'.[129] Decca paid more, up to 8 per cent, but Meek was happy to go to whoever would take his masters. This habit would cause headaches for those trying to untangle his finances following his death and lead to Meek being accused of having little business sense, but filmmaker and musician Russell Caligari sees it differently: 'Joe Meek, cleverly, didn't have a publishing agreement with one company. He did what we call "single song assignments", so he'd make the record, he'd find a label then he'd find a publisher and make a separate deal. It really kept him lean and keen, constantly negotiating. His legal papers show that he was incredibly astute, and while that may have been driven through distrust of the music industry, it served him well.'[130]

Triumph may have failed, but Meek had enjoyed the taste of independence. He now wanted to set up his own company, one where he called the shots. At first, Charles Blackwell suggested that Meek join him in a partnership with John Barry, but when Major Banks decided to open up his chequebook Meek chose to go with him instead. Although his experience with Triumph had left a sour taste, he turned to Major Banks to help finance his new operation, perhaps feeling that he would have more freedom to do his own thing there than he would with Blackwell and Barry, both musicians, arrangers and composers, who would surely be balloting for their own material ahead of Meek's. Despite being branded as 'a thoroughly nasty character'[131] by Tony Kent, Banks clearly saw something in Meek, even if it was just a way to make a quick buck. After the Triumph fiasco, Barrington-Coupe was out, leaving Meek and the Major as equal partners in a new business, RGM Sound Ltd, which the pair announced to the press in the middle of August, at the very same time as EMI decided to mothball the Top Rank label.

Meek's first post-Triumph recording session, for his as yet unnamed new company, had already taken place: on 6 August, at Olympic Studios, Michael Cox taped the two sides of a forthcoming single. Cox, who was suffering with a heavy cold, had to squeeze the session in between live dates, and things began badly after the train from Bournemouth arrived into London forty-five minutes late, meaning that the session had to be cut short. The resulting tracks, 'Along Came Caroline' and the far superior 'Lonely Road', were originally planned for Top Rank, but – with the label on ice – the disc was issued by another EMI imprint, HMV, in September. The A-side was a follow-up to 'Angela Jones', using similar motifs and referencing their romantic association, and EMI expected a hit, boasting of it having secured a US release before the tracks had even been recorded.* Around the same time Meek produced the second single for Peter Jay, 'Paradise Garden' (written by Meek as Robert Duke), recorded at IBC and issued by Pye in September. The disc was praised by television and radio presenter

---

* Despite their boast, 'Along Came Caroline' would not be issued in the USA. In fact, none of Cox's singles received a stateside release.

81

Love and Fury: The Life, Death and Legacy of Joe Meek

Keith Fordyce for having 'remarkable production and arrangement', which offered 'something really out of the ordinary... with throbbing drums and oodles of echo'.[132] But few listening to the song would know that the song's title came from Paradise Park, the name of the cruising ground near to the Madras Place public lavatories in Islington, one of Meek's favoured pick-up places, and somewhere 'where all my dreams come true'.

Pye would issue two further Meek productions that same week, both originally intended for Triumph, the (subtly renamed) Flee-Rekkers' 'Sunday Date' and Ricky Wayne's 'Make Way Baby', written by Robert Duke and published by the Rank-owned Filmusic. A third Ricky Wayne single planned for Triumph, which featured the bodybuilder covering Meek's 'Put a Ring on Her Finger', would not appear, yet Meek boasted that he would 'have at least three of his recordings in the charts by Christmas'.[133]

Like the Michael Cox single, John Leyton's next release, 'The Girl on the Floor Above' (backed with Meek's own composition, 'Terry Brown's in Love with Mary Dee', a song heavily influenced by 'Tell Laura I Love Her'), would also be issued by HMV, but unlike 'Along Came Caroline', which was a minor chart hit, Leyton's disc again faltered. 'The Girl on the Floor Above' – another single originally intended for Triumph – was given a decent push, with reviewer Don Nicholl insisting that 'Leyton will make a big impression with this recording', noting that the song 'seems destined for plenty of air time and juke box spins' and that it 'could even crash the parade if luck is on his side'.[134] The singer's manager, Robert Stigwood, and Meek planned to have Leyton record a version in Italian which would be issued ahead of a fifteen-day tour of the country the following February, and they ran a competition that offered one lucky young lady the chance to join Leyton on a date in Luxembourg, yet it still failed to find an audience. However, it would not be too long before the actor-cum-singer would provide Meek with his first independent chart topper.

Working with Stigwood and Larry Parnes had given Meek a taste for management, a role to which he was spectacularly unqualified and ill-equipped. True, he had found some success in getting publicity for Jimmy Miller and the Barbecues and had managed to get Joy and Dave featured in a couple of newspapers, but he had not had to send a band out on tour, organise photo shoots, book hotel accommodation and transport, pay them wages and deal with their demands. Parnes had his office, his secretary and

I'm Waiting For Tomorrow

a retinue of road managers to help look after his charges; Stigwood had the ever reliable Stephen Komlosy, but Meek had no one, yet his need for control made him eager to learn. His first move was to employ Stigwood to promote his latest offering from Joy and Dave, their remake of the Fats Waller oldie 'My Very Good Friend the Milkman', originally planned for Triumph, but issued by Decca in October; his second was to place his acts with Harry Dawson at the George Cooper Organisation, which opened for business in the heart of the city's theatre district in November 1960 and quickly became Britain's biggest booking agent. By aping Parnes and Stigwood he would be able to muddle his way through. For now.

But if he were to expand his business, Meek needed a new premises to operate from. Meek's landlady at Arundel Gardens had been very accommodating, and although she had occasionally threatened to kick him out she had never quite been able to bring herself to do it. Stories about Meek being given his marching orders after the Jimmy Miller launch party are simply wrong: Meek was still living at 20 Arundel Gardens when he began working with Barrington-Coupe at Triumph. She even turned a blind eye when Meek started sticking and nailing soundproofing to the ceilings and walls of the rooms he used for his makeshift studio, but in the spring of 1960 she decided to sell, and Meek had no choice but to move out and take his burgeoning home-recording empire with him. At first he moved in with Lional at his home in Clifton Gardens, but while he was formulating his exit strategy from Triumph he discovered a three-storey apartment just down the road from the label's offices. The flat he found – and began renting in June 1960 – would go down in history: 304 Holloway Road. No longer would he need to rent time at IBC or Olympic; now he had the space he needed to set up his own professional studio.

During the last decades of the 19th century, 304 Holloway Road had been the site of a milliners, a green grocer and coal merchant. The whole area was extensively remodelled in the mid-1890s into 'a new fine row of shops', and number 304 was one of the first of these new businesses to be occupied when, in 1897, a shoe retailer opened its doors there. The owner of this new business, Edward Challis, had some interesting ideas for attracting patrons into his store and was years ahead of his competitors: in 1899, having spent two years experimenting with various fabrics and processes, he proudly boasted that he had invented an entirely vegetarian shoe, with 'absolutely

Love and Fury: The Life, Death and Legacy of Joe Meek

no paper or leather of any description' in the construction and that, he insisted, would last 'one-third longer than leather shoes'. Challis was an innovative businessman, and following a trip across the pond he decided to remodel his business as the American Boot and Shoe Saloon. Sixty years after Edward Challis established himself as an innovator and forward-thinker, another visionary took up residence, and after several months of remodelling, hammering, cable-laying and equipment shifting (much of that done by his friend Dave Adams), Robert George Meek opened his new company, RGM Sound Ltd.

CHAPTER 8

Dreams Do Come True

RGM Sound offered artists something entirely different to Decca's Broadhurst Gardens or EMI's Abbey Road. Joe's scratch-built studio was, in fact, no more than a collection of rooms spread over two of the upper three floors of number 304 Holloway Road, a building whose ground floor was occupied by A. H. Shenton Leather Goods. The flat above Shenton's was not an obvious choice for a recording studio, but it was affordable, with the Shentons sub-letting the space to Meek for a weekly rent of '£7 10 shillings for the whole three floors'[135] according to Lional Howard, and it was close to one of Meek's favourite cruising places, Paradise Park. It was also near to Major Banks' offices in Holloway's Empire Yard, which meant that Meek should not have to go too far if he needed the Major to sign off on a financial deal or cut him a cheque. At one point an associate of Meek's, Peter de Rouffignac, offered to share the premises with him. De Rouffignac, who had run a small advertising agency in York before moving to London, was keen to set up on his own as a booking agent, something that could easily work in tandem with Meek's aspiration to expand his operation into artist management, and he signed several Meek-related acts, including Peter Jay, George Chakiris, Michael Cox and Neil Christian. However, it soon became obvious that two businesses sharing the same space would not work. Besides, Meek was going to need all of the room himself. The ever-loyal Lional helped him move all of his stuff in: Howard in his Austin A40 and Meek in his recently acquired Sunbeam Rapier, with his furniture tied to the roof. 'It took us about three days using the two cars…' Howard recalled. 'He had hundreds and hundreds of records, and tapes and tapes.'[136]

Love and Fury: The Life, Death and Legacy of Joe Meek

There was only one way into Meek's empire, and that was through a nondescript door which was set in a recess a few paces from the pavement (the entrance has since been remodelled and now opens directly onto Holloway Road), sandwiched between the Shentons' shop and the adjoining electrical goods store, Bellanger Brothers (London) Ltd. Roy Phillips explains: 'As you walked up Holloway Road from the underground you had to turn right, past Shenton's window then straight ahead, five steps past the shop door to the door leading up to Joe's.'[137] Meek left his front door unlocked; the major recording studios had security guards, but word soon got around that RGM Sound was not only open for business but that its owner would grant an audition to just about anyone who crossed its threshold. An endless stream of hopefuls turned up on spec, expecting the powerful Mr Meek to grant them an audience, and often these young aspirants ended up blocking the entrance to Shenton's store, much to the annoyance of Mrs Violet Shenton, Meek's landlady. Later, when Meek tried to call a halt to groups and singers climbing the stairs uninvited by locking his front door, the acts that made their way there would cart their equipment into the store itself until Mrs Shenton – or one of Meek's assistants – was available to escort them upstairs. Even faced with the closed door, Meek's set-up seemed much more approachable than the big studios, and each day the mail brought letters requesting auditions, packages with demos enclosed and reels of tape from emergent songwriters.

Once you had ascended the first flight of stairs and reached the landing of the first floor, you were faced with the business end of RGM, with Meek's own office, and a larger room adjacent. Initially, this served as Meek's own bedsit, but it later became a place where musicians and visitors could wait, help themselves to a coffee (from the small, adjoining kitchen area, part of a single-storey extension above the Shentons' storeroom), watch television or listen to music on Joe's own radiogram. The floor was invariably strewn with records, acetates and ephemera, and the drawers of the sideboard were filled with photos and press releases. Next door, Meek's office was dominated by a large desk that sat in front of the fireplace and mantelpiece, and the wall next to his chair was plastered with photographs of the acts Meek either managed or had worked with. Those photographs would change regularly, not least because when he fell out with one of his acts the first thing he would do would be to rip

Dreams Do Come True

their photo off the wall and tear in in two before throwing it into his wastepaper bin. 'He had a bad, bad temper,' Joy Adams recalls. 'I was afraid of it and I think Dave was too.'[138]

Up another flight of stairs to the second floor you would find Meek's control room, small and windowless. Next to that was the studio itself, which had originally been a bedroom at the front of the building overlooking Holloway Road. At the opposite end of the landing was a separate lavatory, a room that would become infamous as Meek liked the acoustics in there and would occasionally have singers use it to record their vocals. If you went up the final set of stairs, you would encounter the bathroom (which, legend has it, doubled as Meek's echo chamber) and two bedrooms; Joe took over the one at the rear of the building, the other began as a guest room but eventually became a depository for many of the hundreds of reels of tape that would fill the flat and, ultimately, dozens of tea chests.

Peter Jay, leader of The Jaywalkers, recalls that working at 304 in those early days was a bit of a shock, especially as the group had recorded in the relative luxury of Decca's Hampstead studio: 'This was going from something quite posh to, well, chaos. Trying to park in Holloway Road was a nightmare, but you parked outside this little shop front and then had to carry all the gear through... the lady was in there and she wasn't happy. Can you imagine seven people and all their gear traipsing past the shop and then up the stairs? And then making a lot of noise, being there for two or three hours and then coming out again while there was another band coming through! It must have been pretty full-on for her!

'You had to go up the stairs to the studio. Once you got up there, there was a very small room, I'd put the drum kit in there and we'd all squash round, and he had this like two-sided cupboard in the corner full of different things. The floor was knee-deep in tape, and there were wires going straight across. It was amazing when you consider the sound he got out of that... incredible. It was just a small living room above the shop: we had seven of us, and I gave up taking the big drum kit with the two bass drums up there because you could hardly get it in!

'We were never allowed upstairs. Apparently that was because he had his secret echo chamber there. We were expecting some big kind of Tesla set-up, and I never actually saw it but it turned out that the echo chamber, where he had all these fabulous sounds from was just a bathroom, with a

Love and Fury: The Life, Death and Legacy of Joe Meek

speaker on one side and another speaker on the other side – that was it! It was incredible what he created there: when you listen to them and you think he did this from this little shitty room, with the woman banging on the ceiling with a broom, and the tapes all over the floor yet this incredible sound comes out. Those John Leyton records, all the stuff he did there… Amazing.'[139]

'When I first started recording here I used to get a lot of leg-pulls from the musicians, who are top musicians often playing in, say, Mantovani's orchestra, and classical orchestras – really the cream of musicians,' Meek explained. 'They used to come in, look around and say, "Where do you want me? Am I supposed to be in the bathroom?" But after they've heard a playback, I usually don't get any more criticism. They realise what presence there is on their instruments, and that they've really got to be on form or it'll show up in the recording.'[140]

People who knew Meek and who worked at 304 fall into two camps. He polarised opinions: some say he was scruffy, others that he was always immaculately turned out; some of his acquaintances will tell you that he was kind, quiet and benevolent, easy to get along with and endlessly helpful, while others attest to his quick temper, his legendary tantrums and sudden, abrupt mood swings: 'One day he'd be on top of the world, and the next he'd be down in the dumps,' Screaming Lord Sutch succinctly put it.[141] What they all agree on, though, is that the place was knee-deep in boxes and reels of tape. When Meek had money he would buy quality, and he preferred industry standards such as Scotch, EMI and BASF, but when funds were short – or when the Major refused to sign the cheque – he would buy cheap tape, and he was not averse to reusing second-hand tape. 'He was reusing all this old eastern European, Communist Bloc tape,' engineer, producer and musician Alan Wilson explains. 'It appears that the Major was giving him old tapes from Saga; you can still hear parts of the original orchestral recording on some of them.'[142] In September 1964 Meek cancelled a recording session with Flip and the Dateliners, telling them not to come to the studio as he had no tape, a pretty feeble excuse when everyone recalls seeing tapes piled high everywhere.

Something else that almost everyone who passed through the doors of 304 agrees on was the chaos: 'I had nothing to compare it to,' says Mike Berry. 'I'd never been in a studio before, apart from the demo which we'd

Dreams Do Come True

recorded in John Hawkins' front room in Wandsworth. It was obviously a flat that he had converted for recording. He had a vocal booth there, built partly from polythene, and I was shut off there in the corner. Behind that were the windows overlooking the street, which were all boarded up and covered in curtains, and in that same corner would be Bobby Graham on the drums. To my left was Chas Hodges, and Bill Kuy was towards the window more, as was Reggie Hawkins on rhythm guitar. We were all set up in that one room: he had a lovely Neumann U 47 microphone, which are as rare as hen's teeth nowadays; he had all the good stuff, because he was a proper engineer. He knew his equipment and knew what he needed. There was no control room window, like you would get in a proper studio; he just stuck his head round the door and shouted "Ready?"

'I remember there were loads of wires on the floor, all running in and out of the control room from the studio. I never understood why there were so many wires, because all he needed was one microphone for each instrument, plus another two or three for the drums. But all of these wires, like a great snake, led back to the control room, where they all linked up to his recorder and whatever mixer he had... it was all very basic.'[143] Singer Cliff Bennett concurred: 'He had jack plugs hanging down, and wires in knots and things, and tape everywhere. It was unbelievable. I said to him, "How the hell do you know what's going on?", but he knew exactly what he wanted... He was always in there digging about, pulling wires out, plugging wires in, it was incredible. He was always experimenting.'[144]

The studio was indeed basic. Built by Meek and Dave Adams, the window recesses had been filled and then boarded over, and a heavy curtain covered the entire wall, all to block out the noise of the street below and to help deaden the sound in the studio. The other walls were covered in rudimentary soundproofing, which in turn was covered in acoustic, pegboard-style tiles, or baffle boards. A notice read 'Don't bang drums on the walls', a small courtesy to his neighbours. The fireplace was left open, and drums were set up in front, as Meek liked the added echo the void gave him. Meek's niece, Sandra, remembers visiting the studio around Christmas 1966: 'I was so worried because the floor was just covered with wires... I felt as though I could be swallowed up by them. I was trying to step over them but there wasn't any room on the floor, and he said, "Oh, don't worry! Just walk over them!"'[145]

Love and Fury: The Life, Death and Legacy of Joe Meek

Oddest of all, as Berry explains, was that there was no window between the studio and the control room next door, where racks contained a number of customised or homemade gadgets, mixers, equalisers and effects units. Whenever Meek wanted to communicate with the musicians he had to come out of the control room and stick his head around the doorway to the studio; there was no intercom or talkback system, and no coloured light to tell the musicians when the recording process had begun. 'They're completely on their own in the studio,' Meek told John Wells of *Disc* magazine. 'I think it helps a lot. There's nothing to distract them… All they have to do is produce a sound, which is what I'm interested in. When I want them to start a number I go into the studio and tell them.'[146] Luckily, the two doorframes abutted each other. Patrick Doncaster, pop columnist for the *Daily Mirror*, described the room as having 'lines of recording apparatus and, around the floor, miles of tape. Joe knows every inch of it. In this unlikely setting he produces discs of quality that go out on several labels. And he manages somehow to produce, too, most of the effects that come out of the large, up-to-the-minute studios conducted by the recording giants.'[147] Talking to *Record Mirror*, Meek explained his *raison d'être*: 'This is where I like to record. And this is the way I like to record. I stress "informality" because you get the best out of an artist in this business in that way… I'm after a sound, and to get results you have to experiment. That's how this started… as an experiment. Then I thought I could get better results here. I still think so.'[148]

In an aural biography recorded in the autumn of 1962 for his friend Donald Aldous (and later issued on the CD box set *Portrait of a Genius*), Meek went into great detail explaining his equipment and methods:

The main microphones are two U-47s, I think this is a wonderful microphone and I use it for all my vocalists… the others are AKG mics, small microphones, dynamic types that are very popular today; I have about six of those. I have also a couple of Rezlos, I use one of the bass drum and one sometimes for a vocal group working on both side of it. Really, the microphones aren't all that expensive, but they're very efficient, and being such a small studio they're used pretty close to the instruments. Later, in the other control room, I add echo to the different channels, and this way I get what I feel is a more commercial sound than to get the instruments to balance themselves in the studio…

Dreams Do Come True

The main recording machine is a twin-track Lyrec. I usually record the voice on one track and the backing on the other. The other recorder is a TR51, and this I use for dubbing, and I must say it's turned out to be a marvellous little machine, but I would prefer to change it soon for something like an Ampex, which would possibly be a little more reliable as this machine tends to 'pop' just a little bit, sometimes you get a sort of 'bumping' in the background... I have a home-made mixer which has four channels, with 'top' lift on each, then I use a Vortexion mixer, which does a pretty good, solid job... I use a Vortexion tape recorder for delay and the echo, this gives me tape play echo which I use, then above my control room I have a room which I've made into an echo chamber, and it's quite remarkable given the size of it, it really gives me a very, very good echo sound which is on all my records, and also I use an electronic echo which I have a patent on. This is used quite a lot on my records too, especially on guitars and percussive sounds. The vocal mic goes through a little cooker I've made, which has got bass, top and middle lift: it was originally a small amplifier. It has three channels, so I can mix in a vocal group with it, or possibly the frontline instruments...

The first act to record at 304, in September 1960, was Kenny Lord and the Statesmen. The band, with 17-year-old vocalist Michael Bourne, had come to Meek's attention through a mutual friend, Peter 'Yak' Raymond (real name Peter Yaquinandi). Bourne had been fronting the band for a couple of years and Raymond had seen his potential. The youngsters had recently cut a demonstration record, and the budding entrepreneur gave copies to both TV producer Jack Good and Joe Meek.

Bourne had started with skiffle band the Rebels, but like many aspiring young musicians had his head turned by rock 'n' roll. 'The first big impression on me was Little Richard,' he remembers.

I went to see the film *Don't Knock the Rock* and Little Richard sang 'Long Tall Sally'... I was absolutely gobsmacked. Then I heard Elvis, then Tommy Steele who I wasn't that enamoured with but who everyone was calling the English Elvis.

We copied Lonnie Donegan, but we also sang rock 'n' roll – it was pretty dreadful. We used to do things like 'Bony Maronie', we tried to do Little Richard which wasn't overly successful... but Lonnie was the one, and when my brother bought 'Rock Island Line' on a 78 I was just blown away! I thought it was the best thing I'd ever heard. Lonnie had such energy, and his rendition was fantastic. I think most rock 'n' rollers will tell you that was their introduction.

Then the Americans came, and Elvis. When I first heard 'Hound Dog' I thought, 'Woah! What is this?' It was a bit like the Little Richard experience... Gradually we moved over to rock 'n' roll. Eventually I broke away and was introduced to some guys with electric guitars. That became Kenny Lord and the Statesmen. We made a demo in somebody's front room in Wandsworth... [Yak] heard this demo, was impressed and came up to see us in rehearsal. He liked my singing and took the demo we'd made to Joe Meek and to Jack Good via his girlfriend. She was a bit of a dish, and the irony was she was trying to use her charms on Joe Meek! Joe wasn't interested in her, but he was impressed with the demo, particularly with 'Peggy Sue Got Married' because, unbeknown to us, he was looking for his own Buddy Holly. He was obsessed with Holly and used to have séances to try and contact his spirit. [149]

Meek was indeed impressed with the band's take on 'Peggy Sue Got Married': 'I rushed to the original version to compare the two. It was fantastic and I immediately wanted to see the young man with the uncanny voice.'[150] But Meek was not the only music industry insider to show an interest in the singer. 'Jack Good also heard this demo,' Berry explains. 'He sent for me and I went to see him, and he said, "Right. We're in the studio next Tuesday. I've got a song for you called 'Not Guilty' and you're going to be the next Adam Faith!"'[151] Bourne was none too keen with Good's plans for his future, but he liked what Meek was offering. 'Joe had a vision of an album for me, which he described as having "a ghostly picture of Buddy Holly on the front, with you superimposed". It sounded great to me. I thought, "Wow! Fantastic!" I turned down Jack Good, who was the god of rock 'n' roll, as far as television was concerned, and went with Joe Meek.'[152]

Dreams Do Come True

True to form, Meek was none too impressed with the band he had heard on the demo, but he was taken with Bourne. However, being four years under the age of majority (21 at that time) the youngster was unable to sign any contract, and was accompanied by his grandmother to his first meeting with Meek. 'We made a record called 'Set Me Free' which Yak had written and Joe liked enough to record it,' Berry recalls. 'We weren't the most impressive band, but I think I was one of his better singers.'[153] Within a few weeks Meek would jettison the band and gift the singer a new name: Mike Berry.

Dick Rowe, who had returned to Decca after EMI took over Top Rank, turned the song down, suggesting that Berry record a cover of 'Will You Love Me Tomorrow' instead. That song had been a US number 1 hit for the Shirelles, but Decca had been assured that the original version would not be issued in the UK. Charles Blackwell wrote the arrangement and directed the orchestra, and Berry put on a credible, if slightly strained, performance, slathered in echo and backed not by the Statesmen but by a different band, the Stormers. Again, it was Peter Raymond who brought the Stormers to Meek's attention, and Raymond fancied steering the career of Mike Berry too. By the time they came to be paired with Berry, the Stormers' own singer, Billy Gray, had gone and the band consisted of Chas Hodges (bass), Billy Kuy (lead guitar), Reg Hawkins (rhythm guitar) and drummer Bobby Graham. 'They'd just come back from a miserable summer season at Butlins in Filey,' Berry explains. 'And the band was on the verge of breaking up... Pete Raymond spoke to them all, told them that he knew me and I had a record deal and that Joe Meek needed a band. Pete took me round to meet them all, they all said yes, and we got to Joe's. We played a song together to show Joe we knew what's what, my band were dumped and the Stormers were brought in. I remember standing on a landing outside Joe's studio, the Stormers were standing on the stairs, and Joe said, "Right, we can't have Kenny Lord and the Statesmen anymore, I don't like that name. Michael Bourne is no good, it doesn't have a rock 'n' roll ring to it. I'm going to call you Mike Berry, because of Buddy Holly, holly berry, and I'm going to call the band The Outlaws." There was no argument about it; that was it. None of us cared. What's in a name, anyway?'[154] The name the Outlaws had been suggested by guitarist Big Jim Sullivan, who had played on Meek-produced sessions for Lance Fortune and the Flee-Rekkers.

Hodges would later recall that, the first time the band went to 304 to audition for Meek, the producer proudly played them tracks from *I Hear a New World*, several of which would later be adapted for the Outlaws repertoire. 'I'd never heard a sound like it in all my life,' Hodges explained. 'I was so amazed at the sound that he got. We'd been to places like IBC before... big studios with a more expensive, wider range of equipment, but when I went to Joe's I couldn't believe the sound that came out of his speakers. We were really amazed. Me and Reg Hawkins, we came out of there and got on the bus that night, and we were sort of in a daze... I was so knocked out; I couldn't stop thinking about the sound he got.'[155]

Despite the snazzy new names, when 'Will You Love Me Tomorrow' was issued in January 1961, it bombed. 'Joe did that under duress,' Berry adds. The song was backed by one of Meek's own compositions, again in the style of Buddy Holly, called 'My Baby Doll'. 'I always hated that record,' says Berry. 'Joe was not a good songwriter; he copied it from Buddy Holly's 'I'm Gonna Love You Too'. He was always coming up with these clones of Buddy's songs. 'Will You Love Me Tomorrow' wasn't a good record, it was in too high a key.'[156] Despite Berry's own reservations, the recording was well received, with *Disc* claiming that the release 'could establish him swiftly as one of the big British sellers... Joe Meek, who brought him to record, should be very pleased with his Buddy Holly-like discovery. The song flows nicely and Mike is well backed by his own group, the Outlaws. You will want to hear more of Mike.'[157] It would, however, be eight months before the country would hear from Mike Berry again.

While still at Triumph, Meek had been approached by a persistent young man from Hackney called Keith De Groot, a singer in a band called the Spotlights. De Groot thought his band had something, and felt that Meek was the man who could help: 'I figured the big companies were far too important to worry about us,' he explained to *Disc* magazine, 'So when I saw an advertisement for Joe Meek... I decided to try.'[158] Meek duly invited the band to audition for him one Sunday afternoon: Meek preferred to work on a Sunday as there was a reasonable chance that he would not be interrupted too often by the ringing of the telephone. 'Unfortunately he wasn't too keen on the group,' De Groot explained. 'But he signed me.' De Groot came from a family of performers: his sister Myra was an actress, his mother a singer and his father a stage comedian, and despite his young

Dreams Do Come True

years he had long held a fascination for showbusiness. At school he wrote and performed in plays and as a teenager he submitted his own sketches to the popular radio comedy programme *The Goon Show*. He spent a period living in New York as a teen, after Myra married a US serviceman, and met stars including Frankie Vaughan and Patti Page.

Shortly before leaving Triumph, Meek brought De Groot back in to record two sides for a potential single, and he announced that the youngster would now be known as Gerry Temple. Just 16 years old and still studying, working for Meek 'was quite an effort,' he later admitted. 'I was at school five days a week, then would spend Friday, Saturday and Sunday nights singing at various engagements.'[159] Temple's first single, arranged by Charles Blackwell, was eventually issued by HMV on 6 January 1961. The slow and atmospheric rocker 'No More Tomorrows' was written by Len Praverman, who had composed Michael Cox's Triumph side 'Don't Want to Know', and was backed with De Groot's own composition 'So Nice to Walk You Home'. Despite getting plenty of TV and radio exposure, and being given a starring role – alongside RGM alumni Michael Cox and Ricky Wayne – on tour in the package show *1961 All Stars*, when he deputised for a sick Terry Dene, none of Temple's three RGM singles charted.

CHAPTER 9

Time Will Tell

The typical work day would begin around 10 a.m., with Joe trying to get both sides of a 45 on tape and spending three hours or so on the A-side before sending the musicians involved off for lunch. It was not unusual for a singer or a group to turn up and be presented with a new number on the spot. 'You'd walk into the studio, and he'd say, "Right, here's the number, I'll give you half an hour and we'll record it,"' Heinz told interviewers Jim Blake and Chris Knight. 'How the hell are you going to learn a number in half an hour?'[160]

The songs would be recorded again and again and again until Meek felt he had enough different takes to choose from. 'He didn't care about mistakes,' Chas Hodges recalled. 'As long as the feel of the track was right.'[161] During the break he would reconfigure the microphones in the studio, ready for the afternoon session, which would see him record what he had envisioned would be the B-side of his next hit. Many of his recordings were done 'as live', with the band running through the song from start to finish. The reason for this was simple: to obtain a more immediate, fresh and realistic feel, but also because the Musicians Union rate was £7/10 for a three-hour session; if a recording could not be captured in three hours, then Meek – or rather, RGM Sound Ltd– had to pay double and, as a rule, the Major would have already given Meek a series of sealed envelopes containing cash for each of the session musicians coming in that day. Vocals would often be recorded 'on a separate track and [I] don't join it up with the backing until a few days after. That gives me even more time to decide on the sound.'[162] Once the recording was finished and the musicians had called it a day, Meek would get to work on his own, without distractions, editing sections of

Time Will Tell

the various takes together, mixing, adding effects and, if necessary, calling in other musicians to overdub extra instruments or add backing vocals. Terry O'Neil, who became Meek's studio assistant after the departure of Tony Kent, was somewhat in awe of his boss's way of working: 'I think he was really a technical artist. He was just getting a sound from whatever he could. He'd get an artist or a band or a group of session people and build what he had in his mind... after the recording was over he'd spend weeks on mixing it, and remixing it and adding things.'[163]

Meek's ear – and the years he spent collecting sounds back in Newent – kept him attuned to every creak, every clank, every single noise that he might be able to capture on tape and reuse later. 'A track Roger LaVern wrote, 'Costa Monger', there's a cracking sound... that was done on a Jag[uar] ashtray,' Heinz revealed. 'He said, "Oh, that's a good sound," and put that on there.... In the bathroom, he used to drop different weighted things into the water to get the different effect. He would never use these BBC Sound Effects things, he'd rather – if he was going to have sound effects – do his own.'[164]

It was not unusual for Meek to work sixteen hours a day, although he would attempt – at least in his first few years as a resident of Holloway Road – to finish recording by 6 p.m., for fear of upsetting the Shentons' neighbours; on one tape that exists of a composing session with Meek and Geoff Goddard (for an unfinished song, 'Rings and Things'), the producer can be heard telling the somewhat excited songwriter, 'Don't tap your feet too much. The people next door will start tapping on the wall.' Violet Shenton often became irritated at the noise emanating from the studio and the endless parade of musicians coming in and out of the flat, blocking their shop entrance, yet despite all that, Meek and the Shentons mostly got on well, even after Lloyd's Bank opened a branch next door and complaints about the noise increased. The maternal Mrs Shenton became something of a surrogate mother to him and was always happy to stop and chat with Meek over a cup of tea; not that he had much time to socialise. Meek got on well with the Shentons' children and grandchildren, and they would occasionally visit the studio to take a look around and marvel at the famous faces coming and going.

An inveterate tweaker, Meek barely knew when to stop. He would 'bounce' recordings down – mixing two or more tracks down to one to free

Love and Fury: The Life, Death and Legacy of Joe Meek

up space on his tapes – often ending with a compressed, distorted sound on his final masters that was at least in part due to his mono deck – the EMI TR51 – which was notorious for producing 'flutter', caused by variations in the tape speed that would produce disparities in pitch. He would work all hours of the day and night, fuelled by pep pills and endless cups of tea and coffee, in an effort to distil the sounds he heard in his head and capture them on tape. This urgency was, in part, propelled by the widely-held belief that rock 'n' roll was a fleeting fad, which would soon be replaced by the next big thing. Many music papers and record reviewers were convinced that rock 'n' roll had already had its day: the threat to childhood posed by Elvis and Cliff was over now that both were recording more anodyne numbers, and if the British music press had its way the airwaves and jukeboxes would soon be filled with trad jazz and bland, housewife-friendly pop. Meek had to work fast: everyone was telling him that the bubble was about to burst.

Usually thought of as an egomaniac who always wanted to see his own name credited, Joe was also a workaholic, and even after RGM Sound was up and running he would occasionally do work for others knowing full well that his name was unlikely to appear. This inability – or unwillingness – to turn down work would produce its own set of problems, and artists often felt that they were not given enough attention, as Dave 'Screaming Lord' Sutch would explain: 'He always seemed unorganised… He only had one phone; he'd tell you, "Right, phone in for your next appointment," a bit like the dentist, and you'd phone up and phone up and the phone would just ring and ring and no one would answer it, or then you'd phone and it was off the hook because he got fed up with it ringing! He's trying to run his recording production company from there; he's trying to run his songwriting from there; and he's trying to run his personal management from there… He just took on too much. The thing with Joe Meek was that I don't think he trusted anybody… he'd have been a multi-millionaire if he could have got somebody he trusted to run different parts of his business… he could have just concentrated on recording the artists, which he was a genius at doing. He should have stuck to what he was best at.'[165]

Apart from being keen to capitalise on a trend, there was another, far more obvious reason that Meek rarely refused work: money. Royalties from his recordings or from his song writing were welcome, but it could take months, if not years, before he would see a penny (quite literally: he

Time Will Tell

told the *Daily Mirror*'s Patrick Doncaster that, as an independent, RGM Sound earned 'a penny a disc, the same royalty as the artist')[166] from a hit single. His artists would complain about not receiving royalties from their recordings, but most of them were bringing in at least some income from live appearances, studio sessions and from radio and television performances. Meek had no other form of income: RGM Sound Ltd paid Meek a weekly wage of £20, and the Major kept a tight rein on the purse strings. 'If we needed any money,' Cliff Bennett revealed, '[When] we were doing sessions for Joe, Joe used to have to get on to Major Banks, and Major Banks used to have to bring a cheque down. It took ages… it could take fucking weeks to get your money off Major Banks.'[167] Meek did not enjoy having to go cap in hand to him every time he wanted to spend some money, and so he would occasionally accept engineering or production work outside the confines of RGM Sound, so long as they promised to pay quickly and he could keep it a secret from the Major.

The transient nature of pop music turned Meek into a control freak. 'To survive as an independent A & R man I've got to produce records that are different. This is the only advantage I have over the big companies, and working as a small unit like this I can do it. When I first get a song sent to me, I know exactly what sort of sound I want, who is the best person to sing it, who I want to back it and so on. I can only look after all these things if I do it myself.'[168] Meek admitted, however, that many of his artists baulked at his way of working: 'They don't always like it, but in the end they do as I say and it gets them hits.'[169]

Not only did they back Berry in the studio and on tour, but the Outlaws also had a career as a stand-alone instrumental act and backed many of the artists who came through the doors of 304. Meek, a man of many passions, was obsessed with the romance of the American Wild West, a rough place where handsome men rode across the prairie picking off the baddies and winning the hearts of fair maidens. Back at home in Newent he had played Cowboys and Indians with his Market Square Gang, and like much of the country he was often glued to the television, where western serials including *Gunsmoke*, *Bonanza* and *Rawhide* dominated prime time during a period when Britain only had two television channels, and his interest in the spirit world had brought him to believe that he was being guided

Love and Fury: The Life, Death and Legacy of Joe Meek

by the ghost of a Native American. His decision to outfit the Outlaws in a fanciful approximation of cowboy chic, and to have them record country and western-flavoured instrumentals, would culminate in Meek's second concept album, *Dream of the West*, in December 1961.

Their first single, 'Swingin' Low' was issued in March 1961. The Outlaws had recorded several takes of the song at a session just weeks earlier, but Chas Hodges was unhappy with the results: to his ear each take had a problem. The track features several breaks, highlighting the drums, bass and rhythm guitar, but as he explained, 'I'd do a real good bass bit that I was happy with, but the drummer would mess his up... the next one would be a great drum break, and my bass break wasn't as good as the first one. We did about six takes, I think, and Joe Meek went, "Right, OK, we've got it."' Hodges, concerned about the performance, wanted to know what take the producer would be using, but Meek replied, 'Don't worry; you're all going to be happy. You're all going to have your favourite bits.' The band left and Meek got to work, razor blade and adhesive tape in hand, editing the various takes together into a flawless whole. 'When we went back and heard the playback, I said "How did you do it?", and he showed me... He taught me that and that stayed with me.'[170]

To promote 'Swingin' Low', loosely based on the African-American spiritual 'Swing Low, Sweet Chariot' but credited to 'Yak' Raymond as a 'thank you' for bringing the band to Meek's attention, Joe had the group dress as cowboys, put them on a Wild West stagecoach and set off on a tour around London, starting off at the HMV shop on Oxford Street, where the band pretended to hold up one of the store's assistants with their toy guns. Lional was there, cine camera in hand, to capture the madness. Covering the coach in hand-painted posters which announced to the public that 'Swingin' Low' had already been voted a hit on popular TV show *Juke Box Jury*, Meek had the band – complete with an outrider on a white horse – ride on to Leicester Square, via Piccadilly Circus, attracting the ire of traffic wardens and police along the way, while he followed in his cream and red Sunbeam Rapier. Despite all of their hard work, the single peaked at a disappointing number 46 in April. A month later the Outlaws issued their follow-up: Meek's composition 'Ambush' begins with a barrage of gunshots and includes a full-on gun battle, complete with whooping Native Americans and whinnying horses, but although it sold a healthy 30,000 or so, it did not follow its predecessor into the charts.

The publicity stunt for 'Swingin' Low' was just one of many. Always on the lookout for a gimmick that could help him market his productions, Meek had young Joy Adams photographed in a bath full of milk to publicise 'My Very Good Friend the Milkman', which saw the pair return to Decca after their one-off release on Triumph. 'That was Joe's idea,' Joy recalls. 'Everything came from Joe.'[171] George Martin had produced a rather pedestrian version of the same song a few months earlier for singer Johnny Angel, but Joy and Dave's version of the song positively jumps out of the grooves; the disc is only let down by the dreadful flip side, Robert Duke's silly 'Doopey Darling'. 'Joe was a terrible writer,' Joy admits. 'We felt trapped and intimidated into recording what he wanted in his songs.'[172] Meek always liked to have his masters cut as loudly as possible, and despite his dislike of Alan Stagg he would get many of them cut at IBC, where he knew exactly what the equipment was capable of. Initially, he would attend these sessions himself, supervising the cutting and pushing IBC's engineers (and their equipment) to the limit, but as RGM Sound became busier he would delegate this process to his assistant, Tony Kent. Between making cups of tea and running the Outlaws fan club, Kent would often be sent to IBC with reels of tape, with Meek's poorly-spelt instructions to the cutting engineer scribbled on the box.

In the same month that 'Swingin' Low' found its way to the record stores, Meek brought Chris Williams and his Monsters into RGM Sound to cut their third (and final) single for him. Recorded over two sessions, the first on 30 March at 304 Holloway Road, the second a week later at Lansdowne, for this particular release the group was renamed Chris and the Students. The resulting single was a trad jazz version of the folk standard 'The Lass of Richmond Hill', which one reviewer described as a song that 'moves along with the gentle subtlety of bulldozer demolishing bomb-site';[173] the flip side 'Ducks Away From My Fishin'', which announced itself as a Robert Duke original, took its theme from a traditional sea shanty.

Meek's friends in the music industry would often bring their latest discovery to see him. Songwriter Lionel Bart brought 16-year-old piano player Clive Powell to 304; he cut several demos for Meek, including a cover of Bart's

Love and Fury: The Life, Death and Legacy of Joe Meek

'Living Doll', which Cliff Richard and the Drifters took to number 1 the previous year. Meek passed on Powell, but another friend of Bart's, Larry Parnes, took him under contract on the understanding that the Lancashire-born Powell change his name to Georgie Fame. His reputation was such that Meek was soon being sought out by international artists too: Canadian singer Donn Reynolds signed a recording contract with Meek, but with little interest shown by British labels in the 'King of the Yodellers', the singer soon found himself back in Winnipeg, albeit with a newly-acquired British wife.

In late 1960 Bob Kingston, managing director of music publishers Southern Music, introduced Meek to a shy, quietly-spoken young piano player from Ormsby Street, Reading, the 22-year-old son of a butcher, who aspired to make it in the music business. A natural talent, Geoffrey Goddard was bashing away at the family piano from the age of 3; at 6 he began formal piano lessons, at school he wrote hymns by composing music to accompany Bible verses, and by the time he was a teenager he was appearing in local variety shows. Like Meek, Goddard had completed his National Service, although he served his two years in the army, not the RAF, and while there he had performed as part of a military band. Crucially, Goddard shared Meek's fascination in spiritualism, and he would go on to develop interests in some of Meek's other passions, including extraterrestrial life, unidentified flying objects and the occult.

Shortly after he was demobbed, Goddard enrolled in the Royal Academy of Music, but he left in late 1959 once he realised that he was unlikely to earn a living as a classical pianist. Instead, he went looking for work playing piano in pubs and hotels, and quickly landed a job playing light classical music and easy listening favourites in the lounge of a Reading hotel at the weekend. Weekdays were spent looking for something more rewarding and permanent, and he developed a routine, leaving the family home in Reading and catching an early train into London, where mornings were spent feeding pennies into telephone kiosks in the train station (the family had no telephone at home: most private residences in the UK would not have their own telephone until the mid-1970s) setting up appointments before doing the rounds of the city's music publishers. Most of them had offices on Denmark Street, the thoroughfare often referred to as London's Tin Pan Alley, and it was there that he met Bob Kingston. Turning up at

A few weeks after his fifth birthday, **Joe** (back row, left) in 'Daffodils and Pixies' in Churchdown, Gloucester with his brother **Arthur** (back row, right), May 1934. *(The Joe Meek Family Archive)*

George and **Evelyn Meek** on their wedding day, April 1927.
(The Joe Meek Family Archive)

Joe aged nine, Picklenash School, Newent, 1938.
(The Joe Meek Family Archive)

Standing next to his mother **Evelyn** and sister **Pamela**, circa 1949. *(The Joe Meek Family Archive)*

Joe with a **friend** at The Ledern, 1950.
(The Joe Meek Family Archive)

The Foley artists (far right) with friends from one of Newent's amateur dramatic societies, circa 1951.
(right) Taking time out in one of the family cherry orchards, Newent, circa 1950. *(both photos, The Joe Meek Family Archive)*

A rare image of **Joe** hard at work in the cutting room at IBC, circa 1955. *(Shutterstock)*

(top left) **Joe** shortly after moving to London, circa 1955. *(The Joe Meek Family Archive)*

(bottom left) Relaxing in a deck chair, possibly in Arundel Gardens, circa 1955. *(The Joe Meek Family Archive)*

At **Eric** and **Marlene**'s wedding, **Joe** (far right) stands next to his boyfriend **Lional Howard**, behind his **mother** and **sister**, April 1960. *(The Joe Meek Family Archive)*

(top) **Joe** (middle) with **Adrian Kerridge** (right) recording on the road for Radio Luxembourg, circa 1956.
(The Joe Meek Family Archive)

(left) **Clem Cattini** at Holloway Road, 1962.
(John Pratt/Keystone Features/Getty Images)

A very happy **Joe** with his international number one act the **Tornados** in the studio at 304 Holloway Road, late 1962. *(Keystone/Hulton Archive/Getty Images)*
(top) **John Leyton**, 1962. *(Popperfoto via Getty Images/Getty Images)*

Time Will Tell

his office late one Monday afternoon, Goddard impressed Kingston with a more than passable Russ Conway impersonation, playing him three tunes he had written over the previous weekend. Goddard also submitted a song that he thought might be suitable for Cliff Richard, but although Kingston could not use it, he believed that there was some potential in the nervous young scribe from Reading. Kingston signed Goddard to a five-year songwriting contract and invited Meek down to his office to meet him.

At first, Meek – directed by Kingston, who was looking for material in a similar vein – attempted to mould the 22-year-old Goddard into a Russ Conway-style pianist, and to this end they awarded him a new stage name: Anton Hollywood. Solo pianists were big business, with hit singles and plenty of television and radio work, and Meek sent the newly-christened Mr Hollywood out on tour to boost his profile. In January and February 1961, Anton Hollywood appeared as part of a Robert Stigwood-promoted package starring actor Michael Medwin, plus John Leyton, Iain Gregory, Charles Blackwell and his Big Beat Band, and Joy and Dave. However, audiences did not take to the cut-price Liberace; they did not like his habit of humming along while he played – Jack Good called the noise that emanated from Goddard 'an uncanny grumbling groaning wailing sound'[174] – and Goddard did not enjoy the roughhousing that went along backstage between the acts. This was not the life for a man Charles Blackwell described as 'sensitive and temperamental'.[175] Meek tried to interest Decca in signing Anton Hollywood, but they felt that he was too similar to Conway and there was no room in the hit parade for a mediocre version of the king of the jangly piano. Besides, Decca already had Winifred Atwell, the undisputed queen of ragtime key-thumping and the first Black woman to sell a million copies of a disc in the UK. Things might have been different had Meek taken him to see George Martin, as before the year was out Parlophone would unveil their answer to Atwell and Conway in the form of a 43-year-old East London secretary, Mrs Mills.

Meek believed that he had been in communication with the spirit of Buddy Holly, and soon Goddard too became certain that the late star was guiding his songwriting from beyond the grave. In early 1961, at a séance in Reading, Goddard was persuaded that the spiritualist medium present had been channelling the spirit of Holly, and that the singer had come through specifically to give him advice. 'The message she gave me was that he was trying to help me. She said she heard him mention "Oh! Boy" which she couldn't understand – but I knew it was the title of one of his records. She wasn't aware of my interest in songwriting, although she knew I played piano, nor did she know about Buddy Holly.'[176] Goddard was so convinced of the medium's veracity that he began attending sessions with her every Monday evening. 'I've had several more [messages] directly to me from Buddy,' he insisted, 'And these talks with him have given me the encouragement and inspiration I need.'[177]

'Joe was quite obsessed with that,' says Joy Adams. 'And I took part in some of his séances. Even when we were recording, according to Joe, there was always a presence there. We were supposed to believe that there was a presence there, and of course we were kids so we did! There was always talk about ghosts, about people who were dead that were present during recording sessions. He believed that someone was there that was famous, like Buddy Holly. Joe said that he was reaching to the beyond. He discussed that quite a bit; he didn't keep it hidden, not to us, anyway.'[178]

Goddard and Meek were both outsiders, drawn to London because that was where you had to go if you wanted to work in the music industry, and that was where you had to go if you wanted to have any kind of life if you were homosexual, which many assumed the confirmed bachelor to be. 'He was a sweet guy, a lovely guy,' his friend Mike Berry says. 'I'm not sure if he was gay, but that didn't matter. He was a sweetheart.'[179] Sensing a potential comrade-in-arms, Joe put Geoff to work as a songwriter and pianist. Goddard recalled that, in the early days, he found Meek 'a bit eccentric, I suppose, but very friendly though. He always seemed to be quite happy-go-lucky,'[180] although later he would describe Meek as 'a very strange man, very temperamental. He could be very moody: if he was upset he might pick up a chair and throw it at you.'[181]

He remembered too that the studio at 304 was 'very small... he was always tripping over leads and things,' and he would later comment that 'I was no expert on electrical gear, but the equipment at RGM looked like odds and ends Joe had picked up from a junk shop, wired them all up and made something of them.'[182] Usually, Goddard would not write to order, but he would come to RGM Sound several times a month with the songs he had composed and show them to Meek. 'He was interested to see what I had written and wanted to see if it would suit any of the singers,' he said.

Time Will Tell

'I'd make a demo there, usually, just play the piano, and Joe might bang on the door to provide some rhythm accompaniment to it. Then he'd play the tape to whoever he wanted or thought it would suit, and the next thing I'd hear was when he had arranged a session. I'd come up and we'd usually do the backing track first, and the singer would go along on another day and finish it off.'[183] Singer Glenda Collins agreed: 'He did tend to record separately; I think he recorded the backing part first... Invariably he added things on afterwards, especially his effects and his sounds [but] mainly you added the voice on afterwards.'[184] Goddard was able to play almost anything by ear, and equally able to pick out the bones of a tune from Meek's own garbled demos and provide something useable for the artists flooding through the doors of 304. Occasionally, Goddard and Meek would try to write something together, as Goddard later revealed: 'Joe Meek used to say to me, "Play 'Maybe Baby' and that'll get us into the mood." We'd come up with songs like 'Don't You Think It's Time', which was a good one.'[185]

His first tune to see release was an instrumental entitled 'Lone Rider', a Shadows-inspired twangy guitar number which was recorded by the Flee-Rekkers and issued by Piccadilly (Pye's new pop imprint, launched in April) in June 1961. Radio and TV presenter Keith Fordyce seemed convinced that Goddard and Meek were about to enjoy a major success: 'This British group could hit big with the mood instrumental. The tune is gripping, the beat is stirring and the atmosphere conjured up is powerful.' At that time, the Flee-Rekkers were seen as the country's number 1 rival to the Shadows; the previous autumn they had won a huge £10,000 contract to play the Mecca ballroom circuit (the first beat group ever put under contract by the organisation) and they had invested £1,000 of that in the latest PA equipment. Instrumental groups were big business: in the week that the group secured their lucrative deal almost a third of the Top 30 was made up of instrumental acts, with Johnny and the Hurricanes, the John Barry Seven, the Piltdown men, the Viscounts, the Ventures, Bert Weedon, Duane Eddy and two Shadows singles jockeying for position. Sadly, in spite of their increasing fame and Fordyce's enthusiasm for the disc, 'Lone Rider' was not a major seller. Jazz musician Benny Green, commenting on the disc on the popular BBC TV show *Juke Box Jury*, was nonplussed by Meek's effects: 'It sounded like an explosion took place, as if the guitar had electrocuted the guy that was playing it... I wouldn't have been unhappy if it had exploded and killed the guitarist, because it's like 10,000 other guitar records I've heard.' Comedian Spike Milligan found it 'repetitious, boring... trying to keep pace with current trends which are nauseating,' adding, sarcastically, that 'It's bound to be a winner!'

Earlier that spring, Meek had produced a 45 for Piccadilly from a pair of songwriters from Smallheath, Birmingham, John Shakespeare and Ken Hawker, who went under the *noms de plume* Carter–Lewis. Backed by the Outlaws (although the act was credited as Carter, Lewis and the Southerners), the disc featured two originals, 'Back on the Scene' and 'So Much in Love'. Carter–Lewis were managed by Terry Kennedy of Southern Music and had first appeared on Meek's radar while he was running Triumph: the songwriters had recorded for Saga, Triumph's parent company, although their disc went unissued (one of the songs recorded at that time, 'Can't Forget', was later recorded for Parlophone by Johnny Gavotte). When 'Back on the Scene' faltered, Kennedy decided that the pair, who had already appeared on several BBC teen music shows, should record 'Two Timing Baby' a song co-written by Meek's new songwriter Geoff Goddard and Barry White (Southern's Bob Kingston). They agreed to do this on the understanding that one of their own songs, 'Will it Happen to Me?' would appear on the B-side. Recorded at 304 and featuring Goddard, plus Outlaws Chas Hodges and Bobby Graham, the tracks were licensed to Meek's friend Jeff Kruger at Ember. 'Two Timing Baby' sold reasonably well but again did not chart nationally. Carter and Lewis would return to RGM Sound for a further session which resulted in a pair of singles issued within days of each other; a second single for Piccadilly (issued in late 1962), 'Here's Hopin'' (produced not by Meek but by Terry Kennedy for the Southern-owned Iver Records), backed with a cover of Meek's own composition, 'Poor Joe', and a second for Ember, featuring another Geoff Goddard composition on the top side, 'Tell Me', which was again produced by Kennedy under Meek's supervision.

The same month as Piccadilly issued 'Lone Rider', Parlophone released the debut single from Cliff Bennett and the Rebel Rousers, an act brought to Meek's attention by Putney dancehall owner Bob Alexander. Alexander, who managed the Rebel Rousers, the Flee-Rekkers and Emile Ford and the Checkmates, invited Meek along to the Finsbury Park Empire to see the

Time Will Tell

band in action, and Meek was impressed enough to offer them a deal on the spot. Former foundry worker Bennett and his band (who took their name from Duane Eddy's 1958 instrumental hit, 'Rebel Rouser') had already landed a couple of live radio spots on the BBC, and Meek quickly put them to work. The band appeared as the Alexander Combo (the name derived from their manager's surname), backing Danny Rivers on his second RGM single, 'Once Upon a Time', in May 1961; however, Meek's own composition, 'You've Got What I Like', issued in June, would be their first outing under their own name. Both the song and the group's performance were clearly inspired by Jerry Lee Lewis (Bennett acknowledged that Jerry Lee was his idol), and although the flip side, 'I'm in Love With You' was credited to Meek and Bennett, it was a shameless rewrite of the Big Bopper hit 'Chantilly Lace', inspired no doubt by the A-side's title being so close to that song's tag line, 'You know what I like'. 'You've Got What I Like' showcased every trick in Meek's book, with heavy reverb and echo on the vocals, substantial use of flanging on the guitar, the tinny, tack piano and massive compression (a trick from the recording engineer's tool bag to even out sound levels and add extra dynamism or 'punch' to a recording) that would have made the needle jump right out of the groove.

'At first, when I walked in, I thought, "I don't know if this is going to work,"' Bennett admitted. 'But the equipment he had was fantastic... He really had weird ideas. I'd been into places like EMI, not to work, just to observe, but it's only when you heard the results that you appreciated [what he had]. It's not really the size of the studio, it's what you can do with what you've got.'[186] Maureen Cleave, the *Evening Standard* pop critic visited 304 and wrote about what she found there.* She was impressed with the sound Meek achieved on the Danny Rivers single, writing that the performer 'seems to be singing through crystal glass. There are tinkly bits in the upper register while the bass is clean, hard-hitting and exciting. The whole thing doesn't sound English. The company responsible for this artful conception, I learned was RGM Sound...

---

*   Cleave would go on to find everlasting fame in 1966, with a series of articles entitled *How Does a Beatle Live*, which contained John Lennon's infamous remarks about Christianity.

Love and Fury: The Life, Death and Legacy of Joe Meek

'RGM – those are my initials,' explained a Mr Meek as he let me in, 'Though everybody calls me Joe.' We climbed the narrow stairs, past a budgerigar in a cage, wormed our way round a spare mattress propped against the bannisters. Then we were hit by the sound.

'It's the Flee-Rekkers,' mouthed Mr Meek apologetically, ushering me into a room the size of a small front parlour where hell was being knocked out of drums, three guitars and two saxophones. Mr Meek is a gentle-voiced, shy man from Gloucestershire, aged 29, he made the hit Angela Jones, and is the only person I know with a recording studio in his own flat – *small* flat.

If Mr Meek has to record strings as well, he doesn't overcrowd the sitting room. They play from the bathroom.

He padded serenely from room to room, fixing bits of gear, shifting little bits of cardboard.

'There's about £5,000 worth of equipment,' he said, as we waded through spaghetti streels of wiring, where no char had waded since Mr Meek built the set-up a year ago. On a listing book-case were lumps of machinery I couldn't understand.

'This,' said Mr Meek, pointing to a tall thin piece of metal that looked as if it belonged in a lift shaft, 'This is my echo unit. A small thing, but it sounds like a cathedral. Cuts out the echo chamber, you see.

'My methods are a bit unorthodox,' he went on, as I peered into the piano which had a drawing pin stuck in every single hammer, 'But I think I get professional results. If I sell a hit to the recording companies, I might make £5,000.'[187]

Ms Cleave might have been impressed with Danny Rivers, but Cliff Bennett's 'You've Got What I Like' was a staggering recording, with a sound unlike any other rock 'n' roll discs being produced in Britain at that time. Although they gained plenty of exposure, neither 'You've Got What I Like', 'Once Upon a Time' or 'Lone Rider' were hits; however, Goddard's second composition, a number he later claimed to have dashed off in minutes, would be: 'Johnny Remember Me'.

CHAPTER 10

Johnny Remember Me

A few months earlier, following the public's disinterest in John Leyton's second release, 'The Girl on the Floor Above', Joe received a letter from Roland Rennie, a senior manager at EMI. Rennie was not enamoured with Leyton or his discs, and wrote on 10 March to tell Meek bluntly that he should 'please accept this (letter) as authority to place the artiste elsewhere'.[188] Meek, along with Robert Stigwood, Leyton's manager, was convinced that if Leyton was going to be a star he needed a company with the clout of EMI to help make that happen. A stubborn Meek wrote back, telling Rennie about a new song he had for Leyton, written by Geoff Goddard.

Stigwood landed Leyton a role on an ATV evening drama serial, originally known as *Big Store* but now renamed *Harpers West One*, on 24 July playing Johnny St Cyr (pronounced Sincere), a singer who was making a personal appearance in the department store's record concession. Getting Leyton on *Harpers West One* – 'The story of life behind the counter of a big London store'[189] – was a massive coup: the show's first episode attracted a massive audience of 25 million, and the potential for both Leyton and the song featured was huge. Luckily, Goddard had something that was perfect: a sensational, theatrical, almost cinematic tale entitled 'Johnny Remember Me', that the songwriter had penned 'in the early morning, just after I had opened my eyes. I believe I receive direct help from Buddy Holly.'[190] Meek told Rennie that 'I decided it would be far better to find a good song... And offer him to you with a possible hit disc... Well, I'm quite positive this new one will be a very big hit. The song is great and John does a great job with the vocal. It's a song like 'Tell Laura' that will get lots of publicity because it's about a girlfriend that dies... I would like everything done to keep the boy with EMI; he's going to be very big one day, this record will do it.'[191] It would appear that, at this point in time, neither Meek nor Rennie were aware that EMI's chairman, Sir Joseph Lockwood, had taken a personal interest in Leyton's career, and in Leyton himself.

A dramatic and emotional account of lost love, Leyton was none too impressed when he first heard Goddard thump out the song at the piano, but by the time Meek had finished with it, it had been transformed. 'Johnny Remember Me' featured a driving accompaniment from the Outlaws and a superb arrangement from Charles Blackwell, complemented by the disc's major hook, the ethereal backing vocals from classically-trained soprano Lissa Gray. Meek first encountered Lissa when he was recording the George Mitchell Singers, and to give her part a wraithlike feel had her sing from inside the first-floor lavatory. 'The loo was horrendous,' she recalled. 'I remember at one stage, in order to get an echo effect, Joe dangled the microphone actually down the loo!'[192] Meek's eldest brother, Arthur, was visiting at the time: 'I can remember these queer fellows all trooping up the stairs into the room… The room was pretty full. It wasn't a very big studio, but the room was quite full, so I sat downstairs and could hear them recording it over and over again.'[193]

Leyton recalled a typical RGM session: 'I was in the sitting room behind a little screen. The rhythm section was in the room with me. The violin section was on the stairs, the backing singers were practically in the loo, and the brass section was underneath, on another floor altogether and there was Joe next door, playing his machine like another musical instrument. It was quite bizarre. We did it over and over. Joe wanted plenty of exciting atmosphere in it, and it was a really exhilarating sound with the galloping, driving beat.'[194] It was an unusual way for anyone to record, but having everyone perform live added an urgency and dynamism to the finished recording. 'I was lucky in a way, recording with Joe Meek,' Leyton would recognise. 'Joe was very *avant-garde* for his time and he got a unique sound out of his studio.'[195]

With Blackwell, Goddard and himself, Meek had built a brilliant, supremely talented trio, and in the Outlaws he had a superb and versatile backing band, able to play pop, rock or country and western. As Mike Berry explains, 'They seemed to be quite a good team. Joe tended to pull people in who he thought were good, and also he probably fancied them! I don't know what happened with Geoff Goddard, because he wasn't every gay

Johnny Remember Me

man's idea of a dish, and Charles Blackwell was a big, strapping chap who was very happily married. Charlie was a very talented man, as was Geoff Goddard, so Joe did get some big talent around him, which was proved by the work that they did.'[196]

Meek was convinced that 'Johnny Remember Me' was a hit. Buddy Holly had guaranteed as much, as Leyton remembered: 'One morning Joe told me, "Geoff and I made contact with Buddy Holly last night, and we asked him if 'Johnny Remember Me' was going to be a hit. He spelt out that it was going to be a number 1." My reaction was, "in your dreams".' Leyton may have been sceptical, but in his own words, 'it took off like a rocket,' and Meek was not in the least bit surprised. 'He'd expected it. Having contacted Buddy Holly, he was quite convinced it was going to go to number 1. So when it did, it wasn't that much of a surprise to him. But I remember him being ecstatic about it – it was his first number 1.'[197] Goddard recalled that 'using the glass tumbler and cards, Buddy's name was spelled out [and] 'Johnny Remember Me' was forecast as a hit... I don't think the cards are completely reliable, but it is strong evidence nevertheless.'[198] Goddard went on to tell the interviewer that 'I am sure I receive my inspiration from the spirit world'.[199]

Roland Rennie had close ties to Sir Joseph Lockwood, who despite being significantly older was having an affair with Robert Stigwood: 'Sir Joseph Lockwood was his boyfriend,' Mike Berry confirmed. 'They used to come back stage holding hands, the pair of them back when being gay was frowned upon.'[200] Lockwood was also rather taken with Leyton (despite the actor being heterosexual) and would insist that Stigwood bring the handsome young man along to meetings and on dinner dates. This caused a few issues as Stigwood was also keen on his charge and would scarcely let him out of his sight. 'It's general knowledge Joe Meek and Robert Stigwood were gay,' says John Leyton. 'Along with a lot of other pop management in those days. I don't have a problem with that, but I'm not gay – and at some stages with Stigwood it got difficult because there was a predatory element to it and I had to fight him off. I imagine there was a kind of male casting couch but I never went anywhere near it. Joe Meek never made any sort of move at all. He was in a world of his own and didn't seem quite "there". He was a troubled man. A lot of young boys would knock on Joe's door hoping he would record them. But I was already semi-established as an actor in a

Love and Fury: The Life, Death and Legacy of Joe Meek

TV series at the time and I had a manager. So maybe that's what made him stand off a bit... But I had trouble with Stigwood. I was not what he wanted me to be. It was quite difficult at times. He made passes at me and I pushed him off and told him to forget it. At times he would threaten me.'[201]

Leyton was not the only one of Stigwood's artists to have to fight off his advances, as Mike Berry was to discover after the Australian took over as his manager. 'He tried it on with me,' Berry remembers. 'He was going to take me out to dinner but tried to seduce me in his flat and I didn't get out to eat that night! He spent most of the evening getting drunk and trying to get into my trousers... He was on his knees between my legs with his hands on my thigh... I jumped up and said, "You're lucky I'm not a violent man."'[202]

Lockwood brought pressure to bear on Rennie and had EMI issue the record. Although Goddard was convinced that the disc would be a success, telling his local newspaper shortly before its release that 'this could be my first real break',[203] Meek still did not find favour with this version of the song. Although Rennie relented over its suitability, Walter Ridley, A&R manager at HMV, objected to the dark lyrics, and the disc was instead given to the recently reactivated Top Rank, which had issued Leyton's debut, 'Tell Laura I Love Her'. Still things did not go smoothly: the BBC also found the original lyrics unpalatable, and Leyton had to return to 304 to record a slightly cleaned-up version, which altered the offending line from 'The girl I loved *who died* a year ago' to 'The girl I loved *and lost* a year ago'. Even then, people who thought that they knew better, including composer and arranger Martin Slavin, attacked Meek's home recording techniques: 'A recording studio is the place to record. They are there for that specific purpose and they have the best technicians in their employ.'[204]

Slavin had been the orchestra leader for both sides of Joy and David's Parlophone debut in 1958 and was a member of Kenny Graham and His Satellites, so understandably Meek took the attack personally. A fortnight later the *Record Mirror* printed a rebuttal from a furious Meek, who chastised Slavin's narrow mindedness. 'Why did Martin Slavin slate me?' he asked. 'Who is he to say what he did about a studio he has never entered?

First of all, what IS a studio? It is basically a room with acoustic treatment, fitted with mikes, play-back speakers, chairs and music stands. My studio is equipped with the best type of mikes available,

Johnny Remember Me

together with carefully-planned acoustic treatment and all the material I need for recording. The only difference to any other studio is that I use some units I designed and built myself. They add an extra something to my recordings. Fair enough, my studio was originally a large bedroom, but it is now a first class studio in which I have made many hit records – and no one will tell me that is wrong. If Martin Slavin had dug deeper he would have found that most studios started as a room, basement or bedroom in a town house... I would be a fool to listen to an arranger with a bee in his bonnet. I make records to entertain the public, not square connoisseurs who just don't know.[205]

Meek had his supporters, and no doubt would have been heartened somewhat by bandleader and radio personality Jack Payne who, while berating John Leyton as 'manufactured', at least gave begrudging credit where it was due: 'Engineers make records, and not musicians.'[206] Even so, the producer came out fighting, telling readers of the *Melody Maker* that the allegations that Leyton relied on Meek's 'echo chamber and superb techniques' were 'utter rubbish. Certainly I try to inject punch and drive into my productions with John, but he is basically talented. He would have made headway with whoever put him on record.'[207] Jack Good was as effusive as ever: 'Joe is a mastermind,' he trumpeted. 'He creates sounds that have never before existed – not even in your wildest dreams. Needless to say, this causes trouble. Not infrequently his imagination has brought something really wonderful into being and the record firm has rejected it, because they haven't understood it. But Joe persists in making records for teenagers rather than record bosses. This has taken courage, for if the company releasing Joe's record doesn't really have faith in it, it understandably doesn't get the exploitation it deserves. And nothing sells without getting plays. Maybe, following 'Johnny Remember Me', Joe's ideas will be taken more seriously. They should be.'[208]

One week after his appearance on *Harpers West One*, and despite being voted a 'miss' by the members of the panel on *Juke Box Jury* (Spike Milligan dismissed it as 'Son of "Ghost Riders in the Sky"', which was particularly embarrassing as, moments later, Leyton walked out from behind a screen, a surprise guest on the show), 'Johnny Remember Me' entered the *Melody Maker* singles chart at number 19. The following week it leapt to number 7.

113

Leyton and Stigwood were sailing on the Norfolk Broads when they heard that 'Johnny Remember Me' had hit the top spot.

On 7 September Meek attended a party at the Dorchester hotel in London, thrown by Stigwood, to celebrate the sale of 250,000 copies of 'Johnny Remember Me'. Charles Blackwell bought gifts for Goddard, Leyton and Stigwood, cigarette cases which he had inscribed. He bought Joe, a non-smoker, 'something ornamental for his flat. And Joe was so overcome when I gave him this thing that he burst into tears. The next day he was screaming at me like a fishwife over something that didn't please him, something that had happened... An incredible man but so temperamental.'[209] 'He did have a temper,' Chas Hodges agreed. 'You never knew how to handle Joe; he was always a bit on edge. You could never [predict] how he was going to react to anything.'[210] No one was immune, and everyone in the industry knew that Meek was difficult, but so long as he kept producing hits these outbursts were passed off as eccentricity.

Although 'Johnny Remember Me' was an enormous success, selling in excess of a quarter of a million copies in its first four weeks and earning a coveted silver disc award, the song attracted a lot of attention because of its supposed bad-taste lyrics. Since 'Tell Laura I Love Her', the press had been debating the value of so-called 'death discs' – songs more often than not built around the demise of a young lover – but as Arthur Meek explained, 'Joe couldn't have bloody cared less! [He] had his own ideas and he carried them through. He didn't really care about nobody.'[211]

The hit breathed new life into Meek. 'Before "Johnny Remember Me" he used to get very depressed,' Geoff Goddard recalled. 'He seemed to be under some tension,' which, it seemed, Goddard's hit-providing ability was able to ease. Always keen for recognition, his ego would have been bolstered by seeing his name in print again and again, recognised as the genius behind Leyton's success: 'I give a lot of credit to recording man Joe Meek who together with accompanist Charles Blackwell has given the record an authentic feel. It's well in line with Meek's other efforts.'[212] Cliff Bennett agreed with Goddard's assessment. 'He used to get depressed,' he remarked. 'The thing he liked to do was go up and have a good session, that's how he'd come alive. He was a different man. If you went up there and we had, say, two numbers to do and we went in there, no mucking about, straight away everything fell in place and the session was good, he

Johnny Remember Me

was like a little boy... That would really lift him. But so many musicians used to go up there and fuck him about, you know? Really. We were culprits a couple of times, because what he was trying to put over to us we just thought it was funny. But if you could have gone up there and been sincere and worked hard with him, you'd get results.'[213]

Meek may have had very definite ideas about what he wanted, but in those early days he was not totally closed to outside influences. He had planned to record a couple of originals for Michael Cox's next single, but when he caught the singer and band – Marty Wilde's former act the Wildcats, now renamed the Krew Kats – jamming a version of the Chuck Berry hit 'Sweet Little Sixteen' during a break in the session, he decided that number would be the plug side instead. Both band and singer made a valiant effort, with blistering guitar work from Big Jim Sullivan and excellent work from future Shadows drummer Brian Bennet captured by 'a microphone placed right against the bass drum which is "dampened" by a blanket'. Good called the record 'a rock 'n' roll masterpiece' and labelled it Cox's 'best disc yet'; however, despite its claim to fame as one of the first British pop records to use a wah-wah effect, it was dismissed by the *Melody Maker* for its 'excessive echo and electronics overload',[214] and again did not make the national charts.

Geoff Goddard was a proverbial hit machine, and in September, while 'Johnny Remember Me' was at the top of the charts, HMV issued his next winner, 'Tribute to Buddy Holly', recorded at 304 by Mike Berry and the Outlaws. 'When "Will You Love Me Tomorrow" was a flop, Joe got together with Geoff Goddard and came up with "Tribute to Buddy Holly",' Berry recalls. 'He was looking for his own Buddy Holly. He was obsessed with Holly and used to have séances to try and contact his spirit.' Meek's ideas of how to reach the other side were somewhat at odds with Goddard's own, more respectful and serious approach: 'Joe Meek was very interested in the occult,' Goddard commented. 'They were just card and tumbler séances, which is a bit way off-mainstream spiritualism.'[215] Meek convinced himself that 304 was haunted and claimed that, during one séance, an electric organ in the studio began playing by itself: Meek believed the invisible keyboard player was Holly.

Goddard's song was written, primarily, as an attempt to keep Meek happy. 'That was my idea, really,' Goddard recalled. 'I was very influenced

115

Love and Fury: The Life, Death and Legacy of Joe Meek

by Buddy Holly's music; I wrote the song and it appealed to Joe... If I had taken the stuff to somebody else, they would have said, "Oh, we don't understand, we think this is rubbish," but he seemed to like what I wrote.'[216] Once the sessions for 'Tribute...' were completed, Meek hit on a novel idea to promote the release, inviting the members of a Buddy Holly fan club over to 304 to give their opinion. 'We'd recorded it, and then the Outlaws and I performed it at Joe's studio with these kids from the Buddy Holly Appreciation Society,' Berry confirms.[217] Society president John Beecher announced that 'Mike's new disc is a great tribute to Buddy without cheapening his memory'.[218] 'It was all a bit of a charade,' Berry adds. 'But needless to say it got their seal of approval and it was a hit.'[219] One of the young women who attended the reception would later become Mrs Chas Hodges.

As was usually the way, the press was split over the disc's qualities, with the *Liverpool Echo* calling it a 'dramatically delivered piece [with] an attractive melody',[220] while the *Daily Herald* criticised Meek's reliance on studio gadgetry: 'An echo chamber adds a ghostly singing-in-the-shower touch to Berry's voice... There is a piece of pious narration with a suitable sprinkling of oh-oh's and yeah-yeah's... Personally, I prefer my Holly without Berry's.'[221] 'It was a really naive record, written by a really naive man. Geoff Goddard was a real sweet and innocent man, but some of the lyrics were a bit much, you know? "The snow was snowing and the wind was blowing", well what else would they bloody do? Even at my tender age I could see that,' Berry laughs.[222] The singer altered the lyric for his 1975 re-recording, and was rewarded with a Top 5 hit in Belgium.

Again, Goddard was certain that Holly had been guiding his hand through the writing process, and during the same séance that he and Joe had discussed their songs with the spirit of the bespectacled singer, Holly had described 'Tribute...' as 'great', although as Goddard admitted, 'I am aware there is faking in spiritualism – I have seen it for myself – I am convinced that this link between Buddy Holly and me really exists.'[223] Drummer Bobby Graham would later state that Meek's own interest in the beyond concerned him: 'I didn't like his occult thing, I'd seen him and Geoff Goddard on a Ouija board session. He told me he was talking to Buddy Holly and Mario Lanza.'[224] 'Tribute to Buddy Holly' peaked at number 16 in the *Melody Maker* chart, and the song was a significant success

Johnny Remember Me

in other countries too. Both Holly's ex-manager, Norman Petty (who had been fired by Holly days before he embarked on that final, fateful tour), and his parents rated the disc, with Holly's family writing to Berry to thank him:

> Dear Mike, We would like to express our appreciation to you for the wonderful tribute in song which you made to Buddy in your recent release. We think the song is great and you have done it well. You sing a lot like Buddy but most of all there is a sound of sincerity and we wish you a lot of success in the future. We hope you will not mind if the disc-jockeys here are playing your song. They too think it is great. Again thanks! and Good Luck.[225]

Petty added his praise, telling *Record Mirror* that he thought the song was 'pretty good, about the best memorial disc there was',[226] although he was less complimentary about Geoff Goddard's revelation that the spirit of Buddy Holly had helped him compose his hits: 'On the face of it... it sounds like taking advantage of a name. Some artists do inspire others to write. But about this I don't know.' Jack Good, usually a staunch supporter of all things Meek, was unimpressed with Goddard's claims and sniped: 'I wonder if Geoff Goddard ever met Buddy Holly during his lifetime. I did. And if it is Buddy Holly's spirit that is directing Geoff Goddard's song writing now, all I can think is that Buddy has changed or that he's saving the best material for himself.'[227] Good might have been sceptical, but there were many in the British press who took Goddard's claims of help from the ether entirely sincerely, and who could blame them? In October the songwriter, who no one had heard of six months earlier, had three hits in the UK Top 20: 'Johnny Remember Me', its follow-up 'Wild Wind' by John Leyton and 'Tribute to Buddy Holly'.

'Joe did a great job recording it,' says Berry. 'The sound of it was very advanced for its day, and it was very stylised with lots of echo, all very dramatic.'[228] The disc would be issued, in late 1962, in the United States by Coral – the same label that had issued many of Holly's own hits. Holly's former band, the Crickets, were touring the UK at the time and Berry was offered the chance to front the act for a series of stateside dates, although the single's failure to make any headway in the US charts (its progress was hampered somewhat by a note-for-note copy by Canadian band Chad Allen and the Reflections) put paid to any plans.

During the summer of 1961, six-piece instrumental group Peter Jay and the Jaywalkers had been playing at the Windmill, in Great Yarmouth, as part of a variety package, the *Windmill Show of 1961*, headlined by Tommy Steele and comedian Frankie Howerd. It helped that Peter's dad, Jack Jay, not only ran the theatre but was co-promoter (along with Peter's mum, Freda) of the show. The hardworking act had originally come together when Jay was at college in Norwich. 'The band had already started, and they were looking for a drummer,' he says. 'The college had its own theatre, and we talked them into letting us have the back stage at lunch times... there was a little coffee bar there and it was great. Gradually we started doing little local gigs, and the first season we did at the Windmill was with Tommy Steele.'[229]

By September the Jaywalkers were on the road, along with a batch of youngsters from the Parnes' stable, including Billy Fury, Eden Kane, Joe Brown and Georgie Fame, as the *Sensational Disc Stars of 1961*. The Jaywalkers provided the musical accompaniment to the solo singers on the show apart from Fury, who performed with his own band, The Blue Flames, who at the time included a drummer called Clemente Cattini. Jay and Cattini became close friends and would often trade drumming licks backstage. With a similar line-up and sound, the Jaywalkers were soon being compared to Meek's big hit act, the Flee-Rekkers. 'Usually, when you had a band like Peter Jay and the Jaywalkers, or the Flee-Rekkers who backed me a lot, they would do their set first, then you'd have them backing me,' Jess Conrad explains. 'And of course they became a name themselves. Sometimes a band like that would back the whole show, because it was so expensive to put a show on. You couldn't have every act with their own band, so the promoters always tried to get one band to back everybody. And if the band had a name themselves then you were quids in.'[230]

The tour criss-crossed the country throughout the autumn and winter months with barely a night off. By February 1962 – with John Leyton, Shane Fenton (who would score huge hits in the 1970s and 80s as Alvin Stardust) and Larry Parnes' other big act Marty Wilde replacing Kane and Fame – Jay and his band were starting to attract some serious interest from record companies, with news getting back to London that they were an act to keep an eye on.

Johnny Remember Me

Among the many acts who turned up on the doorstep hoping to benefit from a little Meek magic were the Raiders, a five-piece band from Hornsey, fronted by a 16-year-old vocalist and harmonica player called Rod Stewart. Stewart had only recently joined, having replaced their original singer, Robert Farrant: Farrant would later find some small level of fame after Lionel Bart renamed the youngster Bobby Shafto and launched him as a solo artist. The Raiders duly auditioned for Meek, but the producer was none too keen on their new singer, allegedly telling him to his face, 'You look fucking awful, you're ugly, you're short, you sound terrible – fuck off!'[231] Stewart himself recalled that 'Meek was an intimidating bloke in a suit and tie who sported a rather magnificent rock 'n' roll quiff… At the end of the number, Meek came through from the control room, looked me directly in the eye and blew a long raspberry. I got my coat. I guess that was my first official review.'[232]

'Joe did not think a lot of Rod,' says Raiders drummer Tony White, and he would only offer them a contract if they promised to ditch the teenager. Once they had, Joe immediately changed their name to the Moontrekkers and suggested that they record an instrumental written by the group's 15-year-old guitarist, Gary Leport. Called 'Night of the Vampire', Meek set about knocking it into shape for release, adding eerie sound effects including a creaking door and howling wind (previously used on Gary Miller's single 'Moby Dick') to the intro, plus a galloping horse and a woman's bloodcurdling scream to the end – the woman in question being played all-too-convincingly by Meek himself. The unusual, reverb-drenched recording was issued by Parlophone in September, and Meek's labours were rewarded by the disc scraping to the number 50 spot on the national singles chart for one week only in November. Meek's production work on 'Night of the Vampire' would directly influence the sound he would later achieve on the debut release from David 'Screaming Lord' Sutch and his band, the Savages. The Moontrekkers would record two more singles, neither of which would chart, but their recently ousted singer would fare better. After reuniting briefly with Gary Leport in Jimmy Powell and the Five Dimensions, Rod Stewart began his own solo career in 1964, eventually becoming an international icon and one of the biggest-selling British artists of all time.

CHAPTER 11

Can't You Hear the Beat

At the end of October, John Leyton stood in for a sick Billy Fury for several dates on Larry Parnes' latest package tour, *Star Spangled Nights*. The actor turned pop sensation was a big hit with audiences, as was proved by the deafening screams from the auditorium when he walked on stage, and the shows proved an excellent advertisement for Leyton's first long player, issued at the beginning of the following month.

Three of the twelve songs on *Two Sides of John Leyton* (so called because side one of the album comprised of beat songs while side two was made up of ballads) were written by Joe Meek (as Robert Duke) – including 'Can't You Hear the Beat', which Iain Gregory recorded as 'Can't You Hear the Beat of a Broken Heart' – three by Geoff Goddard and one by Charles Blackwell. Other songs included a cover of the Elvis standard 'I Don't Care If the Sun Don't Shine', which featured extra percussion performed on the banister of the stairwell outside Meek's control room. 'He'd try anything that appealed to him,' Leyton explained. 'And if anything odd happened during a session, he'd invariably try and work it in somewhere. The drummer – it might have been Bobby Graham or Clem Cattini – had taken his shoe off and was banging his heel against the stair, probably trying to knock a nail back in or something. Quick as a flash Joe picked up on it, jumped up, asked him to do it again, and taped it. He was delighted with it. He liked the sound so much he kept playing it back to us throughout the session, just like a big kid. He drove us mad with it! And the next thing I knew, when I heard the finished LP, he'd dropped it into the middle of the song! ...When I asked him what it was doing there, Joe just laughed and said: "That'll give them something to

Can't You Hear the Beat

think about!" That was very much Joe, he'd always try and do something different.'[233]

Robert Stigwood acknowledged the production and songwriting team's brilliance in his effusive sleeve notes, which stated that Leyton's 'recording manager, Joe Meek [is] recognised as Britain's most adventurous and talented disc producer. Joe Meek has developed a world-beating production team with the country's youngest musical director, Charles Blackwell, who has won well-deserved acclaim for his clever and exciting arrangements, and Geoffrey Goddard who is surely the most commercial hit writer to emerge in many years.' Meek's name was a recognisable commodity: on 18 November *Disc* printed a letter from a reader suggesting that 'that fabulous man, Joe Meek' was more than a rival for his US counterparts, and perhaps instead of 'stories of the splendour of the "Nashville Sound"', Britain's pop lovers should celebrate their own successes: 'Let's call it "Meeksville".' It was a phrase that would put a smile on his face and stick in Meek's mind.

In the same issue, it was announced that Meek had signed an exclusive, five-year contract with a singer who had made quite an impact on local audiences since he first appeared in the cafés of Soho, 'Screaming Lord' Sutch. Dave Sutch had become a regular at the famous 2i's coffee bar after singer Vince Taylor brought him to the attention of the co-owner (and Taylor's manager), Tom Littlewood. Littlewood convinced the long-haired Sutch that he did not need to be a great singer to be a hit with the teens, so long as he had the right gimmick, a philosophy that could have come straight out of Meek's own playbook. Wearing a hat with a pair of buffalo horns attached, pasting ghoulish white make-up over his face and running through the audience like a demented thing, Sutch made his debut in 1959 and was soon packing them in. His stage get-up grew to incorporate giant plastic feet, a fake leopard-skin coat ('borrowed' from his aunt and cut to ribbons) and a stick with a wig on the end (aping the skull on a cane carried by US singer Screamin' Jay Hawkins) which he lovingly referred to as his 'minge pole'. Soon he had so much equipment that he could be seen pushing his props around Soho in a pram.

Sutch's first appearance outside London, in September 1960, was on a package show starring Lance Fortune, but not everyone in the provinces understood his unique style, with one reviewer summing his act up as 'screaming and shouting, crawling on hands and knees, and prancing about

Love and Fury: The Life, Death and Legacy of Joe Meek

in the strangest of costumes, including what must be the dirtiest fur coat yet used as a prop, and a large horned headdress'.[234] Soon newspapers up and down the country were writing about the long-haired freak who travelled in a fluorescent pink horsebox and candidly admitted that there was more to this rock 'n' roll malarkey than being able to carry a tune: 'I've met people who could really sing,' Sutch admitted. 'But they were getting nowhere. Now I can't sing. Never could. I just scream. That's the way to put rock 'n' roll over. Scream, man.'[235]

Officially, Dave Sutch first became aware of Joe Meek while he was on tour with his band (originally known as the Cannibals but soon renamed the Savages); someone saw Sutch perform on the same bill as the Flee-Rekkers and was so impressed that he passed him one of Meek's business cards. Calling him on the phone, his lordship was delighted to discover that the producer had not only already heard about him but was keen that they should work together; Meek suggested he and his band come along to an audition at 304 when they were back in London. But, like Meek meeting John Leyton at the Blue Angel, this story was concocted for the press: Meek and Sutch first became acquainted while Sutch was still wowing the coffee and Coke crowd at the 2i's, and Meek immediately saw something in the singer. Although it is unlikely that any piece of paper was signed at that time (aged 19, Sutch would have needed a parent or guardian to oversee any contract or legal document), by the summer of 1960 – several months before the singer gained his first national exposure and shortly before Meek left the company – Sutch was advertising himself and his band as 'Triumph Recording Artistes'.[236]

No record by Screaming Lord Sutch (with or without the Savages) would appear on Triumph, but some eighteen months later, in December 1961, HMV issued the first of six singles that Sutch would make with Meek over the next four years. Sutch's song, 'Big Black Coffin', was renamed 'Till the Following Night' for release, to get around a likely ban on the grounds of bad taste. Meek re-employed the howling wind and creaking door effects he had used on 'Night of the Vampire', with additions including Sutch repeatedly dropping the chain from Meek's lavatory cistern into a biscuit tin.

For all of his successes, there were dozens of other acts that entered the hallowed portals of RGM Sound never to be heard of again. Horace Cook,

Can't You Hear the Beat

from Meek's home town of Newent, came to audition along with harmony vocal act the Foresters. The six-piece laid down eight songs during their audition, and Meek had them return later to record two tracks, 'It's Almost Tomorrow' and the David Whitfield number 'The Book', for a single. 'It was a big event,' Cook recalled. 'We came from the country and we were all off up to the smoke! A huge event.'[237] An acetate was cut and submitted for consideration to one of the majors, but the company turned it down, saying that the band's sound was not commercial enough. Likewise, Wally Whyton, the former frontman of the Vipers skiffle group (later to become a famous face on British television) came to 304 looking for a break after a couple of singles for George Martin at Parlophone had failed to ignite his solo career, but any recordings that were made there have yet to see the light of day.

York theatre manager Jack Prendergast came to see Meek. Prendergast was the father of John Barry, but it was not to promote his now highly successful son that the northern impresario came calling but to advocate for another local act, Sammy Browne and the Escorts. 'Jack was a nice guy, an entrepreneur who was very keen on bringing shows to York,' explains singer and guitarist Norman Fowler, aka Sammy Browne. 'Jack heard about us and we went to audition for him, and he put us on shows with Cliff Richard, Adam Faith and Michael Holliday. We were only kids, you know, and we knew five songs probably! But we got better and better and people seemed to like us. We got plenty of work, and then Jack said, "I'm going to take you to London. There's a guy called Joe Meek. He's set up his own studio in Holloway Road." And so we all went down, very excited, to record with Joe Meek. Prendergast paid for us to stay in a hotel for a night, and then we went to Holloway Road studio.

'We got dressed up in our gear, we had band jackets, and we'd gotten changed into all that because it was like an audition. We meet Joe, and take all the gear up the stairs. We then found out he had this intriguing piano, with drawing pins in the ends of the hammers [an innovation Dave Adams had introduced to Joe], and it made this particular sound, and I did it to my mother's piano at home, which she wasn't very pleased about! Of course Joe was amazing for trying new sounds, with people stomping on the stairs or whatever they might be doing that was different. We had this arrangement of the song 'A Shanty in Old Shanty Town', so we recorded

Love and Fury: The Life, Death and Legacy of Joe Meek

that and two or three other songs, and we were amazed when he played it back to us, because we'd never been in a recording studio and heard what we sounded like. Joe was ever so professional and very nice; we were in the studio and he was in his control room, where all the gear was set up. It was like a large broom closet. You couldn't see him and he didn't see you, but he could hear it because everything was mic-ed up.

'We did our stuff and he liked it and he said that it would be released as a record. He cut an acetate there, he gave us his phone number and said to stay in touch and he'd let us know about the release date. He was very pleased; we went to a Chinese restaurant down the Holloway Road, Joe came with us and Prendergast paid for us all.

'A couple of weeks later he got in touch and said that he wanted our guitarist, Ian Early, to go down and overdub the guitar solo. Ian went down the following week on the train and did that. And then a couple of weeks later he rang me – or perhaps I rang him – and he said, "I want you to come down and record two songs for B-sides. The A-side will be 'A Shanty in Old Shanty Town', but I've got two B-side songs that you can record." He sent one down to me; it was called 'Funny Man' [written by Geoff Stephens: the song would also be recorded by Michael Cox]. I said I'd rather do it with the band, but he said, "No, you don't need to bring the band down: you can do it with my band." I wasn't very impressed with the song, but B-sides often weren't very good.'

Meek made it clear that he saw Sammy, or Norman, as the star of the show, and suggested another name change. 'He wanted to call me Johnny April! I'm glad that never happened, but when you're 16 years old, and you're recording with the guy who's had a number 1 hit record, they can call you any bloody name they want to! Sammy Browne was Jack Prendergast's idea. I didn't mind what they called me, as long as I was going to have a record released. You could have called me anything you liked, so long as you were going to promote my band and we were going to be famous!

'So the next week I went down. Prendergast gave me the money to stay in the Royal Hotel in Russell Square in London. I went there on the Friday, booked into the hotel, then I went to Holloway Road to listen to the track and to see if there had been any developments. Joe was there, and I spent the evening with Joe, talking about all sorts of things to do with music. He was a really interesting guy; we were just sitting on a settee in his living room. We talked for hours, and then I said, "Well, I'd better get back to the hotel now, because I usually get up early." He said, "Have you paid a deposit at the hotel, or have you left anything there?" And I said, "No. I haven't," and he said, "Well, stay here." Now, I had no idea that Joe was gay. It didn't occur to me. I didn't know anything about Joe's homosexuality, but here I am, this 16-year-old in his studio, with the offer of staying there, so I think, "Why not save the money from the hotel?" So I go to the bathroom and brush my teeth and I come back into the room where we'd been talking, and there's like a studio couch in there and he's already in bed, so I say to him, "Where am I going to sleep?" And he said, "Here!"

'I think this is weird, but I had an older brother and when we were kids we'd share a bed sometimes, so it wasn't anything that I wasn't going to do. He's already in the bed; I get into the bed next to him. The bed was up against the wall, I'm on the other side that wasn't against the wall, and he's further in. And we're talking still about music, and then I say, "Goodnight, then," like you do eventually, when you're feeling tired, and he put his arm around me. Now I'm thinking, "No, this ain't right; this isn't what I want to do," or whatever. This is alien to me; I had never experienced anything, or even thought of anything like that with regard to Joe. So I was quite disturbed by that and I rolled away so that he wasn't touching me, and I'm thinking, "I just don't know what's going to happen next," and I never slept a wink that night, but he never touched me. He obviously realised that I wasn't going to do that, and that I wasn't homosexual, and that was fair enough.

'Later on you realise, with hindsight, well, that's what I would do with a girl. Find out what she would do and what she would stand for, and if she wasn't willing then that's the end of it. So nothing happened.

'Next day the band come in, and I'm feeling a little bit on edge, but I recorded the B-side with the band, and the recording went okay, and then Joe dropped me off at King's Cross station in his Sunbeam Rapier. He dropped me off to get the train back to York, and nothing was said about anything. I never said anything, he never said anything, but then he said, "Ring me in a week's time and I'll have a release date, probably, for the record." And I rang the following week, and the following week, and the following week, but we never had the record released.'[238]

Love and Fury: The Life, Death and Legacy of Joe Meek

Two years after his experience at RGM Sound, Norman Fowler would re-emerge, thanks to John Barry, with yet another different name, Steve Cassidy. His 1963 single, 'Ecstasy', was co-written by Marty Wilde and actor-musician Mike Pratt.

One signing whose recordings would make it to the stores was Don Charles. Born Walter Scuffham in Hull, Charles had recorded one single for George Martin ('Paintbox Lover', issued in August 1961 as Don Bennett, the surname taken from his stepfather), but he was unhappy with the result, it did not sell and Parlophone dropped him like a stone. The dejected singer was bemoaning his situation to a publicity agent when they suggested he get in touch with Meek. Bennett called that day and was invited to RGM Sound the following morning. Meek immediately set about moulding him into a pop crooner, altering his name to Don Charles (reasoning that he already had one Bennett on the books) and giving him one of his own Robert Duke compositions, a track that had already been recorded by John Leyton for his debut album, 'Walk With Me My Angel'.* Using the same backing track, but with a new string arrangement from Charles Blackwell, the single spent five weeks in the national charts in early 1962, reaching the heady heights of number 39. It would be Charles' only chart placing, but Meek rated Charles as one of the few artists in his ramshackle stable with any real ability, apparently telling the former Royal Navy diver, 'You are my only legit artist. All the others are yugga-dugs,'[239] a term Meek had picked up while in the RAF that stood for a pilot who was unable to fly smoothly in formation. Meek appreciated that Charles, another former forces man, knew how to take direction, unlike some of his other acts who struggled to fly straight.

Robert Stigwood had developed an interest in both Blackwell and Goddard, and he encouraged Meek to promote Geoff as a singer in his own right. During the sessions for *Two Sides of John Leyton*, Goddard recorded his debut single, 'Girl Bride' (backed with Meek's 'For Eternity'). With its slightly dodgy lyric and sped-up vocal – an effect Meek would obtain, according to Clem Cattini, by sticking 'Sellotape around the spindle of the tape recorder so it went slower. When you replayed it, the sound was speeded up,'[240] – 'Girl Bride' would not be a hit. In fact none of Goddard's four solo singles

---

* The same song would be covered by comedian Dick Emery in 1963.

would chart in spite of press coverage and personal appearances on both radio and television, but Stigwood had faith in his abilities, and it would not be long before the Australian entrepreneur would try to poach two thirds of that 'world-beating production team' away from 304 Holloway Road. Stigwood was not the only one paying attention to the talent that Meek had assembled around him; Columbia's A&R man Norrie Paramor swooped in with a recording contract for Charles Blackwell, and Goddard's publishers, Southern Music, had a suggestion for their hot new property: 'I have so many compositions already written that I've been asked to write a musical to fit some of them in,' he revealed, before admitting, 'the trouble is that, living in Reading, I haven't even seen a West End musical yet, so I have no idea what is going on.'[241]

To help push his golden boy's album, and to placate him after he turned down the chance for Leyton to co-star in the Billy Fury vehicle *Play It Cool*, Stigwood had the actor-cum-singer appear in a 10-minute short for cinema release, *The Johnny Leyton Touch*, a quickie that purported to show the singer, his band and orchestra in rehearsals for a show. It was hastily thrown together after much-vaunted plans for a feature based around a day in Leyton's busy life fell through and industrial action from actors' union Equity (which lasted from November 1961 until April 1962 and forbade union members from working for the Independent Television network) effectively kept Leyton off the small screen for six months.

Filmed in December, also appearing in the movie was Iain Gregory (who had been at drama school with Leyton). Stigwood was grooming him for pop stardom despite the fact that he could not sing, something Gregory cheerfully admitted: 'I can't really sing. I just try and put over a personality that people seem to like.'[242] Gregory's first RGM Sound single, 'Time Will Tell', originally slated for Triumph, was issued in late 1960: the B-side, 'The Night You Told a Lie', featured a great arrangement from Charles Blackwell and a trademark Meek thunderstorm, but Gregory's voice proved so weak that on his subsequent releases his voice was 'fattened up' by Dave Adams. The following year Gregory would land a role in television adventure serial *Richard the Lionheart*, playing the part of a medieval minstrel. Again, his singing voice would be dubbed.

As well as Leyton and Gregory, *The Johnny Leyton Touch* also featured Meek's wunderkind musical arranger Charles Blackwell and a four

Love and Fury: The Life, Death and Legacy of Joe Meek

members of arock 'n' roll band that Joe had put together specifically to back Leyton. Unnamed in the film, the band would soon become known as the Tornados, Meek seemingly oblivious to the fact that there was already a band of that name (spelled Tornadoes) playing in Britain.

Meek had been looking for versatile instrumentalists for a while; the Outlaws were in disarray, and Meek was struggling to cope with the amount of work coming his way. Meek had recently had a major argument with the Outlaws' lead guitarist Bill Kuy, and was looking to replace him while keeping mainstay Chas Hodges. Hodges' ability to pick a tune out of Meek's peculiar, often rambling vocal demos was invaluable to him, but there was another reason for Meek wishing to keep him happy: the producer had developed a bit of a crush on the bass player. Hodges ended up on the receiving end of one of Meek's failed attempts at seduction one Saturday afternoon while the pair sat in the bedsit next to Meek's office, drinking coffee and watching wrestling on the television. Meek's preferred way to unwind was watching television, and as well as his beloved cowboy shows and Hollywood musicals (he once told journalist Ray Coleman that 'I want to go into films and write a musical')[243] he enjoyed tuning into televised wrestling bouts. These were immensely popular at that time and millions of viewers would tune in to ITV's weekly wrestling strand.

Hodges recalled that

Joe said to me, 'I love wrestling. Do you?' My whole life flashed before me. I thought, 'Oh no! It's the bums he likes! My mates were right.' Too late! The next minute, there was a hand groping round my bollocks and I froze. Petrified. It must have been only a fraction of a second that I sat there rigid but it was enough to make Joe think, 'He likes it,' cos his hand started scrunching quicker and he started bobbing up and down. My eyes started watering. I looked at Joe. His eyeballs were bulging but he looked ever so happy. I leapt out of that seat like my arse was alight. It very nearly could have been. I found my voice, but the best I could come up with was: 'I've got to be going now. I've got to go and meet my big brother.'[244]

Meek would use the same seduction tactic on more than one occasion. In late 1966, Don Morris, the blond-haired guitarist with the Impac was

Can't You Hear the Beat

surprised to find himself the subject of their producer's ardour. 'We were watching TV during a break, and Joe put his arm around Don,' the band's drummer Nigel Silk recalls. 'All of us, including Don, looked at each other feeling a bit uncomfortable, but it didn't go any further than that.'[245] 'After a while I began to realise that he was gay,' his assistant Tony Kent recalled. 'At that time the word gay wasn't really used; it was queer. I just kept well away from him. I think it would have freaked me out completely if he had made a pass at me… Nowadays one would take it with a pinch of salt, say, "Come on now, I'm straight," and leave it at that; it wouldn't worry you. But in those days it seemed a bit of a frightening thing.'[246]

Hodges, who acknowledged that Meek 'used to have geezers up there that you knew who were sort of queer' and that when Lional Howard was visiting 304 he and Meek would tell endless jokes about 'queers' to gauge people's reactions, kept away from Holloway Road for the following week. Unsure what to do next – or even if he had a job any more – he was relieved when Meek finally telephoned and apologised. The incident was never mentioned again, at least not to Meek's face, but he was well aware of the sniggering and *sotto voce* snarky comments coming from certain other members of the Outlaws, and the producer was not deaf to their none-too-subtle digs.

'All the different groups that went there knew he was gay,' says his friend Tony Grinham. 'Some would take the piss out of him, and if he'd catch on – because he had bloody microphones everywhere – he'd lose his temper.'[247] Joe had been hearing the same comments since he was small; having people laughing about him behind his back was something he had to deal with. Harder to ignore was the Outlaws failing an audition for the BBC. At that time most bands who appeared on BBC Radio played live, and having a group as versatile as the Outlaws, who could turn their collective hands to just about any musical style, was a huge asset for RGM. However, their trial did not go well; producers were incensed at the band's insolent behaviour and bad language, and the BBC refused to have anything to do with them.* The fiasco incensed Meek, but worse was to come. After Bill Kuy demanded to know why the Outlaws were not seeing any royalties

---

* The Outlaws would not appear on BBC Radio until July 1963, when they performed on *Saturday Club*, backing Gene Vincent.

Love and Fury: The Life, Death and Legacy of Joe Meek

for their work, a furious Meek chased after the guitarist with a pair of scissors and, aiming for his head, embedded them into the back of his office door. 'Joe would just throw the first thing he had to hand,' explains Mike Berry. 'He'd suddenly flip his lid. He was quite unbalanced when he lost his temper.' [248] Bass player and singer Heinz Burt remembered witnessing an almost identical argument between Meek and Bobby Graham: 'I was sat in the little lounge watching the television, and he came knocking at the door to ask for his session money. Joe opened the door and said, "What do you want?" He said, "I've come for my session money." Joe said, "I'll give you two minutes to get down those stairs. If not, I'll throw you down." The guy started mouthing off, and the next thing I heard was wallop! Bomp, bomp, bomp, down the stairs. He'd hit him, and both ended up at the bottom of the stairs.' [249]

Peter Jay agrees: 'He was sort of volatile, I suppose. He was okay when things were going alright, and then if it wasn't, he would go into a very stroppy, kind of crazy mode. We had great respect for him; for a while we backed John Leyton on tour and backed him on some of his records, and the sounds that he got, that he came out with, were amazing, you know? He might have been a bit crackers, but you'd go along with it because we all thought of him as the British Phil Spector really, a genius.' [250]

With no exposure from the BBC, Meek put together a series of 15-minute programmes for Radio Luxembourg, *It's the Outlaws*, which aired from December 1961. Tony Kent, who fronted the show, was often witness to his boss's erupting anger: 'He used to go off the deep end quite regularly, for the strangest reasons. I got on fairly well with him [but] he was very strange. He used to have strange ideas suddenly, he was always changing his mind, and getting fantastic ideas that he'd try and put into operation… And forget about them the next day. One had to learn to take that as part of the job.' [251]

Kuy's enquiry about unpaid royalties may have infuriated Meek, but musicians who had spent endless days on the road performing to sell-out audiences who were so broke that they were forced to sleep in their van, who could not afford to have their stage clothes laundered, or who had appeared on several hit records yet were not seeing the financial rewards they might expect were bound to question the set-up at some point. Managers were notorious for paying their artists miserable amounts –

barely enough to exist on in some cases – and others who worked with Meek were also puzzled about why they often had no more than two coins to rub together.

'It was the typical thing,' says Peter Jay. 'When we came to settle up with Decca after the success of "Can Can", we wanted to know where the promised penny per record had gone, only to be told, "Well, we took the front page of the *NME* for you, which you had to pay for, then there's the studio time…" Basically they claimed that we were all square, there was nothing, you know? And that kind of thing went right through, with the Beatles and the Rolling Stones, everybody. They all got taken for a ride at the start. It wasn't until they realised what was at stake with record royalties, songwriting royalties and the rest. The ones that survived, that did well, had to learn the business – when you're in a band, the last thing you want is to be associated with accountants, the men in suits. Nobody was into the business side of it. On those tours we were paid £20 a week each, and we had to pay for our own digs out of that.

'I met Stigwood a few times. And Don Arden. We did the Hollies, Small Faces tour, backing Paul Jones, and that was through Don Arden. The Small Faces were coming to us all the time saying, "You couldn't lend us twenty quid, could you? We haven't got any money." And I said, "But you're top of the bill. You must be getting £700 a night," or whatever it was, and they said, "Yeah, but we don't see any of that," and that was typical of Don Arden. He didn't pay them. There were other gigs, for people like Roy Tempest, and you'd see the acts queuing up the stairs, saying, "All we need is the money to get to the next gig!" The managers were all-powerful, and the record labels were all-powerful.'[252]

Bobby Graham later admitted that 'it's no secret we didn't get on. He was a sad little man, a very lonely person. He couldn't relate to people.'[253] Screaming Lord Sutch would later recall that 'if you criticised any little thing… then instantly from a happy, jolly person he'd get really snappy and nasty'.[254] Meek's attempt to keep Graham happy was to give him a co-writer credit for 'Crazy Drums', the B-side to the Outlaws' September 1961 single 'Valley of the Sioux', but that was not enough. An offer to join Joe Brown's backing band, the Bruvvers, was too tempting to resist. 'Joe was a complete dickhead in so many ways,' adds Berry. 'But he was a sweet man when he was just recording and doing his thing, and [when] the band were

Love and Fury: The Life, Death and Legacy of Joe Meek

up to it he was as happy as Larry… He knew good musicians. He'd worked with some crap, but by the time you had people like Chas Hodges and Bill Kuy and Reggie Hawkins in, they were the best. They were easily the best band in North London; that's why they became his house band.'[255]

Hodges was proving himself indispensable, one of the few people – alongside Dave Adams, Geoff Goddard and Charles Blackwell – able to translate the atonal 'la-la-las' and wild, off-key humming of Meek's demos into actual tunes. 'He would pick a record that was near enough the same tempo, and then he would sing to it, regardless of what tune was playing underneath,' Hodges explained.[256] 'He couldn't sing,' Peter Jay adds. 'But he would try and half-sing it. Luckily we had a good lead guitarist who could pick it up, and Lloyd [pianist Lloyd Baker] could work out the chords and everything, and in about ten minutes we'd have it and then we'd do it.'[257] If Meek had an idea in the studio, he would bang out a rhythm on whatever was close to hand while attempting to sing a guide line. 'The hardest thing was trying to pick up a song when he used to bang on the side of the door and scream things,' reckoned Cliff Bennett. 'Some of the things he was trying to explain were so bloody ridiculous that you'd just burst out laughing. He used to get really emotional, would slam the door… He used to go downstairs and make a cup of tea, and say, "I'll come back up when you can pull yourselves together, you dickheads." He wanted it done his way, and you, being a musician, had always done things a certain way and you'd clash. I used to say to Joe, "No, I don't like it," and he'd say, "You'll bloody do it like I want it, because I'm spending the money! It's my time!"'[258] Glenda Collins concurred: 'Joe and I were a wee bit at odds as to what I recorded, but with Joe's personality one had to record more or less what Joe wanted. There wasn't really a tremendous choice in the matter,' she later confessed, although she conceded that 'in a way [that] could be a good thing because very often an artist doesn't always know what's really the best for them'.[259]

Hodges, despite Meek's failed conquest, was in awe of his abilities: 'I think he really was a genius, in his own way… I always think that a genius never does something in-between: it's either fantastic or terrible, and that's how he was… They're so into what they're doing that they don't stop to think [about things] logically, or of making the best of a bad job or anything like that; he would just go ahead and do it, and follow it right through until the end. Looking back, he was a long way ahead.'[260]

Can't You Hear the Beat

However much he rated the Outlaws, as far as Meek was concerned Kuy was expendable. The demand for money (despite all financial transactions being handled by the Major), the temerity of questioning Meek's integrity, was the last straw. Kuy and Graham were out, and Meek set about trying to build a new version of the band. Michael Cox, one of the many RGM singers who had relied on the backing of the Outlaws, had suggested former Pirates guitarist Alan Caddy as a potential member, but he was out of the country at the time, touring Italy with Tommy Steele's brother Colin Hicks in his group the Cabin Boys. On their return to the UK, Caddy went to see Meek. Hodges was keen to have Caddy in the group and even more pleased when he heard that Caddy had brought a friend along for moral support, drummer Clemente 'Clem' Cattini. Cattini was the son of an Italian restaurateur, had been a member of Billy Fury's live band and, like Caddy, had scored a number 1 hit in the summer of 1960 as part of Johnny Kidd and the Pirates, with 'Shakin' All Over'. Cattini had also been a member of the Cabin Boys and had recently filled the drum seat for Eden Kane's UK number 1 'Well I Ask You'. Caddy and Cattini ran through a couple of numbers and Meek offered them both a job on the spot... but not for the Outlaws. Meek had a new strategy: he wanted to build a second instrumental band around a young bass player he had become infatuated with, Heinz Burt.

Burt worked at the bacon-slicing counter in his local Co-operative store. His parents were German, but following his father's death during World War Two his mother moved to England and remarried. He was brought up in Eastleigh, near Southampton, and, as a teenager, had played with local skiffle group the Falcons. The Falcons already had two guitar players, so Heinz was persuaded by the band's leader to learn bass, and they soon landed a series of dates with the south's answer to Larry Parnes, pop promoter Reg Calvert. In the early 1960s, Calvert built up his own stable of acts and put them through a Parnes-like finishing school at his country home, Clifton Hall near Rugby, before sending them out on the road, many with vibrant new names. Like Parnes, Calvert manufactured teenage idols in the image of the big American rock 'n' roll stars, and his artists included Eddy Sex (real name Johnny Bennett), Ricky Fever, Buddy Britten (Calvert's own Buddy Holly-alike), a diminutive Black rhythm and blues vocalist known as Baby Bubbly (whose name was derived from

TV star Cuddly Dudley), Robby Hood and his band the Merry Men, and Danny Storm. In the summer of 1961 Calvert arranged an audition for the Falcons with Meek, as Meek later recalled: 'I thought he was O.K. but the group was below standard. So I sent them away. Three months later, he came back with what he said was a different sound but I'm afraid he was still below standard.'[261]

What Meek did not pass on to the readers of the *Record Mirror* was that the Falcons had turned up late for their audition and the irate producer had initially told them to 'sod off!' It was only after they pleaded with him and explained that they had travelled all the way from the south coast that he relented and let them in. Despite thinking them 'below standard', Meek was struck by the young bass player's eagerness, and a few months later Heinz and Meek met again. This time the grocery assistant had come to the door of 304 after answering an advertisement for a new bass player for the Outlaws.

When Heinz Burt arrived at RGM Sound the second time, Meek was initially reluctant to let him in. 'No, I can't see you,' he snapped. 'I'm too busy. I'm recording.'[262] After realising that he had already met the handsome young man, he relented, and Heinz plugged his bass in. Chas Hodges was not present at the time, and a conversation with Meek shortly afterwards did not give him much hope. 'I said, "What's he like?" He said, "Well, he's tall, he's quite good looking…" So I said, "No. What does he play like? Is he any good?"'[263] Hodges was unimpressed with Burt's abilities, and his arrogance, but thought he would do for now, as he had already made up his mind to switch from bass to lead guitar himself. With a belief that even the smallest of coincidences was more likely a message from another plane, the similarity between Heinz's surname and that of his own grandparents – Birt – would have amplified Meek's interest. But there was another reason for Meek wanting Burt to stick around. 'Joe took an immediate fancy to him,' Tony Kent revealed, 'and he had to find work for him, so Joe would have forced him into the Outlaws.'[264] Burt left Eastleigh behind him and moved into Meek's flat on the top floor of 304 Holloway Road.

Meek may have been happy, but Hodges soon realised that bringing Burt into the group was a mistake. 'Joe wanted Chas to take over on lead guitar,' Mike Berry adds. 'He'd got rid of Bill Kuy and wanted Chas to play lead guitar so that Heinz could take over on bass. But Chas wasn't having

Can't You Hear the Beat

any of that. Heinz couldn't even hold the bass!'[265] Burt would not join the Outlaws, but instead of packing his bags and returning to the south coast, a besotted Meek decided that he would build a new band around him, and it made sense to create a new act to accompany his other hot property, John Leyton. 'I had a lot of musicians coming to the studios around that time,' Meek later said. 'And the difficulty was finding lads who were both good musicians and strong personalities.'[266] Caddy and Cattini had already been put to work: one of the first tracks Meek had them perform on was the next Leyton single, Geoff Goddard's 'Wild Wind'. Issued by by the temporarily reactivated Top Rank label on 29 September, Meek wanted a similar-sounding disc to follow up 'Johnny Remember Me' (then still number 1 in the charts), and he instructed Cattini to play in a similar galloping style.

Next came rhythm guitarist George Bellamy, who joined the band after answering an advertisement in the *Melody Maker* in October 1961 for 'an answer to the Shadows'.[267] Two saxophone players were added to the initial line-up (although they would not last long, the sound being far too close to the Flee-Rekkers), and last came keyboard player Norman Hale – added to the band to distinguish them from the Outlaws and the Shadows – who had been a member of the Falcons, the same south coast band that had included mousy-haired wannabe pop star Heinz Burt.

CHAPTER 12

Something Better Beginning

Heinz Burt was not the only artist from the south coast whom Joe had plans for, and in late 1961 he was invited to Southampton by Reg Calvert, the man who had originally brought Heinz to his attention. The impresario wanted Meek to appraise a number of his acts via an ad hoc audition in Calvert's office, and although he dismissed most of them as raw and unsophisticated, one shone through: vocal duo David and Gordon Dowland. The Dowlands, among the few acts to refuse one of Calvert's ridiculous stage names, did a passable impersonation of the Everly Brothers, and Meek invited them and their three-piece backing band, the Drovers, to a recording test at RGM Sound.

'Mrs Shenton was the first person we met,' Drovers guitar player Roy Phillips recalls. 'She took us upstairs, together with a cup of tea for Joe.' He remembers the scene that greeted them as 'a mess: ankle deep in cables. It was chaos. Joe was in such a hurry to get people in and out of the studio; there were always people waiting all over the property.'[268] The band and singers ran through a test – a cover of the Everly Brothers hit 'Poor Jenny' – before they set about recording a Dave Dowland original, 'Little Sue', a song with more than a tip of the hat to the Everly's own 'Wake Up Little Susie'. Meek seemed happy with the session, but he was not keen on the name of their band, and the Drovers were immediately rechristened the Soundtracks. 'Joe came up with that name,' Phillips adds.

Mike Berry, recording at the same time as the Dowlands, enjoyed his time at RGM Sound: 'It wasn't that bad,' he says. 'The only time it got chaotic was when Joe was looking for a particular gimmick to put on the record. He'd ask you to blow into a comb and paper, or a kazoo. Or he'd pick something up and say, "Bang that here!" and "Bang that there!" and

Something Better Beginning

stuff like that. It was all a bit Heath Robinson:* he was experimenting all the time to try and get a different sound, which he would then echo up.'[269] Meek would use whatever came to hand – or to mind. Looking for something to approximate the sound of a kettle drum, Meek had assistant Tony Kent bang on the back of an armchair with a drumstick, an effect that turned up on Michael Cox's January 1962 release 'Young Only Once'.

John Leyton was now an established star, and Meek was eager to sprinkle some of that stardust onto his new studio band. The still-unnamed act was seen accompanying Leyton on his new single, 'Wild Wind', in *The Johnny Leyton Touch* (Heinz Burt mimed playing the bass in the film; Chas Hodges appeared on the record), and they also played on the second single from Gerry Temple, Geoff Goddard's 'Seventeen Come Sunday', issued by HMV in November. The demand for Leyton's new record was exceptional with advance sales, according to an EMI spokesman, 'coming in in the volume usually reserved for the really established stars like Cliff Richard, Adam Faith and Elvis Presley'.[270] 'Wild Wind' would crack the Top 10 while 'Johnny Remember Me' was still riding high in the charts, and would reach number 2. Robert Stigwood was soon fending off offers from the States for live appearances, film and television work for his star, and several titles were mooted for Leyton's first starring role. The singer's full-length, big screen debut (he had appeared as an uncredited extra in three movies in 1959) came when he guest-starred in the 1962 British/American musical *It's Trad, Dad* (issued stateside as *Ring-a-Ding Rhythm*), alongside several other Meek-related artists, including Chris Barber, Acker Bilk and Gene Vincent. *It's Trad, Dad* was the directorial debut of Dick Lester, who would go on to direct the Beatles.

Leyton's career consumed him – the singer released six singles, two EPs and a full-length album between October 1961 and October 1962 – but Meek still managed to find time to record his new studio act (the band taped 'Swinging Beefeater' and a very Shadows-sounding 'Theme From "A Summer Place"') and he continued to look for other artists to add to his burgeoning empire, including a young female singer called Carol

---

* William Heath Robinson was a British illustrator and artist. He is best remembered for his drawings of elaborate contraptions designed to accomplish simple tasks, which led to his name being used to describe self-built, complicated machines made out of odds and ends.

Hedges, who had been introduced to him by Cliff Bennett. Stigwood was also looking to expand, and happened to be at 304 one day when Carol was taking part in another of her seemingly endless recording tests. Meek had yet to decide what to do with her; he'd had her tape a few demos with his new band, but nothing was being released (five of these tracks would eventually surface on the 2024 release *Do the Strum!*). More importantly, he had failed to get her under contract: Carol was just 15 years old and needed a parent or guardian to sign any legal documents. Perhaps unwisely, Meek had decided not to bother her parents until he had the right tracks in the can. Leyton's manager saw an opportunity and signed her to his personal management, renaming her Billie Davis in tribute to her two favourite performers, Billie Holiday and Sammy Davis, Jr.

Partly to pacify Meek, Stigwood offered his new band the job of backing John Leyton on an eight-date tour in November 1961. The dates, which also featured Mike Berry, Gary Mills, Charles Blackwell and his new signing Billie Davis proved a perfect training ground for the five-piece, and also provided them with a name: the Tornados, taken from a line in Leyton's song 'Six White Horses'. That tour was a turning point in Mike Berry's career. He had been due to record an album with Meek once the dates were over, to capitalise on the success of 'Tribute to Buddy Holly'. 'The original concept was to make an album, but before we recorded that I was off on tour with John Leyton and Billie Davis for Robert Stigwood,' Berry remembers.[271] The album would not see a release during Meek's lifetime.

Stigwood was in the habit of making his artists promises he could not hope to keep, or simply ditching one offer when something he considered better came along. In November he claimed to have lined up a series of US promotional dates for John Leyton, but these opportunities vanished after 'Johnny Remember Me' had zero impact on American record buyers. There was still the lucrative European market, and Stigwood decided that Leyton should record several foreign language versions of his latest release, the Geoff Goddard song 'Son, This Is She'. He turned to another of his artists, actor and languages student Michael Sarne, to help coach the singer. Issued in December 1961, 'Son, This Is She' had once again been helmed by the Blackwell-Goddard-Meek trio, something that Leyton saw no need to change. 'Geoffrey Goddard knows the sort of song I like and understands the way I sing,' he explained. 'Charles Blackwell is terrific on

Something Better Beginning

arrangements and backing, and Joe is a wizard at recording the sounds we make.' Leyton may have seen no reason to split up a winning team, yet despite entering *Disc* magazine's own chart at number 10 and enjoying the added boost of being featured in *The Johnny Leyton Touch*, sales of 'Son, This is She' were disappointing. Stigwood felt that the ongoing industrial action by actors' union Equity badly affected the disc's chances: '[John] has too big a following already and the advance orders were colossal, but I estimate [the ban] will cost us about 100,000 copies.' Stigwood complained that the ban on working for ITV had also adversely affected the latest Iain Gregory single, 'Can't You Hear the Beat of a Broken Heart': 'We've had to turn down seven dates for Iain, and if this had not been the case I'm sure his record would have been in the charts by now.'[272]

Choral acts were popular, Meek had already produced the George Mitchell Singers for the 1960 release *The Blue and the Grey*, and in January 1962 Parlophone issued another choir production, one of the more esoteric releases in Meek's catalogue, *Sing Me a Souvenir* by radio favourites the Bowman-Hyde Singers and Players. Although the back of the sleeve featured an 'RGM Sound Recording' credit, neither this nor the eponymous album from Brian White and the Magna Jazz Band (issued by HMV around the same time and again credited to RGM Sound) had much – if any – input from Joe. Still, these were just the kind of records that his family back home in Newent would have loved, something which, they could proudly boast to their friends, their Joe had made. No doubt they would have loved the debut single from the Charles Blackwell Orchestra, a cover of the instrumental hit 'Taboo', backed with Meek's own composition, 'Midnight in Luxembourg', issued in mid-January.

Sometime in early February, Heinz was enjoying a coffee at the 2i's when he heard from one of the regulars that Larry Parnes was looking for a new band to back Billy Fury on a British tour. Fury and his previous band – the Blue Flames – had parted company,* and Heinz reckoned that Meek had the

---

* Almost two years earlier, and before Fury was matched with the Blue Flames, he and his manager Larry Parnes had returned to Fury's home town of Liverpool to audition local bands to back the singer on tour. One of the acts that attended the audition, held at the Blue Angel club on 10 May 1960, was a five-piece known as the Silver Beatles.

Love and Fury: The Life, Death and Legacy of Joe Meek

perfect act. The pair telephoned Parnes and a few days later Larry and Billy arrived at 304. Fury was a major star, celebrating three consecutive Top 5 hits, and Meek knew that if he could add the singer to his production roster it would boost his standing in the recording industry. Offering Parnes the use of his Tornados – and space at 304 to rehearse – would surely guarantee that he would be able to work with the young Liverpudlian. The Tornados and Fury hit it off immediately, recording several numbers there and then, and, with encouragement from Heinz, Meek and Parnes struck a deal: the pair would go into partnership to manage the Tornados, with Parnes taking care of their live commitments and Meek continuing to steer their recording career. Fury, under contract to Decca, would not be recording for RGM Sound; however, Meek held out the hope that he would soon get to work with the teen heartthrob.

Clem Cattini, who had already worked with both Fury and Parnes, was none too happy with this arrangement. He liked Billy but had rowed with Parnes over money (or, rather, the lack of it) on more than one occasion, and he warned Meek against going into business with the impresario: 'It was a mistake,' he remembered. 'It was like this cat and dog fighting all the time, and we were stuck in the middle, watching them arguing.'[273] Parnes insisted that the band sign a new contract, as per his arrangement with Meek, that would give him control over every aspect of their career bar their recording commitments. Cattini refused, despite threats from both Parnes and Meek to replace him, while the other members were happy to sign. Work was work, they reasoned, and a regular pay packet was better than none at all: they had been paid so little when loaned out to Stigwood that a couple of them spent Christmas Eve 1961 sleeping in a barn to save money. Eventually, Cattini acquiesced, but he would soon learn that it was not just Parnes he should be wary of; the brilliant and versatile drummer was often at loggerheads with Meek. 'I didn't get on with Joe,' Cattini admitted. 'As far as an engineer, for producing sound he was a genius. But I didn't get on with him at all. We had so many rows over different things, it was unbelievable. He slung a tape recorder once down the stairs at me!' Cattini recalled another similar incident, from early 1966: 'I remember the first day he got his new Ampex four-track tape recorder... the top of that was smashed when Joe threw a stool at me! He was a moody guy... most people like Joe are, he was a real mixed-up guy, but he was a genius for sound.'[274]

Something Better Beginning

Cattini was impressed, however, with the way Meek worked: 'He was the first guy in this country that knew how to record a bass drum... Nobody could record a bass drum; he was the only guy I knew who could do it.' He also marvelled at his inventiveness. 'On one record... we didn't use the bass drum, I used my case... banging along on the bass drum case.'[275] Meek was emulating Jerry Allison, drummer with the Crickets, who had used a cardboard box to get the distinctive sound heard on their 1957 hit 'Not Fade Away'. It became a favourite trick, and Meek used packing cases and cardboard boxes on several occasions to achieve the right percussive effect.

The Tornados backed Fury for the first time in late March: much of the publicity material for the tour had already been prepared, so many of the posters and flyers for *The Big Star Show of 1962* still included the Blue Flames alongside Fury, John Leyton, Peter Jay and the Jaywalkers and others. Booking the Tornados onto a high-profile tour was good business, but around the same time that Fury first came within his orbit Meek made what, in hindsight, could be seen as one of the biggest mistakes of his career. He was approached by a young, gay record-store manager from Liverpool, Brian Epstein, who had recently signed a local group to a management contract, four lads known as the Beatles. On 1 January 1962 the Beatles had recorded fifteen tracks during an audition at Decca's Hampstead studios, and although the company had decided not to sign the group, Epstein had been taking copies of the audition tapes around to anyone in the music industry he could gain an introduction to.

One of the people he was keen to meet with was Joe Meek. The exact date of Epstein's first meeting with Meek is unknown, but it probably would have been in mid-February 1962, after the Beatles' manager had his first meeting with Parlophone's George Martin (an event that took place at EMI's offices in Manchester Square on 13 February), at which Martin tried to dissuade the Liverpudlian store manager from pursuing his dream of obtaining a recording contract for his boys. Epstein, who had been a major supporter of Meek's John Leyton records, took Joe to dinner, but he too thought that Brian was wasting his time. Biographer Mark Lewisohn doubts that Meek was offered the chance to work with the band, and Meek himself would later tell readers of the *Mersey Beat* magazine that 'it surprised me that the Beatles and Gerry and the Pacemakers did not approach me for a recording contract, as it is mostly this kind of music

141

that I have been recording for over a year now. I was naturally upset at not having the chance to record such a great bunch of talented boys.'[276] He may have missed an opportunity, but he was hardly alone: no one outside Epstein and their local fanbase saw the band's potential, and everyone who listened to the Decca audition – a dozen half-hearted covers and three Lennon-McCartney originals (none of which the band thought good enough to record again) – turned them down. By fluke, and only after he was cajoled by Sid Coleman of music publisher Ardmore and Beechwood, George Martin would grant Epstein a second meeting (at EMI's Abbey Road studios on 9 May) before somewhat reluctantly offering them a recording date the following month.

Epstein was certainly not the only manager trying to persuade Meek that his act was going to be the next big thing. In early June Carl Lewis of the Forrester-George theatrical agency, wrote to Meek begging him to meet with one of their artists, Gerry Dorsey, who after a few late-50s releases on Decca and Parlophone was without a contract. Meek would not sign the singer, and he would remain without a deal until 1964, when Tom Jones' manager Gordon Mills took him under contract. Dorsey would eventually find fame after adopting the stage name Engelbert Humperdinck, from the German composer of the opera *Hänsel und Gretel*. Although Meek missed out on the chance to work with either the Beatles or Engelbert, when one new group, the Flintstones, came to 304 to audition he was delighted to discover that the act contained three members of his first house band the Blue Men (aka the Cavaliers or the West Five). Meek suggested they change their name to the Stonehenge Men, an obvious allusion to hit American instrumental act the Piltdown Men, to avoid any potential lawsuit from the American cartoon giant Hanna-Barbera. The band was not happy about the change, although their only single ('Pinto' backed with 'Big Feet', a Robert Duke tune with an alarming similarity to the Moontrekkers' 'There's Something at the Bottom of the Well') was issued under that name in February 1962.

The Tornados' debut single, 'Love and Fury' (written by Meek and featuring Norman Hale on Clavioline, who would be out of the group before the disc hit the shops), was a hastily-conceived replacement for their inaugural recording. Meek had originally planned to release another of his own

Something Better Beginning

compositions, 'Swinging Beefeater', as their first record but ditched that in favour of a tribute to the singer who had given the band their big break. Issued on 30 March 1962, a week earlier Meek had written to Jimmy Grant, producer of BBC radio's popular *Saturday Club* music magazine to ask if he would audition the group with the hope that he could use them on future editions of the show; Meek was lucky to have the Tornados – or any of his acts – appear on the BBC after the debacle with the Outlaws the previous year, and he made it clear to the band how important an opportunity this was. Nonetheless, the band's BBC audition would not take place until that September, and it would be another three months before the Tornados made their debut on *Saturday Club*.[*] 'Love and Fury' sold respectably but failed to chart; however, their second single would see them top his parades on both sides of the Atlantic, as well as in several other countries around the world.

On the same day that Decca issued 'Love and Fury', Parlophone released the third single by Cliff Bennett and the Rebel Rousers, the Robert Duke song 'Poor Joe'. The release of the record angered Bennett, who had believed that the B-side, a cover of Brook Benton's 1959 hit 'Hurtin' Inside', should have been the plug track. Certainly it was a more obvious choice, following on from their previous releases, but either Meek or someone at Parlophone decided that, after two flops, a change of pace was needed. Bennett might have hated 'Poor Joe', but he was even more upset with the treatment Meek gave to 'Hurtin' Inside', which one critic called 'a "doctored" sound. It seemed that every piece of electrical effects apparatus possible had been used to make the recording. The pounding, drowning bass was a backcloth to a tracked vocal saturated in over-reverberation.'[277] With backing vocals supplied by the Pepperminties (a scratch collection of singers including Bennett himself, plus Joy and Dave Adams), Meek had taken the initial inspiration for the ballad 'Poor Joe' from a picture of the same name that hung on the wall over a fireplace at 304, a colour print in a glazed oak frame featuring a barefoot Victorian sweep examining a few coins in his right hand.

---

[*]   The Tornados made their BBC Radio debut in December 1962, on the show *The Talent Spot*.

Love and Fury: The Life, Death and Legacy of Joe Meek

The inspiration may have come from that print, but 'Poor Joe', with lines like 'He's fallen in love, and he vowed that he wouldn't', 'He's ended his fling, he gave his heart away', offers an example of Meek writing a clearly personal lyric. Meek's words, although at best naive, often reflected his state of mind. His earliest songs, written not long after he arrived in London, are for the most part fun and exciting, derivative yet full of drive: 'Sizzlin' Hot' and 'Put a Ring on Her Finger' are forward-looking songs about young love. Meek gave vent to his obsession with space and with the Wild West through 'I Hear a New World' and his instrumentals for the Outlaws, but his songs are usually simple 'boy meets girl' love songs. As life becomes more complicated and the business pressures mount, the words to his songs take on a more wistful air, and elements of heartbreak, longing and loneliness creep in. 'Poor Joe', a song about unrequited love, which he was adamant that Cliff Bennett record, was written after he had split with Lional and not long after meeting Heinz, and there are a few later songs, such as the Honeycombs B-side 'I'm Not Sleeping Too Well Lately', which are also clearly autobiographical. 'Poor Joe' failed to resonate with buyers (six months later Carter–Lewis would issue their vastly superior version of 'Poor Joe' on the B-side of their single 'Here's Hopin''), and after one more single with Meek, Bennett and the Rebel Rousers would be off. The same was true of Danny Rivers. His new single for HMV, a tepid cover of Lorne Lesley's 'We're Gonna Dance', backed by the far superior 'Movin' In', a Dave Adams composition that was later covered by Heinz, was another flop, and it would be the singer's last release for two years.

Irrespective of the irregular hit rate and the constant digs in the press about his reliance on studio trickery, Meek still found himself inundated with approaches from musicians, singers and artist managers, all desperate for the producer to help them on their way. Bennett may have thought little of 'Poor Joe', but Parlophone was more impressed with his work. In 1961 the label had signed instrumental three-piece the Scorpions, yet despite some excellent reviews their two singles for the company failed to set the charts alight. Perhaps Joe Meek and his ramshackle studio in Holloway Road could do a better job than EMI's own set-up in Abbey Road. Meek held two sessions with the Scorpions, but none bore fruit. 'The sessions produced 'Two Brothers',' bass player John Barber recalled. 'It was a rather morbid song about brothers divided by the US Civil War. Joe

Something Better Beginning

Meek actually suggested that we wear Union and Confederate uniforms to perform the song.'[278] Unreleased in his lifetime, the track would eventually appear, credited to the Ferridays, on the album *Hidden Gems Volume One* and again in 2024 on the Tea Chest tapes compilation *Joe Meek: From Taboo to Telstar*.

John Leyton's vocal version of Geoff Goddard's 'Lone Rider' hit the stores at the beginning of March. His manager, Robert Stigwood, now had a new proposition for Meek. Stigwood had been impressed with Mike Sarne, the student who had coached Leyton through his recent European-language recordings, and began looking for the right song for him. Stigwood brought his latest discovery to Meek, but none of the tracks recorded by Sarne for RGM Sound would surface. In May 1962 Parlophone issued Sarne's debut, 'Come Outside', written and produced by Charles Blackwell, with Cattini on drums and Sarne accompanied by a young actress then working as a secretary for Stigwood, Wendy Richard. The flip side, 'Fountain of Love', was by Geoff Goddard, but despite both songs sounding very Meek-like, and Stigwood having originally intended for Meek to produce Sarne, neither side featured any input from Joe, partly because Sarne hated the set-up at RGM Sound. 'It was this dark, dismal, horrible, creepy, smelly place Joe lived in, with pale young boys coming out of the dark like *Night of the Living Dead*,' Sarne later recalled somewhat dramatically. 'Joe coming out with popping-out eyes and this pale face. They lived in the dark. I remember thinking how weird and sick it all was.'[279] With the windows in the studio sealed closed, boarded up and curtained off, it was indeed dark; the lack of ventilation also made it oppressively hot and claustrophobic. It is hardly surprising that the singer was unimpressed, but he would return to do the occasional session, including adding backing vocals – in French – to Glenda Collins' 1966 recording 'Sing C'est La Vie'.

Goddard and Meek had an unwritten understanding that the songwriter would offer Meek first refusal on all of his material. If Meek did not wish to use 'Fountain of Love' (and he did not: it's a pretty terrible song), Goddard was free to take it to anyone else. Stigwood did not care if the song was good or not: he just needed something to fill the second side of the disc, as Mike Berry later recalled: 'I remember when we were recording the B-side to 'On My Mind', a song called 'This Little Girl'. We ran through it, and Stigwood announced "Right, that's it!" I said, "What do you mean, 'That's it'?" and he said, "We've recorded it". He'd recorded the rehearsal, trying to save a few quid!'[280] Sarne's debut would reach number 1 in the singles chart at the end of June 1962, much to Meek's irritation. Having missed out on what could have been his second number 1 hit, Meek put together a copycat version featuring Alan Klein (who had been part of a duo with Tornado George Bellamy) and actress Julie Samuel. Meek's version of 'Come Outside' would not be issued in Britain (although a promotional Scopitones film was made and shown in the UK and Europe); instead, another Meek-produced song, 'Striped Purple Shirt', was chosen for Klein's first solo outing. The singer's second release, his self-penned comedy song 'Three Coins in the Sewer', featured sound effects created by Clem Cattini dropping marbles into the RGM lavatory.

Possibly influenced by his experience with Sarne, although it carried the usual 'RGM Sound Recording' credit, the next John Leyton single, Geoff Goddard's 'Lonely City', would be recorded at EMI's studios in Abbey Road, rather than at RGM Sound, and was produced by Charles Blackwell and Robert Stigwood. Although the single, issued in late April 1962 and featured in the film *It's Trad, Dad*, featured instrumental backing from an uncredited Tornados, Meek's main involvement was as co-writer of the B-side, 'It Would Be Easy', credited to R. Crossley, a one-off pen name used by Meek and Blackwell, the 'R' from Robert, and the 'Crossley' from the famous pickles manufacturer Crosse and Blackwell. Meek attended some of the sessions at Abbey Road (his distinctive voice can be heard on the tapes), but his interference was not welcomed; the follow-up, 'Down the River Nile', would also be recorded at Abbey Road. The singles were taped shortly before Leyton left Britain to make his major feature film debut in *The Great Escape*. Stigwood was planning his artist's future, and that future did not include Joe Meek.

After trying out a series of other musicians – including bass player Alan Brearley, known professionally as Tab Martin – in March 1962 a new line-up of the Outlaws emerged. This incarnation saw Hodges back to playing bass, accompanied by Ken Lundgren on rhythm guitar, Roger Mingay (late of Screaming Lord Sutch and the Savages) on lead and Don Groom on drums. 'Only Charles is left of the old group,' Meek told the *Record Mirror*. 'That's the trouble – personnel changes as better offers come along for

Something Better Beginning

the boys... Personalities can't click with the public though their discs have all sold in the 30,000 each bracket, just missing the charts.'[281] This version of the band would record two singles, 'Ku-Pow!' (credited to Duke) and 'Sioux Serenade', which Meek composed under the rather bizarre pseudonym Dandy Ward, a name purloined from a Scottish boxer of the 1930s. Britain's record reviewers liked 'Ku-Pow', with one going so far as to suggest that the Shadows 'could well take a lead from the exciting new British group the Outlaws, who always seem to come up with a new line in instrumentals'.[282] The reviewer clearly had not heard the Shadows' 1960 recording 'Shotgun', as Meek had stolen that tune's introduction note-for-note. Meek saw 'Sioux Serenade', issued in October 1962, as a potential chart topper, telling *Pop Weekly* that 'the boys have done a great job of work. It's a bit Shadowy, maybe, but I think it could really break through.'[283] One of Meek's more understated productions, it's hard to understand why the disc failed to chart at all.

'Ken was a great bloke,' Hodges would later recall, 'but he had a way of doing the wrong thing as far as Joe went. And Joe would fire off at him, really lay [into him]. Ken was the nicest bloke you could meet, and Joe knew that but he used to rub him up the wrong way.'[284] During one session, Lundgren managed to knock over Meek's latest piece of equipment, an expensive new microphone. An incensed Meek chased Lundgren down the stairs of 304, screaming at the terrified guitar player to 'Fuck off out of it!' Hodges recalled that, invariably, when Meek blew his top he would kick everybody out of the studio until he had cooled down and work could resume. 'We'd just have to get out of there. Just leave. You'd shoot off for a couple of hours and just ring him up or come back in and gauge the situation by how he looked. If he looked happy, then you'd come in! One of his favourite tricks, when he lost his temper, he would just run down the stairs and put a record on at full blast. Turn it on as loud as he could so that the whole building would shake, you know?'[285] It was a habit that would invariably encourage the wrath of the Shentons' neighbours, and of Mrs Shenton herself, who would react by banging on the ceiling of the shop with a broom handle.*

---

* In the 2009 film *Telstar*, Hodges appears in a cameo as a neighbour subjected to Meek's irritation.

CHAPTER 13

Telstar

With the Outlaws once again settled, Joe was able to allow the Tornados out of the studio to fulfil their live commitments. At the end of April, their co-manager Larry Parnes sent them out on a series of one night stands without Billy Fury, but with two new Meek-signed singers, Andy Cavell and Tony Victor. Victor (real name Francis Armitage), a former shoe salesman and electrician from Bradford, would not score big in Britain despite Meek describing him as 'a clean, fresh boy with tremendous sex appeal',[286] but he would go on to find fame in France. He fell out with Meek after his one RGM single – 'Dear One' backed with 'There Was a Time' (by Robert Baker, yet another of Meek's many songwriting pseudonyms)* which saw Victor accompanied by the Tornados – flopped. Despite further live appearances with the Tornados, the promise of a film role and further recording sessions at 304, nothing else was released and the young singer became increasingly difficult to deal with: when Meek made it obvious that he was attracted, Victor suggested that Meek pay for the privilege. An incensed Meek refused to hand over any cash for sex and angrily threw the singer out of his home. That should have been the end of it but, displaying the stubborn streak he so often employed, the aggrieved producer dug his heels in and refused to release Victor from RGM Sound until publicity agent and aspiring artist manager Kenneth Pitt – who would later manage Crispian St Peters and David Bowie – bought out his contract. A suitably chastened Victor would fare better after he crossed the Channel and joined French rock 'n' roll act Les Pirates as replacement for their original singer, Dany Logan.

---

* The same tune would later be adapted for the Tornados' March 1963 single 'Robot'.

Telstar

Meek's other new signing would get a much better deal, and in May 1962 HMV issued the debut single from Andy Cavell, the Meek-written (again as Robert Baker) and produced 'Hey There, Cruel Heart'. Meek first met Cavell – real name Andreas Hatjoullis – when the Greek-born teenager was invited to come along to 304 Holloway Road to take photos at a recording session. The son of a chef who worked at an Italian restaurant in Holloway, Meek was immediately struck with the young man's good looks. 'When Mr Meek saw me he asked if I was a singing photographer,' he later explained to the readers of *Record Mail*, the EMI-financed monthly music magazine. 'He told me that I looked like a singer, offered to hear my voice and advise me of any potential I showed as a commercial vocalist. So, I sang for him – and to my surprise he liked me. That's when everything started to happen.'[287]

Cavell (who would go on to run a highly successful chain of pizza restaurants in Norway) quickly became part of Meek's inner circle, and that summer spent a short break at a caravan park in the country with Meek, Lional and Dave Adams. Home cine film from that brief holiday, captured by Lional, shows a happy, relaxed Meek larking around with his friends, pulling faces for the camera and playing pranks on each other. Meek does a quick impersonation of Fred Scuttle, one of comedian Benny Hill's many characters, and at one point several of the party dodge in and out of the lavatory block, with Adams reappearing, seemingly pregnant. The Joe Meek in that film is a million miles away from the dour, driven demon that many of his associates knew: here, with his guard down and among people he trusted, he is silly and camp and clearly enjoying himself.

Meek was not the only one interested in the attractive, boyish Cavell; young businessman Michael Montague was looking to move into the music industry and he saw potential in the photography student turned singer. Meek and Montague were both part of the same social circle, and Montague was no doubt aware that Meek was perpetually on the lookout for someone who could help him out financially without the Major finding out. Montague's principle business interest was in heating (he had established his own company, Gatehill Beco, before becoming a director of Valor), although he was also involved in plans to launch a commercial radio station in the West Midlands, and the opportunity to get involved in the management of a potential pop star was undoubtedly attractive. The two men set up a new company, Joe Meek Associates Ltd, to handle

Love and Fury: The Life, Death and Legacy of Joe Meek

Cavell and manage other artists in the RGM Sound stable, including the Outlaws, and although Joe Meek Associates was not involved in Meek's recording career, it did manage certain other business operations, including the purchasing and leasing of vehicles. Montague, perhaps after witnessing the haphazard way Meek dealt with business, soon backed away from the deal, and his position on the board of the new company would be taken by one J. W. Croxton.*

Late in the evening of Monday, 23 July 1962, Joe was sat at home glued to his television for a monumental event: the first worldwide public satellite broadcast. It was estimated that, in Europe alone, 200 million people tuned in to see the fuzzy pictures sent around the world via the Telstar satellite, and Meek watched in awe as, at two minutes to eleven, his black-and-white screen was filled by the face of Big Ben, shortly before British television presenter Richard Dimbleby – live, from a studio in Brussels – introduced the rest of the world to what newspapers the next day described as 'an awesome, sometimes bewildering kaleidoscope of sights and sounds'.[288]

The first communications satellite to orbit the earth, Telstar (whose name came from a contraction of the words 'television' and 'star') was a joint project between the United States, Britain and France: a three-foot-wide sphere covered in solar panels and antennae that received signals broadcast from earth, amplified them, and then sent them back out, bringing news reports and other programming live to the television viewer. Meek had been fascinated by the satellite for weeks, and it had inspired him to launch his own addition to that 'kaleidoscope of sounds'. The first test broadcasts had been made in the early hours of Wednesday, 11 July – the day after the satellite had been launched from Cape Canaveral – and the following day Britain beamed its first live broadcast, via the satellite to America. Meek, often up and working all night (Clem Cattini recalls arriving 'at ten o'clock for work and he'd just be going to bed!'), sat watching these early tests, and during one grabbed hold of a magazine open on his lap and furiously began scrawling some notes, later saying that the broadcast reminded him of his own route to stardom. 'I used to be a TV dealer's engineer,' he explained.

---

*   In 1997 Michael Montague would be created a life peer, taking the title Baron Montague of Oxford.

Telstar

'Telstar stirred me up inside. I found myself scribbling down a tune on the back of the *Radio Times*.'[289] Whatever it was that he wrote down (Meek could not then and would never be able to write music), once the broadcast was over he raced into his studio to capture his ideas on tape before they were gone forever.

This urgency, he would later state, was because 'I tried to capture the romance of Telstar. Although the picture was blurred and jumped all over the screen, I knew that I was watching something important.'[290] Meek seized a reel of tape containing the instrumental track for a song called 'Try Once More', originally performed (and left unreleased) by Cliff Bennett and the Rebel Rousers. The Outlaws had recently cut a pass at the song, and their version would appear – with hiccoughing, Buddy Holly-style vocals from Geoff Goddard ('some grotesque Holly-isms,'[291] according to the *New Record Mirror*) – a month later, on the B-side of Goddard's second solo single, 'My Little Girl's Come Home'. On the released version, the composer credit was given to orchestrator and arranger Ivor Raymonde, his name misspelled 'Raymond' on the label. Meek wrote 'Try Once More' himself, but gave Raymonde the rights either as a gift, as payment in kind for the work he was doing for RGM Sound now that Charles Blackwell was increasingly unavailable, or as a way to prevent Major Banks taking a share. Using a pseudonym also allowed Meek to sell the rights to some of his songs (or to Goddard/Meek co-writes) to a different publisher, and have the royalties paid straight into Meek's pocket, rather than to RGM Sound Ltd where they would be split 50/50 with Banks. The Major soon got wind of Meek's deception and was, naturally, angry. He tried to explain to Meek how there were bills to be paid and session fees to cover, but all Meek knew was that he was constantly skint, so broke in fact that at times he was forced to eke out splicing tape by cutting it horizontally in two. Raymonde would remain Meek's go-to arranger for the rest of his life, and with Raymonde doing much of his work at Decca, Meek would often take his tapes to the company's Hampstead studios for the arranger to overdub his orchestrations.

With the Outlaws' recording playing in the background, Meek recorded a live guide vocal onto tape, overdubbing his voice over their instrumental track. The noise he made was little more than a cacophonous racket: 'Uhhh, oh wahhh, la-de-dah, de-doo-wahhh, la-de-dah, de-doo-laaa, la deyyyyy!' But it is clear from the very first bar that the tune for his biggest

Love and Fury: The Life, Death and Legacy of Joe Meek

and most enduring hit – a record that would sell well over 5 million copies worldwide – was born fully formed in his head, as he later explained. 'I was impressed by the tremendous scientific achievement the Americans had made, and translated my thoughts into terms of the tune.'[292]

The Tornados had been scheduled to record the instrumental standard 'The Breeze and I', a favourite from their live set, as a follow-up to 'Love and Fury'. At the time, they were appearing with Billy Fury in summer season at Great Yarmouth's Windmill Theatre: their friendly rivals Peter Jay and the Jaywalkers were on the same bill, as well as appearing every Sunday in another Larry Parnes package alongside Mike Sarne and Shane Fenton and his band the Fentones. Keyboard player Norman Hale had been sacked at Larry Parnes' insistence – and without any of his fellow Tornados being consulted – after missing too many rehearsals, and had been replaced by the end of April 1962 by Roger LaVern (a former Household Cavalry officer whose real name was Roger Jackson), who had come to Meek's attention after the keyboard player asked a contact at EMI if he could introduce him to the producer. Meek, uneasy about sacking Heinz's friend, managed to find Hale employment in another act.

The shows were wild: Fury was a huge star and mobs of teenage girls would hang around outside the theatre hoping to see their idol and, if they were lucky, grab a handful of Fury's carefully sculpted quiff, or a piece of his clothing as a souvenir. Fury was, by now, well versed in making a quick escape: the fans waiting to touch the hem of his garment had no idea that he'd been off the stage and out of the door before the final bars of the last song were played, heading back to his hotel where he would take off his stage make-up and lurex jacket away from prying eyes and grabbing hands. The Tornados, charged with dismantling their equipment and getting it into the tour bus, were not so lucky. They had no choice but to run the gauntlet, often with terrifying results: at one show, after being chased by a crowd of youngsters desperate for a shirt button or a lock of hair, George Bellamy was crushed against the front of a furniture shop, the plate glass window shattered and he was pushed through into the store's display area.

Chatting together in a nearby pub, the Tornados were disheartened to discover that the Fentones also had plans to record 'The Breeze and I' for Parlophone (the tune would be covered again the following year by the Shadows), and Cattini, the Tornados' nominal leader, telephoned Meek to

Telstar

pass on the bad news. Luckily, Meek already had a new tune to present to them, something he called 'The Theme of Telstar'. 'When Clem Cattini came on the phone from Great Yarmouth to talk about ['The Breeze and I'], I realised this was our big chance,' Meek told the readers of teen weekly *Valentine*.[293] Their recording of 'The Breeze and I' would appear on the flip side to their second US hit, 'Ridin' The Wind', and on the British EP *More Sounds from The Tornados*.

With them playing in Great Yarmouth six nights a week, Meek and the band would not have much time to record his tribute to the marvels of satellite communication, but he knew that they had to get it done – and have the record available in the stores – while the public were still fascinated with this new technological marvel. After finishing the show that Saturday night, the band piled into Roger LaVern's Austin A35 and drove straight to London. The Tornados session was to begin at 10.30 a.m. the following morning.

Before they arrived to record the tune, Joe had a more complete demo prepared by Dave Adams. With little interest shown by the public in their recording career, Meek had put the team of Joy and Dave to work as backing vocalists: 'We just used to record these vocals, because that's what Joe would tell us to do, without even knowing who we were backing,' says Joy. Her multi-instrumentalist, songwriting brother was finding plenty of extra work adapting Meek's ear-splitting bleatings into an acceptable form, and it made sense to have them close by. At first the siblings shared a basement flat, but once Joy met her future husband, Dave moved into 304. He would not be there long: with Heinz now living there too, Meek soon found Dave his own flat, above a shop at 284 Holloway Road, just ten doors away. Adams shared the flat with his friend, freelance photographer Tony Leigh, who quickly became Meek's house snapper.

Adams first transcribed Meek's original demo into something more recognisable before recording the distinctive keyboard part (using the same Selmer Clavioline later used on the finished recording) over the backing track of Mike Berry's recent release 'Every Little Kiss'. 'Joe played the demo a few times, and then Alan [Caddy] worked out the chord sequences,' Cattini recalled. 'Joe wanted a moving rhythm; he sang the beat – like dum-diddy-dum – and indicated the guitar sound and bass, and then we just kicked it about, and he'd direct each individual into the

Love and Fury: The Life, Death and Legacy of Joe Meek

shape he wanted it to go. He knew what he was after, but if someone did something he liked, he'd say, "Keep that. I like it." Then he'd say, "Right, that's it up to there," and it went on like that until it was more or less ready. Then he'd record it and change a couple of things here and there. I played the basic beat with brushes on the cymbals.'[294] After working all day Sunday, the band returned to Holloway Road on Monday morning to finish off.

By 2 p.m. everything was in the can, including a second bass part from Heinz, mimicking his original but played with a handkerchief threaded through the strings of his guitar to deaden the sound, and the Tornados were back on the road to Great Yarmouth, where they were due on stage that evening. Knowing that he had to work fast, Meek had already arranged for Geoff Goddard to come in that day and, after waving them off on their journey, Goddard set about recording a second keyboard part, the disc's distinctive Clavioline lead. Goddard recalled that 'the group had to rush off to Great Yarmouth and of course the organist went with them, so I put the organ on, It took me six hours, adding it over the backing track.'[295] He then went to work tidying up 'Jungle Fever', the track that would appear on the B-side of 'Telstar'. A joint composition, Goddard was given a full composer credit for 'Jungle Fever', which would earn him as much in royalties as Meek stood to reap as the composer of the topside.

Then Meek himself got busy. Inspired by his earlier production work on *I Hear a New World*, he began adding a series of incredible electronic effects to the tune, some of which were created by 'blowing into a microphone and using a tape-delay effect to give you the in-orbit sound'.[296] These effects, he boasted, were 'all home-produced. Blowing into the mike… speeding up the tapes… reversing them… echo units… It's bang up to date, the contemporary noise of the 1960s. I'm going to do some more recording with this sound.'[297] Meek's visionary production would help to elevate 'Telstar' above anything else released at that time, but very few people – not even those on the recording – thought that it would be such a huge hit. Clem Cattini certainly had no major expectations for the tune: 'Joe Meek was wildly confident about it. He told us it was going to be a big hit, and we were quite happy with it,' he said modestly. 'Remember, this was our second disc, and our reaction was that if it went as well as our first record we would not be doing too badly.'[298]

Telstar

Issued on 17 August 1962, the British press did not know what to make of 'Telstar'. Meek, the mastermind behind this obvious hit – who at this point had been engineering, producing and writing hit records for six years – was dismissed by the *Sunday Mirror* as nothing more than an 'ex-television engineer',[299] and the *Melody Maker* lambasted the record, claiming that 'topicality [is] the only thing to commend it' and harrumphing that 'Billy Fury's backing group ought to be able to produce something less monotonous than this'.[300] Despite the derision, the single entered the *Melody Maker* singles charts in the first week of September, while the Tornados were still appearing in Great Yarmouth. Larry Parnes, a man who knew all too well what would put teenage bums on seats, insisted that the band introduce the tune into their act, but none of the Tornados knew how to play it. The record that was racing up the charts, complete with Meek's space-age sound effects, was so very different to the instrumental they had recorded a few weeks earlier that they hardly recognised it.

Also on the bill were Peter Jay and the Jaywalkers. 'Larry phoned them up and said, "'Telstar''s gone to number 1, and I want it in the show tonight,"' recalls Jay.

'They said, "We don't really know how it goes." It's a fabulous record, a genius record, but Joe had recorded it in bits and pieces and then stuck it all together, and that was so typical of the way Joe Meek worked. But Larry insisted, saying "I want it in the show tonight", so they had to go out to a record shop in Great Yarmouth, buy 'Telstar', bring it back and practise it all afternoon so they could include it in the show that night.

'Joe was amazing when you consider what he did. He couldn't sing, he couldn't play, but he just had that magic touch. Now when I listen to those records I realise how great he was. At the time it was, "Oh, God, here we go again with that Joe Meek sound," but that Joe Meek sound was just incredible. It's magical. When you hear 'Telstar' come on, it's like going back in a time warp. It takes you right back to that moment.'[301]

The same month that Decca issued 'Telstar', the company paid for a session by Robert Stigwood's latest signing, an 18-year-old actor from Dublin named Billy Boyle. Boyle would issue five singles over the next two years, all of which credited Stigwood as producer, when in reality most of the production work was overseen by his business partner, Stephen Komlosy, and

Love and Fury: The Life, Death and Legacy of Joe Meek

was heavily reliant on the skills Komlosy and Stigwood had picked up from watching Meek and Blackwell at work. For his first single, Stigwood commissioned another tribute song from Geoff Goddard, this time titled 'My Baby's Crazy About Elvis', and gave Charles Blackwell the job of arranging the musicians (and of writing the B-side, 'Held for Questioning'). The team had already given Stigwood a number 1 with Mike Sarne's 'Come Outside', so why mess with a winning formula? 'Charles Blackwell was a nice fellow,' singer Jess Conrad remembers, 'and at the time very sought-after. One was very lucky to get him. He didn't have to work with anybody in particular, he could be quite choosy – people like that wouldn't record you if they thought there was no chance of it being a hit. Around that time the producer or the arranger were almost as famous as the star. If you had a record produced by a big name, it would be played by the disc jockeys, because they would think, "Well, if it's Blackwell it's got to be good."'[302]

Boyle's version of the song was not a hit, but it would appear, alongside several other Geoff Goddard compositions, on Mike Sarne's debut album, *Come Inside*. The Sarne version used the same backing track, slightly sped up: another little trick lifted by Stigwood directly from the Joe Meek playbook. A rift that had begun with Stigwood poaching Billie Davis from under his nose was forming between Meek and Stigwood, and Goddard was witness to it all. 'I was tied to both, which made it very awkward. Really, Joe didn't like my having anything to do with Mr Stigwood by then, and Stigwood wasn't too keen on my having anything to do with Mr Meek. I was doing very well, between the two...'[303] The situation would be further compounded by US trade publication *Cash Box* reporting that 'Meek has been responsible for many hits in recent months including "Come Outside" by Mike Sarne', which of course he had nothing to do with, and by Britain's *New Record Mirror* stating that Blackwood, a man Meek (with some small justification) felt he had discovered, was 'part of a tightly-knit, ambitious show business set-up headed by manager Robert Stigwood'.[304]

Stephen Komlosy accepts that the pair owed a huge debt to Meek and his team, despite the fact that the set-up at RGM Sound was as he puts it: 'All so fundamental. It was all done in this room in Holloway Road, with egg boxes on the walls to keep the sound from going through to the neighbours... Joe's early records were rather good; I thought they were tremendous, very American with a sort of pre-Phil Spector sound, and

Telstar

I'm sure that in a way Phil Spector may have been influenced by some of Joe's records.'[305] Future Yes guitarist Steve Howe remembers that 'it was a strange place if you weren't familiar with it, but you accepted that it was a recording studio. The egg boxes were to keep the noise from the buses away, more than anything else. What was tacky about it, compared to say Kingsway or Abbey Road, was that this was a home studio; there wasn't a purpose-built control room or anything, but he made do with it.'[306] There may well have been egg boxes on the walls, but most of the studio was lined with professional soundproofing. Meek became so used to people making fun of the way he made his records that he began to refer to the studio as 'The Bathroom', even though he refuted the idea that he ever recorded there: 'It just isn't true,' he said. 'I don't make recordings in the bathroom... But I don't mind what they say; it's the results I'm interested in. Some musicians, particularly string sections, ask me if I want them to sit in the bathroom or kitchen when they first come here. But they take everything much more seriously when they hear the results.'[307] Meek's assistant, Tony Kent, backed his former boss up, insisting that 'one of the big stories about Joe was his recording in the bathroom with egg boxes [on the walls]. I never knew that. I don't think he ever recorded anyone in the bathroom except for effect. He used to go everywhere to get an effect, but I don't think he ever put anybody in the bathroom.'[308] Clem Cattini agreed, and recalled Meek using the bathroom on several occasions simply to get a particular sound, because the room had its own echoing ambience; he remembered Meek having string players perched on the edge of the bath as they plucked away at their violins, female backing singers using the room and one occasion where he himself had to sit in there banging two lengths of steel pipe together to obtain just the right result.

The success of 'Telstar' was evidence for Meek that he was right. Major labels had scoffed at his amateur set-up, despite several hits, but now the media wanted to know about the maverick making music from a tiny flat above the bustling Holloway Road. 'We make records on a shoestring,' he told the *New Musical Express*. 'But now there is firm proof that you don't have to record in a plush ultra-modern studio to get the biggest hits.' Masters that had proved impossible to place with the majors were suddenly in demand: Oriole (the small British company that also issued cut-price cover versions on the Embassy label for retail chain Woolworths) took a brace of songs recorded almost a year earlier by south coast act the Dowlands, issuing their first 45: 'Little Sue' backed with 'Julie' (both composed by Dave Dowland) with the label crediting the act as the Dowlands and the Soundtracks. Soundtracks guitarist Roy Phillips – who would find fame as one of the founding members of 1960s hitmakers the Peddlars – decided that this was just the push he needed. He waved goodbye to the *Bournemouth Times* and relocated to London, moving into shared accommodation in White City. With Meek paying his musicians the going union rate of £7/10 for a three-hour session, it was in the young guitar player's best interest to take part in as many sessions as he could. 'I'd go in with my guitar sometimes and just hang around. He would come in and would say "I've got this song. It goes like this." He used to come and hum his new tunes to you, and somehow you had to pick the melody out. Those of us who could got most of the session work!'[309]

Soon the British press were trumpeting that the Tornados were the only viable contenders to the Shadows' crown as kings of the beat instrumental, and writing about how the previously unknown fivesome were now earning enough money for each member to be able to afford to buy a new car. Meek had big plans for the group, and especially for their handsome young bass player. He had already started grooming Heinz for fame, encouraging him to bleach his mousey-brown hair blond (inspired, it is said, by the blond-haired children in the 1960 British sci-fi/horror film *The Village of the Damned*) so that he would stand out from the rest of the band on stage. When in London, Heinz stayed at 304 – which on the surface made sense as it was much more handy than his family home on the south coast – but it soon became an open secret that he and Joe were sleeping together.

Meek felt vindicated: the success of John Leyton had proved he could produce a number 1 hit, but Leyton's achievements had come from songs written by Geoff Goddard. 'Telstar' was *his* baby, and its success made him think that perhaps now was the time to relaunch an earlier project. 'A couple of years ago on the small Triumph label I had a stereophonic long player and EP out called *I Hear a New World*,' he told Ian Dove of the *New Record Mirror*. 'That was full of what I call outer space noises. So the idea of 'Telstar' isn't exactly a new one. I've had it in my mind for a couple of years at least.'[310]

CHAPTER 14

There's Lots More Where This Came From

Peter Jay and the Jaywalkers continued to build a reputation as a formidable live act. Their involvement with the Larry Parnes tour saw them courted by Decca, the same label that already had both Fury and the Tornados. 'Dick Rowe [head of A&R] had come down and seen the show,' Jay remembers. 'There weren't that many groups around in those days, there were only about six main bands, with people like the Shadows, the Flee-Rekkers, Sounds Incorporated, who were a big rival, and Shane Fenton and the Fentones. The rest were just local groups. The interest in groups was only just starting so I think that's why Decca wanted to sign us.'[311]

The band's first single was to be recorded at Decca's Hampstead studio and, following his enormous success with the Tornados, Decca brought Meek in to produce the session. ''You can see why we were put with Joe,' says Jay. 'He was the instrumental guru of the moment; he already had 'Telstar' by then. He had written a song for our first record, called 'Redskins', a typical Joe Meek thing with his usual 'Cowboys and Indians' connection, with a drum solo on – it was a good track.' The author credit on 'Redskins' is Knight, a pseudonym for Meek and Dick Rowe. For the flip side, Rowe was keen that the band record their show closer, a rocked-up version of 'Galop Infernal' from Offenbach's *Orpheus in the Underworld*, better known as the 'Can Can'.

'We had been rehearsing in the winter, and it was so cold that we used to run on the spot to keep warm,' Jay explains, 'And then we introduced that to

Love and Fury: The Life, Death and Legacy of Joe Meek

the act. We were doing things like 'Piltdown Rides Again',* and running on the spot, and the natural thing was to go into the 'Can Can'; it became a big part of our act. I'd go from that into a big drum solo, with my drums lighting up, sparks coming off the cymbals… it was really, really strong. It was an unusual set-up: we used to put the drums at the front, rather than being hidden at the back… we were one of the first to do that. I got very friendly on the tours with Clem Cattini: because I had these lights in my drums he used to call me "Osram"! He used to tease me, "Once those light bulbs go out, you've had it, haven't you?" But I told him I had plenty of spares!'[312]

Because it had been such a highlight of their live act, Decca were convinced that 'Can Can' could be a hit. 'We did the single in Decca's big studio. The studio had a raised control room, with a glass front and Joe had to keep coming up and down the stairs…' Meek was clearly not happy with the endless running up and down the rickety wooden stairs, as by the end of the session he was in a furious rage. 'He gradually lost it with us,' Jay recalls. 'He was in a real temper by the time we got to Take 41. I remember him shouting "Take 42! Don't make any mistakes!" We were all scared stiff of him by that stage; he had turned into a bit of a raving lunatic… although I don't blame him after 41 takes! There was real pressure: you don't want to be the one who makes a mistake and drops everyone in it.

'It was a different world then. If you wanted to take something out, you had to physically cut the tape to try and edit it, and they didn't want to do that… it's so easy now, when you can just drop things in at random. It's wild.' Meek always worked in this way, laying down multiple takes and then editing by hand, splicing and sticking lengths of precious – and expensive – tape together until he had created what, to his mind, was the perfect version of a song. It was a painstaking, laborious process, and one that could not be trusted to anyone but himself. It did not always work. 'Although we did all these live takes, even on 'Can Can' he tweaked it,' Jay continues. 'There's one bar there that's five-and-a-half beats long, and he's speeded it up slightly, but that was typical of Joe. Once he got his hands on the tape he could do what he liked with it. We never got a playback in the studio, never got to hear it until someone gave us an acetate, but by then

---

*   A hit in early 1961 for the Piltdown Men; a rock 'n' roll version of the *William Tell Overture*.

There's Lots More Where This Came From

we were already back on tour. They wanted to put 'Can Can' on the B-side, so we recorded that, and we did something like 42 takes of 'Redskins', and then Decca decided to flip it round, put "Can Can" on the A-side, which worked really well.' [313]

Officially titled 'Can Can '62', the single began its eleven-week chart run in November 1962, while the Jaywalkers were appearing with the Tornados, Billy Fury, Mike Sarne and others in another Larry Parnes package tour, *The Mammoth Star Show of 1962*. 'The tour went on for months and months,' Jay explains. 'Everywhere we played, sales jumped in that town the next day.' Although it only reached number 31 in the *Record Retailer* chart, the disc fared better elsewhere and went on to sell 100,000 copies. 'If it had done that in one week, it would have gone to number 1,' says Jay. 'But that was over a year. It was disappointing; we were going so well in the theatres; we were getting a great reaction that I thought, "This is going to go all the way," and then it made 19 in the *Melody Maker* chart and 30-something in the *NME*. At that same time, 'Love Me Do' came out, and that didn't do so great either!' The Beatles' British debut entered the charts that October and reached its peak, number 17, in January 1963.* 'Love Me Do' was still in the Top 30 when its follow-up, 'Please Please Me' hit the charts. The band that Meek – and just about everyone else in the industry – had dismissed would soon score their first number 1, and they would dominate the pop charts for the rest of his life.

In the same week as Parlophone issued 'Love Me Do' the label also released 'This Song Is Just For You', a country-and-western number and the first of a series of 45s Meek would produce for singer Houston Wells and his band the Marksmen. Meek saw Wells (born the far more prosaic Andrew Smith) as his Frankie Laine or Jim Reeves, and wanted to pair him with the Outlaws, a match surely made in heaven: Meek even had Wells pose for publicity photos, with the singer seemingly forced to sign a contract with the producer while Meek brandished a double-barrelled shotgun, a prescient image that would later haunt the singer. Wells, however, had other ideas and would not sign a deal that excluded his band. In the end, Meek signed Wells as a solo artist, on the understanding that the singer

---

*   Reissued in 1982 to mark its twentieth anniversary, 'Love Me Do' would reach number 4, and it has since been awarded a silver disc in the UK, with sales of over 200,000 copies.

161

Love and Fury: The Life, Death and Legacy of Joe Meek

would not only retain the services of his own band but would pay them out of his own pocket as well. As it turned out, the single was not a hit, and was dismissed in the pages of the *Record Mirror* as 'a nasal type whiner'.[314]

Meek barely noticed. Life was becoming more hectic, and he was used to his innovative records being dismissed by the 'rotten pigs' of the industry. He had recently signed a deal with Jeff Kruger's Ember Records, promising to supply the label with at least six artists a year for a minimum of three recordings each, although only one disc would be released under this new deal, 'It Matters Not' by Mark Douglas, a 19-year-old singer (also known as Billy Dean) who sung with the Outlaws when they were known as Billy Gray and the Stormers. Meek was also heavily occupied with the rapidly advancing career of the Tornados who, unbeknown to Decca, had performed the instrumental backing for 'It Matters Not'. 'Telstar' had been issued in America and was starting to climb the charts there, and there was huge demand for them to make personal appearances on television and on stage. Larry Parnes began to negotiate a US tour for early 1963: the band had dates to fill in Britain in January, but with Billy Fury scheduled to be off the road for much of February that seemed like the perfect time for the Tornados to fill a few dates stateside.

Backstage at one of the Parnes shows, Meek met a teenage record plugger called Andrew Oldham, there to keep an eye on his own act, Mark Wynter. Meek found the young, charismatic Oldham fascinating and asked him to drop by his office when he could, as he might have a project that would interest him. That project was 15-year-old singer from Welwyn Garden City, Kenny Plows, who Meek had rechristened Kenny Hollywood. Following the Parnes/Calvert model, Meek invested in the youngster's future stardom, with voice lessons, workshops in stagecraft and directions for how he should dress and present himself in public. By the time Oldham was introduced to him Meek had already produced a couple of tracks for the teenager, a lush Geoff Goddard ballad, 'The Wonderful Story of Love' and 'Magic Star', a version of 'Telstar' with lyrics by Meek. Recorded not at 304 but at Decca's Hampstead studios, the company issued the disc that November hoping for a Christmas hit, and Meek himself was full of praise for the youngster, telling Oldham that this was the best record he had produced so far in his career.

Meek offered Oldham a job, promoting RGM recordings, but the pair parted ways after 'Magic Star' failed to chart. Despite Meek's belief that the

There's Lots More Where This Came From

singer was 'a boy with a tremendous future, and will do well,'[315] although he recorded several more tracks for RGM Sound over the next year, young Kenny Hollywood was soon reduced to touring British Legion clubs to keep the wolf from the door. The singer would later confide that he believed that Meek had lost interest in him after he refused the producer's advances; it is perfectly possible, although Meek was not generally known to be spiteful, and there were plenty of other musicians who said no to Joe and continued to work for him. US singer Margie Singleton fared better with her version of 'Magic Star', which just missed the *Billboard* charts in January 1963. Meek was convinced that the vocal version of 'Telstar' would emulate the success of the instrumental original, and had Glenda Collins cut her own version of 'Magic Star', accompanied by the Riot Squad, in 1966. Oldham would later remark that 'Joe Meek was terrifying. Just a rude, embittered cunt. Awful man unless he fancied you. Which he did not.'[316] The future Rolling Stones manager has also gone on record to say that 'Meek really scared me! He looked like a real mean-queen Teddy Boy and his eyes were riveting.'[317]

Along with Kenny Hollywood, Meek also signed 18-year-old singer Wes Sands and Neil Christian (real name Christopher Tidmarsh), from Shoreditch, East London, to recording deals. Accompanied by the Outlaws, Sands would issue just one single for Meek, 'There's Lots More Where This Came From', through Columbia the following March, backed by a Meek original, 'Three Cups'. Sands, whose real name was Clive Sarstedt, had been bitten by the singing bug after his band had backed his brother Richard, better known as Eden Kane, in Hamburg, although to appease his mother he agreed to train as an accountant before attempting to hit the big time. It was Meek who persuaded him to leave his band and try for solo stardom: 'Nobody was interested until Joe Meek took a chance with me,' he told the press.[318] Sands promoted the disc on tour, backed by the Stigwood-managed beat group the LeRoys, but 'There's Lots More Where This Came From' would not be a hit, and the teenage hopeful would have to wait another thirteen years before he saw success when, as Robin Sarstedt, he made the UK Top 3 with a cover version of the Hoagy Carmichael song 'My Resistance Is Low'.

Neil Christian's debut single, 'The Road to Love' backed with a Meek co-write, 'The Big Beat Drum', was issued in late November. 'Neil Christian came to my office a while ago with a great number,' Meek told *Disc* magazine. 'It had been written by John Barlow but neither Neil nor John was sure it was the right kind of song for a first disc. I heard the number and flipped, not only over the way Neil sang it, but over the arrangement too. I insisted on recording Neil, and am not sorry about my decision.'[319] He may have had faith in the song and the singer, but seemingly had less in Christian's guitar player, a 17-year-old by the name of Jimmy Page. The future axe superstar's lead guitar is barely audible, buried beneath an otherwise appealing arrangement (from Ivor Raymonde) and a production that featured heavily muted and echo-drenched brass. Page would soon become a fixture at 304, one of the many star musicians who cut their teeth playing on sessions for Joe Meek.

The Outlaws were struggling to settle on a permanent line-up. Musicians came and went (Roger Mingay was replaced by Canadian musician Lorne Greene), with some staying for just a handful of live dates before, after open auditions were held at Soho coffee bar the 2i's in late October 1962, a new team emerged. Hodges and Lundgren were joined by 17-year-old drummer Mick Underwood, who had been recommended to Meek by Dave Sutch, and a shy young guitar player named Ritchie Blackmore. Blackmore had recently been kicked out of Sutch's band, the Savages, because, as he later admitted, 'I wasn't quite good enough!... Joe Meek heard about this and said, "Well, how about joining my band, the Outlaws?" And I said, "Okay! Sounds good to me." I mean, the Outlaws were more well-known than the Savages, so I was quite pleased.'[320] Blackmore, who had made his debut recording in 1961 aged just 16 years old, impressed Meek, and outside recording with the Savages he brought the youngster in to work on other sessions at 304. By happy coincidence, Blackmore and Underwood already knew each other well: both had gone to the same school, and both had been members of skiffle group the Dominators in their early teens.

Meek was full of praise for his new line-up: 'Ritchie Blackmore models his style more on Les Paul than anyone else,' he said, 'But can turn out a big gutty sound when necessary. Micky Underwood has a commercial style that has helped quite a few hit discs. He's not happy with just one sound... keeps on creating new ones. And Ken Lundgren, a Canadian, has a winning Country 'n' Western style and a feel for a power beat. He has also mastered

There's Lots More Where This Came From

the steel guitar and, along with Chas, helped to make that Mike Cox seller "Stand Up"... The time is ripe for them to make it big.'[321] The producer was right to boast about 'Stand Up': Cox's single may have failed to win over many record buyers in the UK, but it topped the charts in Sweden for four weeks at the start of 1963.

In Blackmore, Meek had found a guitarist who sounded different: many of the better-known musicians of the day had been influenced by Hank Marvin of the Shadows, and his signature twangy Fender sound; the noise Blackmore got from his Gibson was more raw, and Meek encouraged this by suggesting that the guitar player make holes in the speaker of his amplifier, to distort the sound still further. With effects pedals rare and expensive commodities, it was a simple yet effective trick that gave Blackmore a unique edge. The still relatively inexperienced Blackmore recalled how Hodges would translate Meek's mumbles into something coherent for the group to play: 'We'd go in in the morning, and [Joe] would say: "This is what I want you to do today." And he would either play us a demo or he would sing it to us. And he couldn't really sing, so that became embarrassing. Chas was brilliant. Chas would make up his own melodies. Chas would go: "What do you want on this, Joe?"... Of course, you could see what was going down. Chas was writing it for him.'[322] Meek was perfectly aware of how much he had come to rely on people like Hodges to help him create his songs and was frank about his importance: 'Charles... is a brilliant boy. He plays bass with a unique style, plus piano, rhythm, organ and harmonica on discs. One day, he'll be a top arranger – and is already a big help to me on sessions.'[323] Hodges' reward was four years of paid session and live work, and writer credits on a handful of Outlaws tracks, including 'Last Stage West' (co-credited to Meek), 'Fort Knox' (credited on demo copies to Robert Baker, a Meek pseudonym, but on stock copies as C. Hodges), and 'Hobo'.

With two instrumentals doing well in the charts, it was hardly surprising that Meek would be called on to add a touch of magic to the next single from the Packabeats, an instrumental four-piece who had issued a single the previous year for Parlophone. That record, 'Gypsy Beat', had spent just one week at number 49 in the charts, but Meek was convinced he could do better. The band, now with a new line-up and signed to Pye, issued 'The Traitors', the theme to the movie of the same name, but Meek – and who would argue with him at this point in his career – decided that the killer instrumental

Love and Fury: The Life, Death and Legacy of Joe Meek

(later used as the opening theme to the movie *Telstar*) should be relegated to the B-side in favour of Meek's own composition, the distinctly mediocre 'Evening in Paris'. Thanks no doubt to Meek's disastrous decision, neither 'Evening in Paris' nor its follow-up, a peculiar instrumental version of the Bobby Darin hit 'Dream Lover' would trouble the charts.

When Preston-based singer Robb Deka came to the door of 304 Holloway Road late in the year to audition for Meek, Joe sent him away with a flea in his ear, telling him that he was hardly in a unique position – 'you and thousands of others' had turned up uninvited – and he told the young hopeful to come back when he had a band together. He duly returned, accompanied by Lancashire three-piece the Bobcats. Deka (later known as Robb Shenton – no relation to Meek's landlords – but whose complicated back story saw him born Terry Ryan but brought up by adoptive parents as Robert Eccles), did not make the grade, but Meek saw something in the trio and had them perform a couple of numbers themselves (including a cover of the doo-wop classic 'Little Bitty Pretty One'), showcasing their harmonies. When they called him a few weeks later to see how their friend had done, Meek told them that 'he didn't pass the audition, but I'd like you three to come back for another hearing'.[324] Meek offered the trio a management contract and changed their name to the Puppets which was fine by the group: 'He knows best,' they told *Record Mirror*. [325] With his current workload, Meek was unable to schedule much time with the act before the following summer, but as he said, 'I felt from the start that these three very bright lads from Preston had something really different. Their voices somehow gelled just right. I honestly think they'll be very big indeed.' [326] Despite Meek's confidence in the group's abilities, he could not help himself, adding his usual layer of echo and speeding up their voices for their debut single, 'Everybody's Talking' backed with a cover of the Coasters' hit 'Poison Ivy', which would be issued in September 1963. 'He made us sound like the Chipmunks,' said drummer Des O'Reilly.*

---

* Before joining the Bobcats, Des O'Reilly had briefly been the drummer for Rory Storm and the Hurricanes, joining after their original drummer, Ringo Starr, left to take over the drum stool for the Beatles.

There's Lots More Where This Came From

Through Meek's connections with the George Cooper organisation, the Puppets would find plenty of work over the next few years, touring under their own name and backing a host of stars including Michael Cox, Billy Fury, Jess Conrad, Gene Vincent and the Ronettes, and would appear on the same bill as the Beatles, the Rolling Stones, the Honeycombs and Millie among countless other big names. However, although their leaning was towards rock 'n' roll, Meek had other plans: 'In our early sessions, we put down tracks like "Roll Over Beethoven" and "Money",' said O'Reilly. 'I remember the expression on Joe's face as he smiled at us and said, "It won't sell." Six months later, after the Beatles broke, everybody was doing those sorts of numbers.'[327]

Although Deka (the stage name was supposed to be Robb Decca, but it was misspelled on an early poster and the musician decided to keep it that way) had not impressed as a solo artist, the following year Meek would invite him back to RGM Sound as a session musician and backing singer. 'I signed an individual recording contract with Joe in 1963,' he explained. 'I recorded four tracks with The Prestons, but these went unreleased because the band split up. In 1964 Joe produced tracks I appeared on with Liverpool band The Nashpool. We'd had an offer from Mickie Most, and the rest of the band wanted to go with him, but I said I was going to stay with Joe. Looking back, it was one of the worst things I did, but I had signed a contract and I just couldn't break it.' It was Deka who had brought the Nashpool to Meek's attention. Originally known as the Nashpool Four (until the addition of Deka on keyboards made them a five-piece) the band recorded several tracks at 304 in May 1964, immediately before they went off on a tour of Britain and Europe, including a three-month stint at the Star Club, in Hamburg. Sadly, the band broke up on their return to the UK, primarily over the inability to accept the offer from Most, and the tracks they recorded with Meek would remain unreleased, but over the next few years Deka would find plenty of work through Meek: he sang backing vocals – often with Vivienne Chering (aka Flip of Flip and the Dateliners) – for acts including Freddie Starr, Bobby Rio (former grocery assistant Bobby McKellar) and Dave Kaye, and would appear as a member of several acts Meek recorded.

Busy as he was, Meek still found time to record an audio biography for his friend Donald Aldous, editor of the *Audio Record Review* and the

Love and Fury: The Life, Death and Legacy of Joe Meek

president of the South Devon Tape Recording Club. The tape was to be played by Aldous for society members at a meeting at the Torquay YMCA in early December and gives a fascinating insight into Meek's working life (the recording was later issued – under the title 'Joe Meek Speaks' – on the CD box set *Portrait of a Genius*). That same month, 'Telstar' became the first single by a British band (renamed 'The Tornadoes' for the US market) to top the *Billboard* chart. Back home in a snow-covered Britain, the Tornados were due on stage at the Memorial Hall in Lydbrook, a dozen or so miles from the Meek family home in Newent, when the news of their stateside success came through. Larry Parnes had tried desperately to break the band's contract with the Lydbrook Old Folks Committee, knowing that his 'Famous Television and Recording Group' (as they were advertised that night) could earn far more than they had been promised for this backwoods appearance, but Meek was not going to allow his near-neighbours to be disappointed. His integrity was rewarded when the Tornados were booked for a return visit in December 1963.

As well as being number 1 in the States, Meek fancied a festive hit in Britain, and had a crack at the Christmas charts with 'Poppin' Party' by the Chaps on Parlophone. The Chaps were the Outlaws, 'Poppin' Party' was a two-part medley of recent hits, including 'Telstar', and this disc marks Ritchie Blackmore's first appearance on an RGM Sound 45. He would follow this up with 'In the Night' by Jamie Lee and the Atlantics (Lee's real name was Ray Walsh, the Atlantics was simply an alternative name for the Outlaws), which would be issued by Decca in early January 1963, and it would not be long before Meek and Goddard would introduce Blackmore to their joint obsession with the afterlife. 'I used to come into a session sometimes and [Meek] would say, "I've been speaking to Buddy last night," the guitarist later revealed. '"Buddy?" "Yes, Buddy Holly, and he told me that we must do this record." He actually thought that he could communicate with Buddy Holly and people like that.'[328]

There was no escaping the fact that Meek had arrived. With 'Telstar' now an international hit, he was approached by Dave Kapp, the president of Kapp Records, to produce masters with the US market in mind. Kapp wanted instrumentals: surf music and twangy guitars were all the rage with stateside teens, and Kapp had done exceedingly well with a series of light instrumental pop albums, but although Meek signed a 16-year-old

There's Lots More Where This Came From

keyboard player, Tony Ashton, specifically to produce masters for Kapp, none of the tracks he cut at 304 would surface. Years later Ashton would join Liverpool band the Remo Four, and appear on George Harrison's first solo album *Wonderwall Music,* before forming Ashton, Gardner and Dyke and scoring his first chart hit with the 1971 Top 3 single 'Resurrection Shuffle'.

The deal with Kapp may have come to nothing, but the enormous international success of 'Telstar' changed Joe Meek's life. From now on he would invariably be referred to as 'Joe "Telstar" Meek', or simply 'Mr Telstar'. He had done all right financially from his earlier hits, but, as he put it himself, 'After selling about 2,000,000 and making £26,000, I can stop watching the pennies.' With all of that money (equivalent to over £680,000 in 2024), Meek had options: 'I'd like a handsome ground-floor studio,' he told Jane Gaskell of the *Daily Express,* 'so the artists don't have to lug so much up and down the stairs. But then again, I like it here,' he added, referring to the set-up at 304.

An unusually open Meek let the young journalist into some of his songwriting secrets: 'I like an out-of-tune piano for composing on; it keeps the last note longer while you're still wondering what to make the next one. I'm not too quick at reading music,' he admitted. 'And I get a nice metallic effect by sticking drawing pins in the pads – cheaper than one of the specially made pianos like Winifred Atwell's.'[329] No one mentioned the sign that sat on the piano, instructing all musicians to tune their own instruments to Meek's distinctly out-of-tune upright. Ms Gaskell clearly made Meek feel at ease, as her short interview was one of the most revealing he would ever give. 'I like anything that's a bit unreal,' he told her. 'I'm not keen at all on the ordinary, the everyday. I like horror stories, horror films.' Meek did not elaborate on this, but he would occasionally take friends – or his recording artists after a long session was over – to the local cinema to watch the latest horror film (Dave Adams recalled the pair going to see the Vincent Price shocker *The Fly* together, and laughing afterwards at Meek's jokes and puns), and he even attempted to write his own original horror story about a haunted bathroom mirror, although because his spelling and grammar were poor he dictated the tale onto tape rather than put pen to paper. While talking to Gaskell he touched on his own state of mind when he revealed that 'my sounds usually come to me on a Sunday, when I'm a

Love and Fury: The Life, Death and Legacy of Joe Meek

bit low and depressed. Then the mood comes first, probably with a mean old title. If nothing else is handy, I'll beat out the rhythm on the door.' Finally, he discussed his thoughts for his own future: 'I don't think I'll get married. It wouldn't be fair to the artists. I just wouldn't have enough time for them.' [330]

CHAPTER 15

Globetrotter

Time was certainly an issue, and late 1962 saw Joe busier than ever. Newcastle-based electrician-turned-tenor singer Patrick Riley came to audition at RGM Sound and was rewarded with a new name, Toby Ventura, and a pair of Goddard/Meek compositions, 'If My Heart Were a Story Book' and 'Vagabond'. The latter was credited to Peter Jacobs, a joint pseudonym for Goddard and Meek, and an act of subterfuge that allowed Meek to assign copyright to Ivy Music, rather than Goddard's usual publisher Southern.

Meek may have felt that 'this boy has a fine voice, and there's no reason why he shouldn't do it',[331] but by February the following year, when the disc reached the shops, the tastes of the record-buying public were already changing, and it and another Meek single issued that same month, Gerry Temple's 'Angel Face', both fell by the wayside. After three flop singles Temple would leave RGM Sound and, later that year, would sign on as vocalist with the Laurie Jay Combo.

At the beginning of 1963 the pop music scene in Britain was on the cusp of the greatest change it had ever seen. Although the charts were dominated by proven stars such as Cliff Richard and Elvis Presley, a batch of new young artists were heading for the big time. At the end of January the Beatles scored their first major hit, and by the early spring fellow Liverpudlians Gerry and the Pacemakers would join them. Merseybeat had arrived. Billie Davis, the singer that Robert Stigwood had snatched from under Meek's nose, landed a Top 10 hit with her debut solo release, 'Tell Him', and big ballads like 'If My Heart Were a Story Book' or 50s-influenced teen pop songs like 'Angel Face' suddenly sounded ridiculously old-fashioned. This

Love and Fury: The Life, Death and Legacy of Joe Meek

new crop of chart acts might have been a challenge, and the failure of Toby Ventura or Gerry Temple to land a hit was obviously disappointing, but Meek was still riding a wave thanks to the unrivalled success of 'Telstar', and the media remained enthralled with the one-man recording conglomerate: 'It's easy to see why Mr Meek is so successful with teenage record buyers,' wrote Thomas Alstone in the *Bristol Evening Post*. 'He creates new sounds, entirely new concepts specially for them and builds up a great, exciting atmosphere.'[332]

Luckily, further success was just around the corner. For Mike Berry's next single, Goddard and Meek came up with a song called 'Don't You Think It's Time', and at the end of January 1963 the singer cracked the Top 10 for the first time. The single would reach number 6, and provide him with the biggest hit of his career, a welcome relief after the relative failure of his two previous singles, as Berry explains: 'The next song, after 'Tribute', was 'Just a Matter of Time'. It didn't happen, it wasn't a very good song. Again it was a Joe song, and Joe didn't write hits. His bloody arse would heal up before he'd write a hit! The B-side [Geoff Goddard's 'Little Boy Blue'] was much better.' Berry is equally dismissive of the follow-up, another Goddard–Meek song, 'Every Little Kiss'. 'It was a complete nick from 'Will You Love Me Tomorrow'. The phrasing was all unnatural, it was singing with a mouthful of spanners! It didn't flow. You don't speak like that, it didn't have that singability, [sic] because he was borrowing the phrasing from 'Will You Love Me Tomorrow'. That was the problem with Joe; he was not averse to plagiarising other people's work.'

Every songwriter was influenced to some degree by another writer or song, but often with Meek it was flagrant. Whereas the Beatles might take a Roy Orbison number as the starting point for a song like 'Please Please Me', and then (often with the aid of their producer, George Martin) twist it, turn it and mould it into something new, Meek was blatant. The Tornados' follow-up to 'Telstar', although recorded back in September, was issued in the first week of January 1963. Meek had been keen to ensure that the band's follow-up would stand out, telling the press that 'it's not an outer space thing. I think that would be a mistake. But it is a colourful type of thing. I went out of my way to try and create a picture again. I like playing with sounds.'[333] Drummer Clem Cattini was unimpressed with the tune Meek gave them, something he called 'Globetrotter', but it was a view he

Globetrotter

would live to regret, as an incensed Meek quickly saw red. 'He said, "What do you think of 'Globetrotter'?" I said I didn't like it, and he got the hump, and threw a stool at me!' A chastened Cattini begrudgingly played on the track, but although 'Globetrotter' was credited as a Meek composition and was a Top 5 hit, it immediately ran into controversy when people began to realise that part of the tune had been snatched (inadvertently or otherwise) from 'Venus in Blue Jeans', a UK hit for Mark Wynter. Meek and Goddard would help themselves to 'Venus in Blue Jeans' again later in the year, when Screaming Lord Sutch released 'Monster in Black Tights', a comedy song that, during its creation, according to Goddard, 'Joe Meek laughed so much he got hiccoughs!'[334]

Berry may have been unhappy with his performance on 'Every Little Kiss', but, unlike the singer, Robert Stigwood liked the song and, within weeks of its release, had taken over as Berry's manager. 'Stigwood signed me up on the strength of that record. He didn't see that it was shit either! Stigwood took me away from Joe. Joe said to me, "He'll try and take you away from me."' Stigwood had a very different approach to Meek: 'He would tell you what you were doing, not ask you. It was a foregone conclusion.'[335]

"Don't You Think It's Time' was a hit because Geoff Goddard had a hand in it. Geoff more or less wrote the song with some of Joe's input. The irony was that Joe used to come up with all this rubbish yet he could have had the pick of any songwriter in the country with the track record that he had. But he thought that he could do it all on his own.'[336] In mid-January 1963, Berry was at the Alpha Television Studios in Birmingham, to record a performance of 'Don't You Think It's Time' for the ATV show *Thank Your Lucky Stars*. Also on that programme were the Beatles, then promoting the release of their second single, 'Please Please Me'. 'It was soon to get to number 1 in the charts of course,' Berry later recalled. 'But at the time they didn't know that was going to happen – their first record 'Love Me Do' had been only a minor hit – and they were eager to push their songs... I was chatting to John Lennon in the canteen and he said, "Oh, we'll write a song for you!" I was with Robert Stigwood who was then my manager and we just didn't follow the offer through! Firstly we didn't know about their writing and secondly we were associated with Joe Meek at the time who wrote all his own stuff or liked to have a say in what was

Love and Fury: The Life, Death and Legacy of Joe Meek

written for me.'[337] The Tornados' appearance on *Thank Your Lucky Stars* on 16 February saw them presented with an International Gold Award from *Cash Box* magazine for reaching number 1 in the US charts with 'Telstar': the band was the first act ever to receive the award. A gold disc, awarded for sales of 2 million copies of 'Telstar', had been stolen from their dressing room at the Granada, Edmonton, on 25 January, but was returned to them – via Patrick Doncaster at the *Daily Mirror* – a few weeks later.

Stigwood's insistence that he take over the management of Berry effectively killed Meek's idea for an album with the singer. Stigwood had plans for his new signing, and although Berry had recorded around a dozen Holly cover versions at 304 (the tapes of which still exist) for the album, his new manager decided that was not the direction he wanted his boy to go in. The album was off, although a similar sleeve design would be employed on Berry's mid-1963 EP, *A Tribute to Buddy Holly*, and on Heinz's 1964 album *Tribute to Eddie*. Berry's next single for Meek, 'My Little Baby' struggled to make the Top 40: 'It was awful! He had that "ooh-pa-pa, ohh-pa-pa" backing vocal because he said he wanted it to be like Del Shannon's 'The Swiss Maid'. That's where that was stolen from. It was typical of Joe to steal the wrong thing! It was a Joe song, mainly, I'm not sure that Geoff had a hand in it [the disc credits Meek and Goddard as co-composers], but Chas was very good at interpreting Joe's wishes. I thought it was godawful!" Critics seemed to agree, with David Nicolson of the *Gloucester Citizen* noting that 'Mike Berry always sounds to me as though he's singing through a wad of soggy cotton wool', although in the same column Nicolson praised Meek as 'the wizard of recording engineering and effects'.[338] 'It only made number 34, and that was on the strength of 'Don't You Think It's Time',' Berry adds. 'Then we did 'It Really Doesn't Matter'; what a bloody awful record that was!'[339]

'It Really Doesn't Matter' would be the last single that Mike Berry recorded at 304, and the two men would not cross paths again. His next release, the self-penned 'On My Mind', was recorded at EMI's studio in St John's Wood, now famously known as Abbey Road, with Stigwood credited as producer. 'Stigwood couldn't produce a piss-up in a brewery,' Berry laughs. 'He would be in the box [the control room] but that would be it.'[340] In December, Stigwood announced that John Leyton would be recording in America (the singer was in the country to film *The Great Escape*), and as he slowly moved to extract himself and his acts from RGM Sound

Globetrotter

he would poach more and more of Meek's collaborators: songwriters John Shakespeare and Ken Hawker, aka Carter and Lewis, were on Stigwood's shopping list, the pair announcing through the pages of *Pop Weekly* that they 'were working over some ideas for John Leyton and Mike Berry',[341] although it would be almost a year before Leyton issued the pair's Stigwood-produced rewrite of the classic 'Beautiful Dreamer'. The following year Stigwood and Sir Joseph Lockwood would fall out over a loan EMI had made to the Australian's company, RSA (Robert Stigwood Associates), and Lockwood vowed never to work with Stigwood again. Berry remained signed to HMV until late 1966, but Stigwood's name would not appear on any of his releases after 1964.

Over the years, Meek's scattershot approach saw him sign dozens of artists, only a small proportion of whom would have any real success. Toby Ventura and Gerry Temple were not exactly fodder for the beat-hungry kids, so perhaps Meek would do better with his next opportunity, a song based on a dance, 'The Sidewalk', performed by Tony Holland, singer with the Packabeats. On paper this seemed destined to be more successful, especially with the demand for vocal groups increasing and the popularity of discs built around dances ('The Locomotion', 'Madison Time', 'Harlem Shuffle' and so on), but 'The Sidewalk' was another miss, and Holland quickly went back to performing with the Packabeats.

Maybe Meek would stand more chance with a female singer? He tried to interest Decca in a young woman known as Doris Jillette, who had co-written the Danny Rivers chart hit 'Can't You Hear My Heart'. Meek wanted to market her as a solo singer, but the company refused to release her single, 'Johnny-O' (on which she was backed by the Tornados), as they considered it unlikely to gain any radio play, clocking in as it did at an uncommercial five minutes long. The ever-stubborn Meek refused to edit it down to a more acceptable three minutes in length, and it went unreleased. Roy Pitt, of Rank's music publishing arm Filmusic, brought actress Jenny Moss to audition at RGM Sound. Moss had made quite an impact as Lucille Hewitt in the ITV soap opera *Coronation Street*, and one episode had featured her singing (along with another *Street* regular, Violet Carson) a version of the Brian Hyland hit 'Sealed With a Kiss'. Moss cut several sides for Meek, including a version of Mike Berry's 'Every Little

Love and Fury: The Life, Death and Legacy of Joe Meek

Kiss' (that would appear on the 2024 collection *Do the Strum!*), but only two of her recordings were issued at the time, 'Hobbies' (co-written by Pitt) and Meek's own composition 'Big Boys', by Columbia in June 1963.

For a man who had spent the last five or six years surrounded by famous people, Meek was on tenterhooks over the thought of having a television star in his studio, and told the Outlaws – who he had chosen to back Miss Moss on her audition – that they had to clean up their act. Chas Hodges recalled Meek telling them to 'smarten yourselves up, polish your shoes, because Jenny Moss is coming down. I said, "Who's Jenny Moss?" "Lucille from *Coronation Street*." So [next day] she introduced herself, pleased to meet you... she said, "Is there a toilet?" So she went to the toilet, and she came in and said, "Guess what, boys? I've just had a shit and I've done a turd that long...'[342] The single got good reviews (the *Liverpool Echo* called it 'catchy and exciting, and at time reminiscent of [Helen] Shapiro')[343], and although Meek would have been incensed once he discovered that the name of his company had been left off the label, he was probably secretly thrilled at having the lines 'Big boys, they don't worry me but I know one day I'll be loved by one of them' played on the radio and broadcast into thousands of homes around the country.

Despite the failures, there was still work to do. Peter Jay and the Jaywalkers were proving a popular live attraction and, with 'Can Can '62' still selling well, Decca and Meek needed to get a follow-up on tape while they had the chance. The tunes chosen were a Meek original, 'Totem Pole' (later re-recorded by the Honeycombs), and 'Jaywalker', a tour-de-force instrumental with Jay and Meek credited as co-writers. 'We did 'Totem Pole', which he'd written, and he'd say, "Go and get a cup of tea," and we'd then go back and do the B-side. That was how it worked.' Today Jay is unsure of how he received co-credit on 'Jaywalker'. 'I think that was just him being kind, because he'd got the A-side,' he suggests. 'We'd all convinced ourselves that this was going to be a huge hit, so it was a bit of a softener I guess. It was the total Joe Meek sound, I remember that he kept wanting more "twang" on the guitar, more tremolo. It was a great record, but it didn't even show in the Top 50. I don't know what happened: I thought, this is tuneful, it's got that Joe Meek sound, it will go to number 1, but it didn't show anywhere. We were playing on the Beatles tour after that, but it just disappeared. So we

Globetrotter

thought, OK, we'll go back to rocking up the classics, and that's why we did 'Poet and Peasant'.'[344]

In the States, London Records were also keen to build on their success with the Tornados but seemed unsure how to do that. 'Globetrotter', which Meek revealed was inspired by the idea of 'sleighs racing through the sky',[345] was issued – retitled 'Globetrottin'' – in America in January 1963, just a fortnight after its British release (the B-side, 'Locomotion With Me' was retitled 'Like Locomotion' for the US market), but within a week, perhaps spurred on by a distinct lack of interest from American radio, London issued 'Ridin' the Wind', their third 45, a remixed version of the song that had appeared on their first British EP, with added wind and explosive effects. Written by George Bellamy (and again credited to the Tornadoes, as all of their US singles would be), 'Ridin' the Wind' reached number 63 on the *Billboard Hot 100* the following month: 'Globetrottin'' did not chart at all.

Much had been made in the press of upcoming live dates stateside, but co-manager Larry Parnes refused to let the band go. Although initially keen, he made it clear that he had no intention of the Tornados appearing anywhere in the States without Billy Fury, and Fury was virtually unknown there. Parnes did everything he could to try and break his boy in America, even finagling a meeting with Elvis (a dumbstruck Fury could barely piece two words together in the presence of the King), but he made no impact. Parnes' intransigence cost the band dearly. They should have been flying high, with the number 1 single in the US charts and multiple advances from promoters to tour, but Parnes turned down every offer they had to go there. 'There's 'Telstar', number 1 all over the world, and the band's sat at home doing nothing,' Dave Sutch would later rue. 'They were starving, and they could have gone out to America and been the first Beatles!'[346] Parnes, naturally, would blame Meek for ruining the Tornados' big chance: 'I wanted them to go out on a world tour,' he later claimed. 'Joe didn't.'[347]

They may have been denied the chance to tour the States, but other markets were opening up to them, and at the same time as the band were celebrating their second US chart success, 'Telstar' reached number 1 on the French charts. The timing was perfect, with the Tornados due to play a series of shows at the famed Olympia theatre in Paris that April; however, the accomplishment came at a cost. Musician Jean Ledrut

Love and Fury: The Life, Death and Legacy of Joe Meek

heard the tune and declared that it sounded like his own composition, 'La Marche d'Austerlitz', from the 1960 movie *Austerlitz*. Ledrut began court proceedings against Meek, and the tune's publisher, Ivy Music, charging them with plagiarism. Meek would not see another penny in his lifetime from his biggest hit; the moment that the claim was filed the court froze all income from the song – the multi-million selling Tornados version as well as dozens of cover versions from around the world – while they debated the tune's authorship. Meek's own legal team assured him that he had no case to answer and the issue would be settled soon.

Meek's solution to this temporary financial hiccough was to keep occupied. Obsessed with Heinz, and convinced he could make his boy a star in his own right, Meek began to distance his prey from the rest of the pack. It began subtly, with Meek designing a special bass cabinet for Heinz to use on stage. Then he upped the ante, insisting that Heinz be dressed differently from the rest of the Tornados, to distinguish him as the group's main focus. Finally, in a move that could have scuppered the band's career but which guaranteed maximum publicity for his decision, at the end of December 1962 Meek announced that Heinz would be exiting the Tornados to go solo the following spring. The announcement was timed to give him plenty of opportunity to find the right replacement, and Meek was keen to tell the press that 'he needn't be a brilliant guitarist. Just competent will do.

'Personality and good looks are what count, and at the moment all the boys seem to be developing nicely, though Heinz is the one all the girls go for... Over Christmas it's really been brought home to me just how fantastically popular Heinz is... I'm going to be his manager and I'll record him. I think he's got tremendous potential, very individual. By this time next year, or even before, he could be one of the biggest names in the pop world.'[348]

Meek explained to the readers of the *New Record Mirror* that he had intended for Heinz to go solo from the outset: 'Heinz was really a bit young for the others in the group and he had a different approach to selling himself to the audience than the others. So I made up my mind that he'd turn solo one day and the sooner the better. I remember how it all happened on the singing side. He had a go at me about another artist on my books – he said this chap was very conceited and wasn't a very good singer. I told Heinz he was being insulting and that I felt the singer had potential and therefore I

Globetrotter

should record him. And Heinz said: "Well, you never give me a voice test." I agreed to give him one. He had that husky quality all right. But he was out of tune – a bit flat.'[349]

But before Heinz was yanked out of the group (a decision that the other Tornados were perfectly happy about), in March 1963 Meek took a few days out of his increasingly busy schedule to escort the Tornados on a profile-raising trip to Paris, ostensibly to promote their upcoming shows at the Olympia and shoot a film for the new Scopitones system to promote their new single, 'Robot'.* A precursor to the video jukebox, Scopitones had been popular in Europe for a couple of years but had only recently been launched in Britain. Accompanied by Norman Miller, who directed the promotional clips for the company Radio Vision, they also shot a film for their recent French number 1, 'Telstar', and Heinz filmed a short for his upcoming solo debut, 'Dreams Do Come True'. The Paris trip would be one of the last Heinz would make with the band. Once their British tour was over at the end of the month, the bleach-blond bass player was out, replaced initially by Chas Hodges and then by Tab Martin (to help the band fulfil their live bookings: Tab also appeared with the Tornados in *Farewell Performance*) before Brian Gregg, who had previously worked with Clem Cattini and Alan Caddy in both the Cabin Boys and Johnny Kidd and the Pirates, was given the job full time. This new line-up of the band was soon off on tour, backing Billy Fury: the dates were accompanied by an EP from Decca, *Billy Fury and the Tornados*, recorded at the Hampstead studios without Meek's involvement. To keep Tornados-mania bubbling, the band made a brief appearance in the British teen comedy *Just for Fun*, playing a new tune 'All the Stars In the Sky'. To achieve a suitably 'sparkly' opening effect on the recording, Meek had a member of the band drag a screwdriver over a serrated glass ashtray.

Meek's tremendous success – in March it was announced that he was to be awarded a coveted gold disc for 'Telstar', the first independent production ever to achieve such a feat – kept him in demand. One of the oddest things that Meek was ever involved with occurred that same month, when he was

---

*   The flipside of 'Robot', 'Life on Venus', featured a spoken intro from Ken Lundgren. Despite rumours to the contrary, the German version was not narrated by Heinz.

Love and Fury: The Life, Death and Legacy of Joe Meek

approached by Henry Blythe, the President of the Gloucester Hypnotic Research Society with a proposition. Blythe had recently hypnotised society girl Philippa Beresford-Pierse, convincing her that she was capable of producing a hit song, and while in a post-hypnotic state the granddaughter of the Earl of Mount Edgcumbe had indeed composed and performed a pop song that, Blythe felt, would be perfect for someone like Meek. Unfortunately, Ms Beresford-Pierse would not have a hit with her unnamed song: Meek may have had a reputation for the extraordinary, but this particularly esoteric project was passed over and quickly forgotten about.

March also saw a new release from the Checkmates – Emile Ford's former backing band – written and produced by Meek, and an answer to the detractors who were accusing him of constantly delving into his bag of tricks: 'You've Got To Have a Gimmick Today'. The disc poked fun at other successful artists and was a precursor to the similar 'Call Up the Groups' from the Barron Knights, but it was painful, forced and did not sell: the song parodied three earlier hit singles, and Meek was lucky not to have been sued as none of the original authors or their publishers were given credit, a situation that would have quickly changed had the record been a hit. Luckily, other acts in the RGM stable were more successful, and any doubt in Meek's abilities as a producer of hit material were quelled when he was presented with an Ivor Novello award for writing the bestselling British single of 1962, 'Telstar'. The awards show was screened by the BBC on 4 May 1963 with the Tornados performing their hit (the band mimed to a recording made the previous day, thanks to the BBC's archaic performance rules): the statuette would be prominently displayed on the desk in his office, next to his gold disc.[*]

In April film composer and pianist Stanley Black issued his version of another of Meek's outer space tunes 'Lullaby of the Stars', one of the very few instances of a Meek composition being recorded without his involvement in the production; the Tornados would also record a version of this instrumental, but it would remain in the vaults until 2023. He was the most famous producer in the country; his name was seldom out of the music press, and this brought an endless parade of hopefuls to the door

---

[*] A copy of the statuette, presented to Decca, was found discarded, wrapped in newspaper, in Greenwich in the 1980s. It was later sold at auction for £1,400.

180

Globetrotter

of 304 Holloway Road. Many of these came from the North of England, inspired by the success of the Beatles to try and forge their own way in the world of pop music. Clearly, they had not heard that Meek had already turned down an opportunity to work with the Fab Four.

When Meek first met Brian Epstein, the Liverpudlian music store manager was desperate, struggling to find anyone who would give the act he had signed a break. By the spring of 1963 – just over a year after they had their initial encounter – Epstein was the manager of an increasingly important stable of stars: the Beatles' third single was sitting on top of the UK's bestsellers lists (and would stay there for seven weeks, two more than Meek had managed with 'Telstar'), Gerry and the Pacemakers had scored their first number 1 with 'How Do You Do It?' (a song the Beatles had turned down) and Billy J. Kramer and the Dakotas had just begun a fifteen-week chart run with 'Do You Want to Know a Secret?', a song written by Beatles John Lennon and Paul McCartney. No one would have blamed Brian Epstein for steering clear of the man who had so casually turned down a chance to work with the hottest property in the country, but Epstein liked Meek, and he was becoming increasingly aware of just how influential gay men (and lesbian and bisexual women) were in the UK music industry. Soon to move his management offices from Liverpool to London, it made good business sense for Epstein to build up his social and work circles. His early experiences of gay life in London had been traumatic: having Joe to introduce him to the city's social scene must have seemed like an excellent idea.

Meek's disinterest in the Beatles has often been passed off as his missing an opportunity and, like Stigwood, pig-headedly ignoring the onslaught of the beat boom. But that's too simplistic: Meek had not closed his ears to what was happening. As he told Ray Coleman of the *Melody Maker*: 'The pop scene in Britain is getting better in quality all the time, in my opinion. It used to be everyone trying to sound and look like Cliff Richard. Now things are much more individual.' But Meek had to do things his way, and work with acts that were easy to guide, even to manipulate. He was convinced that he knew what song should be sung, how it should be performed, what style of production it needed and who was best to put it across. Musicians were simply the tools he employed to get his ideas out there, he would argue, and the people managing the major record companies knew nothing:

Love and Fury: The Life, Death and Legacy of Joe Meek

'My years as a deejay helped me judge what the public wants,' he insisted. 'So few of the people in this business know that.'[350] Meek had very definite ideas about what was best, and Brian Epstein's boys were not going to be as easy to direct as the artists he was used to working with. They had their own thoughts about what they wanted to do, and Lennon and McCartney especially were not going to be happy recording Meek's compositions; Cliff Bennett and the Rebel Rousers might have looked similar on paper, but their first three A-sides had been Robert Duke songs, while every A- and B-side the Beatles issued in Britain during their lifetime was a Lennon and McCartney (or, later, George Harrison) composition.

The Rebel Rousers could be difficult, as Bennett admitted: '[We] weren't the greatest bunch of blokes to get along with, you know? We were in [Joe's studio] and we're just fucking about, and [he] knew we were doing that and he came in and he really got upset... The band didn't want to do the song. And he slammed the door and said "Get out everybody... If you don't want to do the song, pack up your stuff and get out!" He was very hurt.'[351] If he lost his temper with the Rebel Rousers, he would have positively blown his top had he been subjected to the acerbic tongue of John Lennon.

The Beatles and the Rebel Rousers were rivals of sorts, having rubbed shoulders with each other in Hamburg, and although they were around the same age – and the Rebel Rousers had already signed to a major label – the London-based outfit were somewhat in awe of the Liverpool mob. Still, for a while Meek seemed to hold a personal grudge against the band, telling singer Ray Dexter (who, backed by the Outlaws – under the name the Layabouts – recorded 'The Coalman's Lament' and the Buddy Holly rip-off 'Lonely Weekend' for Meek in 1962, and who claimed to have written the John Leyton B-side 'You Took My Love For Granted') that 'someone should have stamped on those Beatles when they started crawling'.[352]

In truth, Meek was alert to the current 'Beat Boom' trend, but he either did not have Epstein's faith in the quality of artists that were filling the northern dance halls, or he was simply jealous of this upstart's success. Meek had been beavering away at the coalface of pop since the mid-1950s, yet here, seemingly from out of nowhere, was this quietly spoken, impeccably mannered and dressed northern shop manager with a burgeoning stable that was disrupting the industry and threatening to take over the world. Epstein was just about to sign another Liverpool singer, Cilla Black, who

Globetrotter

would go on to become a major star and a national treasure. Meek's latest signing was a 12-year-old schoolgirl from Leytonstone called June Harris who he had spotted when she appeared on the Associated-Rediffusion show *Tuesday Rendezvous*. Little June's performance of the standard 'Birth of the Blues' might have caused him to phone the studio and offer the youngster a three-year contract, but she was hardly going to threaten the sudden, unassailable rise of the Beatles and the other Merseyside groups. His sniping in the press that 'Liverpool characters come down here and ask for auditions, and they think that just because they're from up there they run the British music business' was little more than sour grapes, and his insistence that 'there are so many copyist groups around that the fans will wise up to it and pack it all in' was simply barefaced cheek from a man who would take a musical motif, phrase or effect and flog it to death should it turn out a hit or two along the way. When he added that 'managers, agents and everybody concerned have got to learn that to saturate the disc world with hundreds of tunes sounding the same is to invite disaster,'[353] he demonstrated a distinct lack of self-awareness or irony.

Epstein's agency, NEMS (the initials taken from the family business, North End Music Stores), had recently taken Mersey Beat band Freddie Starr And The Midnighters, and Starr's personal manager, Alan Watts, into the fold and was keen to find them work. Dave Adams, who saw them perform at an ice rink in Streatham, was quick to tell Meek about them, and Epstein soon took his latest signing to audition at RGM Sound. Led by former child actor Fred Farrow, the band recorded a live favourite, 'Peter Gunn Locomotion', but for the A-side of their debut, Meek had other ideas. Despite the potential for Epstein to put work his way, he still believed that the Liverpool sound was a flash in the pan, and although the disc – issued in May 1963 – was credited to the band, for the Geoff Goddard/Barry White (Southern Music's Bob Kingston) song 'Who Told You', Freddie Starr was backed by the Outlaws. Mick Underwood later recalled that at the time 'we were doing five or six sessions a day. We'd start around ten and finish at seven in the evening, while Meek wheeled them in and out!'[354] The finished disc was unsatisfactory and sold poorly, partly because Meek significantly sped up Starr's vocal to give the disc a Freddie and the Dreamers feel. Said Meek, 'I just couldn't believe that nobody had snapped them up before… I'll never forget that recording session. Freddie was one bundle of energy,

Love and Fury: The Life, Death and Legacy of Joe Meek

impersonating many other artistes, cracking gags, making with the funny gestures all round the studio. Freddie genuinely is a show-stopper. But all the boys are individual personalities as well as being great musicians.'[355] Meek may have crowed about Starr's boundless energy to the press, but in the studio he found the Liverpudlian a pain: Starr's antics included pretending that his microphone was cutting out – something that would drive Meek to distraction as he searched for a solution – dropping his trousers and attempting to play the piano with his penis.

Freddie Starr's 'funny gestures' were not cutting it with the teenagers, and his capers may have cracked the session musicians up but they did not make Meek laugh. Perhaps he would do better with the new single he had cut for Decca for Screaming Lord Sutch. Opening with heavy breathing, frantic footsteps and a bloodcurdling scream, 'Jack the Ripper' was blasted by many in the press as being in poor taste, and when the BBC refused to air the disc Meek hit on the idea of having Dave Sutch dress as the notorious Victorian mass murderer and retrace the footsteps of the Ripper around the darkened streets of Whitechapel. In spite of Meek's – and Sutch's – best efforts the single still bombed.

Regardless of Epstein's attempts to disperse any bad feeling between himself and Meek, when buttonholed for an opinion by a reporter, he could not help but have a dig. Still keen to prove he could turn just about anyone – including the supremely ordinary Heinz – into a pop idol, Meek took yet another swing at the Beatles in the press. 'There's nothing new about their sound,' he claimed, explaining that 'Cliff Bennett and the Rebel Rousers have been doing the same thing for a year now, and, up to a point, so has Joe Brown!' That he would use the opportunity to plug Bennett, an artist he had produced four singles for over the previous two years, all of which had failed to grace the charts, was no surprise, but for him to state that 'I don't really understand all the fuss about the Liverpool sound' was short sighted, and to dismiss many of the artists in Epstein's stable with a caustic 'I had hundreds of groups down here from Liverpool before the Beatles made it big but none of them had anything very different. Some of them, in fact, were just rubbish'[356] was a slight that would end up costing him dearly. Epstein, more level-headed and astute than the incendiary Meek, would never be drawn into such controversy, but his protective nature towards his artists meant that any real friendship between the two men would, for now, take a back seat.

CHAPTER 16

Chills and Fever

In the spring of 1963, Welsh songwriters Raymond Godfrey and John Glastonbury brought a four-song tape by the group they managed, Tommy Scott and the Senators, to the door of 304. The band had built up a huge following around the Pontypridd area, but their managers had struggled to convince anyone outside the Welsh valleys that the five-piece were going anywhere. Having already been turned down by several labels, they were running out of options, but, like Brian Epstein a year earlier, Godfrey and Glastonbury were convinced that they had a hot property on their hands and were willing to talk to anyone who might be able to offer them a break. Including, naturally, Joe Meek.

The tracks that Godfrey and Glastonbury brought to Meek were recorded on a portable studio by George Sharland. The somewhat less than salubrious venue chosen for this auspicious occasion was the gentlemen's changing room of the Pontypridd YMCA, the same venue where Scott had made his debut with the Senators. It was an unusual setting for a recording – Sharland had his own studio in Cardiff – but one with lots of natural echo, something that Meek would have undoubtedly appreciated. Certainly, he would have enjoyed a wry smile at the parallel between Scott and the Senators performing in a changing room and their being booked for a session at his own studio, the one he and others often referred to as the Bathroom. When the local paper reported on this momentous event it claimed that the session had taken place in Cardiff and that an EP release was imminent: a ruse to save embarrassment and make the band appear more professional.

Tommy Scott's real name was Thomas Jones Woodward, and he had joined the Senators in December 1961 at the insistence of their leader,

Love and Fury: The Life, Death and Legacy of Joe Meek

bass player Vernon Hopkins. Scott had started out as a drummer with Pontypridd's first rock 'n' roll band, the De-Avalons, but since switching to vocals he had impressed all who heard him with the power of his voice. Within two years Scott would become an international superstar after once again changing his name – to Tom Jones.

The band's trips to Holloway Road were fraught with difficulties. On one occasion, Senator Mike Roberts recalls, 'We had finished a gig, and the boys said, "Let's drive up to London and see Joe." It was a case of "Let's drive up tonight instead of tomorrow".' There was no motorway connecting South Wales to London at that time; construction on the M4 would not be completed for years. Instead, the band piled into Roberts' Atlas van ('an old butcher's van which we'd cleaned up… it was quite clapped out') and drove from Wales, with a stop-off at the Silver Fox transport café (dubbed 'The Fly Factory' for its haphazard approach to cleanliness), through Gloucester and onto London. On their first trip, according to Hopkins, by the time they reached Shepherd's Bush the band decided that they had had enough. Navigating London's busy streets was proving impossible; they would leave the van there and catch the underground to Holloway Road. Clutching their equipment, and with Hopkins on crutches following an incident at a gig, the Senators finally made it to the door of RGM Sound Ltd.

Roberts remembers their first meeting well. '[Meek] was an interesting guy, but strange. His hair was all greased back in a big Teddy Boy quiff, and he had really pallid features which, I suppose, was due to all the drugs he was taking at the time. I remember thinking, "This bugger's weird."'[357] 'He was a bit of a lad,' Raymond Godfrey recalled of his association with Meek. 'He was very short-tempered, very full of anxieties, very hyper and homosexual. He was very difficult to deal with, he wouldn't talk logically.'[358]

The songs the band performed included several written by Godfrey and Glastonbury, using the pseudonym Myron and Byron, and one penned by guitarist Mike Roberts. Roberts remembers Meek insisting that the band 'tune their instruments to the organ he had there, the one he used on 'Telstar'. He also told the drummer that he could only use his own snare drum, and had to use the drum kit that was already set up there,' a kit that Hopkins recalls as 'being set right in front of this big fireplace'.[359] Meek knew how to make the most of the room's natural ambience, and had already set his microphones exactly how he wanted them before the

Chills and Fever

group arrived to record. He was in no mood to alter things around for a bunch of Welsh chancers.

Meek paid for a photo session. 'We went to a park with a photographer and had to find ways to hide Vernon's broken leg, so we were sat in the trees,' Roberts says, and he had clearly made some promises to the group or their management team about getting the tracks placed, because by October they were being advertised back home in Pontypridd as 'Decca recording artistes'.[360] A few weeks later the same newspaper was boasting about how two of the tracks recorded at Meek's studio, 'Lonely Joe' backed with Myron and Byron's 'I Was a Fool', would be the band's first release, due to be issued by Decca in December.

Yet in spite of the excitement locally, nothing happened. Unsurprisingly, the band were disappointed, but as Roberts says, 'It didn't stop us progressing.' The original release date was put back until mid-January 1964, but again this deadline passed with nothing reaching the shops. Meek felt that the tracks were 'not "beaty" enough for a first release',[361] and insisted that the band return for another session to cut four further tunes, including 'Chills and Fever', 'Little Lonely One' and another Myron and Byron original, 'Baby I'm in Love'. This time it was announced that the band's debut would see the light of day in early March. Again, no disc would appear. Roberts recalls inadvertently upsetting Meek on that visit. 'Dave Berry had recorded "My Baby Left Me",' he says, 'and it sounded like Meek's music [although it was produced by Decca's Mike Smith, the guitarist on the session was one of Meek's session men, Jimmy Page]. Well, we went up and said that "Oh, we like the single you did with Dave Berry. You did well there," and he scowled and said, "That's nothing to do with me!"'[362]

It was only a minor upset: with recording sessions going well and the promise of an imminent release, the band and their managers started to make plans to move to London. However, they were only going to do that once they had Meek's guarantee that their first single had a release date. Godfrey and Glastonbury spent days on the telephone trying to get through to Meek, just to be told that the producer was too busy to take their call. 'Tom was signed through us to Joe as a record producer,' Godfrey revealed. 'And then Joe would do a tape-lease deal with one of the majors. We kept pestering him about when there would be a release…

Love and Fury: The Life, Death and Legacy of Joe Meek

Very often we would ring Joe and he would never come to the telephone. He seemed to have an army of people around him. Eventually, we thought it had to be now or never. So we saw Tom and said, "Look, Tom, we are not happy with the way things are going and we are going to lay the law down because this could go on indefinitely."

'So we went to see Joe Meek and knocked at his door at 10 a.m. after driving up from Wales through the night. At first he wouldn't see us, but we insisted and at last he came and we confronted him. He put his hands on his head and shouted and screamed. We said we didn't want to hear that. What we wanted to hear was what was happening and why we didn't have a release. Then he said he had had enough anyway and wanted to break the contract. We said that was fine by us because nothing was happening. So we agreed to break the contract with him and went back to Wales and told Tom and the boys we had broken with Joe.'[363] Hopkins recalls an incensed Meek later remonstrating with him 'in a thick Gloucestershire accent that "You buggers cost me £20 for them photos! I want my money back!"' Jones was furious that his management team had left London without the tapes that the band had worked so hard on and went to see Meek himself. 'He was saying that he was going to get these tapes released. EMI were going to have it, and I went to EMI, and they didn't know anything about it, and then I went to Decca, and they didn't know... and then I went for him. I went back up to [his office], and I said, "You fucker!" I went across the desk at him, and it was the first time I ever saw anybody fly! It's unbelievable, he was like Peter Pan! One minute he was standing there, behind the desk, and the next minute he was sitting on the mantelpiece. I thought, "How the fuck did he get up there?"'[364] Meek later recalled the incident far less colourfully: 'Tom, the group, his manager and all arrived on my doorstep one morning and Tom asked me, "How can people turn down a powerful record like 'Little Lonely One' when the hit parade is full of ****?" Well, what could I say? I'd done everything I could – in fact spent £300. There really wasn't much else I could do, so I said if they wanted I would cancel my contract with them, which although it would mean the tapes we had cut were now my property and I could place them with a record company if I liked, would enable them to approach the recording companies direct.'[365]

Godfrey could not understand why Meek, so enthusiastic about their future when he first met the band, had lost interest so quickly, but the

Chills and Fever

management team were unaware that the members of the Senators – like other artists who passed through 304 – had been gossiping about Meek's sexuality. Vernon Hopkins recalled seeing a naked Heinz in Joe's bed one morning. 'The story was that Heinz was his boyfriend,' Mike Roberts confirms. 'And Heinz always seemed to be there, but in those days I really didn't know what homosexuality was. Joe lived on the upper floor, in a flat, and Heinz was always coming up and down the stairs from there.' (Meek's former assistant Tony Kent told Jim Blake and Chris Knight that 'Heinz was definitely bisexual... As far as I know he used to sleep in Joe's bed.')[366] Jones himself scarpered down the stairs of 304 during one session after loudly claiming that the producer had become a little over-friendly and placed one of his hands in the pocket of Tom's rather tight and revealing jeans: 'He tried touching Tom up,' says Hopkins. 'We were loading up the van outside Joe's, and Tom came running down the stairs shouting: "He just touched my bollocks! That bastard grabbed my balls!"'[367]

'To each his own; I don't hold it against him,' Jones admitted to director Mike Figgis for his film *Red, White and Blues*, part of the seven-episode documentary series *The Blues*. 'He was like, "Those jeans fit you well, don't they?... It looks like you've got a bit of a..." And I said, "Well, yeah, it serves its purpose!" I thought, "What the fuck's he on about?"'[368] Following Meek's clumsy move on Jones, the band and singer were somewhat reluctant to continue working with the producer; however, they would return for one final session to finish off the recordings. In Jones' autobiography, *Over the Top and Back*, the singer recalled how a disagreement over microphone technique quickly developed into a furious, and frightening, altercation.

'"You won't need to be so close to the microphone," he tells me. "You have a very loud voice." After the first take he returns from the control room looking like thunder. In his hand is a gun. "Didn't I tell you to back off from the microphone?"

He points the gun right at me, at arm's length from himself.

"Jesus Christ!" I shout.

Bang!

My ears ring and the room reels in shock. It's a starting pistol.'[369]

'I remember the incident well,' says Roberts. 'We had four numbers to do. At one point Tom went into a higher register, and Meek stopped recording, came into the studio and said, "Tom, when you hit that register

Love and Fury: The Life, Death and Legacy of Joe Meek

move the mic away from your mouth. So that you don't peak too much on the recording equipment." So we started again and Tom did the same thing; he didn't move the mic away. I can't remember if it was the second time or the third time, but he did it at least twice, and having done that he was singing when Meek stopped, and he dived into the room with a pistol and he said, "I told you to move the fucking mic away when you hit that note!" And he fired the gun! Tom clutched his chest, and our mouths just dropped.'[370]

Luckily for them, although Meek could not help the band get their big break, Decca remained interested. However, the issue was further complicated by Decca signing a second singer called Tommy Scott, and insisting that the Welshman change his name. Scott adopted his mother's maiden name, becoming Tom Jones; the band, after learning of another act called the Senators, changed their name too, initially to the Playboys before settling on the Squires. Their debut, a re-recorded version of 'Chills and Fever' (produced by Decca staffer Peter Sullivan), finally made it to the shops at the end of August, almost eighteen months after they first met Meek.

Another RGM Sound production from around this time, but issued early the following year, came about almost by accident. Coventry-based act the Atlantic Showband had been in London to play a show at an Irish club, but were also interested in scoring a record deal for themselves and their lead singer, Jimmy Lennon (no relation to the Beatle). The following day three of the band – Lennon, guitarist Philip 'Pip' Witcher and drummer Bruce Finlay were in a car heading back to the Midlands. 'We were on the way home,' says Witcher. 'We passed his studio and I recognised it. I said, "Wait here," and I went up to the door and spoke to Joe.'[371] Witcher had a tenuous connection to Meek: their mothers knew each other (Witcher's grandmother was from Newent, and his family would visit often) and, watching a television show that featured Meek and Heinz, his mother had commented, 'Oh, that must be Biddy Meek's son.' Tenuous indeed, but it was enough for Meek to allow them over the threshold. 'I told him that our guy had written a song and he said, "Come up." We recorded it there and then. That was the first studio I'd been in,' Witcher recalls. 'I didn't know any better.' The guitarist would later record at Decca's studio in Hampstead and at Pye in Great Cumberland Place. 'Then I got to know what a studio was really like!'[372]

Chills and Fever

In one short session Meek recorded the song that Jimmy Lennon had written, a country-and-western-tinged novelty track entitled 'I Learned To Yodel', with Lennon doing a more than passable job at yodelling, and a cover of Gene Pitney's 'Louisiana Mama', which was marred by Lennon performing a pastiche Presley vocal and by Meek's inability to resist tinkering, speeding up the backing vocals until they resembled Elvis's own Jordanaires on helium. His mother's friend's grandson might not have made it, but Meek was always keen to give anyone with a local connection a break, and that October he brought in Gloucestershire's top jazz band, the seven-piece Bill Nile and the Delta Jazzmen to audition at 304, an act that had once included a young, blond-haired saxophone player from Cheltenham called Brian Jones.

While the Tornados were appearing in theatres around the country, the band's former bassist, soon to be known by the monomym Heinz, made his debut as a solo singer. On 3 May, Decca released Meek's own composition 'Dreams Do Come True' backed with the Meek/Burt co-write 'Been Invited to a Party'. The following night, supported by the Outlaws, he unveiled his live act for the first time to a paying audience at the Matrix Ballroom in Coventry, while viewers at home could see him perform the song on that evening's edition of the popular ABC-TV show *Thank Your Lucky Stars* (the Tornados appeared on the same episode, performing their latest single, 'Robot'). Two days later he was in Birmingham, on a bill that included Jerry Lee Lewis, Gene Vincent, the Outlaws and Andy Cavell. This onslaught of activity should have ensured a hit, especially as 'Dreams Do Come True' had the added cachet of being included in the upcoming British beat movie *Farewell Performance*, a potboiler about the murder of a pop singer for which Meek had been employed as musical director. Meek secured a guest spot for the Tornados (who had already appeared, albeit briefly, in the comedy *Just for Fun*), and Heinz was given a small but significant acting role that dramatised the launch of his solo career. 'He starts as a member of a group backing a pop singer,' Meek enthused. 'Then, half way through, the singer goes off – and Heinz gets his solo chance. It's a good film, with an interesting story. And I think you'll be very impressed with the way Heinz works. He's star material, all right.'[373]

Although Meek was keen to tell the media that the boy 'will be the biggest star in the pop world within a year',[374] his transition from bass player to solo

Love and Fury: The Life, Death and Legacy of Joe Meek

singer got off to a shaky start, and after several attempts to capture a decent take for the A-side, Meek employed a second vocalist to thicken out the sound: what sounds like a double-tracked vocal from Heinz is actually two singers, Heinz and Billy Dean, singing the same part. Heinz's vocal performance, while more than adequate for the film, simply would not cut it on a hit record, so Meek had session singer Dean (aka Billy Gray and Mark Douglas) 'enhance' Heinz's voice. 'I used to hit a few duff notes,' the singer acknowledged. 'Everyone does occasionally... I'm not embarrassed about it.'[375]

Disker, of the *Liverpool Echo*, was none too impressed with Meek's bag of production tricks, which he described as 'a clanking, clanging, tinkling, thudding network of unreal instrumental sounds',[376] and the disc-buying public seemed to agree: the disc is reputed to have sold less than 400 copies. A second single from the movie, performed by Irish bricklayer Chad Carson (who dubbed the singing voice of the film's lead, actor David Kernan), featured the Meek originals 'They Were Wrong' and 'Don't Pick On Me' (which had its title altered to 'Stop Picking on Me' on stock copies) sold even fewer. Twenty-year-old Desmond Carson (his real name) had auditioned for Meek in late 1962 and had already cut what he thought would be his first single, a song called 'Jesse James'. Heinz would later cover 'Don't Pick On Me', but 'Jesse James', featuring a young Ritchie Blackmore on lead guitar, would remain unissued for twenty-five years. Carson's voice drew comparisons to Elvis, which caused one irate fan to write to the *Record Mirror* demanding that the single be banned, as it was 'ruining Elvis's name and reputation'.[377]

Ignoring the odd complaint from the even odder Elvis fan, the film was well-enough received to persuade producers Rank to offer Heinz another role, this time as Ron, a motorbike-riding postal messenger and erstwhile pop star in the B-movie musical *Live It Up!* (released in the US as *Sing and Swing*). Meek boasted that 'he was so good in "Farewell Performance" that he was immediately snapped up by the same company for another major movie',[378] although his acting in *Live It Up!* – which began shooting at Pinewood studios on 29 April 1963 – would prove so wooden that he would not be offered any further film roles. Meek was brought in by Columbia's Norrie Paramor and wrote and produced the majority of music used in the film, a silly tale about four GPO messengers putting together their own rock 'n' roll act co-starring future Small Face Steve Marriott, Jenny Moss (who would sing another Meek

Chills and Fever

composition, 'Please Let it Happen to Me' in the film) and briefly featuring Mitch Mitchell, who would later work as a session man for Meek before joining the Jimi Hendrix Experience. For years it was believed that Marriott recorded an unreleased song, 'Love Gone Away', at 304, but research has revealed this to be by another act, the Birds of Prey.

Outside his work on the big screen, Meek reasoned that the best way to promote his boy as a solo star was to keep him out on the road, and during May Heinz appeared, backed by the Outlaws, sandwiched on a bill between rock idols Gene Vincent and Jerry Lee Lewis. Following his one-off appearance in Coventry, these would be the nervous young singer's first solo appearances since leaving the Tornados, and a doting Meek had spent money to make sure that he stood out, dressing him in an expensive black suit and buying him a brand new, black-and-white electric guitar. The first show of the tour was at the Town Hall, Birmingham. The singer had been filming in Pinewood, and he had to drive over 100 miles after a full day's shooting in around two and a half hours if he was to make his entrance on time. The shattered star arrived at the venue with minutes to spare, and he later described the welcome that greeted him as akin to 'a boxer coming out of his corner and running smack into a sucker punch'. He was only on stage for ten minutes, just four numbers, but the end could not come quickly enough. 'My mere appearance seemed to trigger off a barrage of full force-hostility,' [379] he ruminated.

If Meek had bothered to turn up to Birmingham, or to any of these shows, he would have been appalled to hear the audience chanting 'Off! Off! Off!' before his star had sung his first note. Perhaps if he had witnessed the response, he would have been less vitriolic towards the newcomers from Liverpool, but as Dave Sutch noted, 'He had too many commitments. He'd say to you, "Yes, I'll come and see your act," on a certain day... "Oh, I'd love to see it," and then he'd find that he'd overbooked, that he'd got about five groups on that day which he often did.' [380] Heinz himself was badly shaken by the reaction, and if it had not been for Gene Vincent, who came to see him backstage after he had finished his spot to offer his encouragement, he may have given up on the idea of solo stardom right then and there.

Heinz may have faltered, but the Outlaws made a big impact with the visiting American talent, and Jerry Lee Lewis decided to keep them on as his backing band for further British dates his management had lined up. Meek had little choice but to put together a new band to back Heinz, and built a three-piece outfit around Soundtracks guitarist Roy Phillips. 'He formed the Saints,' Phillips recalls, 'with Tab Martin on bass and Ricky Winter on drums for us to back Heinz and many more of the acts that arrived at the studio, including Andy Cavell.'

The Saints appeared, backing Cavell, as the opening credits ran in *Live It Up!*, performing Meek's composition 'Don't Take You From Me'. 'I was getting a lot of sessions from Joe,' says Phillips, who was starting to see more and more of Joe's infamous temper. 'He was a fiery person anyway. When he kicked off we all tripped down to the fish and chip shop, three doors down on Holloway Road. Joe was always professional in the studio until something broke normality, then it was all down to the chippy!'[381] Cavell had already recorded a couple of singles for Meek, including compositions by Dave Adams ('Lonely Soldier Boy') and by Meek himself, who had written the A-side of Cavell's debut single, 'Hey There, Cruel Heart'. Most of the film's musical interludes featured Meek acts, including Cavell, Heinz and the Outlaws and his recent signing Rosemary Cottnam, who recorded under the name Kim Roberts (Meek having ditched her chosen stage name of Kim Rayner). The film also featured a number of other acts performing Meek-written material, such as hit instrumental act Sounds Incorporated (who had recently signed to Brian Epstein's NEMS organisation: Sounds Inc. would issue Meek's composition 'Keep Moving' from the film, backed with 'Order of the Keys', written by Meek again, using his Duke pseudonym) and US rocker Gene Vincent, who appeared in the film singing 'Temptation Baby', a song that was recorded by Meek at 304 in late April 1963 and that would later be issued (in an alternate version, not produced by Meek) as the B-side to his 1963 single 'Where Have You Been All My Life'.*

Having Vincent sing one of his numbers in the film was a considerable accomplishment for Meek. Their meeting – and the subsequent recording – came about by pure luck, after Outlaw Ken Lundgren saw an advertisement placed by Vincent's management for a group to back the singer on his UK tour. Vincent was now living in Britain, in a flat in Notting Hill, after US

---

* A take from the Meek-produced sessions for 'Temptation Baby' would finally surface in 2024, on the 10-inch album *Live It Up*.

Chills and Fever

fame waned and the tax man came calling. Often in severe pain after a motorbike accident which had almost resulted in the amputation of his leg (an injury exacerbated by his involvement in the crash that killed Eddie Cochran), Vincent could be just as volatile as Meek, especially if he had been drinking. On tour in early 1963 he pulled a gun on former Shadows bassist Jet Harris, almost taking John Leyton out into the bargain. An audition for the Outlaws was set up at 304, and the band (Hodges, Blackmore, Underwood and Lundgren) would also back Vincent at Hamburg's famous Star Club as well as on episodes of the BBC radio show *Saturday Club* in July and September: Meek effectively signed them over to Don Arden, who was able to get them on the show as Vincent's band.

Within a fortnight of the release of his solo single, Meek announced that he was accompanying Heinz on a trip to Paris to line up live dates, secure the release of a French-language version of 'Dreams Do Come True' and to discuss the singer's appearance in a French movie. Meek had already seen success with French- and German-language versions of John Leyton hits, but it looks like the sudden interest from the French in the German-born singer's career was little more than a smokescreen to cover the pair enjoying a short Parisian holiday, paid for by the newly established Heinz Burt Ltd, a company set up to manage the career of the object of Meek's desire. Major Banks was not involved, having already made it clear he was unhappy with the amount of time, effort and money Meek was expending on the bass player-cum-singer, and nor was he asked to become a partner in another company Meek set up around the same time, Joe Meek Enterprises Ltd.

Meek's co-director in both of these new companies was Thomas Edwin Southey Shanks, an accountant, property investor and former solicitor's clerk who tried to rein in Meek's spending by suggesting that the company lease the pop star's expensive new toys – the boat (originally called the *Golden Heinz* but quickly renamed *Globetrotter*) and a Ford Zephyr car – rather than buy them outright. It was a sensible decision that would save the company tax, but one that would come back and bite Meek on the ass a few years down the line. Initially though, Meek was just happy to get Heinz off his beloved motorbike and into something a little safer.

Shanks had been involved in the entertainment world for a long time: he was a partner in early pop video company Telebroadcasts Ltd, and had been on the management teams of singer Petula Clark and orchestra leader Ray Martin. He was also a musician, a former orchestral conductor and choirmaster, which in Meek's eyes made him a much more suitable business partner than the decidedly unmusical Major. Perhaps buoyed by this new business success, Meek successfully renegotiated his contract with the Major, putting him on a better deal and setting it out for the first time that any songwriting royalties due to Meek were to be accounted for separately to his production and A&R work for RGM Sound. With that guarantee in print, Meek stopped using his Robert Duke pseudonym. Completing a trifecta of new companies Meek set up without the Major's knowledge or involvement, in the summer of 1963 he formed a new music publishing company, Blue Bell Music, with Charles Blackwell. The company did not last long, but among the songs published were compositions by Meek for Mike Berry and Andy Cavell.

Meek's family could not understand Joe's conviction that Heinz was going to be a huge star. 'He spent thousands on Heinz,' Eric Meek later revealed. 'But he had no power in his voice. In my opinion he couldn't bloody sing! He wouldn't have gone anywhere without Joe.' His older brother, Arthur, believed that Meek's attempt to turn Heinz into a solo star was swayed by pressure from the fans: 'When Heinz was in the Tornados, the Tornados were doing very well… but all the mail that came to the Tornados was addressed to Heinz, because he was the best-looking of the five, and Joe thought he'd do well on his own.' 'He came and stayed with us a couple of times,' Eric added. 'He'd bring the Wild Boys, or Heinz, or Tab Martin… and Lional of course.'[382]

The reason that Meek was happy to invest so much time and effort into Heinz's career was simple, and although Heinz – and his family – would always deny that there was any kind of sexual relationship between the two men, those who saw them on a regular basis were convinced otherwise. Meek regularly tried it on with the young men he took a fancy too, although just as many went through 304 unscathed, including Tony Kent who revealed that 'he never made advances to me. Bob Stigwood did, but not Joe Meek. Maybe it was because I was working for him, that may have been the reason, and at the time Heinz was living there…'[383]

Heinz had indeed moved in, and, as Peter Jay notes, 'it couldn't have been easy living with Joe'.[384] After he was pulled over following a minor car

Chills and Fever

accident in Stoke-on-Trent, Heinz gave his home address as 304 Holloway Road. Graham Sharp, guitarist with Flip and the Dateliners, recalls an incident that many of Joe's artists would gossip about: 'It was Heinz, or one of his group, who told me that they had all gone out to a restaurant. For some reason Heinz and Joe had a disagreement and Joe shoved Heinz's meal right in his face.'[385] However tempestuous their relationship was, the singer was soon boasting about how he was enjoying all the trappings of a pop star lifestyle: 'Most of my money goes on clothes,' he revealed. 'I have 14 suits and 40 shirts. I pay around £40 for a suit because it has to look just right. I have a 28ft motor-cruiser back home in Southampton. It cost £3,000 and is made of fibre glass. I share this with my recording manager Joe Meek.'[386]

CHAPTER 17

Just Like Eddie

Having filmed their segments for *Live It Up!*, in June 1963 Heinz and the Saints were off on tour. 'Heinz was OK,' says Phillips, 'but he was quite a prima donna. That didn't bother us as we were getting paid for this rubbish!' What did bother him, though, was the constant threat of being hit in the face by a flying tin of baked beans, a favourite prank from Teddy Boys wanting Heinz off stage so that Gene Vincent could begin his twenty minutes. 'That was rather a worry at times. I was always worried about when the next open tin of baked beans would missile from the audience, especially as we wore white suits when working with Heinz. Luckily, I was only ever caught once.'[387] Not one to take things lying down, at one show Heinz retaliated by taking off a shoe and aiming it at one of his bean-laden assailants.

While on tour, the Saints issued their first single under their own name, their only chart hit, a cover of the surfing instrumental 'Wipe Out', the original of which (by the Surfaris) was then riding high in the US charts, and which became the original theme tune to the TV pop show *Ready Steady Go!* The Savages' Tony Dangerfield would recall another attempt by Meek to capture something suitable to introduce the show: 'We were recording a try out for a new *Ready Steady Go!* theme he'd been asked to do. He kept singing this weird tune to us and we tried desperately to translate it for him. It just wasn't working and I remember him running out of the studio crying.'[388] "Wipe Out' was the first single the Saints ever put out,' Phillips explains. 'The laugh on the end was Ricky Winter after making a mistake at the coda. Joe kept it in.'[389]

It seemed as if everyone who worked at 304 was busy. While the Saints went marching off with Heinz, the Outlaws were backing Gene Vincent on

Just Like Eddie

tour and, with the band playing shows around the country, HMV decided that the timing was right for a new release. In June, Meek brought the Outlaws back into RGM Sound to cut four new tracks for an EP. Only one would surface, the Chas Hodges-penned instrumental, 'Hobo'. Hodges' composition was considered too good to be wasted on an EP and would, in fact, grace the A-side of a new single, but after spending the morning recording it, they realised that they had not decided on what would appear on the reverse. In typical fashion, according to an article in *Record Mirror*, 'when they went to lunch from Joe's place he penned the flip side for them – arranged it and cut a demo. When they returned they found a new song awaiting them.' Meek's composition, 'That Set The Wild West Free', should have been the B-side, and the performance was captured in a couple of hours but, with a fine double-tracked vocal from Hodges, it was instead chosen as the plug side. The tracks laid down for the aborted EP would languish in the Tea Chests for decades.

By now Meek could have the choice of any number of better-positioned – or equipped – premises for his studio, but he chose to stay in the ramshackle collection of rooms above the Shentons' leather goods store. 'I like it here,' he told journalist Leslie Thomas.* 'But we can't record after six o'clock because of the neighbours. The old dump has been lucky for me and I want to stay.' Although he boasted that he had made 'around thirty thousand quid now' from 'Telstar', that was not his main motivation: 'I don't care much about money,' he said before explaining his approach as he showed Thomas around his control room. 'I made some of this gear myself. I like making new sounds, fiddling about until I get the right one.' [390] He did not reveal that he had yet to see much in the way of financial gain from the multi-million-selling tune.

Meek may have thought the place lucky, but anyone studying his results might have had a different opinion. In the last week of May, Meek had no less than four singles issued: Peter Jay and the Jaywalkers' 'Poet and Peasant' (a rocking rewrite of an overture by Franz von Suppé), Freddie Starr and the Midnighters with the Geoff Goddard co-write 'Who Told You', and 'Ice Cream Man' from the Tornados (composed by Meek and featured in *Farewell Performance*), all on Decca, and Glenda Collins with 'I

---

* Thomas would become an author, best known for his 1966 novel *The Virgin Soldiers*.

Lost My Heart at the Fairground' on HMV. Only one would chart, with the Tornados' latest offering peaking at number 18 nationally.

At least one of those other releases deserved better; in fact, its success had been written in the stars. Glenda Collins had already made a name for herself on television and radio as a 16-year-old when, in 1960, she was signed to Decca. Despite heavy press promotion none of her three singles sold well and she was dropped by the company. Although she still found work on the BBC Radio programme *The Beat Show*, no one was interested in signing her as a recording artist, and she had all but given up hope when her father decided to pay Joe Meek a visit. By May 1963 Meek had signed her to an exclusive contract and she had recorded her first single for RGM Sound, Meek's composition 'I Lost My Heart at the Fairground', with backing provided by the Outlaws.

The pair worked well together, with Glenda telling the *New Record Mirror* that she was impressed with Meek's work ethic: 'He has young ideas and it's a pleasure working with him. He lets me sing out and I'm sure he's captured the real me on disc for the first time. And at the first go. I've never been completely satisfied with my recording in the past but this one suits me. Let's hope it suits the fans.'[391] More than a decade later her view had not changed: 'I was very happy working with Joe Meek, I got on extremely well with him and I was very fond of him... He did believe in me, and of course that's a very big thing when you're an artist.'[392] Meek's trust in otherworldly signs convinced him that the disc would be a hit: television clairvoyant and newspaper astrologer Maurice Woodruff had already predicted that Glenda's next release would sell in excess of a quarter of a million, and Meek swathed her performance in authentic fairground sound effects to help bolster its appeal, but sadly to little benefit.

Critics judged the production harshly, claiming that Collins would be unable to perform the song on stage: 'To do it justice she would need the backing of a hurdy-gurdy, clattery dodgem cars and a few hundred yelping extras,' wrote Mike Nevard in the *Daily Herald*, who had an extra dig at Meek's usual collection of 'spacecraft effects, howling winds and other noises'.[393] 'Roll up and get your gimmicks galore,' snarked Disker in the *Liverpool Echo*. 'Tornado-type sounds tumble about our ears on this deck and somewhere behind the mass of irrelevant noises the voice of songstress Glenda Collins echoes through,' although he did offer some scant praise:

Just Like Eddie

'I hate to admit it because I don't like his methods of studio-doctoring every disc he makes, but I enjoyed Meek's 'Fairground' recording for all its obvious faults.'[394] Meek was used to being knocked: 'I have a lot of critics in the business,' he told *Melody Maker*. 'They are just damned jealous because one man has done so well... Why are people so jealous of anybody who gets up and works?'[395] Sadly, Woodruff's prediction did not come true, and despite plenty of television, radio and press coverage 'I Lost My Heart at the Fairground' became the first in a series of eight singles that the singer made for Meek that offered much but continually missed the mark.

Although he already had a perfectly good backing band in the Saints, Meek opted for the latest version of the Outlaws to accompany Heinz on his new single. Issued in July 1963, 'Just Like Eddie' was another Geoff Goddard tribute to a late rock idol, this time Eddie Cochran, who died after the car he was travelling in went off the road between Bath and Chippenham in 1960.

The song was initially recorded as an instrumental; that was not unusual for Outlaws sessions, as Meek would bring the band in to record track after track, and often the first they would know about whose voice would end up accompanying them was when they heard the song on the radio. This time, Heinz was present, but he was unwilling to record his vocal with the rest of the band. 'We never really liked him,' Chas Hodges recalled. 'But when he first became a singer, we started backing him. We used to do the backing tracks, but he wouldn't sing. We'd say, "Come on, Heinz, what key do you want the song in?"... But he wouldn't sing. I think he was a bit embarrassed. We'd say, "Are you sure?" because we've got to do the backing track and if you do your voice later and it's in the wrong key, then it's all that time wasted. "Yeah, that's all right," he said.' It was a decision that would cause a huge headache for the band. Several days later, when Ken Lundgren and Ritchie Blackmore paid a visit to Meek to check on any upcoming live bookings, the producer flew into a rage. 'He went berserk,' Hodges reported. 'He grabbed the phone and threw the phone on the floor, threw everything around the room... There was no reason at all for it.' After the pair told Hodges about their recording manager's sudden, unprovoked outburst, the bass player called Meek to find out what had happened. 'I said, "What's the matter, Joe?" And he said, "I know what

201

Love and Fury: The Life, Death and Legacy of Joe Meek

you've fucking done! I fucking know what you've done! You've played that song in the wrong key for Heinz on purpose because you don't like him. I know you fucking done it!" I was taken aback, you know? I said, "You're joking! We tried our hardest to get Heinz to sing it..." He said, "I spent a whole day trying to get him to sing it and he couldn't do it." I mean, he couldn't sing anyway, but he would not have it that we hadn't done it on purpose. I said, "I swear to you, Joe, we never." We used to get up to a lot of pranks, but to spend hours on a recording for a joke is something that we wouldn't do.'[396]

The red mist that had descended over the producer did not last for long, fortunately, as Meek and the Outlaws had plenty of work to get on with, including having them re-record 'Just Like Eddie' in a suitable key for his prima donna singer. 'Just Like Eddie', with its distinctive guitar work from Ritchie Blackmore, entered the charts in August and by the beginning of October was in the Top 5. Cochran's bereaved mother was so moved by the tribute that she wrote to Heinz to thank him. "Just Like Eddie' was a fabulous thing,' Peter Jay acknowledges. 'Nobody else could have done it other than Joe. It has that magic.'[397] Robert Stigwood had Mike Sarne record a copycat version for Parlophone accompanied by Mike Berry's new backing band the Innocents (a troupe from Manchester formerly known as Bobby Angelo and the Tuxedos). Credited as a Robert Stigwood Production, the mix is unmistakably influenced by Meek's methods, with his trademark drum dampening, close miking and heavy reverb.

On 13 July 1963, shortly before 'Just Like Eddie' hit the shops, while touring with a Don Arden-promoted package that saw Gene Vincent and Heinz share top billing, a queue of people waiting patiently at a bus stop in Shrewsbury were 'enveloped in a cloud of white flour' when a 3lb bag was hurled at them from a passing vehicle. The culprit was one 'Richard Hugh Blackmore (18), a guitarist', who, to relieve the boredom of travelling between gigs had taken to jettisoning flour bombs from the window of the Outlaws' van, a habit he had caught after witnessing Tab Martin of the Saints lobbing cheese rolls at passers-by as their own van sped off down the highway. When Meek learned of the pranks his acts were pulling he found it funny at first; however, he soon decided that Blackmore had gone too far when the Outlaws were summoned to court. 'I did it as a joke,' Blackmore told the police. 'I didn't mean to hit them. I meant the bag to burst behind

Just Like Eddie

them. I am very sorry.'[398] He was fined £2. The van, which was leased by Joe Meek Associates Ltd, would be taken back by the owners after one too many of Blackmore's pranks.

It was not the only trick the teenager pulled – on one occasion, according to fellow Outlaw Ken Lundgren, he 'laid a series of turds around Brenda Lee's dressing-room toilet' (during March 1963 the band backed Miss Lee and Mike Berry on tour) – and he and Heinz baited each other mercilessly. Blackmore's practical jokes could get other members of the Outlaws in trouble, and Lundgren recalled other incidents, including throwing things at 'a policeman in Guernsey doing point duty [and at] a pedestrian on Oxford Street',[399] which brought on a severe dressing-down from Meek'. These shenanigans were annoying, but whatever anger Meek had was soon forgotten: three days after the flour-bag incident the Outlaws were due to record a session for the BBC (their guitarist referred to on the contract for this and all subsequent BBC Radio shows as Ricky Lackmoor), but it was claimed that the band were under contract to Don Arden's Anglo-American Artists company, rather than RGM Sound, a little subterfuge to ensure that the Outlaws – having failed their original audition – could be employed to back Gene Vincent on *Saturday Club*.

Blackmore's juvenile behaviour was annoying, but having Larry Parnes or Don Arden take money out of his pocket was worse. The already overstretched Meek decided to promote his own package, and sent Heinz out on a short tour supported by the Outlaws, along with other acts from 304, including Freddie Starr and the Midnighters, Glenda Collins and Andy Cavell and the Saints. It was hardly the best-planned line-up, as none of the acts on the bill, apart from Heinz, were making much headway with teen audiences: Cavell's latest single, the saccharine death disc 'Andy', failed to click and its proposed follow-up, 'Hey Sugar' was aborted. Starr would record three singles with Meek, none of which seemed to gel with record buyers. By the time of the last one, September 1964's 'Never Cry on Someone's Shoulder', he had already been dropped by Brian Epstein's NEMS agency and, with the public seemingly indifferent to his talents, he would not release a single again until 1971, by which time he was making a name for himself as a comedian. Starr would claim, in a 2002 autobiography, that one night, after a recording session went on into the early hours, he slept in Meek's spare bedroom and awoke to find the producer naked and

Love and Fury: The Life, Death and Legacy of Joe Meek

tumescent in his bed, and that Meek only left after Starr threatened to 'beat seven kinds of shit out of him'.[400] No one who knew Meek has ever corroborated this story; it would have been highly unusual for a recording session at 304 to have gone on until 1 a.m., as Starr maintained, and no one else has ever claimed that Meek had climbed uninvited under the sheets with them.

The massive, insuperable success of the Beatles and the other Merseybeat acts knocked Meek's confidence in his own abilities. Talking to the *Daily Mail*, he berated the Liverpool sound: 'For eight months it has been bash, bash, bash. They could have taken a nursery rhyme and accompanied it with guitar and bass and it would have been as good as anything else. It was even true of some of the Beatles records. They were very catchy, but half-way through they would get boring. Nothing new happened.'[401] Even so, he plagued Chas Hodges and the other artists in his stable for information about the band. Having struck out with Freddie Starr, in another fruitless effort to get a foothold in the beat boom, Meek recorded Manchester band the Beat Boys, whose sole single, 'That's My Plan' was issued by Decca in September 1963: the song, which starts with the line 'I want to hold your hand', was released more than a month before the Beatles would record their international chart topper 'I Want to Hold Your Hand', the single that broke them in the United States.

But before Liverpool took on America, the city first had to conquer London, and a stream of Scouse aspirants continued to beat a path to RGM Sound. One Saturday, three young girls from Liverpool turned up unannounced on Meek's doorstep. The suitcases that they carried were painted with their names – Christine, Pauline and Sheila – and that of their vocal trio, the Blue Notes. Meek, as usual, was working and too busy to see them. Terry O'Neil politely tried to turn them away, but the girls were persistent and, having travelled all the way to the capital in the hope of meeting the great man himself, were not going to be turned away without a few minutes of his company. Reluctantly, O'Neil let them in.

Luckily for them, the trio happened to turn up on the very day that Meek was being filmed by a television documentary crew; interest in the girls from the film crew forced Meek's hand, and he not only met with them but signed them on the spot. Several sessions with the Blue Notes

Just Like Eddie

would take place over the next six months, some with the girls backed by the Tornados, but although Meek was impressed with Pauline Burke's songwriting abilities, between them they failed to find the right material for single release. Frustrated with the lack of progress, and the commuting back and forth from Liverpool to London, the trio split up before anything could be issued.

Anxious to climb aboard the big beat train, Meek turned his attention to the new Peter Jay and the Jaywalkers single. It was an astute move: the group had already been booked to join the Beatles on a tour which would kick off in Cheltenham on 1 November, and it seemed sensible to find something more 'Beatley' for their next release.* The song chosen was 'Kansas City', the Jerry Leiber and Mike Stoller classic which had been a staple of the Beatles' live set for a couple of years. 'The problem with the band was that none of us could sing!' Jay laughs.

'As soon as the Beatles hit, all the A&R people were saying that they wanted us to record a song, so we did 'Kansas City' and had a close miss with 'Do You Love Me', which we thought, "That's going to be a hit", like 'Twist and Shout'. Brian Poole and the Tremeloes did it as well: we were both with Decca, and it went to the head of the company to decide. The Tremeloes had already had a hit with "Twist and Shout", and so they went with their version. We had 50,000 fans in our fan club, and a load of them decided to attack the Tremeloes' van because they'd nicked our record. I had to plead with them to leave them alone, tell them, "Look, it's not their fault," but they were letting their tyres down!

'Decca didn't really know what to do with us: we had a big presence everywhere, we were on the front pages of the pop weeklies for a couple of years, but they couldn't find the right thing for us and neither could we. We were working continually, we never had any studio time – we'd go to Joe Meek's, we'd have a couple of hours to do an A-Side, have a cup of tea, do the B-side and then get back in the van and drive to Leeds, do two shows, come back to London... It was difficult, but of course that would all

---

* The Beatles' 1 November appearance in Cheltenham is principally remembered today for the first appearance of the word 'Beatlemania' in the national press, in the *Daily Mirror*'s report on the show the following day. However, 'Beatlemania' had already been used on the front page of the *Newcastle Evening Chronicle* a full week earlier, on 25 October 1963.

Love and Fury: The Life, Death and Legacy of Joe Meek

change. We were working with Joe at a time when the balance of power was shifting between the artists and the record companies. Then, an A&R guy would say, "This is what you're doing," and you would practise it and come in and do it as quickly as possible and go. After that bands were given the time to go in there and create something in the studio, like the Beatles and the Stones did. We were just slightly too early.'[402]

'The Parade of the Tin Soldiers' (the B-side of 'Kansas City') would be their last Meek production. 'We didn't see him again. We never really had a life apart from on the road, we were working every day.' They made one further single before changing labels. 'After we left Decca and went to Piccadilly, we were put with John Schroeder, who had a hit [with Sounds Orchestral] with 'Cast Your Fate to the Wind'.'[403]

In August, the same month as Houston Wells and the Marksmen saw their hard work rewarded with chart success for 'Only the Heartaches' and Screaming Lord Sutch began his long political career by standing in the Stratford-upon-Avon by-election (caused by the resignation of disgraced minister John Profumo) for the National Teenage Party, it was announced that both Heinz and the Tornados were to appear, separately, along with the Saints in a short film for the European market titled *A Swinging Location*. The film would not make it to the screen, but Wells' single (originally recorded by Tex Allen as 'Only the Hangman') would peak at number 22 and spend ten weeks on the UK singles chart. Wells would record several more singles for Meek, but none would chart, something the singer put down to Meek's tinkering. 'The basic tracks would sound fine in the studio,' he said, 'But then, when we heard them on record they didn't sound the same and my voice sounded much higher than it really was.'[404] Although he had a hit on his hands, Wells would not see any money from his recordings, and at times he was so poor that he could barely scrape the cash together to pay for transport to his concert appearances. 'The contract I had with the Meek organisation stated that I was entitled to one penny for every record sold... With all the records we moved, that should have come to a quid or two; however, I've yet to see a penny from them,' he later complained.[405] 'Joe never paid anybody,' Steve Howe confirms. 'This business has a reputation for being incredibly bad because of things like that, where artists didn't get paid or they got

Just Like Eddie

bought a car instead. I don't want to sound too cynical, but it was very much a rip-off.'[406]

Still more acts made their way up the rickety wooden stairs to the RGM studio, including Welsh musicians Charles and Kingsley Ward, who formed their own band, the Tornados-inspired Charles Kingsley Combo. The group had already been turned down by Parlophone, but George Martin suggested that they get in touch with Meek, a man who, he reasoned, might be more attuned to the sound they made. Meek produced their only single, an original entitled 'Lost Planet' backed with his own composition, the Tornados-sounding 'March of the Spacemen', which was issued in the USA that June, credited to Thunderbolts,* as part of a deal with US publisher George Pincus for the release of several singles and at least one album. Pincus, in turn, had leased Meek's recordings to Randy Wood at Dot records. Dot planned to inaugurate the agreement with the US release of Andy Cavell's single 'Hey There, Cruel Heart', published by Ambassador Music (owned by George Pincus's brother Irwin), although that was later cancelled. *Cash Box* magazine called the Thunderbolts' disc 'a fascinating instrumental with a steady foot-stomp-like beat [that] has that hit orbit sound',[407] and it was released in several other countries – including Belgium, Brazil and Sweden – but 'Lost Planet' would not be issued in the UK, despite UK publishing rights being assigned to Ambassador Music.

The Wards, dairy farmers from Monmouth, would rename their group the Charles Kingsley Creation and again record with Meek in 1965, after Kingsley wrote offering to sell him some used studio equipment, but the brothers would become better known as the founders of Rockfield studios. Despite their lack of success with Meek, the pair held the producer in high regard. 'He was really clever,' said Kingsley Ward. 'He could do more with two microphones than a major producer could do with a [Solid State Logic] console. He was far cleverer than the producers in his day and certainly more original.'[408]

Day after day young men would knock on the front door in the hope of meeting the great man, and singers and bands around the country would send spools of tape or acetate records to Holloway Road in the hope that

---

* The Thunderbolts who issued the single 'Fugitive' on Decca in 1962 were a different band.

Love and Fury: The Life, Death and Legacy of Joe Meek

they might catch the ear of the great and powerful Wizard of Odd. He signed a 20-year-old blind piano player from Wrexham, Gwilym Jones, thinking he had discovered Britain's answer to Ray Charles (he hadn't), and in September he took Lee Starr and the Astrals, from Hereford, under exclusive contract. Although they recorded several songs at 304, including 'I Get Up in the Morning', which was later covered by Heinz, none of their tracks were issued until 2005. The Paladins, from Catford, fronted by 14-year-old guitar player Mike Rossi and featuring bass player Alan Lancaster, were one such cluster of contenders. Meek auditioned them, liked them and brought them back for a proper session, recording three tracks: 'I Gave My Heart',' I Won't Miss You', and 'Love My Life Away'. Meek suggested that they change their name to the Palominos; they opted for the Spectres. In August 1967, after several line-up changes, Rossi and Lancaster would finally settle on the name that would bring them international fame: Status Quo.

According to fellow band member David Hadfield, David Jones, a saxophone player and singer from Brixton, arrived at 304 with his group the Konrads (also occasionally spelled the Kon-Rads), to audition for Meek. Drummer Hadfield remembered that 'we went to his studio in the Holloway Road. It was a real eye opener as he had equipment all over the place. The musicians were scattered all around the lounge, the amps were behind the settee and the kitchen doubled as Joe's control room. It was hard to imagine that this was where he was turning out all those hits. As you might imagine, Joe took quite a shine to David, though we were so innocent that we didn't realise why until much later. Otherwise, I don't think Joe said more than half a dozen words all the time we were there.' The Konrads' audition was barely worth noting, and Meek opted not to sign the band – originally backing vocalists for Jess Conrad – to a recording contract. The audition, at which the group ran through several original numbers and recorded a cover of the Inez and Charlie Foxx hit 'Mockingbird', was followed by a recording session at Decca's Hampstead studios at the end of August 1963 (sans Meek), which too yielded no fruit. Both sessions would have been all but forgotten about, even by those who took part, had the saxophone player not later changed his name to David Bowie, although Bowie himself would insist that he had not appeared on the recording: 'I never worked with Joe Meek, never even met him...

Just Like Eddie

Would have loved to have though. But I believe The Konrads did do a track or two with him.'[409]

Gunnar Bergström of Sonet Records brought hit Swedish singer Jerry Williams, lead singer with the Violents, to 304 and recorded a couple of tracks for his first attempt at the English market, 'Live and Learn' and 'The Wonder of Your Love', with Ritchie Blackmore on guitar. Despite his huge popularity in his home country (he was voted Sweden's top star of 1962) the songs would never make it to the Sonet offices in Stockholm and to this day they remain unreleased, part of the fabled Tea Chest tapes.

Meek may have struck out with these acts, but during the summer of 1963 he met two people who would become close friends: Tony Grinham and Patrick Pink. Aspiring singer-songwriter Tony Grinham came to 304 to record some demos for Meek. 'I had some mates that had been in his studio,' he reminisces, 'They told me he was gay, and that I should "watch out" for myself, but that didn't worry me, I'm not prejudiced, and we got on quite well.'[410] Meek was unable to interest any label in Grinham as a singer, but he hoped that he might be able to use some of his songs, and the pair became good friends. Grinham was also interested in the supernatural, and he was less sceptical than others when the producer explained how, he believed, he was being guided by the spirit of Buddy Holly. 'He was very open about his beliefs, right from the start,' Grinham explains.[411]

Not everyone who came knocking was looking for a recording contract or a hit record. Living just around the corner from 304 Holloway Road, on Rollit Street, was a 16-year-old by the name of William Patrick Pink. A good-looking young man with a Teddy Boy quiff, like many teenagers Patrick (as he was usually known; in 1974 he would change his name by deed poll to Robert Duke) had stars in his eyes, but he was anxious to meet Meek not because he wanted to become a singer, but simply to get an autograph from the man who had produced his favourite Mike Berry records.

On his first visit, in 1963, the eager youngster was met by a locked door. After ringing the bell several times, the door was opened by the Saints' Tab Martin: 'He told me that there was nobody home. He was lying, but obviously Joe had told him to say that to anybody… and to get them to clear off. I went back the next day, about seven o'clock in the evening, and I waited and waited and I rang the bell, I banged on the door, I kicked it… I just wanted to meet him, get an autograph; I was still at school. In the end [Joe] came down in his pyjamas and asked me what I wanted. He was a very charming person… Really friendly.'[412] Before long Patrick was visiting on a regular basis, the starry-eyed teenager gleefully offering a helping hand, stacking tapes, running the occasional errand for Meek and making endless cups of tea and coffee for the stars who passed through the doors. 'It had a distinct smell, like a restaurant,' Pink recalled. 'I'll always remember that… he lived on chips, steak and chips. Every day. Sainsbury's was next door: I used to go and get his steak for him.'[413] Meek would often offer visitors a fried egg sandwich, a hangover from his days in Newent, when sausages and eggs were always to hand. Over the next few years Pink would drift in and out of 304, helping out for short periods of time before eventually becoming Meek's assistant.

Meek was fiercely loyal to the few people he trusted, and both Grinham and Pink would become part of his inner circle. After a series of radio appearances in October 1962 (almost a year after their final release, 'Joe's Been A-Gittin' There'), Joy Adams had retired from the music industry, married and moved to the States, and in an attempt to reignite her brother's career Meek and Dave Adams came up with the idea of relaunching him as a country-and-western singer under the name Burr Bailey. Bailey's first single, 'San Francisco Bay', with instrumental backing from the Outlaws (this time billed as the Six Shooters) was more like a 6-year-old Lonnie Donegan record than a contemporary country hit, and after it stiffed Meek and Adams resurrected a previously unissued Joy and Dave recording, remixed it to boost Dave's voice over his sisters, added a few effects and issued it as 'Chahawki' in January 1964. Like its predecessor, it too barely sold, and Burr Bailey's career – and the album's worth of material he had recorded – were shelved for good. One of Meek's deepest regrets was his inability to reward Dave Adams' loyalty with a hit single. Luckily, he was at least able to put plenty of session work his (and his sister's) way. 'He's always had faith that we'd make it one day,' Adams told *Disc* magazine. 'And he's been a terrific help. Apart from making our discs, Joe also gives us as much other work as he can. We do a lot of demonstration discs for him and help out on backings wherever possible. He's always on at us to keep on trying.'[414]

★

Just Like Eddie

By the end of September 1963, further changes to the line-up meant that only two of the original Tornados – Clem Cattini and Alan Caddy – remained in place. Fury and the Tornados, including new boy Brian Irwin, had recently recorded the 'live in the studio' album *We Want Billy!* (recorded at Decca's Hampstead studios without Meek's involvement), which was receiving excellent reviews, but Larry Parnes was unhappy with the constant alterations and, in a heated argument with Meek, threatened to ditch his boys and find a new act to back Fury unless they settle on one line-up long enough to finish upcoming dates in the UK, Europe and Scandinavia. Meek did not like being held to ransom by Parnes but had little choice but to sort things out. After auditioning potential members at 304 he dispatched organ player Jimmy O'Brien and bass player Ray Randell to Great Yarmouth, where the band had recently completed a summer season and the three remaining members were about to begin rehearsing for a tour with Fury and Marty Wilde that was due to continue into December.

In October, the same month that the newly reinvigorated Tornados set off on the road, Meek issued the only British single from Swedish actress and singer Gunilla Thorn, 'Merry Go Round', a song written by Geoff Goddard (previously recorded by Billie Davis and the Tornados while she was still known as Carol Hedges), backed with Meek's own 'Go On Then'. Thorn and her manager Jan Olofsson had been introduced to Meek by Southern Music's Bob Kingston, and expecting their big break to be on the horizon, the pair moved to London, working menial jobs to pay the rent while Meek prevaricated over her recording. Thorn recorded both sides at 304, with Heinz and the Saints as her backing band, but she was dismayed with the results: Meek speeding up her naturally deep, sultry voice to make her sound more childlike. The *Record Mirror* review noted that, due to Meek's trickery, 'in parts, she sounds as if she's played at the wrong speed'.[415]

It took almost a year from their first meeting to the disc's release, and Meek kept the Scandinavian duo waiting for news: often they were so broke that they could barely afford to eat. Sometime around October 1963 Gunilla was paired with British beat combo the Strollers (from Norfolk) for a recording, but again nothing came of this session. She appeared on ATV's *Five O'Clock Club* to promote her single, but Olofsson's continued trips to 304 to check on the progress of 'Merry Go Round' and try to confirm the release of its follow-up would often be met with anger. On one occasion, in

Love and Fury: The Life, Death and Legacy of Joe Meek

early February 1964, both Olofsson and Thorn were let in by Terry O'Neil, only for a furious Meek to shove them back out the door with so much force that the pair fell backwards down the stairwell. The following day Meek acted as if nothing had happened, and the Swedish duo nervously laughed it off, but his off-hand attitude continued: Meek nicknamed the singer 'Gorilla' and referred to her that way on the box of her master tape. Pink revealed that this hostility was not unusual and that he often heard Meek say of the many hopefuls who came to visit that 'they need me, I don't need them... They think they're coming here with something to offer me, but they can fuck off. They think they're doing me a favour, but I don't need them.'[416] His antipathy towards Thorn may have been exacerbated by the fact that the disgruntled singer, kept waiting for an hour in the studio for Meek to appear, was shocked to discover her producer in the first-floor lounge, kissing another man. A highly embarrassed Meek crept up the stairs, and a second session took place, to record two tracks with the Outlaws for a second single, 'He's Mine' and 'Blueberry Hill', but these would remain in the can due to the poor sales of 'Merry Go Round'.

CHAPTER 18

Boy Trouble

Directly opposite Islington Central Library, Madras Place was not named to honour a trader who brought exotic spices from India, or as a tip of the hat to Britain's long and troublesome history with that country, but after a now widely discredited educational system, based on mutual instruction, which at that time was practised in the classrooms of St Mary Magdalene's school. It is a quiet side road, a few minutes' walk from 304 Holloway Road, with one side dominated by the St Mary Magdalene Church, its adjacent cemetery and gardens. This quiet park would have been the perfect place for Meek to conduct his attempts at contacting the dead, armed with a portable reel-to-reel tape recorder and hand-held microphone. But he had other reasons for visiting the area.

The public conveniences in Madras Place were a well-known cottaging destination for the local gay population. Actor and comedian Stanley Baxter, who lived in nearby Bewdley Street, was arrested there in March 1962, charged with 'committing an act of indecency in the street', although further charges of 'outraging public decency and of committing an act of indecency in a public place' were dropped.[417] The arrest – and the subsequent scandal – was so traumatic that it led Baxter to consider suicide: 'I was going to top myself. I thought, "My career will never survive this. And if I don't have a career, what do I have?"'[418] Playwright Joe Orton, who would die in a frenzied hammer attack at the hands of his lover just a few months after Meek's own death, was a keen cottager and is rumoured to have also frequented the same public lavatory.

Attitudes towards gay men (and LGBTQ people in general) were slowly changing in Britain, but in 1963 'queers', 'poofs' and 'fairies' were, by and

213

Love and Fury: The Life, Death and Legacy of Joe Meek

large, reviled, treated as mentally-ill perverts, criminals and outcasts. A series of high-profile court cases in the first half of the 1950s had finally persuaded the government that now could be the right time to overhaul laws pertaining to homosexuality, then still a criminal offence, punishable by fines, imprisonment and/or barbaric medical 'therapies' including electroshock treatment and chemical castration. However, despite setting up a committee to investigate and report on the issue, the findings (published in October 1957 after a three-and-a-half year inquiry) that 'homosexual behaviour between consenting adults in private should no longer be considered a criminal offence' would not be acted upon. It would take another decade before the Report of the Committee on Homosexual Offences and Prostitution, forever known as the Wolfenden Report, would finally lead to the passing of the Sexual Offences Act 1967. Sadly, Meek would not live long enough to see the law change.

Yet, although they could not be open about their own sexuality, LGBTQ people were involved in all aspects of life: The music industry of the time was dominated by a cadre of homosexual men – producers, label heads, A&R men, publicists, managers and the like – but the vast majority of these men avoided the potential pitfalls of casual, anonymous sex in public places. A few, such as Brian Epstein and Joe Meek, seem to have been drawn to the thrill of cottaging. It was dangerous, seedy and totally unpredictable: you were just as likely to get physically attacked (a frighteningly regular occurrence, which in the 1970s would be given its own term, Gay Bashing) as you were to be on the receiving end of a quick hand shandy. And if you were lucky enough to avoid being beaten up, there was always the possibility of entrapment: undercover policemen regularly hung around places where homosexual men would meet, attempt to lure them into revealing what they were looking for and then arrest them. Even though the laws governing sex between men would change, arrests for cottaging – and instances of police entrapment – would continue for decades to follow.

Up until now, Meek had been relatively brazen about his visits to the city's cottages. His friend Adrian Kerridge had been shocked by Meek's frankness and how he would 'openly hang around known meeting places for homosexual men – a huge risk... If Joe had been caught and convicted, a prison sentence would have been inevitable and our recording industry would have been a much poorer place.'[419] Graham Sharp, guitarist with

Boy Trouble

Flip and the Dateliners, recalls being puzzled by Meek's interest in these seemingly sordid encounters: 'With the access he had to young men, it's hard to understand why he was caught up in "cottaging". Maybe it was a bit of a thrill, an encounter with danger?'[420]

Meek enjoyed camp comedy and double entendres: while at Triumph, he had produced a session with female impersonator Lee Sutton (born Leonard Sutch, but not closely related to David 'Screaming Lord' Sutch) for a comedy album, *Not For Teenagers*, which, sadly, remains unreleased. Sutton regularly performed in drag at the Bal Tabarin, a cabaret restaurant in Hanover Square, and would later hold a residency (and record an album) at the Union Tavern in Camberwell. Earlier in 1963, Meek and Dave Adams (using the nom de plume Silas Dooley Junior), recorded a whole album's worth of similar material. Backed by the Outlaws, the pair came up with twelve peculiar tracks about sex, bowel movements and gender fluidity. Most of the humour is rather juvenile, but it predates Meek's best-known gay-themed work by three years. Chas Hodges claimed that, although Meek could camp it up for comic effect, 'Lional was quite obvious, but with Joe it wasn't... he was a bit of a shy person, if you didn't really know him, and that's all you would think, that he was a bit nervous and a bit shy... I wouldn't have said it was obvious that he was queer.'[421] Meek was no stranger to the Madras Place lavatory, or to other comparable establishments. Yet despite his bravado, he was absolutely terrified of the consequences of arrest.

On 11 November 1963, shortly after descending the steps into the public convenience, he was apprehended by a policeman and frogmarched out of Madras Place and onto the busy Holloway Road, where anyone – including his neighbours – could have seen him. Unbeknown to Meek, the police had been staking out the lavatory for a while, using the nearby public library as their base. Islington Council were keen to rejuvenate the area and were buying up property as it became available, and arrests for importuning or soliciting had been on the increase. The police staking out the Madras Place conveniences must have felt that they had hit the jackpot when they took the hit songwriter and producer into custody. Meek, apparently, was detained after he had been seen smiling at an older man. That's all it took. You did not have to be caught in flagrante: just a furtive look, a smile, a knowing wink was enough for the police to pounce. 'I don't go smiling at old men! It's young chickens I'm after!' an indignant Meek confided in Kerridge after his

Love and Fury: The Life, Death and Legacy of Joe Meek

arrest.[422] 'He couldn't help his sexuality,' reasons Mike Berry. 'What was he supposed to do? At that time, people thought you were ill; it was ridiculous. It was just the way he was born. He never made a pass at me. They were shitbags, the cops; they used to hang around and wait in line for people.'[423]

The pattern would have been the same as the many men who had been arrested there before him. He would have been forced to walk approximately half a mile, in handcuffs, to the police station in Caledonian Road, where he would have been formally charged and required to register as a homosexual. After being released on police bail, he called his friend Don Charles, as the singer later recounted: 'He phoned me at three in the morning. He was crying and frightened. Joe had a great fear of the police, but the one thing that really frightened him above all else was that his mother would find out. Joe loved his mum and couldn't bear the thought of her discovering the sordid details. I spent about thirty minutes talking to him, trying to pacify him, but it was no good. He was very depressed.'[424]

The arrest caused a massive change in Meek's attitude towards his sexuality. His family had known and welcomed Lional into their home, and he often dropped his guard around friends, discussing his theories about homosexuality with singer Eddie Silver and others. Adrian Kerridge remembered that Meek often had a young man in tow, and that he and other colleagues at IBC knew about Joe's relationship with Lional, so much so that they would make comments about Joe behind his back. However, following the arrest, and its mention in the local press, Joe became much more guarded; more than anything he was devastated by the thought that he would have embarrassed his family. 'This appeared in the newspaper and he was terribly upset about that,' Geoff Goddard later disclosed. 'From then on everything went wrong.'[425] A cloud descended over Meek and the whole of RGM Sound. 'Obviously he was upset over it,' says Tony Grinham. 'But you've got to remember that in those days it was illegal. The worst thing about it was that it got on the front page of the *Evening News*.'

The newspaper report, which appeared on the front page of the *Evening News and Star* on 12 November 1963 under the headline 'The Man Who Wrote 'Telstar'' told all and sundry that:

Song writer and recording manager Joe Meek, aged 33, was fined £15 at Clerkenwell today after pleading guilty to persistently importuning

Boy Trouble

for an immoral purpose yesterday at Madras Place, Holloway. Meek, of Holloway Road, Holloway, composed the tune 'Telstar', which sold more than two million copies and was the top-selling record of 1962.

On the same day as Meek was fined, 35-year-old labourer Vincent McDonagh was arrested in Madras Place and offered the choice of a £20 fine or a month in jail for the same crime. A fortnight later another man, Sevki Hassan, was threatened with two months' imprisonment unless he also paid £20 for importuning in Madras Place. The short news item covering Meek's arrest was almost lost on a page dominated by a photograph of Paul McCartney and a story about the Beatles' latest exploits: ironically, Brian Epstein had experienced a similar brush with the law. He too had been arrested for importuning and had been savagely beaten up in Liverpool by a man he had picked up who would later attempt to blackmail him.

Meek was already known to be a soft touch to many of the young gay men who had gravitated to London in search of a better life, and if you were broke, he could often be relied on for a few bob or a couple of pounds to help out. Some of these young men had taken advantage of his generosity in the past, and some of those now resorted to blackmail, threatening to go to the police or the press with a scandalous, usually untrue, story unless Meek paid up. Meek's anger at his arrest infected everything, including his relationship with Lional Howard, who had recently been given a job as Heinz's road manager after his own restaurant venture failed. Joe and Lional had often experienced volatile moments during their years together, but Lional had been a stabilising influence on him. 'They had no friction before,' Eric Meek recalled. 'Lional used to say, "Oh, he's got a terrible temper," but he used to accept him as he was. They used to get on like a house on fire, and Joe thought the world of Lional, I believe he was very good to Lional.'[426]

Not long after the Madras Place incident, the couple would part for good as Lional was unable – or unwilling – to cope with Joe's increasingly frequent mood swings.* Even Heinz would suffer. He had recently returned from a short promotional tour of Sweden, where 'Just Like Eddie' had topped the

---

*   Lional Howard died in late 2023, aged 91.

Love and Fury: The Life, Death and Legacy of Joe Meek

local singles charts. While away he had picked up a handful of records, including a cover of the Isley Brothers hit 'Shout' by American band Joey Dee and the Starliters. Heinz felt that the song could provide him with a surefire hit, and played the disc to Meek. 'I said, "What do you think of this number?" He picked it up after it had played... slung it across the room and said, "Bloody rubbish!" Four months later, wallop with Lulu! Joe, once he'd made his mind up, you couldn't change it. He was right and that was it.'[427]

All of this upheaval caused Meek to become more insular. The visits to Decca or EMI became less frequent: going outside meant having to dodge the roughs who would occasionally hang around outside to jeer at him, but it also meant having to deal with office staff gossip. He refused invitations to record company events, and – according to Honeycombs singer Dennis D'Ell – when he had to attend a launch party for one of his records or a reception for one of his acts, 'He'd just stick his nose in for about half an hour and that was it.'[428] When he did go outside he would hide behind dark glasses, aping the style of Phil Spector and Andrew Oldham. Some of those closest to him believed he developed agoraphobia: 'He had a phobia about going out,'[429] Guy Fletcher confirmed. 'He very rarely went out,' Dave Sutch agreed. 'He just stuck in the house. He was frightened.'[430] Certainly, he became more anxious about what might await him outside the confines of his home. 'I think at the time, with all the scandal in the papers, he withdrew a bit,' Kim Roberts would later comment. 'The next time I saw him he seemed very embarrassed. I mean, it was obvious I'd read [about] it... He wouldn't look anybody in the eye.'[431] As he drew away from the world outside his paranoia increased, and he became less likely to take on suggestions from other people in his circle. Chas Hodges recalled that, in the early days, despite having a singular vision, Meek was reasonably receptive to other people's input: 'He was good in that way, he respected our ideas. Even though he could become a bit obstinate... In the end, if you really went against him, he would go the opposite way, but if you suggested something, he would try... which was a bit unusual at the time, as far as recording went. We were only in our teens, the band, nobody really respected our opinion, but Joe did.'[432]

From now on, visitors to 304 would be greeted by Meek's assistant Terry O'Neil, his secretary Pip Sharpe or one of the Shentons who – if the visitor or act in question had no appointment – might tell them that Mister Meek

Boy Trouble

could not see them today or that he was ill. Occasionally, a visitor would be receiving some such missive when it would be accompanied by Meek shouting down the stairs 'Tell them to bugger off' or something even more salty: singer Gunilla Thorn remembered that if you dared to ascend the stairs at 304 without Meek's permission you took a risk as to how he would be that day: 'Going up those stairs, he would scream and tell you to "Fuck off".'[433]

He would stay up all night, working away on his own in his control room, splicing tapes and layering on effects, these nights fuelled by the increasing use of amphetamines (the blue triangular Drinamyl tablets known as purple hearts – prescribed as a slimming aid and antidepressant but widely abused for its qualities as a stimulant). Overuse of the drug could bring on 'amphetamine psychosis', with symptoms including both audio and visual hallucinations and delusions of persecution, characteristics that those who knew Meek would attest to him suffering from.

The arrest took place the same month that Albert Hand, editor and publisher of several music titles including the *Elvis Monthly* magazine and *Pop Weekly*, brought a band from Derbyshire to RGM Sound: Dave Kaye and the Dykons. Kaye (real name David Knowles) did passable impersonations of several pop singers including Elvis and Roy Orbison, and Hand saw the band as a way to break into the management field. Meek signed Kaye and his troupe, but the first single (issued the following March), a cover of the Elvis hit 'A Fool Such As I', was credited to a solo Davy Kaye, with the singer backed not by the Dykons but the Outlaws. The flip side, 'It's Nice In't It', featured Kaye with the Saints. Meek had decided that the Dykons were not up to scratch for recording, but he was more than happy with Kaye's performance, boasting that the tracks were 'so good, they both ought to be the top side' and adding that 'it might be a good idea to make history, and issue a one-sided EP!'[434] Kaye would later recall Meek as 'a quiet, softly spoken man with this gentle Gloucestershire voice, but he had a terrific temper'.[435] That same month Decca released 'Dodge City', another Goddard-written instrumental from Ilford five-piece the Ramblers,* who had recently been touring with Billy Fury and the Tornados. Despite the trend towards vocal-

---

* The Flee-Rekkers were originally called the Ramblers, but there is no connection.

Love and Fury: The Life, Death and Legacy of Joe Meek

led beat groups, Meek was still convinced that there was room for instrumental acts in the charts, telling *Disc* magazine: 'There's been a lot of vocal-instrumental groups coming up lately, and I feel the time is now ripe for some of the purely instrumental teams to make their mark. To my mind, the Saints – who back Heinz on all his dates – and the Ramblers are among the best on today's scene. Both groups are capable of creating tremendous excitement, and I'm confident they will click in a big way before long.'[436] 'Dodge City' appealed to Meek's continued fascination with the Wild West, but despite some decent press interest the disc would not chart and the group soon disbanded.

By now, Robert Stigwood's working relationship with Meek was over, their inevitable break if not hastened by Meek's arrest, then certainly underlined by it. Their relationship had turned sour: the perpetually broke Stigwood – an inveterate gambler who often could not pay his way – regularly tried to borrow money from Meek (whose only regular income was his £20 weekly pay packet from the Major), and Meek became convinced that the Australian entrepreneur was trying to lure Charles Blackwell and Geoff Goddard away from him. But Blackwell was a freelance arranger and could work for anyone he chose, and Goddard had already agreed with Meek that he could offer other people his compositions so long as Meek had first refusal, after Meek's notoriously penny-pinching ways began to drive a wedge between the two. Goddard, rightly, wanted to know why he was seeing so little financial remuneration for his work at RGM Sound, when Stigwood seemed happy to pay the songwriter for his songs. Goddard began to feel caught in the middle, with both Meek and Stigwood bad-mouthing the other. Stigwood had also been instrumental in encouraging Goddard to pursue a solo career, but his fourth and last disc as a singer, 'Sky Men', was another non-starter. No one took the song, about visitors from outer space, seriously: Goddard's heavily-accented vocals sounded ridiculous after Meek did his usual trick of speeding them up, and the alien voice on the spoken interlude sounded like nothing less than one of *Dr Who*'s Daleks. The *Evening Standard*'s Maureen Cleave said that 'Sky Men' was 'in the worst possible taste' and pilloried it as having 'the ugliest sound ever'.[437]

Stigwood's next move to distance himself from RGM Sound was to issue an album, recorded live at the Granada, Edmonton, featuring John

Boy Trouble

Leyton and Mike Berry, alongside Stigwood-signed singers Don Spencer and Mike Sarne. Meek's name appears on the sleeve of *One Night Stand*, but only as co-composer of two Mike Berry songs. 'Joe didn't like Robert Stigwood,' Eric Meek insisted. 'Joe always thought that he was crooked... a bit devious,'[438] a conviction compounded when Stigwood attempted to hijack Meek's work with Gene Vincent, taking the singer to Olympic Studios and having him re-record Joe's soundtrack song 'Temptation Baby' for a November 1963 single.

John Leyton may have still been tied to Meek by a recording contract, and he had no intention of letting him go, but although future releases would still carry an RGM Sound credit Leyton would never record at 304 Holloway Road again. With no major hits since the summer of 1962, Stigwood was desperate to push his boy in another direction. His success with Mike Sarne had given Stigwood a financial boost, and he relished the opportunity to establish himself as an independent producer. Stephen Komlosy had been trying to persuade Stigwood that he needed to get on the beat bandwagon before it was too late, so matched Leyton with his own band, the Le Roys, in the hope of scoring a hit, but their first record together – 'Make Love to Me' – scraped in at number 49 for one week only.

In the same week as Columbia issued the re-recorded 'Temptation Baby', sister label Parlophone put out 'Christmas Star' by the Ants, a name obviously chosen to poke a little fun at the Beatles, but a tune – co-written by Komlosy – that sounded as if Stigwood, who claimed a producer's credit for the disc, had stolen it from the pile of tapes on Meek's control-room floor. The similarity did not escape Disker, the *Liverpool Echo* record reviewer (a role filled by the Beatles' publicist Tony Barrow before being taken over by Brian Mulligan): 'Joe Meek doesn't get a credit on 'Christmas Star',' he wrote, '... although there's a strong Tornado-type flavour to this pulsating instrumental.'[439] Komlosy says that he and Stigwood were after the same sound that Meek had been getting on the records he made with his musical director. 'Charles Blackwell was a huge influence on all of our artists. He was really quite a genius,' says Komlosy. 'I think we were sort of schooled in sound to a certain extent, Robert and I... Joe's early records were rather good; I thought they were tremendous.'[440] Stigwood's efforts to recreate the atmosphere of RGM Sound on his early discs fuelled Meek's obsession that people were coming to 304 Holloway Road simply to steal his secrets, but, as Stephen Kolmlosy puts it: 'His secrets were so rudimentary. He made his first records on a two-track Grundig, with his bathroom as the echo chamber. It was all a bit basic.'[441]

In an effort to thwart Stigwood's festive release, Meek, via Decca, issued 'Christmas Stocking', a seasonal instrumental from Roger LaVern, the Tornados' recently departed keyboard player, who had first played the Russ Conway/Winifred Atwell-style jaunty piano number to Meek when he auditioned for the band. Meek was clearly keen to have a festive hit: during a long studio session he and Geoff Goddard had worked up an original song, 'Make It a Merry Christmas', but despite several finished takes, it would remain unreleased until 2023. Meek did enjoy a minor hit with the Dowlands' December release, but it would have stuck in his craw that the act's only chart entry was with a cover of a Lennon and McCartney song, 'All My Loving'.

The split from Stigwood was followed by another crushing blow: Larry Parnes decided to extricate himself from his ties to Meek and terminated his contract with the Tornados. From now on Meek would act alone as their manager, and once their current commitments with Billy Fury were taken care of (the last date booked was 19 December), Fury would be paired with a new backing band, the Gamblers. Officially, Parnes decided to ditch the Tornados because he was fed up with the line-up changes, but to Meek it seemed that both Stigwood and Parnes wanted nothing to do with him following his arrest. The Tornados, naturally, were devastated but had little time to lick their wounds: Meek had them booked for three nights in Belfast over Christmas. Fearful of a ban by the BBC, he let it be known that he was no longer managing certain acts; on the day Meek was arrested, the Outlaws' Ken Lundgren wrote to the BBC to inform them that the group had cut ties with both Joe Meek Associates and Don Arden's Anglo-American Productions, and from now on the band would be representing itself.

Meek was being given the cold shoulder by his peers, but a shocking event that took place in Dallas, Texas, less than a fortnight after his arrest blew him and just about every other news story off the front pages. The only disc credited to the Joe Meek Orchestra, 'The Kennedy March' was issued in the UK in December 1963, with a US release on London following swiftly behind. Like the rest of the world, Meek was stunned by

Boy Trouble

the assassination of the US President, and he announced that any royalties from the disc would be paid to his widow Jackie to distribute to charity. The sentiment may have been worthy or it could simply have been an effort by Meek to deflect attention away from his recent difficulties, but the *Liverpool Echo* found the record distasteful and questioned if it was simply a piece Meek had left gathering dust on the shelf, given a new title and hurriedly released to cash in on the world's anguish. It was: the instrumental had originally been composed in tribute to Joy Adams' son and titled 'Smiley's Theme'.

'The Kennedy March' stiffed in Britain, and in America, despite the tune being performed several times on television by accordionist and bandleader Lawrence Welk. Its dismal sales meant it was unlikely to have raised more than a few dollars for good causes, but by the time it was issued there Meek was already on to other things. Over the next few months 304 became even more of a factory, with Meek pumping out masters in a desperate hunt for a hit that might exonerate him. The flurry of activity following his arrest meant that within weeks he would have four new singles in the shops: in January 1964, Decca issued Jimmy Lennon's 'I Learned to Yodel', the 'gimmicky and interesting' (according to one review) 'Dumb Head' by the Sharades and 'I'll Prove It', the debut single from Kim Roberts. The Sharades was a one-off name for a female vocal group consisting of former members of the Liverpool pop act the Vernons Girls; 'I'll Prove It' was an answer record of sorts to Brian Poole and the Tremeloes' recent hit 'Do You Love Me'. Kim Roberts was a 17-year-old from Bridlington who Heinz had encountered in Halifax in early 1963. Keen to impress the young singer and her friends, Heinz telephoned Meek who brought her down for an audition – accompanied by Dave Adams on piano – in March 1963. On 'I'll Prove It' she was backed by members of the Checkmates and the Saints; the flip side, 'For Loving Me This Way', was the song she had performed in *Live It Up!*, and features the teenager backed by the Outlaws and vocal act the Cameos, who had just had their second single, 'My Baby's Coming Home', issued. Roberts would record an album's worth of material for Meek, including compositions from Dave Adams, Geoff Goddard and Meek himself, but none would be released in his, or her, lifetime. 'I'll Prove It' flopped, and Kim Roberts would not make it as a star in Britain, but thanks to Screaming Lord Sutch she was able to find work in Germany.

Love and Fury: The Life, Death and Legacy of Joe Meek

'My Baby's Coming Home' was written by Southern Music's Bob Kingston, using the pseudonym Barry White. The Cameos (a name awarded the trio by Meek) featured jazz trumpeter, singer and nascent songwriter Guy Fletcher, his brother Ted, and Ted's wife Barbara; Guy and Ted had started out as one half of vocal act the Guy Fletcher Quartet, but had recently been working with Barbara as the Guy Fletcher Trio. 'We met Alan Hawkshaw at the finals of a talent competition at a London theatre in 1963,' says Ted Fletcher. 'He was playing keyboards for the Original Checkmates; they won and we came second! Al became a great friend and I worked with him many times over the years. He suggested to Joe Meek that we might be good as backing singers. Joe phoned me and we went for an audition.'[442] 'He put us in this little room, and he said, "Okay, sing!" It was just the three of us; we had no accompaniment or anything,' Guy Fletcher remembered. 'He disappeared into the back room, into the control room, and we just sang. He came in and he said, "No! No! I hate it! It's all wrong! It's terrible! I can't stand it! Get out!" And we were absolutely, completely shattered, but he just looked at us and a smile spread across his face, and he said, "I'm only kidding!" He was very humorous, you know? And he said, "Great. I liked it very much. When can you start?"'[443] Meek immediately put the trio to work, showing Ted Fletcher how to use his tape machines and playing them several unfinished recordings he wanted them to provide backing vocals for. An hour after their initial audition, the trio were back in the studio for what Ted Fletcher describes as 'a recording session with us taping impromptu backing vocals for some Tornados tracks'.[444]

Often compared in the press to the Springfields (and not always favourably: *Record Mirror's* review of their debut release lambasted it for its 'nightmare-ish Springfield sound'),[445] 'My Baby's Coming Home' was their second single for RGM, the siblings having previously issued Guy Fletcher's own composition 'Powercut' (with the trio backed by the Checkmates) as a top side in August 1963. The Cameos would not strike a chord with the record-buying public, but Meek found plenty of work for the singing family, and over the next two years Guy, Ted and Barbara would be put to good use, recording dozens of sessions for Meek, exclusively at his Holloway Road studio. 'I'd sung on over 100 singles before I was 20 and I was meeting some of the biggest names in music too,' Guy added. That list of names included Heinz, the Tornados, Gene Vincent, Michael Cox (they

Boy Trouble

appear on his October 1963 'Gee What a Party', credited as the Fletchers), Jenny Moss and Glenda Collins. 'So many people wanted to record with Joe,' Guy observes. 'He was known either as a genius or a lunatic, and I think there was a little bit of both in him.'[446] 'The accent was always on work,' Ted remembers. 'We had little to do with him outside the studio. I used to have discussions with him about EQ and compression; he was very knowledgeable about the technical side.'[447]

Like many of Meek's acts, the trio would occasionally get to glimpse the producer's temper, although as Ted recalls, 'Joe was always fine with us. He often got frustrated by our "corpsing" during a take; Barbara would often collapse laughing at the sounds we had to produce. Joe used to storm out of the control room and disappear for ten minutes before returning when we had pulled ourselves together.' In 1993 Ted Fletcher, after many years as a successful audio engineer and electronics expert, launched a new range of professional analogue studio equipment, which he dubbed the Joemeek brand in honour of his former mentor. 'I used Joe's name for my company as a reference to his work,' Ted explains, 'particularly with the use of volume compression. This became my own speciality, and some of my later design work was based on sounds that Joe produced.'[448] After almost three decades as a professional musician Guy Fletcher was elected to the board of the Performing Rights Society (the successor to the MCPS), acting as director and, later, chairman, and he also spent twelve years as the chairman of the British Academy of Songwriters, Composers and Authors.

In January 1964, American producer Phil Spector – who Meek had often been compared to in flattering terms – was in London and wanted to meet his British counterpart. Andrew Oldham, who had briefly worked for Brian Epstein as well as for Meek and who had recently taken over the management of a rising young band called the Rolling Stones, encouraged Spector to telephone Meek and introduce himself. The call, witnessed by Clem Cattini, was explosive. The American hitmaker had barely introduced himself when Meek spat an expletive-filled rant back down the phone, accusing Spector of stealing his ideas and copying his methods before slamming the receiver of his red telephone down with such force that it shattered. 'Joe really gave him some verbal on the phone,' Cattini remembered. 'He told him, "Don't you phone me up... You're pinching all my ideas, listening

225

to my records and stealing my sounds.' Unsurprisingly, Spector would not attempt to reach out to Meek again,* although Joe would later, perhaps begrudgingly, recognise Spector's 'genius' and his 'talent as a producer'.[449] The American was not the only one to have to deal with a stream of abuse during a telephone call with Meek, as Heinz recollected: 'The way I heard him speak to directors of record companies... When they've got hold of him and he's lost his temper, effing and blinding on the phone, slamming the phone down and calling them "Those peasants!... I don't need them, they'll come crawling to me on their hands and knees." Even if you've got ten number ones, you don't have that attitude, but that was Joe, and the reason for it, I've always maintained, was the pressure of work.'[450]

Kim Roberts' 'I'll Prove It' would be the last RGM session that Roy Phillips would work on. Heinz now had a steady girlfriend; Meek resented the women in Heinz's life and did his best to keep them apart, sending Heinz and the Saints back out on the road, accompanied by the Flee-Rekkers, on a series of dates in which they shared top billing with Johnny Kidd. It was not a happy experience, and after the tour was over the Saints parted company with Meek. 'Tab Martin and I had had enough of our music not progressing,' explains Phillips. They were also fed up with Joe's increasingly erratic behaviour and the lack of money coming their way. 'We did an overnight trip up to Tab's parents' place in Brighouse to work a few working men's clubs trying to get an act together. We finally did that in Manchester with the Peddlers.' The duo met up with Liverpudlian drummer Trevor Morais, the man who had replaced Ringo Starr in Rory Storm and the Hurricanes, forming a three-piece soul/jazz-influenced band initially known as the Song Peddlers, but who shortened their name on signing to Philips in 1965. With Phillips switching from guitar to keyboards and vocals, the band scored several minor hits in Britain, but for many years they were a popular live act, often appearing on British television and enjoying great popularity in several other countries.

---

* On 3 February 2003, the 36th anniversary of Meek's death – and forty-four years to the day of the plane crash that took the lives of Buddy Holly, the Big Bopper and Richie Valens – Spector took a gun and shot dead actress Lana Clarkson at his home in California. A coincidence, for sure, but a chilling one, nevertheless.

Boy Trouble

With the Saints gone, Meek needed a new act to back Heinz. Letters from home had brought news of a local band, Robb Gayle and the Whirlwinds, which included brothers Pete and Roger Holder, the sons of a Newent greengrocer who was a friend of the Meek family. The singer in the band was a Gloucester boy, Robert Huxley, who had taken the stage name Robb Gayle. The band were doing well locally, playing regularly in Gloucester, Whitminster and in other towns and villages in the area, and the Holder's parents had suggested to Meek's brothers that he should check them out. Meek decided to invite the band to an audition, as Huxley recalls: 'The first time we met Joe was when we went for an audition at Holloway Road. Joe knew pretty much nothing about us or what kind of music we played. All he really knew was that the Holder Brothers, Roger and Pete, were from Dymock, just outside Newent, and that they were friends of the Meek Family.'[451]

'He was smartly dressed in a blue mohair suit, with a shirt and tie and his hair was neatly combed. He always looked exactly the same on all future visits we made to him and throughout our time with him professionally,' Huxley adds. 'He spoke to us in a very soft voice with the distinct traces of a Gloucestershire country accent. The most memorable thing I remember is how he looked at us in a way like he was checking out the way we looked. As far as the set-up at 304 was concerned, we had never been in a recording studio before so we had no idea what to expect. Had we recorded in a professional studio like Lansdowne Studios before going to Joe we would have probably perceived Joe's set-up as rather amateur-looking, with tapes all over the floor and wires disappearing into unknown places. Also when we arrived at 304 for the first time we thought that we had been given the wrong address as we were parked outside Shenton's, a leather goods shop. We saw a side door where someone had scribbled Heinz on the wall, we opened the door and presumed that Joe's studio was upstairs. There was an office where a young lady [Joe's secretary, Pip] sat by a broken red telephone, a young man by the name of Terry and several glossy black-and-white photos on the walls. There was also another room with a kitchen which were Joe's living quarters, but we didn't know that at the time. There was a twisting staircase which led up to a landing where there was a bathroom and Joe's control room and the studio which was about the size of a regular bedroom. Another staircase led up to Joe's bedroom.'

Love and Fury: The Life, Death and Legacy of Joe Meek

Over the next few months they played several sessions for him, even appearing briefly (performing an unreleased song, 'It's Raining') in an episode of the ITV documentary series *World in Action* which was partly filmed at RGM Sound.

Meek was very taken with Huxley in particular, declaring, in a letter to the Holders' parents, that the singer was 'gifted with one of those original voices'[452] and comparing him to his idol, Buddy Holly. Huxley recalled that, when he was putting down the vocals while the rest of the band took a break, Meek made a clumsy, unusually forceful pass: 'It was upstairs in the studio. He kept me upstairs to put on vocals while the rest of the band was sent downstairs. There was really nothing I could do, because of the circumstances, but to give in to his advances. When I told him that I was not "like that" his reply was, "Oh! We're all like that in this business." I was obviously in a state of shock, and it was a secret that I kept inside me for probably thirty years or so.'[453] Interrupted by Terry O'Neil, Meek returned to his control room and Huxley carried on as if nothing had happened. At the end of the session, Joe invited Robb to spend the weekend with him, but the singer declined, telling him that he would not be able to take time off from his day job, at the Bon Marché department store in Gloucester's King's Square, opposite where Joe himself had worked for the Midlands Electricity Board.

Sometime later, Meek made another attempt to seduce the singer. 'We lived in a flat just a few doors up from Joe's studio in Holloway Road. Joe sent Terry to the flat on a Friday saying that Joe wanted to see me on Sunday afternoon at 2 p.m. I was a nervous wreck and kept telling the Holder brothers that I wasn't going to go. They wanted to know but I was too ashamed to say why. All I could say was that I had heard things about Joe to which they laughed and said that those rumours were untrue.

'As soon as Joe started with the approach, fiddling with my zipper, I told him that I thought that I had only come to see him to talk. He said, "OK," and immediately showed me out of the flat. I ran down the stairs rejoicing that I had made it through unscarred and that Joe had been kind and polite. He could have taken advantage of me and tried to force himself upon me, but he didn't do that. Once he realised that I was uncomfortable with the situation he let me go. He never made any kind of advances toward me after that.'[454]

CHAPTER 19

Have I the Right?

At the beginning of 1964, there was speculation that Joe would be cutting back on the number of artists he worked with. The arrest, and his battles with Larry Parnes and Robert Stigwood, had taken a strain. His inability to score a number 1 in Britain in 1963, having achieved that in both of the previous years, was vexing, and then there was the ascent of the Beatles and the other Liverpudlian acts managed by Brian Epstein's NEMS organisation, which had become too great to ignore. By now Epstein had relocated permanently to the capital, and he began to sign up London-based artists for his burgeoning empire, including Meek's own no-hit wonders Cliff Bennett and the Rebel Rousers. Meek's relationship with the Rebel Rousers had come to an unpleasant end after a row over the kind of material Meek was insisting they recorded: 'It got to the stage where he said, "Either you record what I want you to record, or I'll fuck off!"'[455] With bitter irony, within weeks of signing with NEMS the Rebel Rousers would secure their first Top 10 hit with their soulful cover of the Drifters' 'One Way Love'.

RGM Sound productions continued to appear at an incredible rate, Meek still fuelled by the desperate urge to absolve himself. In January, Lionel Bart brought singer Deke Arlon, frontman with a band called the Tremors, to meet the producer. Bart had seen Arlon (the Clacton-born Anthony Howard Wilson) and his band performing at the Top Hat in Littlehampton, West Sussex, and the songwriter immediately took a fancy to the singer, who based his act on Elvis (the name was poached from Deke Rivers, the character Elvis played in the film *Loving You*). Arlon's first session at 304 produced the unremarkable Freddie and the Dreamers-inspired 'I'm Just a Boy', written by Alan Hawkshaw of the Checkmates and with Arlon backed by a four-piece Meek knew called the Off-Beats (featuring Bobby Ross, and who had previously backed Ricky Wayne), but a later session was memorable: 'The rhythm section was in the front room, I was in the bathroom, and the string section, conducted by Charlie [Blackwell], was on the staircase! ... [Joe would] make you sing a song forty times, and of course you didn't know why, but he knew what he was doing. He was a genius, and great to work with. You would work there, non-stop, for ten hours and he would come in with a box of ice creams! There were no hard drugs; we were living on ice creams and cups of tea!'[456]

Arlon would only issue one single from his RGM sessions, but he would continue to record for the next two years before leaving the performance side of the business to work in music publishing, setting up the York record label (where he issued albums by both John Leyton and Mike Berry) before becoming head of the Sanctuary Music Group in January 2001. Although not produced by Meek or recorded at 304, the second single from Deke Arlon and the Off-Beats, 'I Must Go and Tell Her' (issued in October 1964, in the same week as Heinz issued his Columbia debut, 'Questions I Can't Answer'), was mixed by Joe who would only agree to release Arlon from his contract if he were allowed final approval of their sophomore release.

Early that year Decca had signed the Pete Best Four, finally giving a contract to a member of the band they had summarily dismissed back in 1962 with the now infamous assertion that 'guitar groups are on the way out'. Best's band, formed from the remnants of Liverpool's Lee Curtis and the Allstars, had at least one session with Meek at 304: bass player Wayne Bickerton would later comment that 'God knows what happened to those recordings. We were dotted around his house – someone was in the toilets – the usual thing with Joe.'[457] The session yielded no fruit, and the group went instead to Decca's Hampsted studios where they recorded their only single for the company, 'I'm Gonna Knock on Your Door'. To compound his anxiety around the Beatles and Brian Epstein, on 6 February Heinz was due to play the Beatles' old stomping ground the Cavern, and Decca had decided to capture that performance for an upcoming album they had planned. Although the sessions for Decca's *At The Cavern* LP were to be helmed by Mike Smith, Meek decided to travel to Liverpool to oversee his boy's recording himself.

Have I the Right?

Meek had enjoyed a fruitful association with the company, but was starting to believe that Decca was either paying his associates to spy on him or had his studio bugged. His conviction was compounded when the company dropped a planned Meek-produced single from Burton-on-Trent's Shane Spencer and the Casuals, 'I Believe', in favour of a version of the same song by the Bachelors, which was issued in March and reached number 2 in the charts. Perhaps he would have done better had he something worth offering the company, but the next release from the Tornados was 'Hot Pot', a crass reworking of 'Jungle Fever'. This time credited to Meek rather than Goddard (although the original should probably have been credited to the Tornados), the single failed to chart.

Maybe the trip up north opened his eyes, but it had become blindingly obvious that if Meek were to continue to have hits then he could no longer ignore the beat group boom, and his next signing, an R&B four-piece that featured 16-year-old guitarist Steve Howe, might be the act to help. Once managed by his old friend Chico Arnéz, the Syndicats were now being handled by Petronella Driscoll, mother of the band's bass player Kevin Driscoll. After getting nowhere with the BBC, Mrs Driscoll decided to phone Meek and see if she could secure them an audition at 304 Holloway Road. 'She wasn't in the business,' Howe recalls, 'but she was a go-ahead sort of woman. She had a real fire in her eyes: she believed that the band was good, and of course her son was in it, so she went knocking!' Meek initially told her that he was not taking on any new groups, but she persisted, and eventually he gave in. 'We got the audition strictly because of her,' Howe laughs. 'That was quite something!' Meek signed them on the spot and had them record their first single, a cover of the Chuck Berry classic 'Maybelline', which was issued in mid-March 1964.

Steve Howe grew up in Holloway, and for a period worked in a record store, Saville's, a couple of blocks from Meek's studio. He was also a regular visitor to the music shop a few doors away, purchasing one of his earliest guitars from the store, but was unaware that there was a recording studio hiding behind the door of 304: 'The day that we went up there to audition was when I first realised it was there,' he admits.[458] By coincidence, a few months earlier Meek had auditioned Lancashire group the Warriors, featuring vocalist Jon Anderson, who would later join Steve Howe in progressive rock supergroup Yes.

Love and Fury: The Life, Death and Legacy of Joe Meek

'It looked a bit shambolic, and it always was. You'd come up the stairs, and halfway up was the loo, the famous toilet where vocals were recorded because that got a nice, bright sound. You went up another flight of stairs and on the left was his control room; and the floor was covered in tape because he did his editing in there and didn't tidy up, and then the studio was this square room next door. There were no doors, he had to keep popping round the corner, although when we played he was in the control room, doing his stuff. It was fun, and I remember when we went in there and he played it back. That was an experience, a first for me, to hear the track back. It was very much like I imagined it; this is what I had hoped would happen, that we'd record something, then listen to it and go, "Is that good enough?" If Joe said, "That's OK," well, then that's fine, but obviously you had to practise it a few times and we had to keep playing the same thing over and over again. It was so fundamentally basic.'[459]

Meek hoped that signing the Syndicats would prove that he was not unresponsive to the changing tastes of the record buyer. Chuck Berry had recently enjoyed a resurgence in his career – bolstered by his lionisation by the Beatles, the Rolling Stones and the like – and had returned to the British singles charts after a five-year gap. The Beatles' influence was also on display when, shortly after his return from Liverpool, Heinz issued 'You Were There', a new Geoff Goddard composition that the songwriter admitted was him 'trying to do a Beatles'. The song itself was weak, but the vocal arrangements have a distinct Hollies feel and musically 'You Were There' has touches of the Beatles' 'I'll Get You'. Backed by 'No Matter What They Say', a Meek co-write that again has distinct Merseybeat traces, in spite of proud boasts from RGM that the single had sold 30,000 in advance orders, it reached a paltry number 26 on the UK singles chart. It was the only single from Meek that charted in the first half of the year.

Royalties from 'Telstar' were still on hold, but Meek's team assured him that they expected the legal issues would be sorted imminently. He began to spend money wildly and, according to *Variety*, he 'spruced up his north London first floor waxery with $10,000 worth of recording gear'.[460] But where did the money come from? Although he had several other hits to his name and liked to boast that he was well-off, without the 'Telstar' money he had nothing like that amount of cash hanging around. One of the ways Meek got around this problem was to give credit for his songwriting to

Have I the Right?

friends, who would then pass the royalties back to him when the cheque arrived. But that was a long process: songwriting royalties could take years to filter through, so when the Major would not open up his chequebook, he simply took to buying equipment on hire purchase, the dreaded 'never never', a risky business that could involve the equipment being repossessed should he fail to keep up with the repayments: an expensive new Ampex multitrack tape recorder, which Meek took delivery of in early 1966, vanished almost as soon as it had arrived. Was this the four-track machine Clem Cattini recalled being trashed when Meek threw a stool in his direction, or was it removed by the suppliers when Meek could not (or would not) honour his monthly instalment plan?

A celebrity in his own right, he lent his name and likeness to equipment manufacturers Watkins Electric Music (WEM) – whose range now included the 'Telstar Organ', a snip at 235 guineas – and used the money they paid him to acquire the rest of the equipment he coveted. The WEM deal saw the company give Meek several of their new 'GR60/Starfinder' amplifiers, a state-of-the-art piece of equipment then selling for a massive 145 guineas apiece, and had Meek work with the company on a guitar/organ hybrid, the Fifth Man, the prototype of which was first seen in the autumn of 1964 but was soon scrapped. A revolutionary instrument, that 'at the touch of a switch, can be used as a standard guitar, six string bass or organ-guitar',[461] the Fifth Man was lambasted by company owner Charlie Watkins as 'the biggest commercial disaster I ever invented. It was too big, too expensive and took too long for me to realise that a guy buys a guitar because that's the sound he wants in his ear. If he wanted organ sound he would probably buy an organ!'[462] The Saxons had attempted to use the Fifth Man on the unreleased track 'Song of the Sun God', but the machine was unreliable and continually made a noise that sounded like someone passing wind.

With no big hit, and the fallout from his arrest still weighing heavily on his mind, Meek started to sink into a deep depression. He knew that teenage tastes had changed, and while there were still plenty of hopefuls beating a path to the door of 304 Holloway Road, he began to question his ability to pick a hit. Although they had barely spoken in months, Larry Parnes recalled that a dejected Meek telephoned him and begged him to come over and give his opinion on some of the recordings he had been working on. 'He seemed to think that he was a failure,' Parnes remembered.

Love and Fury: The Life, Death and Legacy of Joe Meek

'That he'd lost his touch, that everything he did wasn't right. But I found this ridiculous. He played me so many tapes that night, I must have been there about seven hours... and some of the material I heard was just tremendous.'[463] Desperate and miserable, Meek threatened to burn several reels of tape in front of Parnes, including the original master of the track that would give him his next big hit, 'Have I the Right?'

The Sheratons had been formed in late 1962 by hairdresser Martin Murray. Initially rehearsing in Murray's bedroom, after a few months the act had landed a regular spot at Islington's Mildmay Tavern. Feeling that the group, which also featured Murray's salon assistant, Anne Margot 'Honey' Lantree, on drums, were doing well and building a fair reputation, Murray phoned Joe Meek's studio, hoping to persuade the producer to take a look at his band. As luck would have it, Meek answered the telephone himself and invited Murray and the Sheratons to an audition. The tryout went well, and Meek booked them in for a full recording session, to take place in February 1964.

One evening Ken Howard and Alan Blaikley, two BBC television production staffers looking to break into the world of songwriting, caught their act. 'We were on a pub-crawl one evening in the Balls Pond Road and visited the gangsterish Mildmay Tavern where, unusually for 1963, a pop group, the Sheratons, had a residency,' Howard explains. 'The most striking thing about them, apart from their excellent lead singer Denny D'Ell [a phonetic spelling of his real surname Dalziel], was the fact that they had an attractive and proficient girl drummer, Ann Lantree – a rarity at the time.'[464] Howard also recalled that 'because Denny D'Ell had such a great voice and range, a lot of their repertoire showcased him. I seem to remember him singing the Platters hit, 'The Great Pretender'.'[465]

Howard and Blaikley had been friends since childhood. 'We ran school magazines and began to compose songs and lyrics and in our early teens, and even sketched ideas for musicals, inspired by the success of the Rodgers and Hammerstein films,' Blaikley explained.[466] University had seen them sent to different parts of Britain – Ken to Edinburgh where he formed a folk duo (which soon landed a weekly spot on Scottish television) and Alan to Oxford – but by the mid-1950s they had regrouped and rekindled their mutual love of writing. Emboldened by a few pints from the Mildmay bar, Howard and

Have I the Right?

Blaikley went to the small backstage area after the Sheratons had finished their set and introduced themselves. 'We announced that we were songwriters – and from the BBC! The latter undoubtedly impressed them, and they told us they had an upcoming session with the legendary record producer Joe Meek and needed some original songs. We arranged to meet them a week later with a selection of our material,' the pair later recalled. [467]

The songs that Howard and Blaikley were writing seemed, on the surface, much like most of the pop material of the day: bright, quirky and with a driving beat. But if a listener or performer had scratched beneath the surface sheen, they would have discovered a decidedly 'queer' sensibility to a number of their lyrics. 'We covered a very wide range of subjects,' Blaikley explained. 'Some were simply melodic pop, designed to be catchy earworms; others reflected and sometimes anticipated momentous changes in social and sexual mores.' One such song, and one the songwriting duo were keen to offer to the Sheratons, was a thing they had worked on while travelling on the London Underground called 'Have I the Right?'. 'We had already written 'Have I the Right?' when we met the group,' Howard remembers. 'The title was inspired by the last line of Radclyffe Hall's famous lesbian-themed novel from 1928, *The Well of Loneliness*, which was "Give us also the right to our existence". We had mapped out the construction of the song on the tube going to our jobs at the BBC in White City.' [468]

Learning that the Sheratons already had a session with Meek lined up, it made sense that Howard and Blaikley call in to RGM Sound and introduce themselves; however, the first meeting between the nascent songwriters and the record producer did not go well at all: 'When we arrived at the appointed time it was rather like *Waiting for Godot*, when [Meek's assistant] Terry O'Neil informed us that "Mister Meek is unwell. You will have to come another time",' says Howard. Meek's assistants were used to fobbing people off with excuses when he was not up to seeing people, and visitors were often told that the production maestro was 'unwell'. These bouts of 'illness' increased following Meek's arrest and were exacerbated by his habit of working all night, kept alert by the prodigious use of Preludin and other pep pills. 'Meek had a reputation and we had heard that he had possibly been arrested,' Howard adds. 'Joe was always somewhat manic. He took offence easily and would complain about being badly treated in his business associations.' [469]

Love and Fury: The Life, Death and Legacy of Joe Meek

When they finally got to see Meek's workspace, the pair – schooled in conformity and tidiness at the BBC – were shocked. Howard recalls that 'there were two rooms; the control room was an absolute tip, with tape boxes strewn across the floor and bulging files overflowing with papers and his twin tape recorders... The studio was also pretty full of files, with a cleared space for the musicians to set up equipment. There was some primitive attempt at soundproofing on the walls with egg boxes. Since it looked out onto the busy Holloway Road it wasn't that effective and I recall hearing car horns quite clearly.'[470]

When the duo returned with the band to fulfil their pre-arranged recording date, Friday, 13 March 1964, Meek was in a foul mood, having already aborted one session that day with a band and sent them packing with a flea in their ear and their heads ringing from the barrage of curses that followed them as they rushed down the stairs and out into the cold. Eventually, the Sheratons got the go-ahead to play. 'Halfway through their session, having performed 'Have I The Right?', Joe stopped the session and announced to the group, "That's a number one! I'm going to record it right away!" And he did, including the celebrated stomping up and down his stairs for added percussion.'[471] That sound – which Joe captured by clamping microphones to the banisters around the bare wooden stairs with bicycle clips and having the band march up and down – took hours to get right, much to the chagrin of Mrs Shenton's cleaner, who had to endure a tirade of abuse from Meek as she tried to go about her work. Even then, he was not happy with the result, and called the Fletchers in to beef up the backing vocals and add extra oomph: 'We tried for about half an hour to find the right sound for the marching feet effect,' Ted Fletcher explains. 'It was finally achieved by Guy smashing a tambourine onto the top of an old AKG D19 microphone, completely destroying it!'[472]

Singer Dennis D'Ell was not happy with the way Joe messed around with his voice, speeding it up and raising the pitch, but with its stomping beat, catchy vocal and unusual (if hidden) subject material, everyone knew that this was going to be a hit. Everyone, that is, except for Britain's record labels. Three companies turned Joe's master down – someone at EMI had the temerity to tell Meek that 'Have I the Right?' had 'no commercial value' – before Pye finally accepted it for release. Only Louis Benjamin,

236

Have I the Right?

head of A&R at Pye, didn't like their name, and shortly before the disc was issued he suggested that the Sheratons be rechristened the Honeycombs, in a nod to their drummer's nickname and to the fact that the act's leader was a former salon owner.

In the early 1960s a beat group that featured a female instrumentalist challenged gender stereotypes and was seen as quite a novelty, even shocking. Decca had recently signed West Midlands' group the Applejacks, which included Megan Davies on bass guitar, and Liverpool had the Liverbirds, a four-piece all-female act who did rather well for themselves in Germany (following the well-trodden path between the Cavern and Hamburg's Star Club, where they were billed as 'The Female Beatles'), but prior to that female pop stars had been almost exclusively singers, not players. American instrumental act the Ramrods – who scored a UK Top 10 in 1961 with 'Riders in the Sky' – had featured a female drummer, Claire Lane, but they were thin on the ground. The folk and jazz world had seen women who both sang and played an instrument, but they were making serious music for people to discuss and dismantle, not something as disposable as pop music. The Liverbirds, Honey and Megan were breaking new ground, and all found it hard to be taken seriously. 'I was a bit doubtful about it at first, joining the group, but I was talked into it,' Lantree told journalist Ray Coleman.[473] 'I promise you it wasn't a gimmick. And anyway, why on earth shouldn't a girl be allowed to be a drummer? I don't see why people are so narrowminded about it.' Her fellow band members baulked at the suggestion that having a pretty young woman occupy the drum stool was no more than a gimmick: 'Honey plays with us purely and simply because she is the right drummer for the job,' said D'Ell. 'If she wasn't any good, she wouldn't hold down the job.'[474]

It wasn't just the critics; audiences could be hostile too, as Honey discovered after a particularly terrifying incident when she was dragged off stage during a show in Cornwall. At a later show in Manchester in March 1965 the band (and headliners the Kinks) were bottled off stage by boisterous students, and the Honeycombs refused to return in case Honey was hurt. Founder Martin Murray suffered the most: he too had been manhandled off stage by over-exuberant fans (in Peterborough) breaking a leg and his right hand. The Honeycombs' success saw other companies snap up similar-sounding acts: Parlophone were quick off the mark with

Love and Fury: The Life, Death and Legacy of Joe Meek

all-girl six-piece Sally and the Alley Cats, whose sole single, 'Is It Something That I Said?' even featured dampened drums in the Meek-patented style.

Issued on 23 June, it was not until Radio Caroline's Tony Blackburn started to play it that it began to sell; by the end of August 'Have I the Right?' was at number 1, the single taking pole position in the same week as the group's drummer celebrated her 21st birthday. The Honeycombs were a sensation. Offers of television spots, foreign tours and major British dates flooded in, and Howard and Blaikley – who had been offered the option of returning to the BBC once they had got this pop music nonsense out of their system – found that they were suddenly full-time professional songwriters and artist managers. With an eye on the demands of the foreign markets, Pye's Louis Benjamin loaned Meek some of their own studio equipment, so that he might record them in stereo, and Meek dispatched Patrick Pink off to Pye's Great Cumberland Place studios to collect it. Honey Lantree became an icon overnight and helped empower a generation of young women to pick up an instrument, so much so that it was claimed that 'in every coffee bar in the country girls are studiously tapping the tables, waiting to be discovered'.[475]

It had been two years since his last number 1, but his persistence had paid off; once again Meek had captured something special, and he knew what that was. 'Originality. If you can create something new, you're halfway there,' he disclosed. 'All of my records are aimed at fans between the ages of 13 and 25, and I am constantly trying to produce new sounds and styles.'[476]

The success of the Honeycombs, plus the news that American star singer and songwriter Gene Pitney – who had been in London working with the Rolling Stones – had recorded one of Meek's own compositions, 'Lips Are Redder On You' (also recorded by Freddie Starr and the Midnighters), gave Meek reason to believe that, after a rocky eight months, his career was back on top. Meek was aware that the Shentons were considering retirement when their lease ran out on the shop, and he harboured ideas of expansion, telling reporter Jay Martin, 'I hope to have my own record label distributed through a major company,' and confiding that he had designs on the leather goods store downstairs, with the possibility of taking over 'the entire building soon and then building a larger studio on the ground floor'.[477] But not everything went his way: in September Meek cut a single

Have I the Right?

with Tony Dangerfield, bass player with Screaming Lord Sutch and the Savages, having signed him to a solo management contract. Dangerfield was horrified to learn that his striking dyed-blond locks – an asset on stage with the Savages – would have to be dyed black as Joe did not want him to be seen to compete with Heinz. The disc, the beat ballad 'I've Seen Such Things', written by Manfred Mann singer Paul Jones, his wife Sheila MacLeod and Manfred's bassist Tom McGuiness, was backed by a raucous, Jerry Lee Lewis-inspired Meek co-write 'She's Too Way Out', reworking the Cliff Bennett and the Rebel Rousers B-side, 'I'm In Love With You'. Although Dangerfield had his own band, Wolverhampton's the Thrills, the act appearing on the disc was the then-current line-up of the Savages, minus their leader.

Howard and Blaikley were not the only songwriters that Meek showed an interest in. Early in the year he was sent a batch of acetates by his own publisher, Ivy Music, containing demos from an unknown songwriter, Chad Christian. Looking for a suitable number for the flip side to the debut single from Dave Kaye, 'A Fool Such As I', Meek had chosen one of Christian's songs, adapting it to incorporate a phrase Kaye often used himself, 'It's Nice, In't It'. Kaye's single was not a hit, and it would be a full year before a follow-up emerged from RGM Sound, but by all accounts Meek was particularly 'knocked out'[478] by another of Christian's songs, the Merseybeat-inspired 'Please Little Girl' and had Heinz record it for the top side of his next Decca single. It would be the last single Heinz would release through Decca: although the company promoted the single by giving away a free colour portrait of the singer with the first 30,000 copies, it was not a big seller.

Once the song had been cut, Meek wrote to Mr Christian, inviting him along to 304 to hear the result. A few days later a 20-year-old woman from Ellesmere Port, Christine Chadwick, turned up on Meek's doorstep asking to meet him. Meek invited her in, and the pair got talking. Christine had been in London for a few months, trying to make her own way as a journalist. She also aspired to be a songwriter. Before she had opportunity to say much else, Meek played her the new Heinz single, telling her, 'One of these days you might be able to write a song as good as this.' Meek soon checked his patronising air when she pulled out the letter that Meek had sent, telling him that Christine Chadwick and Chad Christian were one

Love and Fury: The Life, Death and Legacy of Joe Meek

and the same person. 'It was a heck of a surprise,' Christine told Patrick Doncaster of the *Daily Mirror*, adding that 'Joe is considering some of my other songs for other artists'.[479]

Now that the Saints were no more, Heinz was accompanied on the disc by an uncredited Outlaws, the track featuring some wild guitar from Ritchie Blackmore. The Outlaws' own early 1964 release, a cover of the Little Richard favourite 'Keep A-Knockin'', was another attempt by Meek to jump on the beat bandwagon and perhaps to mould his act in the Beatles' image, although it is the B-side that is more widely remembered today. For 'Shake With Me' Meek encouraged Blackmore to 'go crazy; play a very weird solo. Bend the notes and play with lots of distortion and a very freaky effect.'[480] Blackmore was happy to oblige, and happier still when he later discovered that particular track was a favourite of Jimi Hendrix. However, this would be the last single recorded by the Outlaws for RGM Sound. Blackmore joined Heinz's backing band the Wild Ones* – he was replaced by Harvey Hinsley – and before long Chas Hodges was off too, joining the ranks of the Rebel Rousers.

Early in July 1964, Meek decided he needed a break, and he spent the best part of a week out of London. Heinz and the Wild Ones (which, as well as Ritchie Blackmore, now included Dave Adams) were appearing in a ten-week summer season in the North Wales seaside town Rhyl, in a variety package headed by veteran comedian Arthur Askey, and the Tornados were in Blackpool. It would be a chance for him to spend some time with his golden boy who, apparently, was under siege night after night from screaming fans, some of whom had broken into his rented home and had covered his car with whitewashed declarations of their love. It was also an opportunity to visit with the Tornados and to record their stage act, with a view to releasing a live single or perhaps an EP or album, influenced no doubt by the reception to *We Want Billy!* By now, Clem Cattini was the only original member left, the rest of the band made up of guitarist Stuart Taylor, bass player Ray Randall (who joined in late 1963), Bryan Irwin on rhythm guitar and keyboard player Jimmy O'Brien.

---

* Heinz and the Wild Ones made their live debut on 10 May, at the Beat City Club on London's Oxford Street.

Have I the Right?

Meek was keen to capitalise on Heinz's success; the pair let it be known that as well as his yacht, *Globetrotter*, the singer was now the proud owner of a brand new Chevrolet Corvette, and while he was making headlines in Rhyl, it was announced that he had been signed to play Aladdin in pantomime at Blackpool that winter. Heinz would not star in *Aladdin*, but he and his band would appear in several cities in the North and the Midlands, alongside Lulu and Marty Wilde in *Once Upon a Fairy Tale.** However, a 'live' Tornados single was issued that August, their rendition of 'Exodus', the theme to the biblical epic which had been such a showstopper for Peter Jay and the Jaywalkers and had proved just as popular with the Tornados' audience. Although the label claimed that 'Exodus' had been 'recorded live at the South Pier, Blackpool', Joe could not stop himself from adding studio overdubs and some Meek magic to the rather poor-quality live tape. The single scraped into the bottom of the *Melody Maker* chart but did not show nationally.

Meek could not stay out of London for long: he was due to produce a new session for Screaming Lord Sutch, and, what's more, the BBC were coming to 304 Holloway Road to film a restaging of the recording for a documentary they were making about his lordship: the programme (a 35-minute film entitled *Screamin' Lord Sutch*) would be broadcast on BBC Two in April 1965. The singer was keen to continue to combine his twin loves, rock 'n' roll and horror movies, and songwriters Tony Day and Allan Zeffertt – who would also write for another Meek-related singer, Ricky Wayne – had the perfect song. Meek was almost as obsessed with horror movies as Dave Sutch, and the resulting single, 'Dracula's Daughter', featured a new line-up of the Savages (uncredited on the disc's label) which included guitarist Geoff Mew and a young keyboard player who became better known as an actor, Paul Nicholas. Mew and Nicholas can be seen in the footage, with Nicholas sharing vocals with his lordship. Once again, Meek had fun adding effects to the master tape, with a storm, heavy footsteps, screams, peculiar electronic gurgles (made, Sutch later recalled, by blowing through a straw into a glass of water) and plenty of echo.

---

* A second version of *Once Upon a Fairy Tale* ran concurrently in the South of England, starring Jess Conrad and Millie 'My Boy Lollipop' Small. The Tornados were also due to appear but would be replaced by the Flee-Rekkers.

CHAPTER 20

Questions I Can't Answer

Sadly, the success of 'Have I the Right?' signalled the end of Joe's association with Geoff Goddard. Robert Stigwood's interference might have damaged their relationship, but 'Have I The Right?' brought a previously rewarding and supportive friendship to an abrupt and messy finale. Goddard was adamant that Howard and Blaikley had plagiarised their hit from a song he had demoed called 'Give Me the Chance', the composition of which he attributed to himself and Meek equally. An enormous row ensued: Meek, knowing who he stood a better chance of future success with, sided with the duo. Goddard, who had not come up with a major hit for RGM for more than a year, felt betrayed by Meek and sued Howard and Blaikley, and publisher Ivy Music, for copyright infringement. Ivy Music countersued for slander. In a frustrating echo of the 'Telstar' situation, royalty payments for 'Have I the Right?' were frozen: no one would see a penny from the international bestseller until a court decided who actually owned the rights to the song.

Although they had not always seen eye-to-eye, especially when it came to money (or the lack thereof), Goddard had valued his friendship with Meek. 'He was like a brother to me,' the songwriter said. 'He was very erratic, of course, but I liked him straight away. Unfortunately, later on – whether it was a mental illness or what – he did change. I remember, in 1963, him telling me he thought there was something growing inside his head.' Goddard was just as likely as anyone else to be on the receiving end of one of Meek's rages, but these outbursts became much worse following the Madras Place incident, and the previous six months had not been fun. 'He was like Jekyll and Hyde,' Goddard claimed.[481] Once, after he bought

242

Questions I Can't Answer

Meek an expensive gift, a gold watch, Meek screamed at him that it should have been engraved before he smashed it to pieces in front of the shocked songwriter.

During his career as an independent producer, Meek placed forty singles in the UK Top 50 charts: more than a quarter of those written – or co-written – by Goddard. The last new Goddard composition that Meek would produce was 'We'll Remember You', a tribute to singer Jim Reeves who died in a plane crash in July 1964, performed by Houston Wells and Irish showband the Masters. That track would remain unreleased until 2008.

In August, Meek was presented with a silver disc by Pye for 'Have I the Right?'. He had recently been filmed, talking quite candidly in his control room, for the ITV current affairs series *World in Action* (the episode, *The Flip Side*, aired on 22 September), and there was talk of his starring in a colour documentary about his career to date, but the sheen would have been taken off this news by the row with Goddard and a newspaper feature on independent producers ignoring his achievements, despite mentioning both the Honeycombs and his former associate Andrew Oldham (now enjoying huge success with the Rolling Stones), alongside singer turned producer Mickie Most, Island head Chris Blackwell and Meek's former assistant at IBC Adrian Kerridge. The article was titled 'Too Old at 30?'.[482] Meek was now 35, and if the premise was to be believed, past his sell-by date in the fast-moving world of pop music.

That same month Meek announced that Heinz would be moving from Decca to Columbia, and his next single, 'Questions I Can't Answer' appeared on the label at the beginning of October 1964. The Tornados would follow their former bassist from their next release, 'Granada', and another signing, Shane Spencer and the Casuals, would join them, although their disc – like their aborted Decca debut, 'I Believe' – would remain unreleased. It had been more than a year since Heinz had hit the Top 5 with 'Just Like Eddie'. Heinz and the Wild Boys (the band had changed its name to avoid confusion with another act called the Wild Ones, recently signed to Fontana) were soon back out on tour, and although the singer plugged its release with an appearance on *Thank Your Lucky Stars*, 'Questions I Can't Answer' was not a big hit, barely scraping the national Top 40. Meek would have been incensed had he read the review by Peter Aldersley in *Pop Weekly* where the journalist had the temerity to claim that the production was

243

Love and Fury: The Life, Death and Legacy of Joe Meek

'slightly reminiscent of the Phil Spector sound'.[483] Thankfully, the B-side, Meek's own composition 'The Beating of My Heart', supplied the singer with a surprise hit in Australia, which came just as Meek was preparing to send his boy down under for a fortnight of live appearances.

'Questions I Can't Answer' had hardly registered, yet there were many who felt that the singer was too cocky for his own good, and his prima donna attitude was proving unpopular with the other artists on the bill. Backstage one night, Heinz had a run-in with singer Jess Conrad. 'I toured with Heinz a lot,' Conrad says. 'He was one of Joe Meek's favourites. We had a history.' The behind-the-scenes confrontation between the pair was portrayed in the 2009 film *Telstar*. 'It was so vicious!' Conrad explains. 'When they filmed it [for *Telstar*] they made it into a comedy, but it wasn't funny; I bashed him up. Afterwards, of course, I became very friendly with Heinz, we were good mates, but in those days we were all doing the same show: it was very competitive and it became very difficult.'[484]

Heinz came in for a lot of criticism for his live act, and the letters pages of the music weeklies were often filled with complaints from concertgoers about him stealing from Eddie Cochran or others. 'Joe Meek and I work out the routines that I do on stage,' he told *New Musical Express*, 'and we put a lot of thought and hard work into them... I try to be different and still I am criticised. The thing is to fight it. Some of them are really hard digs, and it has been going on ever since I left the Tornados.'[485] The infamous altercation between the pair came after Heinz accused Conrad of stealing his act: Conrad had jumped on top of one of the guitar amplifiers his backing band was using, something Heinz – and others – would also do to get the audience going.

'Before you even sang it would be "How are you walking on?",' Conrad continues. 'You had to have a gimmick. P. J. Proby's roadie would put the same sort of boots on as him: he'd stick a leg out stage left, from behind the curtain, and the girls would scream because they thought it was Proby, then he would walk on from the other side. My gimmick was getting a mirror out and checking how I looked. These entrances were worked on. Rock 'n' roll almost became like a comedy situation, although the fans would not know it. You were always trying to do outrageous things just to outdo the other pop stars. In most of these concerts every act was a name... The order in which you would go on was very important. No one wanted

244

Questions I Can't Answer

to go on first, and sometimes the only way that would happen was for the promoter, secretly, to slip you a fiver.

'Backstage we would all bet on who would have the first rundown: that was when the girls got up out of their seats and ran down to the stage. Now, I knew that always happened to me: they'd get up and run to the stage. And for all the other pop stars it was a thing: if they couldn't get them to get up and run forward, then you knew you were struggling. We used to have bets. I would say that I would get the first rundown, and the others would say, "No, I will."'

Conrad was leaving the stage when a furious Heinz accosted him and accused him of stealing his act. The two got into a fight and, during the exchange Conrad pushed Heinz up against a wall and bit him hard on the nose. A yelping, bloody Heinz limped back to his dressing room, shouting threats to Conrad about his never working again. The incident has gone down in rock 'n' roll history, but the real reason Heinz was upset was not because Conrad had stolen his moves; it was an angry response to the endless backstage gossip about his domestic arrangements. 'Backstage there were all sorts of things going on, apart from a girl being passed around to shag, you know? We were into all sorts of things!' Conrad recalls. 'Everything was going on backstage, because we were all randy boys! And it was common knowledge that Heinz was Joe's boyfriend. We all knew that Joe Meek was a gay man, so there were no surprises there. He had quite a good-looking boy there that did little odd jobs, and there was Heinz upstairs, running in and out. He had to take it on the chin. We knew he lived upstairs; we knew he was recording him and we all knew that he couldn't sing to save his life!'[486]

Back in April 1964, the BBC had launched a new television series, *KYC 64: Know Your Car* (originally to be called *Family Car*) and chose a new track from the Tornados as its theme: 'Monte Carlo'. The B-side, a Brian Irwin original, 'Blue, Blue, Blue Beat', made the most of a short craze for ska and bluebeat discs – the record was issued in the same week as Millie's 'My Boy Lollipop' hit the UK Top 10 – and the band could be seen in glorious Eastmancolor performing the track in the Harold Baim 'quota quickie' *UK Swings Again* that played in cinemas up and down the country. Yet in spite of a push from the BBC, and a tip for Top 50 success from the *Record Mirror*, the single did not chart, nor would any subsequent Tornados release.

Love and Fury: The Life, Death and Legacy of Joe Meek

Their time as chart contenders may have been over, but 'Have I the Right?' was proving to be a massive international success, a number 1 in Canada, Australia, New Zealand and Sweden as well as in the UK, and Top 5 in the USA, Ireland and the Netherlands. Unfortunately, the court case brought by Geoff Goddard sucked much of the life out of what should have been a time of celebration.

The controversy around 'Have I the Right?' would have been easier to handle had Meek, or Howard and Blaikley, been able to come up with a second hit for the group. Within a week of its reaching the top, Meek was telling *Record Mirror* that 'we will probably try to keep the tempo up on the next single and then issue a slower one after that',[487] and although he was true to his word, their follow-up single, 'Is It Because?' (issued in October, the same month as 'Have I the Right?' hit a million sales) peaked at a miserable number 38 during its six-week run on the national charts. Howard and Blaikley had wanted a different song, 'Colour Slide' as the band's second single, but Louis Benjamin was adamant that their follow-up should sound similar to their chart-topping debut. Meek duly provided Pye with 'Is It Because?', but the lack of interest shown by the public fuelled his conviction that the men at the top of the industry were clueless, something that would have irked the man feted as 'Britain's most *avant garde* producer in terms of dramatic teen slanted studio sound' by trade magazine *Cash Box*.[488]

Sensing the need to reverse such a swift and ignominious downfall, just six weeks after the release of 'Is It Because?' the third single arrived. 'Eyes', another Howard–Blaikley composition, was far superior to its predecessor, but it failed to chart at all. Many of Howard and Blaikley's songs have gay overtones, and 'Eyes' was no different. Although Meek's place in the history of LGBTQ-themed recorded music is mostly based on the outrageous late Tornados B-side 'Do You Come Here Often?', several earlier releases – including 'Have I the Right?' and 'Eyes' – have a gay or lesbian subtext that would not be obvious to the casual listener but is there, nonetheless. Says Ken Howard: 'The early 60s were a sexually repressive time and the gay scene mostly took place in clubs or, more dangerously, in cottaging and open-air night cruising. Positive eye contact was the prelude to a conversation. That was what 'Eyes' was about.'[489] Meek may not have been aware of Howard and Blaikley introducing these themes

246

Joe poses for the press in his control room, Holloway Road, December 1962. *(Tony Gibson/Daily Express/Hulton Archive/Getty Images)*
Surrounded by tapes and equipment, at Holloway Road, December 1962. *(Tony Gibson/Daily Express/Hulton Archive/Getty Images)*

A young **David Jones** (later to become David Bowie) with his band the **Konrads**, January 1963. *(Mark and Colleen Hayward/Getty Images)*

(left) **Joe** in his control room, searching for an elusive tape, April 1963. *(John Pratt/Keystone Features/Getty Images)*

Seated in his office, holding his Ivor Novello Award, in front of his wall of stars, April 1964.
(Daily Herald/Mirrorpix via Getty Images)

(right) The producer and his protégé: **Joe** and **Heinz**, 1963.
(Bryan Wharton/Express/Hulton Archive/Getty Images)

Joe outside the front door of 304 Holloway Road.
(The Joe Meek Family Archive)

(top left) **The Honeycombs** at 304 Holloway Road, August 1964. *(Len Trievnor/Express/Getty Images)*

(bottom left) **Screaming Lord Sutch and the Savages**, February 1965. *(Pace/Getty Images)*

(top second left) **Geoff Goddard** during the 'How Do You Do It?' court hearing, June 1965.
(Harold Clements/Express/Hulton Archive/Getty Images)

(bottom second left) **Alan Blaikley**, **Ken Howard** and **Joe** outside the High Court, June 1965.
(Harold Clements/Daily Express/Hulton Archive/Getty Images)

(top) Officiating at a charity event in the Forest of Dean, summer 1966. *(The Joe Meek Family Archive)*

(bottom left) A policeman stands guard outside 304 Holloway Road, February 1967.
(Harry Dempster/Daily Express/Hulton Archive/Getty Images)

(bottom right) In front of one of his own abstract paintings, photographed by his friend **David Peters** at Holloway Road, early 1966. *(David Peters/Redferns)*

Questions I Can't Answer

into their work, but he too had been including the occasional nod to his own clandestine life in his songwriting: the 1963 single from Pamela Blue (Pamela Jean Berry), the Geoff Goddard composition 'My Friend Bobby' was backed with Meek's own 'Hey There Stranger', a song that on the surface seems innocent enough but may have suggested casual sex with a bit of rough.

The sudden *volte face* of the British public was not lost on the members of the group, nor the press. *Pop Weekly*, usually supportive of Meek's endeavours, blasted the band for being 'one-hit wonders', harrumphing that 'fans and readers know instinctively when a group are just lucky, and when they are talented'.[490] Not long after the Peterborough incident Martin Murray left and, as Honey Lantree ruminated, 'Our decline has been hard to take of course but we're compensated by the fact that although this country seems to have rejected us we're very big abroad... We've just returned from a very successful tour of Australia and New Zealand – where 'Eyes' our third single which did nothing here topped their charts – and we've toured Scandinavia and Holland. In Sweden a track from our LP – "That's the Way" – is top and we're soon to Japan where "Have I the Right?" has just been released.'[491] Meek's inability to provide the band with a second massive hit in their home country had a negative effect on his mood, and singer Dennis D'Ell revealed: 'I'll never forget one occasion, just after 'Have I The Right?' got to number 1, ITN [Independent Television News] wanted to interview us, and they sent Peter Snow down. Joe started muttering about lights and cameras and about how he wasn't having it, and they arrived right in the middle of the LP session; we were cutting our first album. They started setting up all this equipment, and Joe swore and stormed off out of the studio and said, "Let me know when it's all over," and he went down into his little room, which nobody was allowed to go in... By this time we were pretty used to Joe, you know. Peter Snow said, "I want the record on in the background... can someone go down and ask Mr Meek?" I said, "I shouldn't do that!"...' D'Ell's warning went unheeded by the veteran news reporter, who gingerly went to knock on Meek's office door. Receiving no answer, Snow pushed the door open. 'All of a sudden this bloody electric razor came flying across the room and smashed to smithereens.'[492]

*

247

Love and Fury: The Life, Death and Legacy of Joe Meek

Floundering, Meek continued to take on acts no matter how unsuitable they might seem. He was still looking for his own beat band, even though he continued to play down the importance and longevity of those very acts in the press: 'Beat is terribly important,' he said, 'and I concentrate on the rhythm tracks first. I go after a colourful sound and try to create a picture with material originality. Groups are going to stay around although not so popular as they have been and I think big orchestral accompaniments are coming back.'[493] Meek auditioned Jeff Curtis and the Flames, who had been playing around the London area for a couple of years and had come into Meek's orbit via support slots with the Flee-Rekkers. Then, from North Wales came four-piece beat combo the Anglesey Strangers, who recorded several tracks at 304. The band were soon advertising themselves as 'Decca recording artists', but a projected single, 'Susanne', was not picked up by the company and after several frustrating months trying to get Meek or someone at Decca to commit to a release date, the band split.

In June Meek auditioned four-man beat group the Combo D'Ecosse, from Kingussie in the Scottish Highlands, after their manager had phoned Meek and convinced him to see the band. Meek had already auditioned another group from the same area, Tommy Dene and the Tremors,* but had decided that he wanted Dene as a solo singer, as his band 'didn't have an original enough sound'.[494] Meek invited the Combo D'Ecosse to visit him in London, but that meant hiking the two youngest members, aged 16 and 17 respectively, out of school for the trip – something their parents were none too keen on. They passed the audition, and Meek brought them back in July to record their first single, having first sent them contracts to sign. The youngsters duly recorded a song, 'Shirley', at 304, played several dates in Cornwall and even performed six songs on a long-forgotten half-hour television programme aired in Japan, but no RGM Sound master would be released, and the four lads would soon be on their way back home to Inverness-shire.

In September 1964 Parlophone released the only single by the oddly named Shade Joey and the Night Owls, a band made up of former members of the John Barry Seven fronted by a singer whose real name was the far less starry Brendan Claypole, who hit on his unusual stage name after appearing

---

*   Not connected to Deke Arlon and the Tremors.

Questions I Can't Answer

at the Manchester club Chez Joey. The band chose a cover of 'Bluebirds Over the Mountain' for the A-side, but when the time came to record something for the flip side they realised that they had nothing suitable. Unusually, rather than insisting that they record one of his own compositions, Meek gave Night Owls saxophone player Bob Downes fifteen minutes to come up with something better, which he immediately did with the proto-Freakbeat* number 'That's When I Need You Baby'. The single failed to find favour, and Parlophone showed no interest in a follow-up. Shade Joey dropped the Night Owls and became front man of another group, the Colnsiders from Essex before reverting to his original name and becoming a Baptist minister. Meek took on Liverpool-based combo Earl Royce and the Olympics. The band had appeared in Gerry and the Pacemakers film, *Ferry Cross the Mersey*, and had recently added a female singer to their line-up. Meek intended to record a heavily Beatles-influenced number written by Liverpudlian songwriter Ron Anderson, 'I Really Do', but when the song appeared – as the B-side to their cover of the standard 'Que Sera, Sera' – the production was by George Martin, not Joe Meek.

None of these would make the grade. Perhaps feeling that Ken Howard and Alan Blaikley would offer him the best chance of another hit, Meek took a chance on another act that the pair had recently taken on. Alan Dean and His Problems, a six-piece band from Peterborough who had been gigging since early 1963, already had the time-honoured stint in Hamburg – and a summer season in Scarborough – under their belts. They had previously issued one flop single on Decca in early 1964, but were now being offered a lifeline thanks to Meek, Howard and Blaikley and Pye records. The frantic 'Thunder and Rain', backed with Meek's 'As Time Goes By' (another Buddy Holly-style song, which borrowed a motif from Geoff Goddard's 'Sky Men'), failed to find an audience: Ringo Starr dismissed it, not unfairly, as 'another group doing a Honeycombs. It's too fast to be any good. It sounds as if he's doing a race – like he's been given a quarter of an hour to make a record... There's just nothing good about it.'[495] The Problems

---

*   Freakbeat: a loosely defined term, coined in the 1980s by music archivist Phil Smee, for harder-edged British pop music from the mid-1960s with a foot in R&B, often seen as a bridge between the beat boom and psychedelia.

249

Love and Fury: The Life, Death and Legacy of Joe Meek

were soon reduced to a five-man act when guitarist Peter Pye left to replace Martin Murry in the Honeycombs.

At least Alan Dean and His Problems got to release a record: the next act Howard and Blaikley brought to Meek would be sent back down the wooden stairs from the studio to the street faster than they had come up them.

Alan Blaikley first discovered the Salisbury-based group Dave Dee and the Bostons when they were supporting the Honeycombs in the summer of 1964. The songwriter admitted to being 'mesmerised by their athletic and acrobatic stage antics while they maintained flawless vocal harmonies. Dave himself was a strong masculine presence and his previous training as a police cadet had doubtless contributed to his powers of leadership.' [496] A couple of weeks later, when the Honeycombs were playing in North London, the Bostons hooked up with Howard and Blaikley backstage. 'They wrote us a song and put us in with Joe Meek, who was the producer for the Honeycombs, but we didn't get on with him very well and he threw us out,' Dave Harman, aka Dave Dee, recalled.

'He had very strange recording techniques,' Dee continued. 'He wanted us to play the song at half speed and then he would speed it up and put all these little tricks on it. We said we couldn't do it that way. He exploded, threw coffee all over the studio and stormed up to his room. His assistant came in and said, "Mr Meek will not be doing any more recording today." That was it. We lugged all our gear out and went back home.' [497]

Meek would not work with the Bostons again, but after changing the band's name to the tongue-twisting Dave Dee, Dozy, Beaky, Mick & Tich in January 1965 (based on the members' nicknames), Howard and Blaikley would secure them their first television appearance, on the iconic *Ready Steady Go!* that March. Before the end of the year, the songwriters gave them a minor hit – the first of thirteen Top 30 placings – with their third release, 'You Make It Move', and DD,DBM&T would go on to give the team their second number 1 hit 'The Legend Of Xanadu'. He may have dismissed the future chart toppers, but in mid-1966 Meek would take the Howard–Blaikley track 'Hard to Love You', originally written for DD,DBM&T, and produce a version by the Honeycombs (retitled 'It's So Hard') for single release. Despite the song's close resemblance to DD,DBM &T's Top 5 hit 'Hold Tight!', once again the single failed to click with the record-buying public.

Questions I Can't Answer

Around the same time a group called the Davernettes, featuring electric guitar-playing female singer Viv Chering, her brother Dave Chering on bass, Graham Sharp on guitar and drummer Dave Donnison, came to record at 304. Meek had enjoyed a hit featuring a female drummer, so why not try a female guitarist? The band had already recorded a four-track demo the previous year (for Curly Clayton),* and the Cherings had given it to Meek in the hope that he could help them on their way to stardom. But nothing happened. Meek seemed to forget all about the act, so Viv took it upon herself to change his mind: 'I phoned [him] more than 50 times – pestered him for months,' she told the *Daily Mirror*. 'In the end he saw us and recorded us.'[498] Meek hated the name: luckily, the band were in the midst of changing it anyway, renaming themselves Flip and the Dateliners after Viv's family nickname and a television news programme, *Dateline*. The band recorded several tracks for Meek, but only two saw the light of day: 'My Johnny Doesn't Come Around Anymore' (originally recorded by US soul singer Debbie Rollins) and 'Listen to Me', a track written by the Chering siblings.

'Joe was professional and as nice as pie to us,' Graham Sharp remembers. 'He was forever combing his hair – it was literally every two to three minutes, even when he was recording. I suppose there were no more than four or five sessions with the band, and with us all being somewhat overawed, we didn't offer much of a challenge or experience a big reaction from him. One of our number asked him where he could find an ashtray, and Joe was not pleased, as he saw it, to be treated as a gofer. On one of the later sessions, I was involved in a bit of a conversation with another member of the band and unaware that Joe had emerged and was waiting to speak to me. He threw a bit of a fit because I hadn't noticed him and had turned up the volume on my amp considerably. On what I think must have been the last of the sessions with the group, Joe became dissatisfied with what Mick Cook, the drummer by then, was doing. Amid some recriminations, everything came to a halt, while Joe rang Clem Cattini and we had to wait for him to come in and set up before continuing. Mick, who

---

*   Guitarist Clayton (real name Harvey Ormerod) owned a small studio and booking agency, originally located in Highbury Place before moving to Islington's Swan Yard. He is best remembered today for recording the first Rolling Stones demo, in October 1962.

Love and Fury: The Life, Death and Legacy of Joe Meek

was an accomplished drummer, had to perform on just hi-hat and snare for the rest of the session.

'The room where Joe's equipment was set up was as chaotic as is usually described, but as far as we knew that's how technicians worked. I once witnessed him wind the reels on a deck very slowly and find the exact point at which to make a splice, which, to me, was genius, particularly having regard to the tape speed at which recording was made: he used a one-inch tape running at fifteen inches per second. He manoeuvred the tape with his hands until he got to the precise point where he wanted to splice it. He'd be listening through his cans and knew exactly the right point to make an edit. There were no counter measurements: it was all down to manual perfection. His biggest talent was being able to hear an end product in his head, and then, with his limited resources, make it happen. That, along with his self-made compressor and use of echo, was very special.'[499]

There was no let-up in his workload, but clearly Meek was spreading himself too thin. US star Brenda Lee was booked for a six-week tour of Britain and Ireland, beginning with the prestigious Royal Command Performance at the London Palladium on 2 November. Appearing on stage with Meek artists including Heinz, the Flee-Rekkers and the Tornados, her UK agent Harry Dawson (of the George Cooper organisation) suggested that the chanteuse could record for Meek, but despite the singer and her mother meeting with Joe, no session took place. Meek signed Islington five-piece the Blue Rondos after they turned up begging for an audition. Member Bill Pitt-Jones, who had gone to the same school as Steve Howe of the Syndicats, remembered that first meeting as a somewhat frightening experience: 'The door creaked open just enough to show a slight chink of light and [Joe's assistant] Patrick Pink stuck his nose through the opening. "Hi," we said in unison. "We understand these are the studios of Joe Meek." Another voice informed us, "We don't do auditions. Go away!" Roger [Hall, the band's 21-year-old singer] said, "Well, at least listen to our demo record, made at Curly Clayton's." The response was for the door to open completely, blinding us with electric light, and Joe Meek himself confronting us in a half-rage saying, "I don't listen to demo disks made by amateurs like that fucker!" Or words to that effect. And maybe as an afterthought, when he saw that he was dealing with young lads and not the heavy mob, added, "Come back at nine o'clock Monday morning and play the song to me."'[500]

Luckily for them, Meek's attitude had mellowed somewhat over the weekend, and after running through several takes of the song 'Little Baby', Meek thought he had enough. He had a meeting with Pye executives that afternoon, and he took the band's demo with him, leaving them at 304 to keep working. Pye, who at this point would take just about anything from Meek, were impressed enough to agree to release a single by the band. Although he usually did not record in the evening, Meek and the band got to work as soon as he returned from his meeting, and by the end of the day the Blue Rondos had taped the first of their two singles with him. Pye should have scored a winner with the band (who took their name from a racehorse, rather than from the Dave Brubeck composition 'Blue Rondo à la Turk'), but neither 'Little Baby' (which featured the Meek co-write 'Baby I Go For You' on the flip, and included some blistering guitar work from Roger Hall) nor 'Don't Want Your Loving No More', issued in April 1965, sent folk rushing to the record store.

A second single from the Syndicats might fare better. The band recorded a cover of the Howlin' Wolf classic 'Howlin' For My Baby', featuring bass player Kevin Driscoll on vocals as singer Tom Ladd had left, reducing the group to a four-piece, but the sessions did not go well. A frustrated Meek lost his temper with the band and stormed out of the building, as Steve Howe recalls: 'He said, "I'll be back in an hour and you'd better know how to play this song properly by the time I get back!"' It's possible that Meek's mood that day may have been affected by Howe rejecting his advances. 'He took a liking to me, which got a little bit difficult. He said to me, "Oh, I like your trousers," and I knew where this was going so I said, "I'm sorry, but I've got a girlfriend in Tottenham." And that was the line; it was my ticket out, you know? Obviously being gay at that time was pretty hellish; I knew other gay people and they were all pretty secretive about it; well, they had to be as they were so oppressed. He never took it any further, and I respected him for that.'[501]

Terry and the Avengers, from Mildenhall in Suffolk, had been offered a one-off deal with Decca, and recorded a song written by Chic Williams at 304, but both Decca and then EMI decided against releasing the tracks. One set of Avengers was not enough: Meek also took on Gravesend act the

Love and Fury: The Life, Death and Legacy of Joe Meek

Four Avengers, finalists in a local newspaper talent competition, but their self-penned tune 'I Don't Need You Now' would remain hidden among the ever-increasing pile of tape spilling from the shelves of the control room. Although their one chance of success via Meek would be lost to the Tea Chests, after a few line-up changes the band would mutate into late 60s hit makers Vanity Fare. Meek had better luck with singer Johnny Garfield, whose late 1964 cover of 'Stranger in Paradise', coupled with Meek's ballad 'Anyone Can Lose A Heart' was issued by Pye in January 1965, although the poor sales garnered by the release meant that Pye turned down the opportunity to issue a second Garfield single, 'Still You Pass Me By'.

Since they last met, Coventry-based guitar player Pip Witcher and drummer Bruce Finley had left the Atlantic Showband and formed a new group, the Sorrows. Witcher had been moved to jump from Irish showband music to the beat group sound after seeing the Beatles perform in Coventry, and readily admits that they built the new band around Finley: 'The best drummer I ever knew. Bruce was an amazing drummer, and other drummers used to come to see him play; Keith Moon came to see us once because of him.' The band had an audition at Decca's Hampstead studios under the watchful eye of producer and songwriter Tony Hatch, but, as Witcher says, 'They turned us down. We were a bit upset at the time, but we knew that they had turned the Beatles down too, so we didn't feel too bad, and then I said, "Let's go and see Joe Meek." So we went and recorded some tracks with him.'

Once again Meek let Witcher and his friends through the door without an invitation; however, the guitar player noticed a change in Meek's demeanour since the last time he was there. 'He was really grumpy,' Witcher recalls. 'When I was with the Atlantics he was really nice and friendly, but this time when I went into his playback room and I stood in front of the speaker he went mad at me! He could get very grumpy, very quickly.' Meek may have lost his temper with Witcher, but any anger soon passed. 'He fancied me,' Pip laughs. 'I could tell. He sort of cuddled me while I was listening, he put his arm around me. At the time I didn't really realise but when you look back it was obvious. Not that it matters. He was in the business and there were a lot of gay people in the business. You got used to it.'

'We didn't really know if it was an audition or a recording session,' Witcher adds. 'We went up to the studio and set up... There was tape

254

Questions I Can't Answer

and rubbish all over the floor; it was a right mess. We set up our amps, he put mics in and we started playing. We just went ahead and did it.'[502] The Sorrows would record at least five tracks over several sessions at 304, but none of this Meek-produced material would be issued at the time and they would eventually be signed by John Schroder, who was heading Pye imprint Piccadilly. Signed to an exclusive contract by Meek at the end of 1964, the Matadors, another Midlands-based band (from Hinckley, a town close to Coventry), would suffer a similar fate to the Sorrows: although they made their way to 304 for several sessions and their local newspaper announced at the end of February that a release was imminent, nothing was issued. The band had already recorded several tracks for Decca with no result, and being given the runaround by Meek was proving to be the last straw. Meek and the band did not get on well; they found him arrogant and claimed that he would not listen to their suggestions, and drummer Harry Heppinstall would later say that 'I recall how very bossy he was. I put my drumsticks down at the end of a take and he shouted at me to pick my sticks up again: "I'll tell you when you can stop!"'[503]

Terse discussions between Meek and the band's manager, Mike James, resulted in James threatening to break their contract. In November 1965, a year after they began working together, the frustrated manager told the *Coventry Standard* that, 'We can't wait around for ever, in fact, we are fed up about the whole business and from now on we are going to try and deal with a major recording company direct. Absolutely nothing was happening, as far as we could see, toward getting a disc released. We cut three discs with Joe Meek, but none have been released. Fans keep asking about our disc and we can't tell them anything.' Finally, in January 1966, and no doubt spurred on by the criticism of him in the *Coventry Standard*, two of the tracks the band cut for Meek emerged. 'A Man's Gotta Stand Tall' / 'Fast Cars and Money' was issued by Columbia, credited to the Four Matadors. The disc sold well locally but failed to trouble the national charts.

Meek was approached by Gordon Williams, manager of another Coventry-based band, the Chicanes, a man who ex-band member Barry Kingsbeer describes as 'a former beach photographer in Blackpool and a third-rate chancer. He wanted us to have our heads shaved and targets painted on them as this had worked for another band and they got pictures in the press!'[504] 'He was pretty good at pushing doors open,' fellow Chicanes member Rob Cumner accepts. 'We were excited about going to London. Like most bands we wanted nothing more than a record release, a number 1! We understood that Joe Meek was an independent producer and had to sell his recordings to record companies.'[505] At the end of September 1965, Meek decided that a change of name was in order, and re-christened them the Money Spiders, which caused some confusion at home: the band had a series of gigs lined up in Coventry; for some they were advertised as the Chicanes, but for others the Money Spiders, occasionally using both names in the same week. 'I don't know whose idea it was to change the band's name,' says Cumner. 'All I remember is Gordon bringing it up, but I don't remember who thought of the name Money Spiders, which we all liked.'[506]

Meek presented the band with an acetate of a previously unpublished song he was keen for them to learn, which they duly did, but although tracks for a potential single were laid down, once again nothing emerged. Kingsbeer, bass player and founding member of the Chicanes, did not agree with Williams about the direction he was taking the band and quit before their first session at 304. 'Meek didn't have a good name among most musicians then, as I recall. He was a bit of a corny anachronism to most of us young musos. In his field, in the early days, he didn't have much in the way of competition and was something of a trailblazer... I'm not putting him down per se, he had an influence on early British rock, but his music was simply never my personal cup of tea.'[507] 'We got on okay with Joe,' Cumner adds, 'although he did not like our harmony rendition of the song, 'Bells', written by the writer of 'The Crying Game' [Geoff Stephens, who had written for RGM Sound artists Michael Cox, John Leyton and Carter–Lewis]. To be fair, our harmonies may have been out due to nerves. He suggested that I should sing the song alone. Personally, I wasn't happy with this, but we did as he asked. He was without doubt a bizarre character; he would change his suit two or three times during a session. He did make a move on me. He wanted to see what we wear on stage: he approached me and touched me but I quickly stepped back and he got the message.'[508]

The Sorrows' Pip Witcher feels that was one of the reasons Meek was signing so many bands: 'Joe Meek would take anybody in those days, especially if he fancied you. If he liked one of you, then you were in.' The other reason was that Meek may have been looking for his own Beatles. 'Wasn't everybody?' Witcher asks. 'It was like that for us when we signed

Questions I Can't Answer

with Pye; John Schroeder liked the look of us and thought we were a bit Beatle-y.'[509]

With his friend Reg Calvert now firmly established in Rugby, perhaps the towns and cities around the area were where he would uncover the 'next big thing'? But if Meek was mining the Midlands for his own version of the Liverpool sound, he would not be successful. The Sorrows would not hit the charts until 1966, two years after their encounter with Meek. Hopefully, he was able to console himself with having two of his acts – the Honeycombs and Valerie Masters, with her festive offering 'Christmas Calling' – appear on the Christmas edition of *Thank Your Lucky Stars*. As his family indulged in this opportunity to gather around their television and toast his success, they could not have suspected that their Joe's golden period was already over.

When the promised Money Spiders single failed to materialise, the band were, naturally, dejected. 'We became a little concerned, having heard nothing from Joe, so we took a trip to London,' says Rob Cumner. 'Gordon [Williams, the band's manager] asked me and another band member to go up and ask Joe if he had any success with the single. We left with nothing, apart from Joe shouting as we left, "Don't slam the door!" We didn't slam any door. It was just another example of his bad temper. We concluded from this that our hopes of some success via Joe Meek no longer existed. We were very disappointed.'[510]

Other aspiring pop stars were going to end up disappointed too. Singer Reg Smart, renamed Reg Austin for his sole release, issued a single on Pye, 'My Saddest Day' backed with 'I'll Find Her', produced by Meek at 304 and credited not as an RGM Sound but, unusually, as 'a Joe Meek Production', possibly because Meek was in the process of switching his credits from RGM, which was half owned by Major Banks, to his new set-up, Meeksville, which was 99 per cent owned by Meek himself. The disc received no press, next-to-no radio play and, consequently, no sales. A projected follow-up, 'Every Second of the Day', would go unreleased.

CHAPTER 21

Nice While It Lasted

The final Tornados release involving Clem Cattini was the single 'Granada'. Recorded in October 1964 but not issued until the following January, rhythm guitarist Bryan Irwin wrote a rare vocal for the flip side. But Irwin and his bandmates – which now included guitarist Stuart Taylor, a former member of the Savages – were surprised when the disc was released to discover that his song, 'One Day I'll Smile Again', had been replaced by Joe's own composition 'Ragunboneman'. Inspired by the hit BBC television sitcom *Steptoe and Son*, the song had a weak vocal that was once again rendered unpleasant by Meek's insistence on speeding it up, although the *Record Mirror* insisted that it 'should have been the top side – it has strong chart potential'.[511] The Tornados were due to appear in Hamburg's famous Star Club immediately following a short British tour, then go straight into pantomime – in the second touring version of *Once Upon a Fairy Tale* – over Christmas, but after a furious row with Joe – which began after Meek grabbed a stool and threw it at the drummer's head and ended with the producer picking up a new reel-to-reel tape deck and hurling it down the stairs of 304 after the speedily exiting percussionist – Cattini, the only remaining original member, was off. The band honoured their German commitments, but their role in *Once Upon a Fairy Tale* was filled by the Flee-Rekkers, and Cattini officially left the Tornados on 10 February 1965: 'I'd had enough… I said to Joe, "I can't handle this anymore. I'm leaving."' He was not the only one defecting: Ritchie Blackmore had had enough of backing Heinz, and left to join Neil Christian's band the Crusaders, although, like Cattini, he would continue to perform on sessions for Meek.

Nice While It Lasted

If Meek had been ostracised by the industry following his arrest, the success he had with the Honeycombs should have put an end to that. The pop music world was a fast-moving one, and very much a closed shop. If you were part of the in crowd, your friends looked after you, and if you were gay, this was doubly so. Meek's associates – including Sir Joseph Lockwood and Brian Epstein – closed ranks, and the first few months of 1965 saw him as busy as ever. Heinz's first release of the year, 'Digging My Potatoes', was issued in February, and the reviews looked promising, but regardless of being tipped for great things the public were not buying. Credited to Heinz and the Wild Boys, Meek was unhappy with the original take of 'Digging My Potatoes' and called in Jimmy Page to add some magic. 'I had done a number of sessions for Joe,' Page recalls. 'But this one I particularly remember as he'd asked me to overdub a solo onto the track.' Despite the star guitarist's work, and the *Sunday Mirror* predicting that it 'should go to the top',[512] the first single to feature the producer credit 'Meeksville Sound' debuted at number 29 in the *New Musical Express* chart at the beginning of March. Although EMI hosted a launch party for the release, which featured the Wild Boys playing live and Heinz miming to his recording – with those present digging into baked potatoes – this would be Heinz's last British hit. A year or so after Meek's death, and after a short stint working for Ford in Dagenham, Heinz could be found running a mobile fruit and veg round, delivering potatoes door to door.

Meek had planned to record a second album with Heinz, and his friend Tony Grinham wrote a song for the project, 'Leggy Peggy'. 'Altogether I wrote about sixty-six different songs,' Grinham explains. One of those songs, 'The Long Drop', would be issued in 2020, with a new vocal from Glenda Collins dubbed over the original acetate Meek gave to Grinham. 'I sang a vocal demo for Joe, and then he's played that for his musicians – I think Ritchie Blackmore is on there – and they did the backing track. It was about a year later that Joe got me to sing over the backing track, and Joe was knocked out by it. He was really overjoyed with it, but it never got released.'[513] Grinham also painted a portrait of the singer to use on the cover. Meek was impressed, and Grinham encouraged the producer to pick up the paint brushes himself, suggesting that it would be a good way to relax after a hard day's work. 'He was always very tense,' Grinham explains. 'He was juggling different things all the time.'[514] Meek would paint several canvasses, some of which he proudly displayed in his office and sitting room, including the abstract *Eye View of a Room* and his infamous portrait, inspired by Judy Garland, *The Lady with the Crying Eyes*, which ended up in the possession of Eric Meek after his brother's death. A pen-and-ink drawing Meek did of Patrick Pink was sold at auction in 2017; other paintings, including one of his mother, a square oil-on-canvas of a blond-haired young man holding hands with another man with a dark quiff (representing Heinz and Joe) and a second which featured a favourite fishing spot near to the family home in Newent, were kept by his siblings. Grinham's portrait of Heinz was gifted by Meek to the singer, who still owned it at the time of his death.

A few days before 'Digging My Potatoes' hit the stores Decca had issued the second single from Meek's very own Elvis, Dave Kaye. It seems that Meek had learned nothing from the failure of their first foray a year before: he chose another Elvis song for the singer to cover, 'In My Way', tacking on an embarrassing spoken-word tribute to the King to the beginning. Kaye hated it, but Meek was insistent: 'It was a lovely song, but Joe wanted this gimmick, and to be honest it was embarrassing,' he explained. 'We fell out when Joe suggested another tribute song. He said he had been talking to Buddy Holly. When I pointed out that Buddy Holly had been dead for [six] years Joe just looked at me and said: "I know. I am a spiritualist." Joe had recorded Mike Berry's hit dedicated to Buddy some years earlier and he reckoned Buddy had told him it was time to do it again – I don't know if he asked Joe to get me to do it! Anyway I told Joe, "No more tribute records," and he went up the wall.' [515] Kaye and Meek would not talk to each other for over a year.

Still the records kept coming: in March Parlophone issued the second single from David John and the Mood, the group's first Meeksville Sound production, 'Bring It to Jerome'. A stomping R&B number, the group had come to Meek via their friends the Puppets, after their debut single, 'Pretty Thing', had flopped. To add some extra drive to the mix, singer David John Smith came up with what he thought was a novel approach. 'We felt we'd needed something different to add to it,' he told *It's Psychedelic, Baby* magazine. 'I went to the toilet and dismantled the metal chain... And when I got back to the studio, Joe's eyes lit up and he immediately left the room, returning with an old biscuit tin. We dropped the chain into the tin on the beat, and Joe layered it with echo and mixed it into the recording. It sounded fantastic.'[516] It was not the first time Meek had employed the effect (he used it on Screaming Lord Sutch's 1961 single 'Till the Following Night'), and despite the extra attention to the percussion, the single stiffed. With little income, Meek gratefully accepted a fee from BBC Radio to record a short interview for a programme they were producing called *Ten Years of Pop*. It meant his having to leave the confines of 304 to go to the BBC's studio at the Aeolian Hall on New Bond Street on 24 March, but it put five very welcome guineas into his pocket. It had been a very different situation two years earlier, when a similar fee for Meek appearing on the programme *Pop Inn* went unclaimed.

Through David John and the Mood, Meek met Northern club promoter Clive Kelly, a friend of Brian Epstein's and close associate of the Beatles' former manager Allan Williams. Kelly ran several clubs in the north, including the Cubiklub in Rochdale, where David John and the Mood had often played. Another of Kelly's friends, pop singer Donovan, had introduced the club owner to a 17-year-old folk singer, Davy Morgan, originally from Woking in Surrey. Kelly took on the role of manager, tried to style Morgan as a modern-day wandering minstrel and successfully persuaded Meek to cut a single with his protégé: one contemporary press report suggests that he recorded an album's worth of material with Meek, and several other tracks, including the song 'Cocaine' do exist in the vaults. Issued by Columbia in July, Morgan's solitary, Dylan-esque release – containing two self-penned numbers, 'Tomorrow I'll Be Gone' and 'Ain't Got Much More To See' – would not grace the charts, but Meek, with his connections at Radio Luxembourg, would attempt to help Kelly secure a job as a DJ at the station.

Both Morgan and Kelly were prodigious LSD users, and it was around this time that Meek tried it for the first time. 'He used to listen to all the freaks in the business, and of course at that time it was the in thing to take speed and all that sort of thing, and there was a lot of it going around,' Dennis D'Ell disclosed. 'In fact I'm sure that Joe had a dabble with acid and god knows what several times which is the only thing really that would account for such irrational behaviour.'[517] Lysergic acid diethylamide, or acid as it was known, was popular among the big names of the American counterculture but was most widely known in Britain for treating schizophrenia and other mental health issues. Michael Hollingshead, an associate of Timothy Leary, had recently moved to Chelsea and opened the grandly named World Psychedelic Centre, selling books about psychedelics and spreading the word about the drug. Meek's own encounter with LSD, he told Tony Grinham, resulted in a bad trip: 'He told me that he was under the influence for about eight hours, and all that time he thought that he was on a raft at sea. He didn't like it, and he never took LSD again, but he was on a lot of different drugs.'[518]

'Alcohol and substance misuse is rife in the music industry,' psychotherapist and author Tamsin Embleton observes. 'What other workplaces have drug use built into how they operate? It's used to celebrate, commiserate, pass the time, tap into creativity (though this often isn't effective), to assuage performance anxiety, to flatter, to control. It's a bit less obvious now, and some of the younger generation are cleaner-living, but it's still around. There have been countless artists who have died through issues with substance misuse – accidental overdoses, polypharmacy, secondary issues such as liver disease and so on.'[519]

In the same month as David John and the Mood issued 'Bring It to Jerome' Tom Jones, the Welsh singer who Meek had once made a pass at, reached number 1 in the British singles charts with his second Decca 45, 'It's Not Unusual'. At that very same time Meek was desperate to find some money. The working relationship between the producer and Major Banks had completely broken down, and Meek wanted to extricate himself from their contract. With royalties from his two biggest hits embargoed by court action, Meek needed to find a way to make some money, and in May 1965 he licensed two of his Tommy Scott and the Senators tracks to Columbia. Credited to Tom Jones, 'Little Lonely One' (a cover of a 1961 Jimmy Justice B-side) and the Myron and Byron composition 'That's What We'll All Do' did not chart in Great Britain (although its release certainly hampered the sales of Tom Jones' latest Decca single 'Once Upon a Time'), but, issued in July in the United States, the same coupling reached number 42 on the *Billboard* chart.

Meek came in for a lot of flak for issuing the single, not least from Tom Jones himself, who was keen to separate himself from the recordings. 'When someone tries to make money by releasing a "name"'s record cut

Nice While It Lasted

in his struggling days, well that really makes me mad!' he told *Music Echo*. 'This is one thing in the business which has always annoyed me, and now it's actually happened to me, I'm just plain furious... I did everything I could to stop that number coming out! Those records are not nearly as good as the ones I am making now.'[520] Not everyone agreed, and some reviewers happily stated that Jones was 'sounding good on the re-release of a song he made a long time ago... In my opinion it's better than 'Once Upon a Time' – even if Mr Jones himself disagrees.'[521] Gloucester's *Citizen* newspaper, usually fulsome in its praise of Meek's work, avoided criticising the local hero but remarked that 'EMI's ethics in digging it out of the archives are questionable'.[522] Meek hit back at the critics, telling them that the decision to issue 'Little Lonely One' was 'a business move which no one with any commonsense would not have taken.

> The general opinion is that I am trying to cash in now because Tom Jones is a big name, but I should like to point out that I certainly would not release just any old record simply to make money. For example, I have in my possession right now, tapes I recorded with THE SWINGING BLUE JEANS, CLIFF BENNETT and SOUNDS INC., who all recorded with me at one time but none of the recordings are up to the standard I consider would be a commercial proposition... so I have no intention of releasing them... It was only when I heard Tom's follow-up to 'It's Not Unusual' that I realised I had a disc which was – to my mind – far better. Even then, I checked my legal position first before farming the tape out to a major record company – who incidentally agreed with me straight away about the disc's potentiality because they decided straight away to rush release it.'[523]

In October, Columbia (and Tower in the US) would issue another brace of tracks from the vault, the aborted late 1963 debut, 'Lonely Joe' and 'I Was a Fool'. This disc would not chart, and one month later Columbia compiled all four tracks onto an EP, which was also issued in several European territories. In November, a third single from the Meek sessions appeared in the States, 'Chills and Fever' backed with 'Baby I'm in Love', but this time there would be no British release. This version of 'Chills and Fever' had been

263

Love and Fury: The Life, Death and Legacy of Joe Meek

recorded in January 1964, before Jones re-recorded the song for Decca; Senators guitarist Mike Roberts recalls that 'we did a version in Meek's studio, but I think my solo was overdubbed by Ritchie Blackmore'.[524]

Meek could no longer handle the Major's parsimony, but extracting himself from the partnership was not going to be easy. In August 1964 Banks had offered to sell Meek his shares in RGM Sound for £2,000, knowing full well that Meek did not have the money. More than a year later, at a heated meeting in October, Banks finally sold his entire stake in the business to Meek for £14,999 4s 6d, almost six times his original investment. He would have settled for less, but in a foolhardy act of bravado Meek once again gave too much away; according to an article in the *Sun*, buying the Major out had 'cost him all he had made so far'.[525] It was a bold move, and one he would not have made had he not expected his financial situation to improve dramatically, but it plunged Meek into massive debt. Meek's new company, Meeksville Sound Ltd, had been registered on 14 April 1965, although he had been using the name since the previous December: an advertisement in the Christmas edition of *Record Mirror* featured his then-current roster of artists under the heading 'Meeksville – where hits are born'. Of the hundred shares, Joe held on to ninety-nine; the remaining one share went to Thomas Edwin Southey Shanks, his partner in Heinz Burt Ltd and Joe Meek Enterprises. Major Banks would later be involved in a tax avoidance scandal similar to that which would see Barrington-Coupe in the dock, when his company, Dorai Giftware, was accused of selling goods direct to dealers for cash, with no invoice, to evade tax. More than a decade after Meek's death, Banks would write to the solicitors handling his estate, claiming that he still had a financial interest in RGM Sound Ltd. The solicitors, Tucker, Turner & Co., wrote back telling the Major that 'we cannot see that you have any grounds for a claim against the estate'.[526]

Meek was not the only one having financial issues: in May Robert Stigwood Associates went into liquidation. Stigwood had milked his company dry, leaving bands owed money, staff unpaid, EMI owed thousands from a loan that had been personally guaranteed by Sir Joseph Lockwood, and his former partner, Stephen Komlosy, carrying the can. The artists he had taken to Meek – including John Leyton – were suddenly without an agent or management, and Leyton would not release another record for nine years. His acts may have suffered, but the ever-resourceful Stigwood

Nice While It Lasted

would resurface with a new business partner, new financial backing from Polydor records, a new company and a new record label: Reaction. Meek would always curse Stigwood for having taken Leyton away from him, but unlike Stigwood, whose label would score hits with The Who and Cream and who would eventually reach stratospheric heights with the Bee Gees, Meek would never again climb as high as he had once been with the hit-making team of Geoff Goddard, Charles Blackwell and John Leyton.

Perhaps it was the knowledge that he was finally in control of his own business, but regardless of the lack of chart success Meek certainly seemed to be in a good mood, as witnessed by one man who, in other circumstances, could have expected a tongue lashing from the producer: Jess Conrad. 'I used to hang about a lot with Michael Cox, who was my best friend,' the singer explains. 'We used to go to Joe Meek's place because it was somewhere to hang out; we'd sit there all day having coffee and just being social… It was just sort of, "What shall we do today? Shall we go and visit Joe Meek?" It was a place to go. You'd sit there all day having coffee; people were coming in and out – lots of people we knew. It was like our playground; other people might go to a certain coffee shop in the West End and hang around with people like Michael Caine and the like, but at Joe Meek's place you'd meet people who were not there to make a record, they'd just popped in to say hello.'[527]

Meek seemed to have forgotten any animosity he was harbouring against Conrad following his backstage rumble with Heinz. In fact, by this point, Conrad and Heinz were getting on reasonably well, and in time they would become good friends. 'Heinz was always upstairs,' Conrad reveals. 'We never went upstairs, but we assumed that was where Joe Meek lived or slept or whatever, and we assumed that Heinz was his boyfriend. He would appear now and then, he'd come down the stairs and go outside, go wherever he was going.' Meek knew that there had been gossip about his relationship with Heinz, but the subject was never broached. 'It wasn't an issue,' says Conrad. 'We just knew that either Heinz was his boyfriend because he liked him or because he recorded him, and he was very successful as a pop star. We didn't think anything about the sexual thing, it wasn't important. We knew that Joe was a gay man, but it was just he was in showbusiness, you know, and people in showbusiness knew about that. It was not a big thing.'[528]

Love and Fury: The Life, Death and Legacy of Joe Meek

In May 1965 Pye released 'Hurt Me', credited on the label as 'a Joe Meek production' rather than a product of RGM Sound or Meeksville. Backed by Meek's own composition 'It Can Happen to You', the A-side featured female vocals from Pat Booth, a successful model who the media claimed had been Conrad's childhood crush. The story was that he had spied Pat while window shopping in Chelsea but was too embarrassed to approach her himself, so had Meek contact her and offer her the chance to perform on the disc. In truth, Meek was hoping to use his contacts at Pye to secure a recent chart topper. 'He said that I was going to duet with a girl who was a big name then,' says Conrad. 'He named all these people who were going to play opposite me, including Sandie Shaw. It was meant to be two big names duetting. There were other people doing that type of record, and I thought it would be quite something. He did it, and then he dubbed the other voice on later on. I was upset that it wasn't Sandie, because that's who he had promised.'[529]

Far from being at loggerheads with each other, Conrad remembers the recording as a happy, fun-filled time. 'We made these records in the front room there, which was overlooking the street, and the windows were all sort of bunged up so that the sound wouldn't go out. Clem Cattini, who was on so many of Joe's records, was a good friend of mine, and it was a very happy atmosphere. We were like a little gang. 'The recording was done in the front room, then next to that was his control room. He came through the doorway to give me a note, and he was wearing a woman's hat, a bonnet like you might see in a western film, that tied in a bow under his chin! He popped his head round now and then in this strange lady's hat and give me notes! We knew he was an extrovert; it was all part and parcel of what made up Joe Meek.'[530]

The result, though no doubt fun for those involved, was spectacularly dull, but 'It Can Happen to You' was one of the best tracks Conrad cut during his 1960s heyday and featured excellent session work from Cattini on drums (who, despite having a tape deck aimed at his head and having left the Tornados, would still join in the occasional session at 304), Ritchie Blackmore on lead guitar and an unnamed saxophone player. 'If you recorded for Joe Meek, it was like you'd got the cherry on the cake, because he used to take care of you and he made very good records,' Conrad remarks. 'I didn't plan it, I just went there a lot and I thought to myself, "It

Nice While It Lasted

would be great if Joe Meek would record me," and in the end he did. I'm not sure if I said to Joe, "Will you record me?" or if he said to me, "Do you fancy making a record?" But I was thrilled when it happened. The recording I made wasn't bad, but he wasn't that pleased with the result. The record wasn't a great success, it didn't chart, but he was anxious to make another one.'[531] With Conrad's busy work schedule – and a planned tour of South Africa on the cards – the pair agreed that when both men were available, and they had the right song, they would reconvene to record a follow-up.

Conrad and Cox may have enjoyed hanging around 304, but after a battle over his latest recording, Cox and Meek would part ways. Cox was rightly proud of his performance of an old Ben E. King B-side, 'Gypsy', but Meek once again sped up the recording by around 10 per cent, leaving the singer sounding like he was trying to pull off a third-rate impersonation of Gene Pitney. Cox was furious with the result. 'I said, "Look, Joe, as far as I'm concerned, it's ruined." But you could never argue with Joe. I liked him, but he couldn't take criticism. That was his one failing. If anyone criticised him, he went to pieces… It was a beautiful song, the rhythm tracks were terrific, and then he goes and screws it up. I said, "Joe, this is stupid." "I want it like this! This is the way!" And I said, "Well, I'm sorry."'[532] Cox and Meek would never work together again.

By the time of the next Tornados release, 'Early Bird' (May 1965) the band included former Flee-Rekkers guitarist Dave Cameron. The group were now referred to as the Tornados 65 in publicity material, although they kept their usual name for record releases. In the hope of emulating their earlier success, this track was also written by Meek and named after a satellite, and once again the original concept came to him while watching television: 'As I watched, I got that urge again,' he explained. 'The melody came into my mind and I went straight away and tapped it out on the piano.'[533] Although it has often been said that Meek could not play any instrument, his brothers both insisted that Joe played the piano, and in one 1962 interview he discussed his abilities, admitting that he played 'enough piano to get by. And guitar, rather poorly. I'm just settling down to learning how to read music properly.'[534]

Part of Meek's fascination with satellites was their ability to foster international communication, as he explained: 'What makes Early Bird so

Love and Fury: The Life, Death and Legacy of Joe Meek

different is its ability to transmit first-class pictures, sound and information from one side of the world to the other. This, in my opinion, could change the outlook of the different nations and bring them together in peace, for it is no longer possible for any country to be independent with such scientific inventions available.'[535] He had great hopes that the song, and the new version of the band – supplemented by saxophone player Roger Warwick for this particular disc – would provide him with another hit, but 'Early Bird' did not sell, appearing on the *Melody Maker* chart for one week only at 49.

A third single from the Syndicats, a cover of the R&B number 'Leave My Kitten Alone' was refused by EMI (the Beatles had recorded a version in August 1964, but that would remain unreleased until 1995), leaving Meek to quickly come up with an alternative. The band pulled out the magnificent 'On the Horizon', a cover of a Leiber and Stoller song originally recorded by Ben E King, backed with 'Crawdaddy Simone', now acknowledged as a freakbeat masterpiece. Problems within the band, coupled with EMI's refusal of their chosen A-side, led to Steve Howe quitting: Howe plays on the A-side but was replaced by Ray Fenwick on 'Crawdaddy Simone'. Howe joined the In Crowd, who would soon morph into Tomorrow and record the psychedelic pop classic 'My White Bicycle'. Line-up changes with the Syndicats aside, Meek's thirst for work continued unabated. He auditioned Liverpudlian foursome the City Kings, and was impressed enough with singer Gerry de Ville (real name Gerry Hale) to offer him a recording contract. He booked de Ville into 304 Holloway Road to record four tracks at the end of June 1965, on the understanding that the economics student finish his degree first. 'That isn't the right image for a pop singer,' Meek explained. 'We had better wait until you have completed your studies and left university.'[536] Shortly afterwards he signed another singer from Liverpool, Al Trent, and his band the Centremen. (The Centremen had been together since 1962, originally as Vance Williams and the Rhythm Four: when he joined them in early 1964 they became Al Trent and the Centremen.) Trent had auditioned for Meek two years earlier, while fronting a different band, but although Meek was keen to sign him, his group broke up, and Trent returned to the family home in the Dingle without issuing a note.

This time around either Meek, Trent or his manager felt that the time was right for a new name. The former butcher was rechristened Jason

Nice While It Lasted

Eddie, but his real name was Albie Wycherley, and he was the younger brother of Billy Fury. Meek would record a number of tracks with Eddie and issue two singles, the organ-driven 'Whatcha Gonna Do Baby?', issued by Parlophone in December 1965, and a frankly unhinged, proto-freakbeat version of the old Guy Mitchell/Tommy Steele hit 'Singing the Blues' in the summer of 1966, with manic guitar work overdubbed by Meek onto the Centremen's original take. 'It was better before Joe messed around with it,' Albie rued. 'He added some fuzz guitar, speeded it up and ruined it.'[537] Despite being issued in both Britain and America, neither 'Singing the Blues' nor its predecessor provided the act with a hit, and although 'Singing the Blues' would become a highly prized collectable amongst freakbeat collectors decades later, neither Eddie nor the Centremen would record for Meek again.

Although Heinz was still living at 304, he now had a new girlfriend, Della, which put further strain on Meek's patience. The rows were endless, and to ease tensions Meek's new business partner Tom Shanks gave the lovebirds the use of one of the flats he had in his own property portfolio, 54 Great Peter Street, Westminster. Previously inhabited by singer Petula Clark, Shanks had encouraged Meek to spend a few days at the flat whenever he wanted to get a break from his work at 304, but Meek tended to use it mostly when his family came to visit.

Joe's temper tantrums may have been legendary, but not everyone got to see that side of him. To many who knew him, he was a gentle soul, quiet-spoken, charming and endlessly kind, as one teenage musician discovered. 'I was nearly 15, and I was walking down the Holloway Road – I'd been to a music shop called Berry's [Nathaniel Berry & Sons Ltd, 320 Holloway Road], which was a few doors away from number 304. I came out of Berry's with the guitar strings I had just bought, and down the road I could see people moving some musical equipment into a shop; I thought, "Hello! What's going on down there?" So, being the nosey little toad that I was, I walked down and saw this leather shop, called Shenton's. I went into the shop and the lady there, who turned out to be Mrs Shenton, said to me, "Hello, dear. Can I help you?" I said, "Yes, what's going on here, with all this gear going in?" And she said, "It's all right, dear, there's a recording studio upstairs, and it belongs to a man called Joe Meek. Would you like to

269

Love and Fury: The Life, Death and Legacy of Joe Meek

go and see him? He'll make you welcome." So I thought, well, yeah.. I'm a musician anyway, I'll go and see him. So I went upstairs – the stairs were so steep you needed an abseiling kit to go up them – but I got up there, knocked on the door, and he answered. "Yes?" he said, and I told him about the lady downstairs and explained that I was a musician, and he said, "Well, come in and I'll show you around."'

The 15-year-old guitarist was Paul Burns, then known by his given name Christopher Paul Barnes. He was Holloway born and bred, having been brought up around half a mile away, at 23 Comus Road. He acquired his first guitar when he was still just 9 years old, and by the time he was 14 was playing in bands at the local pub, the Half Moon (now known as the Owl and the Hitchhiker). In 1969 the Barnes' family home – like those of his neighbours – was subject to a compulsory purchase order by the local council: the houses were levelled and the foundations are now beneath the grounds of Whittington Park.

'He was very quiet, very polite,' Paul recalls. 'I went in and he showed me around. As you went through the door, to the left, there was a kind of sitting room. Straight on was his office. As you go up the next set of stairs there was the recording studio. He took me up there. There were two entrances, one was to the studio, and one was to the control room... The control room was on the left. He said, "This is my studio," and I went into the studio itself, which was at the front of the building. The first thing I noticed was a great, orange-coloured velvet curtain – absolutely massive, I'd never seen such a big curtain in my life – and that covered the whole of the front wall up – the windows and everything. On the right-hand side was a Lowry organ, with a piano stool in front of it, and as I turned around, on the left, was his piano. The front had been taken off the piano, and the top was open. To the right of that was a clear space and then a cream-coloured folding screen. He was very nice, very interested in what I was doing, and said, "Would you like to come up with your band, and audition?" Of course I said yes, although I didn't take him up on it straight away. Then he showed me the control room: "This is where I do all of my recording..." The equipment he had in there was unbelievable. To the right was a big rack of stuff, and his soldering iron was hanging from it, always on. Right in front was a whopping great machine, with two 10½-inch tape spools on it. That was his main machine. He had, to the left, just underneath the window, a massive grey speaker, which had a metal case with a mesh front. It was enormous. He played his stuff back through that, that was his playback. The sound he got through that was fantastic.'[538]

Rob Cumner of the Money Spiders remembers that 'unlike today's recording desks his equipment was vertical and he would stand at the equipment keeping time by swivelling one foot into the other.'[539]

Burns continues: 'I said to him, "I'd like to learn how to record, maybe learn how to do what you're doing but on a smaller scale," and he said, "Yes, I can show you some of my techniques." He was very helpful. He showed me how he recorded bands. Obviously I was never going to be as good as he was, but he was very kind, very soft-spoken; he never ever shouted at me once. People have said that he was horrible and loud, but he wasn't. He was a gentle person, a gentleman.'[540] A gentleman, certainly, but also a man looking for an outlet for his sexual appetite, as Paul soon discovered: 'At the very beginning, he did make a pass at me, but I rejected it straight away. I made it clear that I wasn't interested, and after that he was respectful. He respected me anyway, and that was it.

'I was in there one day, and I'd brought my dad around to see him. He was standing in the doorway of his control room, and he had a massive microphone on a short stand, standing on top of a cabinet, and he was banging, putting his hand on the top and going up and down, *bomp, bomp, bomp* to the beat of a tune, actually recording that. Obviously that was one of the ways he got a bit of drive on his records. He recorded them very, very loud. I saw him recording, when the needles have gone up into the red, and I actually said to him one day, "Aren't you worried about it going over the top, worried about distortion?" And he said, "No, because it's only for a split second. It doesn't count." He got that to such an art where he could do it without any distortion, but still get it the loudest he could possibly get. And, by God, it didn't half work! One day, I went into his office, and he had the radio on. And as I walked through the door, Heinz came on the radio, singing 'Digging My Potatoes'. "There's one of my songs," he beamed, very proudly. "There's one of my songs." He was a proud man, and very, very clever.'[541]

CHAPTER 22

Wipe Out

That July, Joe Meek, Ken Howard and Alan Blaikley finally delivered another significant hit for the Honeycombs, and 'That's the Way' (backed with a Meek original, 'Can't Get Through to You') would spend fourteen weeks in the UK charts, peaking at number 12. Their previous single, 'Something Better Beginning' penned by label mate Ray Davies of the Kinks, had barely scraped into the Top 40. The tune had not been helped by the over-the-top brass and string arrangement from Ivor Raymonde, which Meek had overdubbed onto the original take after the band had finished work for the day.

The Honeycombs managed four hits in a little over twelve months but would not enjoy another chart placing in the UK. Still, the band had tremendous respect for Meek and continued to champion him. That summer, they brought a new act to meet Meek, Diane and the Javelins, who they had seen performing at a club in early 1965. He recorded two sides with them, a pop rewrite of the Hoagy Carmichael and Frank Loesser standard 'Heart and Soul', backed with 'Who's the Girl', an original number written by the band's lead guitarist Peter London. Confusingly, that same year Meek issued a 45 by a blind, piano-playing singer called Peter Cook, a cover version of another Hoagy Carmichael/Ray Charles classic, 'Georgia' (backed with an instrumental, 'There and Bach Again', co-credited to Cook and Meek), but as the comedian of the same name was establishing himself around the same time, Meek thought that his artist should change his name, and had the readers of the *Record Mirror* choose a new moniker for him: Peter London. Meek had either forgotten, or perhaps did not care, that he already had another Peter London on the books, the Javelins' guitar player.

Wipe Out

Meek's association with Howard and Blaikley would continue until the end of 1966. 'We got to know Joe Meek quite well,' the songwriters would later recall, 'and managed to establish a mutual respect. He used to offer us tea in his sitting room, served in dainty cups. However, his conversation often veered into the paranoid, describing not only communication with his dead pop idols, but also his conviction that he was under constant surveillance, spied upon and overheard by rivals keen to steal his unique "magic". He used the same word to describe his technique of speeding and manipulating tracks to give them a strangely hysterical feel.'[542]

'Joe was always quite secretive,' Howard adds. 'I don't recall the last time we were at Holloway Road, but we never fell out with him and I clearly recall the emotional, tear-stained letter he sent after we presented him with an elegant fountain pen at Christmas, and thanked him for all the good work he had put in on our behalf. He said that it was the best present he had ever been given. I think that Joe was a great record producer and one of the major and most original figures in the recording industry in the early 60s.'[543]

Renewed success with the Honeycombs impressed Pye, and the company offered him unlimited access to one of their own studios. Meek, naturally, refused, preferring to remain at 304 Holloway Road. On the same day as the label issued 'That's the Way', they also released the second single from his recent signing Bobby Rio and the Revelles, 'Everything in the Garden', backed by a Meek original, 'When Love Was Young'. Hailing from Dagenham, the singer had toured with John Leyton back in early 1963, later replacing future Small Face Steve Marriott in the band the Frantics. The Frantics were renamed Bobby Cristo and the Rebels and had recorded a single for Meek, 'The Other Side of the Track', issued by Decca in May 1964.

A bouncy, soulful tune from hit songwriters Cook and Greenaway that had already been recorded by Petula Clark, 'Everything in the Garden' should have done well, but Bobby Rio's bid for chart stardom was hampered by Brian Epstein's act, the Fourmost, releasing their version of the same song just one week later. 'Everything in the Garden' deserved to be a hit, as did 'The Very First Day I Met You', from Australian vocalist Judy Cannon, also issued that month. The A-side was written by Terry O'Neill, the English-born host of the popular Australian variety show *Time*

273

Love and Fury: The Life, Death and Legacy of Joe Meek

for Terry.[*] The track features a storming string and brass section, scored and directed by Ivor Raymonde, with (it is alleged) lead guitar work from Jimmy Page. Page can be heard more prominently on the flip side, 'Hello Heartache'.

While Meek was happily mining his collection of unfinished Senators recordings and promoting his new releases from the Tornados and Jess Conrad, in July a disc appeared on Columbia entitled 'Space Walk' backed with 'Goodbye Joe', reputedly recorded by the original Tornados under the pseudonym The Gemini' (named after NASA's Project Gemini, America's second manned space project, the immediate precursor to the *Apollo* mission) and produced by Don Charles, who had recorded half a dozen singles for Meek between 1962 and 1964, and had been one of the first friends Meek turned to for comfort following his November 1963 arrest. Since leaving RGM, Charles and former Tornado Alan Caddy had set up their own production company, Sound Venture; more proof, as if Meek's mounting suspicion needed it, that people were indeed stealing his ideas. George Bellamy had written a solo single for Caddy, 'Workout', that had been backed by a Charles–Caddy composition (complete with the requisite Meek-esque sound effects), 'Tornado': Charles would later record his own vocal version of the same song, renaming it 'A Long Time Ago'. To add to Meek's belief that his former friends were conspiring against him, the A-side of the Don Charles single was written by Guy Fletcher. Shortly afterwards Caddy and Charles approached Meek with a request that they be allowed to use the Tornados' name, but Meek had plans for that and had no intention of allowing a bunch of disaffected former RGM session players use it.

'Space Walk' had a strange and tortuous birth. Two months earlier, Roger LaVern had told the *Daily Mirror* that the band – without Heinz, who was still signed to Meek – had planned to record a tune he had written, 'Gemini', under the name the Original Tornados, explaining that the band were 'going to send a copy to President Johnson to mark the launching of the Gemini Space project'.[544] To say that Meek was unhappy with the

---

[*]   Although he was occasionally credited as co-writer on some of Meek's compositions, this was not Meek's studio assistant Terry O'Neil, but the comedian, musician and television presenter with the similar name.

Wipe Out

news would be an understatement. The tune that the keyboard player was talking about had started out life as a Roger LaVern solo project, produced by Meek, under the title 'Moon Rocket'. Meek had, in true Meek style, sped up the original recording and added a bunch of effects to the introduction and, when Decca decided against releasing 'Moon Rocket' (following the dismal performance of the first LaVern single), he reused the effects tape for the Tornados' single 'Early Bird'. Hearing about LaVern's plans for the tune, Meek threatened to sue, and regardless of the keyboard player's claims in the press, 'Moon Rocket'/'Gemini' would not appear... at least not yet. In the interim another former Tornado, George Bellamy, issued his first solo effort, 'Where I'm Bound', that featured both Clem Cattini and Alan Caddy and members of the Ivy League (formerly Carter-Lewis), and Cattini issued his own instrumental single 'No Time to Think'/'Impact', credited to the Clem Cattini Ork.

The disc that finally saw light of day, 'Space Walk', was a new tune, unrelated to LaVern's 'Gemini', and no Tornado, former or current, appeared on it; although credited to The Gemini', 'Space Walk' was performed by a then-unknown band called the Vikings, and had been produced by Meek's adversary Curly Clayton at his studio in Swan Yard, Islington. However, Meek was stung when he learned that the flip side, 'Goodbye Joe', composed by his former friend Don Charles, featured most of the original Tornados, and the title was meant as a none-too-subtle dig at their former recording manager. A copy of the single was posted, anonymously, through the letterbox of 304 Holloway Road, and reputedly smashed to pieces by Meek. A different recording of Roger LaVern's 'Gemini' tune would finally surface, retitled 'Red Rocket' and issued as the flip side of the reformed Tornados' re-recording of 'Telstar', issued by George Bellamy's SRT company in 1975.

This act of blatant cruelty, from a group of men he had once considered his friends, hurt Meek badly. He considered himself a fair man: hot-headed certainly, but apart from the rather shabby and cowardly way he had acted over Geoff Goddard, he was not known for being heartless. It's true that he could be easily led, and his more selfish business decisions usually had someone else – such as Robert Stigwood or Major Banks – pulling the strings, but when he was acting on his own he was generous to a fault, often gifting composer royalties to friends to pay them back for some kindness or

Love and Fury: The Life, Death and Legacy of Joe Meek

other. Even on those occasions when his temper got the better of him and he fell out with people, they usually ended up forgiving him. But this was different and, with the exception of Heinz and Cattini, he would not work with an original member of the Tornados again.

One of the reasons that Meek was so reluctant to let his former musicians use the name was that there would soon be yet another version of the Tornados to contend with. In June 1965 he had issued a single by a band called the Saxons – the instrumental 'Saxon Warcry' backed with the beat vocal 'Click-ete-Clack', co-written by Meek. The Saxons were, in fact, Robb Gayle and the Whirlwinds, the band from Gloucestershire that he had auditioned a year earlier. In March 1964, after not clicking for Joe, they decided that they needed a new name and a look.

'Not long after we started recording with Joe, he told us that Robb Gayle and the Whirlwinds sounded like a skiffle group and suggested that we change the name of the band,' explains Robb Huxley. 'At that time, with the whole Merseybeat scene exploding, most bands with a few exceptions were just called things like the Searchers or the Hollies, and did not feature a frontman like in the days of Cliff Richard and the Shadows. We talked about the Holder family, and as their family tree went back to the days of the Norsemen we explored names connected with that period. We came up with the Vikings, but that name had already been used by several groups. Then we hit on the Saxons. There was another group by that name, but Joe didn't care about that and told us all to dye our hair and the next time we came up to record we should all be blond. He also paid for new stage suits for us that were Beatle-esque in style and we had them made by Dougie Millings in London who made the Beatles' suits.

'We were fine with Joe's ideas because all we wanted to do was play in a band and make records. We would have done absolutely anything Joe asked us to do. We never questioned anything.'[545]

The four lads bleached their hair blond (their original drummer refused and was replaced by an obliging tub-thumper from Cheltenham) and donned leatherette tunics and Viking helmets, fashioned from horns picked up from a local slaughterhouse stuck to horse-riding hats. A change in name and a bold new look certainly helped attract attention; after writing a letter to the Holders' parents in February 1965, telling them of 'how tremendously

Wipe Out

pleased' he was with the act and that he was convinced that they had 'made a hit record' together,[546] Meek signed them to a management and recording deal, and the band were soon being advertised as 'EMI recording artistes'. The bold claim was somewhat presumptuous: EMI would not issue any recordings by the band, but 'Saxon Warcry' would appear a few months later on Decca.

Meek had big ambitions for the Saxons. In his letter to the Holders, he wrote that 'I felt I must write to tell you how great they are, and I am sure you must be very proud of them... It is not often you find such a talented group and of course I am thrilled to think that they come from my part of the world.'[547] Meek knew that the Holder family farm was involved with the legend of Dick Whittington (the man who would become Lord Mayor of London had been born in the village of Pauntley in the Forest of Dean), and he felt that there may be an angle there to interest the press. He accompanied them on a trip back to Newent, where Meek and the Holder brothers could spend time with their respective families in advance of an appearance, on 26 June, at a fête in nearby Cinderford in aid of children with disabilities. Much as he did when he was younger, most summers Meek would take time out of his punishing schedule to return to the Forest of Dean and have one of his acts appear at a local charity event or two. Although he would seldom make a fuss about it, he always gave his time freely and distributed stacks of his latest recordings among the crowd. Meek was due to perform the grand opening of the fête and judge a talent competition, and he decided that this would be the perfect opportunity for them to perform: a home audience was bound to be appreciative, and the performance should garner some local press interest. Meek would later tell the band that 'that fête at Cinderford with you is the best time I've had this year' and assure them that 'I think we're destined to be a success together and must always stick together, and bring up the problems when they come along'.[548]

The following weekend, on 3 July, Meek had been booked to officiate at another local event, the Longhope Carnival (7 miles south of Newent), with Heinz and the Wild Boys playing the carnival marquee during the afternoon. Again, Meek used the event to help publicise the Saxons and their latest release, giving copies away to many of the teenagers who attended. Expecting their big break to be just around the corner, the

Love and Fury: The Life, Death and Legacy of Joe Meek

Holder brothers and Robb Huxley moved into a flat together in Notting Hill; however, 'Saxon Warcry' – which Meek had planned to promote by having the band drive from their Gloucestershire home to London in a chariot fashioned in part from an old cider barrel (footage still exists of the band fooling around on the family farm in this self-built contraption) – would be their only release as the Saxons.

That same month, the court case over the ownership of 'Have I the Right?' was finally heard. Geoff Goddard told the court that he and Meek wrote a song called 'Give Me the Chance' sometime around April 1964, and that 'Have I the Right?' stole some of the melody from their tune; Howard and Blaikley claimed that they had written 'Have I the Right?' some six months earlier, in November 1963, and that the Honeycombs (then still known as the Sheratons) were performing it regularly long before Goddard claimed to have co-composed 'Give Me the Chance'. Meek wrote to the court denying having anything to do with the composition of either song.

Had Meek, who had form when it came to 'borrowing' other people's ideas for his own songs or simply recycling and repackaging his own tunes (the Andy Cavell single 'Andy' and John Leyton track 'Johnny, My Johnny' are the same song, with just the singer's name altered), planted the seed for 'Give Me the Chance' in Goddard's head, helping himself to the melody of the Howard–Blaikley composition? Ken Howard has no idea: 'I can't surmise what Joe had talked to him about,' he says, adding that 'we had not heard his composition'.[549] Not only had they not heard the song, the court case was the first time that either Howard or Blaikley had clapped eyes on Goddard: 'We had not met, but Joe had often mentioned him as a partner of some sort. When we saw him for the first time in court he presented a rather pathetic appearance, looking very uncomfortable and finally scribbling a note saying, "I give up".'[550]

Charles Blackwell certainly thought that Meek was being less than truthful: 'Knowing Geoff as I did, I was convinced he was telling the truth,' he said some years later. 'But that was the end of the Goddard–Meek relationship... they didn't ever associate again after that.' Meek would not work with Blackwell again, either. 'Nearly all his success, with John Leyton, me, Heinz, was all thanks to Geoff Goddard,' says Mike Berry. 'And he got ripped off, poor old Geoff... He got taken to the fucking cleaners by Joe. I remember thinking, "You bastard, you've stitched him up." Geoff was such

Wipe Out

an introvert, a bit of a mummy's boy, but he was a great musician and the sweetest guy. He couldn't have stood up in court; that would have killed him. The lawyers would have torn him to shreds.'[551]

'Geoff wasn't the sort of guy to make things up,' Berry adds. 'It was totally out of character; the man was completely honest and a real innocent. Joe cheated him, and although I never raised that with him, I feel that probably played on Joe's mind; it was all part of the build-up to him killing himself. He wasn't being honest with himself or with other people. Joe was, basically, an honest man but he was corrupted by the likes of Stigwood.'[552]

In July 1965, Goddard agreed to drop any and all allegations that he had a hand in writing 'Have I the Right?', and Alan Blaikley and Ken Howard were acknowledged by the court as the composers. Howard and Blaikley, and publishers Ivy Music, were awarded costs against Goddard. Geoff had not been keen on appearing in court, and the case left a bitter aftertaste. Beyond submitting a few tunes to Norrie Paramor in 1969, one of which ('My Head Goes Around') ended up on Cliff Richard's 1970 album *Tracks and Grooves*, he would not work in the music industry again. Instead, he went back to Reading, back to his parents' home and took up a job in the catering department of Reading University, occasionally playing piano in a local pub at weekends and attending spiritualist meetings. In the early 1970s, while Heinz's career was experiencing a small upsurge thanks to the rock 'n' roll nostalgia circuit, CBS showed some interest in releasing new material from the singer, especially if Goddard could be persuaded to come out of his self-imposed retirement. 'I got on to him,' Heinz revealed, 'but he just didn't seem interested.'[553] Goddard would sign a new contract with his publishers Southern Music, but no new tunes would surface. 'I need someone driving me forward,' he admitted. 'And Joe used to do that for me.'[554]

In September 1965 what was left of the Tornados, now without a single original member, recorded the two themes from the Gerry Anderson puppet animation show *Stingray* for their next single. This was not the first time Meek had covered the music from one of Anderson's shows: the Flee-Rekkers had issued a surprisingly laid-back cover of the theme from *Fireball XL-5* in February 1963, but for this release Meek pulled out all the stops: '[The effects] on 'Stingray' include an aeroplane breaking through the sound barrier, gun shots and bombs dropping, plus bubbling water, created

Love and Fury: The Life, Death and Legacy of Joe Meek

by a method I can't disclose,' Meek coyly revealed. 'All the sound effects came from my library of over 2,000 different noises recorded since I started experimenting at the age of 14.' This version of the band would implode shortly after, and, on 1 January 1966, after keyboard player Dave Watts (the only remaining member of the previous line-up) joined the Saxons, they officially became the Tornados.

'It all happened so quickly,' says Robb Huxley. 'There wasn't really any time to think about that. In December we were playing as the Saxons, and on 1 January we were appearing as the Tornados in Scunthorpe as an opening act for Heinz and the Wild Boys. Although I was happy that I had achieved my ambition to become a professional musician, I felt that we were stepping into dead men's shoes, and instead of ascending the ladder of success we were now a group that was on the way down, if not already at the bottom. I would have preferred that we would have entered the world of professional musicians as the Saxons, with our own music and style. We also ran into a lot of trouble when we appeared at some gigs when some guys would approach us and say, "You're not the Tornados. Where's Heinz?"'[555]

In October 1965 Joe had produced a demo for his young friend Chris Barnes (later known as Paul Burns), with the singer and guitarist backed by his brother's band the Rapids. This tape was one of the more than 1,800 sold after Joe's death to Cliff Cooper (whose own band the Millionaires had a single, 'Wishing Well', issued by Decca in August 1966 which had been produced by Meek) that became known as the Tea Chest tapes, so called because they were sold to Cooper in sixty-seven tea chests.*

'My brother was 20 years old, and he'd got this band together with these two younger guys. Joe was interested in recording my sound, so he said, "Come along and I'll do a recording of you as an audition." So we went along and we recorded about six or seven tunes. We did one at the beginning, a sound check just to get all the mics right, and then we went straight through the tunes, taped one after the other without any mess-ups at all. At the end he said to me, "OK, fair enough, we'll leave it like that." He gave me a tape which had four tunes on it, which we sent off to have acetates made.

---

* In 1968, using an IBC mixing console previously owned by Meek, Cliff Cooper established Orange, a recording studio and amplifier manufacturer, in New Compton Street.

Wipe Out

'After that, I was going to the studio regularly, just doing general bits and pieces, and he said to me one day, "I'd like to make a comic record with you."' The song Meek had in mind was an answer record to 'Terry', a Top 5 hit for Twinkle in January 1965. 'Twinkle had sung "He rode into the night", and this was going to be "She rode into the night"... and that was his idea. So I said, "OK, we'll do it," but soon after the Rapids packed up.' The youngster soon found work with other local acts, including a band called the Lariats, who regularly played at the Half Moon pub in Holloway. 'The guitar I was using at the time was a Hofner Verythin, which I played through a 15-watt Selmer amp. That sounded pretty good! Playing at the Half Moon, I had started to do "Apache" by the Shadows, but I didn't have an echo unit. I asked Joe if he knew where I could get an echo unit. I told him that I didn't have any money, I was looking for one to borrow, and he gave me this Klemt Echolette, a gold-coloured unit in a case with little slots all along the top, brass-plated I guess. Cream-coloured knobs along the front, three little switches, again a cream colour, and DIN sockets on the front. And it was fabulous.' The valve-driven Echolette, with multiple record and playback heads, contained a 20-inch loop of magnetic tape. 'I plugged it in to an amp, to try it out, and as I turned it on it made the same noise as the beginning of 'Telstar'.'[556]

Shortly afterwards, Meek began working with London pop act the Riot Squad. Signed to Pye, the band had already recorded three singles with the Kinks' co-manager Larry Page, but with few sales to boast of the band split and founding member Bob Evans put together a new line-up. Evans had been doing the occasional session for Meek, playing flute on 'Our Day Will Come', a track from the second Honeycombs album *All Systems Go*, and on the recent Heinz single, 'Heart Full of Sorrow', and it made sense to bring this new version of the Riot Squad to work at 304. The band recorded the top side of their first Meeksville 45 on 16 December. 'Cry Cry Cry', backed with 'How It's Done', was issued in January 1966, and the Riot Squad quickly became Meek's session group of choice – no doubt in part because several members of the group shared Meek's interest in spiritualism.

The lack of sleep, combined with the diet of coffee and pep pills, was harming Meek's health. His insistence on total control over his recordings was alienating his friends, as did his turning up, unannounced and uninvited, to

Love and Fury: The Life, Death and Legacy of Joe Meek

a recording of *The New London Palladium* Show in December. The Honeycombs had been booked to appear and, once again, Meek decided he was the only person who could possibly look after their sound. Staff continued to come and go, and as 1965 closed Meek found himself once again without a full-time assistant. Meek claimed to have received 'over one hundred letters requesting an interview'[557] from the advertisement he placed and, having whittled the list of prospective employees down to around three dozen, he invited each of them along for a ten-minute chat. Meek needed help: he was snowed under with recording and production work, and, frustrated by the lack of resolution in the 'Telstar' case, in January he also began renewed efforts to free the substantial royalties held up in legal red tape. 'I want all the money I am owed,' he said. 'It must be thousands of pounds.' Meek insisted that Ledrut's claim of copyright infringement was 'absolute nonsense' and that he had 'already spent more than £1,500 on legal fees – lawyers in London and Paris are fighting the case for me. It is amazing, but I have not received a penny piece from this tune – one of the most successful I have ever written – since all this started... Now I feel I am being taken for a ride.'[558]

Ted Fletcher was a witness to Meek's mental health issues. 'We were aware of Joe's difficulties,' he admits today, 'but he always kept his personal problems to himself. The pressure of work was too much, his finances were not in good order... and his style of production was being copied by other producers while other sounds were appearing from across the Atlantic. He became generally disliked in the business for his unpredictable rages and unconventional behaviour, and his own paranoia became more and more obvious. He was convinced that the engineers at Decca had "bugs" planted in the walls at Holloway Road and he started to live the life of a recluse.'

Meek was becoming irrational and was starting to turn on people he had once considered friends, including the Fletchers. The end came after Meek sent Ted Fletcher a four-page, handwritten letter. 'I had built a primitive studio at my home and produced some audio work for adverts via friends in the music business,' Ted adds. 'Joe seemed to think I was setting up in competition to him. We had been totally friendly; in fact he had lent and given several items of old professional gear to me to help in our work in the Cameos. The idea of competing with him was a nonsense but he wrote to me accusing me of "undermining his business". After the letter he refused

Wipe Out

to talk to me. In hindsight it's clear that he was mentally very unstable and suffered seriously from a belief that he was being persecuted.'[559]

The knocks kept coming. Having seen off dissent from the former Tornados the previous summer, now it was time for his other studio group, the Outlaws, to put the boot in. In February 1966 a single appeared on the US Smash label credited to the Outlaws but not written, recorded or produced by Meek. Issued two years after their last RGM single, 'Keep A-Knockin'', 'Don't Cry' featured Harvey Hinsley on lead guitar (later to join Hot Chocolate), alongside Ken Lundgren, Chas Hodges and Mick Underwood; flip side, the Hodges-sung 'Only For You' featured Hodges and Underwood, plus Ritchie Blackmore on lead guitar and Nicky Hopkins on piano.

All of these tracks were produced by Derek Lawrence, who first met Meek in late 1963. Lawrence – who worked for the Rank Organisation's Filmusic publishing house – had been managing an act called Laurie Black and the Men of Mystery, who won a local talent show and had been invited to audition at 304. Meek was unimpressed with the band but saw something in Lawrence and offered him a job. Lawrence spent much of 1964 shadowing Meek, learning the tricks of the trade and occasionally producing sessions at 304. He was credited, with Meek, as co-writer of 'Please Don't Pretend Again', the B-side of the Honeycombs' 'Have I the Right?'. 'Joe had a large influence on my production style,' he admitted in a 2003 interview. 'I used a lot of Joe's echo ideas and his in your face drum sounds.' Lawrence recorded the Outlaws in late 1964, shortly before Ken Lundgren left to return to his native Canada. 'I worked at Meek's on and off for about a year and then I just drifted off to do my own thing.' Keen to set up his own production company, Lawrence enticed Ritchie Blackmore to cut his first solo single, the 1965 release 'Getaway' (written by Blackmore and Chas Hodges). The disc had a very Meek sound, which was hardly surprising when it also featured the rest of the Outlaws. Lawrence would go on to work with top names including Deep Purple and Wishbone Ash.

Harvey Hinsley was soon replaced by Ed Hamilton, but the Outlaws had already called it a day before 'Don't Cry' was issued, having grown tired of working with Meek and having to deal with his rages. 'We were getting fed up,' Hodges remembered. 'Aside from his good points he had a lot of bad points. He had too many artists to look after and he wouldn't allow too many people in to help him look after them, because he didn't trust anybody. He would try and do everything himself... In the end some of the artists are going to lose out, and we felt that we weren't getting the attention we deserved.'[560] Their demise left several other Lawrence-produced tracks in the can. Hodges joined Cliff Bennett and the Rebel Rousers, and Mick Underwood joined a new band, the Herd, who would soon sign with Howard and Blaikley.

Over a period of eighteen months or so Meek had lost Geoff Goddard, Don Charles, the Tornados, the Outlaws, the Fletchers, Michael Cox and Derek Lawrence, and he was still dealing with the anger he felt towards Robert Stigwood for having taken John Leyton, Mike Berry and Charles Blackwell away from him. His only coping mechanism was to throw himself further into his work.

With the Outlaws no more, Meek felt he needed another act to fulfil his dreams of the west. Luckily he had recently been contacted by a young singer from a bluegrass act called the Levisa River Boys. He offered them an audition, liked what he heard and recorded their version of the Appalachian murder ballad 'Knoxville Girl'. Typically, he hated their name, and suggested that they change it to the James Boys, in honour of outlaws Frank and Jesse James. He also suggested that they adapt their sound to something more country and western in style, and that they consider taking on a female singer. The band were open to the proposals, but when Meek found it impossible to get 'Knoxville Girl' released – the lyrics tell of the violent murder of the girl in the song's title – they soon fell out with the producer. Member Mike Batory, keen to make it as a songwriter, maintained his connection with Meek and, in 1966, would have songs recorded by Meeksville acts Peter Chris and the Outcasts, and the Riot Squad.

In March 1966, a few days in advance of their debut release, Meek announced that he had signed Scots quartet the Buzz. Although the act was relatively new, the individual members had been involved with other bands in Edinburgh and Falkirk, most notably the Boston Dexters, who had been signed to Columbia but had failed to make an impact. Their Meeksville Sound debut, the freakbeat classic 'You're Holding Me Down' (written by guitarist John Turnbull), was backed by a strange, discordant Meek original

Wipe Out

entitled 'I've Gotta Buzz'. Their local newspaper, the *West Lothian Courier*, hated it. 'I don't like this particular disc one little bit', harrumphed the paper's *Teen Topics* column, castigating Meek's production: 'The backing is far too loud and any attempt to hear the vocal is soon discouraged.' Sales were poor, and the band soon split. Now incredibly hard to find, the disc gained notoriety when it began to appear on David Bowie bootleg releases, although he had nothing whatsoever to do with the tracks: Bowie was involved with a band with the same name, but they were an entirely different outfit.

Another act that attracted Meek's interest was Cornish group the Undecided. The band's manager, former postman David Peters, had written to Meek in January, asking if he would meet with him the next time Peters was in the area. Meek wrote back, telling Peters that 'I would be only to please [sic] to meet you while you are in London and sujest prity [sic] soon, because I have to leave for Italy soon to record a special LP with the Honeycombs'.[561] Meek did go to Italy, and he recorded several tracks with the band – some in Italian – at the RCA studios in Rome for the planned follow-up to their 1965 Italian release *The Honeycombs*, although those tracks have yet to surface. Meek took Terry O'Neil to the San Remo Music Festival, which takes place annually in the northern Italian town each February, but after things turned sour between the pair O'Neil quit.

Once back in London, and now without a full-time assistant, Meek met with David Peters and he invited the Undecided (so called because none of them could agree on a name) to an audition at 304. He liked them, signed them to an exclusive recording contract and changed their name to Danny's Passion (after the band's lead singer, Danny Gill). The band recorded several tracks for Meek, including the Geoff Stephens number 'It's All Leading Up to Saturday Night' (Meek presented the band with an acetate of the song and insisted that they learn it as he wanted it to be the A-side to their first single) and their own composition, 'Wanna Lover'. Sadly, none of their recordings would be released, but David Peters got to know Meek well and saw both sides of the man. 'A mate of the group came down [to 304] too, and Joe flew into a rage about that. Then the lead guitarist snapped a string, and didn't Joe give me hell! It wasn't my fault, but he flew off the handle and stormed out.' Meek left the studio in

285

Love and Fury: The Life, Death and Legacy of Joe Meek

a rage and thundered down the stairs. The band had no idea what would happen next, or if they should simply pack up and go, but a few minutes later Meek returned, all smiles, with a fresh guitar string he had bought from the music shop a few doors away on Holloway Road. 'As a friend, Joe was as good as gold,' Peters adds. 'He would do anything for you. But when it came to work it was easy to upset him.'[562]

CHAPTER 23

Please Stay

Hoping to provide Glenda Collins with a much-needed hit, Joe moved her from HMV to Pye, and at the beginning of February 1966 brought her in for a two-day session with his recent signing the Riot Squad. One of the tracks recorded was the Howard–Blaikley song 'Something I've Got to Tell You',* originally performed by Honey Lantree on the second Honeycombs album. Sandie Shaw, Cilla Black, Petula Clark and Dusty Springfield were all waving the flag for Britain's female vocalists in the singles charts, and US heavyweights Barbra Streisand and Nancy Sinatra (sitting at number 1 with 'These Boots Are Made For Walkin'') were also doing great business. Meek had high hopes, writing that 'without a doubt this is the best disc from Glenda Collins' and claiming, 'it has hit written all over it',[563] but Meek's only credible female singer was again overlooked by pop fans. 'Why wasn't this a massive hit?' Recording engineer John Pickford asks. 'Glenda's vocal performance is first rate; Ivor Raymonde's arrangement is superb and Joe's sound balance is just perfect. It's quite remarkable when you consider that when he recorded the original backing he had to envisage how that would blend with the strings, horns and choir he overdubbed later on. But that was Joe's real genius. He knew how it was going to sound before the musicians had even played a note.'

---

*   Among several versions of the disc's B-side, the Meek composition 'My Heart Didn't Lie' included on the 2023 compilation *Glenda Collins: Baby It Hurts: The Holloway Road Sessions 1963–1966* is one featuring Joe, who overdubbed his own vocal onto the original track. It's a fascinating, albeit unpleasant, listening experience.

Love and Fury: The Life, Death and Legacy of Joe Meek

As Eric Meek later ruminated: 'One of Joe's biggest disappointments was Glenda Collins not getting a hit, because he thought that she was a terrifically good artist. He was very, very fond of Glenda Collins and was hoping all the time that she would get a hit.'[564] 'She seemed very protective towards him,' says guitarist Paul Burns,[565] although gossip circulating about Joe's desire to marry her was furiously rebuffed by Glenda herself. 'It's all utter nonsense,' she told *Thunderbolt* magazine. 'Joe was homosexual. He was never interested in women the way he was with men.'[566]

Meek's continual post-production fiddling almost brought about the end of the Honeycombs. A projected single, the four minute-long 'Our Day Will Come' (taken from the band's second album *All Systems Go*), was dropped after the BBC would only air a severely edited version, but Dennis D'Ell was so unhappy with the sound of the chosen replacement, the February 1966 release 'Who Is Sylvia?', that he quit the band. Inspired by the recent hit for the Toys, 'A Lover's Concerto', this update of a classical air did no one involved any favours. 'He always used to speed the tracks up,' D'Ell complained. 'He used to say that it made for excitement, but as far as I was concerned it made me sound like Mickey Mouse!'[567] D'Ell's discomfiture was intensified when, while on tour of Australia in January 1965, Rolling Stone Brian Jones telephoned a local radio station and insisted that they play 'Have I the Right?' at 78 rpm. D'Ell was replaced by singer and guitarist Colin Boyd. Luckily, one of Meek's other February 1966 releases would fare better, and 'Please Stay' by the Cryin' Shames would provide Meek with his last hit single in the UK.

Six-piece Liverpudlian combo the Cryin' Shames had come together from the ashes of three other groups, the Aztecs, the Bumblies and the Calderstones. Their debut session at 304 took place on 7 October 1965, while they were still known as the Bumblies, a name they took from a 1950s children's television programme devised by ex-Goon Michael Bentine. Meek is reported to have bestowed their new name upon them after singer Paul 'Charlie' Crane spontaneously burst into tears during the recording of 'Please Stay', a song originally performed by the Drifters, although another tale has it that Meek purposely upset the singer in order to get the performance he was after. However it happened, they were performing as the Cryin' Shames by December 1965.

288

Please Stay

Picked up for British release by Decca – and for distribution in America by London – regardless of a significant push and plenty of airplay, sales of the single were hampered stateside by Columbia Records promoting the Chicago-based Cryan' Shames, and when CBS issued the Cryan' Shames debut in the UK the band's name was altered to the Shames in an attempt to avoid any confusion. It didn't work. 'Please Stay' (backed with 'What's News Pussycat', a pastiche of Bob Dylan's 'On the Road Again') peaked at number 26 on the UK singles charts. Through the Cryin' Shames he was introduced to another Liverpudlian beat group, the Maracas, who trekked down to London to record for Meek, but their session – which included the psychedelic-tinged track 'A Different Drummer' – would remain unissued, another casualty of Meek's downward spiral.

The Cryin' Shames were enormously popular in their home city and would go down in Merseyside history for their part in the infamous Siege of the Cavern, which took place a few weeks after the single's release, on 28 February 1966. Club owner Ray McFall had declared bankruptcy, and Liverpool City Council wanted the internationally renowned 'best of cellars' back. Two groups, the Cryin' Shames and the Hideaways, kept fans (known variously as Cavernites or Troglodytes) entertained while they barricaded themselves inside the club, but council staff and police soon broke through and took control of the building. New owners were brought in, who reopened the club in July, and it would remain open until March 1973, when British Rail, backed by the council, served a compulsory purchase order on the building, claiming it was needed to provide air ducts for the Merseyrail underground rail loop. A new Cavern opened in the basement of the building opposite the original site before, in 1984, a replica Cavern – which occupies part of the footprint of the original club – opened its doors for business.

In May 1966, as 'Please Stay' reached its chart peak, Meek's former business partner William Barrington-Coupe was jailed for a year for his part in an attempt at tax avoidance. In what was, at that time, the longest and most expensive trial of its kind ever held at the Old Bailey, Barrington-Coupe and three of his co-conspirators were sent to prison for importing thousands of cheap transistor radios from Hong Kong and selling them without paying £84,000 tax. Barrington-Coupe also pleaded guilty to 'being knowingly concerned in the fraudulent evasion of purchase tax in respect of gramophone records and furnishing false returns with intent to deceive'.[568] Meek should have been happy that he had long since severed any ties with Barrington-Coupe, but the news that tax officials were digging around in his ex-associate's shady past would only have added to his mounting paranoia.*

That same month, the Tornados recorded what would turn out to be their final single for Meek, 'Is That a Ship I Hear'. The A-side featured a new Meek invention, something he called a 'splatter board', which he described as 'a chunk of gear fixed to the piano and it looks rather like the inside of a grandfather clock after somebody's trodden on it!'[569] Session bass player Roger J. Simmonds described it as 'a builder's plank of wood, which was around fifteen feet or maybe longer. Bedsprings were stretched along the length of the board, with nails holding the springs taut. At one end of the board there was a box of electronics that would take the standard jack lead, then a lead that went into another box placed on the floor, and from there into his vertical mixing units on the wall. Joe was unbelievably inventive.'[570] The B-side of the single, 'Do You Come Here Often', would go down in history as one of the most outré gay-themed songs issued in

---

* Forty years after Meek's death it was revealed that Barrington-Coupe had been perpetuating a fraud for more than a decade, issuing recordings by his wife, pianist Joyce Hatto, that were actually recorded by obscure classical artists from Eastern Europe. Hatto was suffering from ovarian cancer (she died in June 2006), and Barrington-Coupe claimed that he had been editing other artists' work into her recordings to cover up her mistakes and to mask any cries of pain she made while performing. He might have got away with it, had it not been for the advent of the compact disc: his deception was only uncovered after owners of Hatto CDs found that when they copied them into their digital libraries, identifying software (such as Gracenote) recognised them as being by different performers. Barrington-Coupe declared that he had only done this because he loved his wife and wished to save her embarrassment, and his financial backer declined to prosecute, feeling he had suffered enough. This heart-breaking tale of devotion was only marred by the fact that this was exactly the same trick Barrington-Coupe had been pulling in the 1950s and 60s, taking recordings by unknown artists and marketing them under made-up names, including Wilhelm Havagesse (will he? Have a guess!) and Herta Wöbbel (heard her wobble), and that he had recently been issuing discs by other performers, including the late pianist Sergio Fiorentino, that also turned out to have been faked.

Please Stay

the period before the partial decriminalisation of homosexuality in England and Wales.

The jaunty, organ-led instrumental features a spoken-word bridge that allows the listener to eavesdrop on a conversation between two camp young men who discuss music, fashion and sex and agree to meet again 'down the Dilly' (Piccadilly), an area notorious for both male and female prostitutes. The band, and Meek, had been discussing the idea of recording a comedy album, and the Tornados had been introducing the occasional comedy routine into their act with a view to the band's potential future in cabaret, but 'Do You Come Here Often' was the only taster of this possible direction issued during the band's – and Meek's – lifetime. Issued at a time when a man could be arrested for being homosexual, this would be Meek's most flagrant attempt to introduce audiences to camp humour and Polari, gay slang.

May was another busy month for Meek: members of two acts who had already recorded for him, Willesden's the Hotrods and Mr Lee and Co. from Birkenhead, decided to join forces and form a new act named Peter, Chris and the Outcasts. After relocating to London in January 1966, Mr Lee and Co. had recorded with Meek at 304, but the sessions did not go well and the band split, with most of the act deciding to return to Merseyside. The Hotrods had issued a single the previous September, 'I Don't Love You No More', a Carter–Lewis song that had already been cut by the Honeycombs, backed with the Meek composition 'Ain't Coming Back No More', a fairly standard beat number that begins, atypically, with the phone in Meek's office ringing and the producer answering with a simple 'Hello?'. Meek struck guitarist Peter Meer as a somewhat pathetic figure. 'One time he put his arm around me. I said to him, "What's going on?" He said, "People put their arms around each other in pubs" I said, "This isn't a pub." He looked a bit embarrassed and said, "I'm just trying to be friendly; I'm just trying to see what you're like. I'll still listen to your songs." There was something really sad about that when I think back. A real loneliness.'[571]

Meek was still experiencing severe staffing issues, partly brought on by his guarded nature. There was no end of young men willing to work for him, to learn the tricks of the trade, but Meek did not want to pass on his secrets to anyone, especially after the perceived betrayal of Derek Lawrence, Don Charles and the Fletchers. Aspiring engineers and producers would come

291

Love and Fury: The Life, Death and Legacy of Joe Meek

to him, hoping to get a foot in the door of the music industry, but instead of explaining how he got his effects or showing them exactly how to mic up a room for a recording, they ended up doing little more than making cups of tea, answering the phone and fending off the press. His secretary, Pip Sharpe, acted as a wall of defence against the outside world, as an increasingly agitated Meek beavered away in his control room, mumbling incessantly about how his lack of success was down to the major studios stealing his ideas, but even she would suffer from her boss's mania, as had her predecessors. 'He lost his personal secretaries all the time,' Dave Sutch reported. 'He kept sacking them because [he thought] they were always selling his material, selling his ideas.'[572]

Meek was exhibiting symptoms of manic depression, now known as bipolar disorder, including mood swings (he would often go from intense highs to terrible, crushing lows), hearing voices, being unable to sleep and the conviction that he was being spied upon. The management of mental health issues was improving, thanks to the Mental Health Act 1959 which meant that patients with psychological problems were no longer automatically locked away, but treatment usually involved long spells in hospitals or secure units, electro-convulsive therapy (often forced onto unwilling patients) and high doses of sedatives such as barbiturates. And that was only if you could get a diagnosis in the first place: to do that you had to be referred to a psychiatrist by your own doctor, and if Meek was not aware of his own worsening mental health, he was unlikely to be able to discuss his situation with his own GP.

'Perhaps his loved ones knew something wasn't right,' posits therapist and writer Tamsin Embleton. 'Especially those who might have known him before his symptoms worsened, but I doubt they'd have felt confident in knowing where to get him the best care. They might have felt reluctant to hospitalise him, or to encourage him to engage in medical intervention, because of the sort of "care" he would have received. Hospitalising Joe would have cut him off from activities he enjoyed and was good at – sources of self-esteem and relief.'[573]

After another round of interviews he took on a new studio assistant, Roger Bruton, but the pair parted ways before his month's trial was up. In a letter sent to Bruton after leaving 304, Meek apologised for his bad behaviour, telling him that 'I think you would have been the right person

292

Please Stay

to work for me, but through bad misuse by othere [sic] people, I could not face letting it happen again, and so the slightest things seemed huge to me.' Complimenting him on his work, he admitted that 'it upset me to have to moan at you for things that were not caused by you' and added: 'If ever you are in need of advice or help in any way, I'm only to please [sic] to do my best for you, give me a ring or drop me a line.' His parting advice was for Bruton to 'always do that extra bit to please, smile at people when you have the chance, and shake hands at the slightest chance, personal contact leave's [sic] a lasting memory, Keep your nails and hands nice, as you did here and try not to be quite so serious.'

The letter also revealed something of Joe's own state of mind. 'I'm prity [sic] low at the moment and I need cheering up more often,' he confessed, adding that although he 'badly' needed a hit, 'with a hit more people come around (for what they can get)'. The letter also contained a stark admission from Meek: 'I realise now I'm really overloaded with work, and if I let it go on I'll be finished.'[574] It was something Meek had been aware of for months: in March he had written to singer Jonathan King, then looking to move into a more managerial role in the industry, telling him to heed 'one little piece of advice from an old trouper. Don't make the mistake I did and sign up too many people, they mop up your ideas and time and you'll end up an overworked idiot like myself.' King had previously recorded for Meek, and the producer joked that he might finally release 'the nasty record you made with me... so I could cop a bit of lolly now you've become famous'.[575]

At the end of May, Meek went with Brian Epstein to see Bob Dylan perform at the Albert Hall. News of Meek's increasingly odd behaviour had spread through London's 'Velvet Mafia', the group of gay men at the heart of showbiz life, and Epstein – who had had a soft spot for Meek despite the many times Meek had slighted his acts – was interested in his company, NEMS, taking over the management of the Cryin' Shames. Epstein was intrigued by reports reaching him from Liverpool about the group's wild live shows and the near-riots that often broke out. At one show, back in February, one dedicated fan broke her leg as dozens of screaming girls stormed the stage. It was a scene reminiscent of the early days of Beatlemania, and Epstein no doubt felt he could relive that halcyon period through this new combo, now that the Beatles were moving away from live performances.

293

Love and Fury: The Life, Death and Legacy of Joe Meek

When he discovered that one of the members of the band, 16-year-old guitarist Ritchie Routledge, worked for *Music Echo*, the short-lived pop weekly set up by *Mersey Beat*'s Bill Harry and bankrolled by Epstein, he decided that he had to have them. Members of the Cryin' Shames met with Epstein at the Adelphi Hotel in Liverpool, but in an act of bravado decided to turn down his offer.

The band's administration had been a bone of contention for months: originally managed by Norman Eastwood, Meek had not only given them a recording contract but assumed – or perhaps had been led to believe by one or more members of the group – that he would be their personal manager too. In February the band was offered (via Eastwood) a five-year deal, new equipment and a new van by Maurice King of Capable Management Ltd. Epstein fired off a warning shot, telling Eastwood in no uncertain terms to stay out of it, having been assured by the group that they owed no loyalty and had no contractual obligations to him. Meek, in turn, wrote to Capable Management (who were already handling the career of his former artist Bobby Rio), insisting that he now had the band under exclusive recording contract and that he intended to remain in charge of their recording career. Meek was used to having his plans scuppered by an act's management, but he would have known that Maurice King was not a man to be messed with. The pop manager and owner of infamous underground hangout the Starlight Club was an associate of the Kray twins and, like Don Arden, had a reputation for using intimidation and threats of physical violence to keep his artists in line. Arden had taken over the management of the Small Faces, fronted by former child actor Steve Marriott, from King the previous year.

Meek was keen to encourage Epstein's friendship. Epstein, he reasoned, would be far easier to deal with than Maurice King and therefore prove a better prospective manager for the Cryin' Shames. In the summer of 1966, when the controversy broke in America over John Lennon's comments about religion and the influence that the Beatles held over the youth, Meek took to the pages of the *Melody Maker* to declare his 'complete admiration' for the band[576]and state that he was shocked by 'the fact that supposed Christian men can pose for photographers while burning Beatles LPs, and the Ku Klux Klan can state that they will do their best to destroy the Beatles' success. These actions are heathen not Christian.' Meek took the opportunity to state that 'many times in the past some of my artists and

Please Stay

I have been misquoted in the press' concerning the Fab Four and admit that the Beatles 'opened the doors for hundreds of other artists to benefit with their talents in other parts of the world.' For good measure, and in a clear nod to the people holding his destiny in his hands, he added that he was 'sure that each talented member of the Beatles blesses the day Epstein, Martin and EMI started to work with them to create the greatest achievement that has ever happened in the record industry'. [577]

Epstein was touched by Meek's intervention, and in another gesture of friendship brought Gerry Marsden, on the cusp of a split with his band the Pacemakers, to 304 to record some demos. Following one more single for Columbia, Gerry and the Pacemakers would be no more, and one of the tracks that Marsden had attempted at 304, 'Strolling', was seriously considered for release by his new label, CBS.

In a last-ditch effort to get the Cryin' Shames to work with Epstein, Meek visited the NEMS offices in London and made a show of using their phone to call the group and ask them to reconsider Epstein's offer. According to bass player George Robinson, 'he desperately wanted to work with NEMS, but we were emphatic. Unfortunately, one of our members told them both to "f*** off". Meek broke down and cried in front of the NEMS staff. I know this was a fact, and he never forgave me because he thought I was the instigator in the revolt... Refusing to sign with NEMS was probably our biggest mistake, and may possibly have contributed to Meek's depression.' [578] Incensed with his treatment, Meek fired Robinson and replaced him with Derek Cleary. This line-up would record their second single, 'Nobody Waved Goodbye', and lay down enough material for a projected (unreleased) album containing mostly covers of R&B standards. Cleary impressed Meek so much that the producer offered him a job as a trainee engineer at Meeksville Sound, replacing Roger Bruton.

Despite losing Robinson, the Cryin' Shames (or at least some of them) were still adamant that neither Epstein nor Meek were going to tell them what to do; and instead, they elected to sign with Capable Management. Meek wrote to Cleary, telling him that he felt this was a mistake:

> I have advised you correctly. But you have lissened [sic] to others and wasted some good opportunities. I work my best with people who lissen [sic]... I hope you explain to the group that I know what I'm

Love and Fury: The Life, Death and Legacy of Joe Meek

about and must try out any ideals nessary [sic] to create a new sound and a new image, it's not easy and I must have all the help you can give, so let them know this recording session can change your lives, as I have for so many before, and you, with a good disc will enjoy the success you deserve.[579]

The move to Capable was disastrous, and the group split up almost immediately; lead singer Paul Crane and guitarist Richard Routledge formed a new act, initially billed as Paul Crane and the Cryin' Shames before settling on Paul and Ritchie and the Crying Shames, but their one single under this name for Meek, 'September in the Rain' (previously recorded at 304 by the original incarnation of the band), reached a lowly number 48 on the *Melody Maker* chart. A planned follow-up, 'She's Gone', co-written by Billy Kinsley of the Merseys, was scheduled for February 1967 but would not appear.

Meek may have been struggling, but some of his associates were faring far better. Thanks to their success with the Honeycombs and with Dave Dee, Dozy, Beaky, Mick and Tich, Ken Howard and Alan Blaikley had become one of the hottest properties in the UK music business, setting up their own management and production company and able to pick and choose who they worked with. Without the hit-writing pair to fall back on, Meek began searching for new young songwriters who might be more attuned to the demands of the day and perhaps be able to emulate some of the success he had previously enjoyed, such as Leonard Moseley (who used the stage name Lee Paul) and Leslie Hall, of Manchester band the Wheels. The pair had recently moved to London, and through their association with Heinz and his former girlfriend, Angie – who was now dating Len Moseley – they were introduced to Meek. On 29 November they signed a contract promising Joe first refusal on their material and set up camp at 304, writing songs for Glenda Collins and others.

Joe's relationship with Heinz had come to a tumultuous end. The singer had already moved into the flat at Great Peter Street, but it soon became obvious that was not going to work. Joe knew the flat, he knew the phone number and was not going to let go easily. In April 1965, after a short stay at the Royal Hotel in Woburn Place (later renamed the Royal National Hotel), Heinz set up home in Westbourne Terrace, close to Paddington

Please Stay

Station, with his new girlfriend (and later wife) Della; he did not tell Meek that he was moving and he made Tom Shanks promise him that he would not give Meek the phone number. 'At the end, I was being forced to do material I didn't want to do,' Heinz conceded, 'because Joe thought it was good. I didn't want to do something particularly, I'd rather do something else that was good, but he'd just say, "Bloody rubbish!"'[580]

Meek, unsurprisingly, threw a massive fit and cut Heinz off. With next to no contact between the two men, what little money Heinz had soon dried up, and he was forced to borrow cash from his girlfriend. 'There were times when Della was giving me her wages, after work... She'd slogged all week for me to get petrol to go to a gig, when I knew damned well that gig would probably earn me 180 quid, which I would never see.'[581] This lack of income saw his car and his beloved boat repossessed, with Heinz blaming his downfall entirely on Meek. Meek, meanwhile, saw the singer's bid for independence as a personal slight. Heinz refused to communicate directly with him, sending all correspondence via Shanks and demanding an itemised breakdown of accounts, including royalty payments, which Meek (or more likely Pip Sharpe) dutifully supplied. Letters sent between the two men at this time are very revealing: when Heinz first announces that he wishes to move out of 304 Meek is consolatory, offering help and proposing ways that the pair could continue working together: 'I have no objection at all to considering any suggestions you have for improving the practical working of the contract,' Meek wrote on 14 April 1965. 'Do realise that you can always have a word with me if you have something on your mind. Don't let us forget that our association has had its share of successes...'[582] The following year, when they were barely communicating and Heinz was blaming Meek for his financial woes, Meek blasts that 'whatever has taken place... is entirely your doing – not mine. If as in the past these things had been discussed together in a friendly and businesslike manner you'd still have a car, and my respect, and continued guidance.' Meek was on the offensive, telling his former protégé that 'I should think I'm entitled to at least regain the monies I've kindly and without question forwarded to you and used on you to build and keep alive your name in this precarious pop business. I couldn't be more disappointed and upset over your recent underhandedness. Fortunately, I've grown out of the habit of being too concerned, life's too short.'[583]

Love and Fury: The Life, Death and Legacy of Joe Meek

The fact that Meek was still willing to work with people who came to him via a connection with Heinz shows that, whatever had transpired, he still had deep feelings for the singer: their last collaboration had been issued back in June, an Eddie Cochran-inspired single written by Dave Adams called 'Movin' In', originally recorded by Danny Rivers four years earlier. Despite the single featuring some blistering lead guitar from Ritchie Blackmore, it failed to chart and they would not release any further work together, although Heinz continued to visit Joe sporadically throughout 1966. The pair had been due to cut another single together, but the session ended in acrimony, with Joe and Heinz at loggerheads over money. The singer was convinced that his producer was holding on to his royalties and, after another row, Heinz stormed out, with Meek screaming after him that he would never work again. Sadly, as well as his career, Heinz also left his shotgun behind him that day. Meek later asked if he could hang on to it; perhaps having the weapon there would offer him some sense of security. 'A couple of times people had tried to break in,' the singer revealed. 'His car was broken into...'[584] Meek also realised that, by retaining possession of the gun, keen shooter Heinz would have a reason to visit. The gun would be kept in a locked cupboard in Meek's office, the cartridges in a box on another shelf.

'I saw Heinz coming out of there a couple of times,' Paul Burns recalls. 'He was standoffish. The last time I went there, Heinz told me, "Joe's busy at the moment, you can't come in." Twice that happened to me: the first time with Glenda Collins a good few weeks earlier, but I don't know why. It was very strange.'[585] One of Glenda's last visits to 304 took place on 11 November 1966, for a session that also featured Ritchie Blackmore and drummer Jimmy Evans, a member of early Jimmy Page outfit the Redcaps, who had played with Blackmore in the Savages. Three tracks were recorded that day including 'Run to Me', a title by Joe's new musical director, Harvey Richards, and a song from Moseley and Hall, 'Self Portrait'. Richards had come to join Meeksville after Meek promised him £20 a week, double what he had been earning under Columbia's Norman Newell. The budding songwriter felt that the chances of having his material recorded were better with Meek, and the fact that both men came from Gloucestershire helped seal the deal.

In an effort to gain media coverage for Moseley and Hall, Joe introduced them to his friend, radio DJ Tony Windsor; he also encouraged them to

Please Stay

join him in séances, where he would again attempt to summon up the spirit of Buddy Holly to help guide their careers. The craziness soon became too much for the fledgling hitmakers, who made it clear that they preferred to work at the flat Les Hall had rented in London (Len and Angie were sharing a house in Chigwell, and would soon become Mr and Mrs Moseley).

According to Patrick Pink (Robbie Duke), 'Tony and Joe had a bit of a thing' and the Tornados' instrumental 'Is That a Ship I Hear' 'was done to please him':[586] earlier working titles for the tune had been the less obscure 'Is That a Pirate Ship I Hear?' and 'Carry On Pirates'. Windsor, or TW as he was known to listeners, was one of the most influential presenters on Radio London, a mentor to a young Maurice Cole (who would soon change his name to Kenny Everett) and the chief compiler of the station's playlist. He had been one of the first DJs employed by Radio London, and one of the few with any experience. Under his real name, Tony Withers, he had been a star in Australia, working on radio and in television in Sydney, but he left the country when his drinking became a problem for his employers and the local media began to gossip about his homosexuality. Withers came to Britain and, after a short period working for the pirate ship Radio Atlanta, reinvented himself as Tony Windsor, first with Radio Caroline and then with the 'Big L'.

Windsor had a regular boyfriend, with whom he shared a home in London's Baron's Court when he was not on the ship (presenters tended to spend three weeks on board, one week off). His relationship with Meek began in 1965, with Meek keen to court him if only to gain more exposure for his acts. Meek was not averse to slipping Windsor, Everett or other pirate DJs a fistful of fivers to ensure his pet projects got plenty of airplay. He also provided them with exclusive content; he had Glenda Collins and the Tornados record a series of jingles in May 1965 which he gave to Windsor one night at dinner, and he produced a similar sales aid for Screaming Lord Sutch's release 'The Train Kept A-Rollin''. When it seemed that the adverts had either been ignored by the station or simply not passed on by Windsor, Meek wrote to Radio London's programme director, Ben Toney, offering to treat him to lunch and discuss how the station and Meek could work more closely together.

Meek had few friends outside the industry, but in 1966 he made the acquaintance of David Farrant, a young man who was similarly obsessed

Love and Fury: The Life, Death and Legacy of Joe Meek

with the occult. Farrant was an associate of David Sutch, and Meek and Farrant began exchanging letters before they met in person at Farrant's Highgate flat. 'He came to my home one evening, and I learned that he had a profound interest in things of an occult nature, indeed all things spiritual,' Farrant later recalled. 'I remember that he was completely dedicated to contacting (and recording) "spirits of the dead" and, to this end, he told me he had some very interesting recordings of "spirit voices" he had recorded in London's Highgate Cemetery. He had spent the night there on several occasions, he told me, and if we could meet again, he could let me hear some of these.

> We did meet again, and he played me a couple of tapes. And not long after that, we both visited Highgate Cemetery. It was open by day, in those days, but I was interested in finding the locations he told me he had made these recordings. I had listened to these recordings with interest; but again, although made at night, with the absence of any London sounds, it was difficult to discern some distinct 'voices' from the sounds of owls calling in the distance or the wind as it made its passage through the still trees. But Joe was convinced that one high-pitched female voice on one of the tapes, was trying to convey some message to him personally, and he was convinced this was a message that had been given to him as it was meant to convey some guidance from the 'spirit world' that could affect his life personally. I really didn't know. But I was sure at least he was sincere. And I was sure, at least, he would not have spent several night in the darkened Highgate Cemetery, unless these recordings were of essential importance to him.[587]

As well as recording in Highgate Cemetery, Joe would travel with his friend Tony Grinham to various locations around the area to capture background noise and atmosphere to use on recordings, but also in the hope that he might stumble upon something supernatural. 'We first went to this old church in Basildon,' Grinham explains. 'There was a story that someone had seen the ghosts of Roman centurions in this churchyard. We didn't see anything, but Joe was really enjoying himself. He was scared, but he enjoyed being scared, like he did when he went to see horror films. The

Please Stay

most unusual recording Joe got there was of me having a piss up against the church wall!' Grinham would later take a BBC camera crew to the same church to film scenes for the *Arena* documentary *The Very Strange Story of the Legendary Joe Meek*. 'I told him that I knew of this place that was really haunted, Warley Lea Farm.' It was there, on the night of 31 August 1965, that Meek and Grinham recorded the miaowing of a cat and convinced themselves that the animal was trying to communicate. 'We went in Joe's car. We got there at about two o'clock in the morning. We had a wander around this disused farmyard, found a few cold spots but not much else. We got back into the car, intending to drive back to Joe's studio and play our tape recordings, and this cat came and sat in front of Joe's car. Joe beeped it, but it just sat there. So we got out with our tape recorders going, and the cat seemed to say, "Hello!" And of course cats can sound a lot like a human voice, and we took the piss out of it, but then the cat seemed to say, "Help me! Help me!" Joe played it back in his studio and was knocked out by it.'[588]

Grinham's tape ('an inferior tape compared to Joe's,' he admits) was loaned to paranormal investigators the Society for Psychical Research the following year and, thanks mostly to its being used in the *Arena* documentary, has gained legendary status as an example of Meek's fascination with communicating with the dead. 'We both believed in the supernatural,' Grinham adds. 'But it was also a boys' night out; he was scared, but he was enjoying himself at the same time.'

Meek's attraction to life after death led to an interest in the culture of ancient Egypt. He was absorbed with tales of mummies and the tombs of the Pharaohs and invested in several Egyptian artefacts, including a pair of obelisks and a statue which set him back £3,000, and a gold ring engraved with hieroglyphs.* He became convinced, during séances, of his ability to conjure up the spirit of Rameses the Great as well as that of Buddy Holly, and that both would help to guide him.

---

*   Grinham says that Meek lost the ring while buying potatoes to promote Heinz's single 'Diggin' My Potatoes'.

CHAPTER 24

It's Hard to Believe It

By the summer of 1966, Joe's life was spiralling out of control. With Ted and Guy Fletcher, Don Charles and Alan Caddy, and Derek Lawrence all setting up their own recording operations within months of each other he felt perfectly justified in believing that his former pupils were stealing his ideas and inventions, and the occasional thoughts he had had about other companies bugging his studio became an obsession. 'He definitely was paranoid,' Dennis D'Ell commented. 'On several occasions he'd just stop recording, or whatever he was doing, and stand there. You went to say something, you know, like "What's the matter, Joe?", and he'd stand there for about ten minutes, then start looking all around the place and everything, and in the end he'd say something like, "It's those bastards at Decca or EMI. They've got this studio bugged and I'm trying to find out where the bugs are," which obviously was a load of rubbish, because nobody could get in there to put bugs around anyway.'[589] Meek's fragile grip on reality was shaken further when, in June, his friend Reg Calvert was shot dead.

Calvert, who brought the Dowlands and guitar player Roy Phillips to Meek, and who was instrumental in bringing Heinz into his orbit, had taken over the management of Screaming Lord Sutch. Calvert encouraged Sutch to get involved with politics (for publicity purposes) and suggested the singer front his own pirate radio station, Radio Sutch, based on an abandoned World War Two fort, Shivering Sands, in the Thames estuary. Advertised as 'Britain's first teenage radio station', the first disc played, in May 1964, was, appropriately, 'Jack the Ripper'. The station was immediately threatened with eviction by the government, and Sutch quickly

302

It's Hard to Believe It

lost interest. By September Radio Sutch had become Radio City, with Calvert buying Sutch out for a reported £5,000. Sutch had other interests anyway: now signed as a solo act to CBS, the singer let it be known that he was thinking of suing Meek over the lack of royalty payments from RGM Sound and Meeksville. Meek had no money to pay any costly legal fees, and Sutch was equally broke, having lost his deposit when he decided to stand against Prime Minister Harold Wilson in the general election earlier that year. An agreement resulted in Sutch obtaining the master tapes for his recordings from 304, making him the only artist signed to Meek to own his own recordings at the time of Meek's death.

Radio City very quickly became one of the most successful of all of Britain's pirate stations. Calvert sold Clifton Hall, his pop finishing school in Rugby, and expanded the reach of Radio City by setting up a booster transmitter in the Bristol Channel. However, after getting involved in some shady financial dealings with rival station Radio Caroline, Calvert was killed by Major Oliver Smedley in what he claimed was an act of self-defence. Radio Caroline director Smedley was acquitted of manslaughter.

Calvert's death shook Meek; as someone who had not been averse to slipping the occasional DJ, presenter or press officer a few fivers to get his records played, with his burgeoning persecution complex it must have felt as though danger was on his doorstep. Still, he kept working; in early summer 1966 Meek auditioned a young singer from Weymouth, Denise Scott, and her band the Soundsmen. Denise had recently appeared on the ITV pop show *Ready Steady Go!* and in July Meek brought her in to record the song 'Your Love Keeps Me Going', although it would remain unreleased until 1996. Denise and the band may not have had what Meek was looking for, but years later Graham Cole, guitarist with the Soundsmen, would play an important role in helping untangle the red tape surrounding Meek's estate.

Meek's low mood – and the crippling state of his finances – were conveyed in a letter he wrote to the members of the Tornados. The group were playing a summer season at the South Pier, Blackpool (with Adam Faith) that would keep them occupied from the last week of June until the end of September. 'Harry Dawson [of the George Cooper Organisation] is very pleased,' Meek wrote, 'and I got a cheque for twenty pounds this week. It couldn't have arrived at a better time. With luck the Telstar case could be over in November then I shall have your disc in... I think it's a

303

Love and Fury: The Life, Death and Legacy of Joe Meek

sure hit this time, I hope so it would be wonderful for us all. I've got Eric to bring mum up here next Sunday for the day, it will do us both good, I'm very run down with worry over the company and the muck Shanks has put me in, I can't really turn to anyone except my folks and you but give me a few more weeks and I should be on my feet again.' [590]

The issue with Shanks, who only owned 1 per cent of Meeksville Sound Ltd, was not elaborated on, but Meek had come to blame his current financial situation on him, and in letters between Meek and his solicitor, John Frederick Ginnett, he would claim that Shanks had ripped him off. Shanks had tried to keep a rein on the company's purse strings, but Meek was convinced that he was milking him dry. He came to distrust any move that Shanks made and felt as though he treated him like a Gloucestershire bumpkin. Meek often complained about Tom Shanks, just as he had complained about Denis Preston, Barry Barrington-Coupe and Wilfred Alonzo Banks before him, but others paint a picture of a generous, helpful man who was very fond of Meek but found his partner's profligacy frustrating. A row ensued, and Shanks threw in the towel, leaving Meek's companies and demanding thousands of pounds in back pay. Shanks' claim put such a strain on Meek's finances that so welcome and unusual a bonus as a cheque for a meagre twenty quid warranted mention in a letter.

In what would seem like a bizarre request by anyone else the letter ended with an appeal from Meek that the band try to get in touch with him via ethereal means: 'If you have a séance try to get through to me, I'm up till about 1 each morning ask that I get three taps on the sideboard. I'll ask for the same, you must be sincere and believe...' [591] Money was tight, but it was a peculiar way to save the cost of a stamp or a phone call and, needless to say, no one in the band tried to contact their manager in this way.

Meek's worsening mental health had a detrimental effect on his work. The flow of new acts coming to his door remained constant, but his ability to pick a hit had gone. He could no longer rely on his 'commercial ear', and as far as Britain's pop critics and record buyers could see, his once bright star had barely a glimmer left. Britain's teenagers were becoming ever more sophisticated, and pop music reflected this: psychedelia was making inroads into the singles charts, and the Beatles were on the cusp of changing the face of pop music once again. 'I remember going up there one day;

It's Hard to Believe It

he couldn't let me into the studio, but he let me into the sitting room,' Paul Burns recalls. 'I sat down and he made me a cup of coffee. He said, "I won't be long, I've got to nip down the road for a minute, but when I come back we'll have a chat." So I was sitting there having this cup of coffee and I noticed his record collection, and at the very front of the collection was the *Revolver* album by the Beatles, which surprised me, because I'd heard that he had rejected the Beatles.'[592]

Meek's attempts to join the beat group boom had found little success, but maybe a shift in direction could help him regain his chart crown. Pop stars were being asked to comment on everything from the war in Vietnam to the state of religion, and at the end of July Pye issued their second single from Glenda Collins, a disjointed protest song which took in subjects from alien life to starvation and all-out war, 'It's Hard to Believe It'. Written by Meek, and featuring Glenda backed by an uncredited Riot Squad, the single came almost a year after the release of Barry McGuire's 'Eve of Destruction', the song that had clearly influenced it, and perhaps if it had appeared in 1965 rather than the summer of 1966 it may have stood a better chance. Pye had already turned down one version of the song, Meek's original lyrics, which included his insistence that 'flying saucers are here to stay' being a bit too 'out there' for the company, but the second version – which opened with the sound of a bomb exploding – also proved too much for many. 'This load of rubbish,' wrote one reviewer, '[is] a pseudo protest song with a Tin Pan Alley gloss. Glenda had a good voice but I'm afraid this drivel sinks her completely.'[593] For a man eager to appear relevant, the reviews were shattering.

In September the Honeycombs issued 'That Loving Feeling', an original Colin Boyd composition, backed with one of Meek's own songs, 'Should a Man Cry'. Only Honey and John Lantree remained of the original band, but 'That Loving Feeling', with its contemporary, California folk-rock feel, pointed towards an interesting new direction. Yet, sadly, despite some good reviews the public were not buying. It did not help matters that the band were out of the country when the disc was issued and unable to promote it in the UK, and 'That Loving Feeling' would be the last new Honeycombs single issued during Meek's lifetime. That same month Meek made a rare appearance outside 304 when he accompanied Paul and Ritchie and the Crying Shames to Rediffusion TV studios for a recording of *Ready Steady*

305

Love and Fury: The Life, Death and Legacy of Joe Meek

Go! The band were due to promote their new single, 'September in the Rain', but after the performance was taped a furious row broke out in the control room, with the band's management accusing Meek of trying to interfere with the group's sound. Word was getting around that Meek was trouble.

But despite the darkness that seemed to be enveloping him, there were still occasional patches of bright light. In late 1966 Meek began to boast about having agreed a deal with EMI for exclusive distribution of his productions. As well as becoming more openly friendly with Brian Epstein, Meek had several meetings with Sir Joseph Lockwood, chairman of EMI, and it certainly looked as if the company was interested in employing Meek in some capacity. George Martin had left to set up his own company, AIR, and other long-standing staff were looking to follow him. Lockwood, it seems, was investigating the idea of Meek coming to work for the company; Meek told Patrick Pink that a move to EMI was imminent and, according to his brother Eric, 'his solicitor had tidied everything up and he was going to work for EMI. They would have first refusal on everything he'd done, but anything they didn't want he was welcome to sell freelance.' 'That's why we couldn't understand the tragic end that happened,' Eric added. 'Everything was pretty sorted out. He had plenty of money, as far as that went, and a lot more money to come, provided they sorted out the 'Telstar' muddle.'[594]

In truth, Meek had built up a lot of debt – some estimates put it at around £15,000, around the same amount he had paid to the Major – and he was having trouble paying his bills. Meek's assistants became adept at keeping debt collectors out of his studio; however, Ginnett had been working hard to sort out the financial muddle Meek was in. With his assurance that the 'Telstar' case would soon be settled in Meek's favour, plus a potential position at EMI, things were starting to look better. Yet Ted Fletcher recalled that, in his last weeks, 'his condition rapidly deteriorated until he was barricaded into the flat and studio, never venturing out'.[595]

One reason he locked himself away may have been that, around this time, notorious East End gangsters Ronnie and Reggie Kray became a thorn in Meek's side. In November the Tornados were approached by British guitar legend Bert Weedon, who they were appearing with in Coventry. Weedon wanted to know if they would join him at a benefit concert, to be held in

It's Hard to Believe It

Cardiff on 20 November, that was being organised to help raise funds for the families of the victims of the Aberfan disaster, when a colliery spoil tip collapsed and engulfed part of the town, including the local school, killing 116 children and 28 adults. Of course the band would take part.

In the audience were the Kray twins. That night they donated a cheque for £100 to the Cardiff Committee for Aid to Aberfan, and, following a charity football match at Cardiff's Ninian Park, had offered up a signed football for auction. 'When we were on stage we noticed two gentlemen in tuxedos in the royal box, and one of them kept waving to us. We were puzzled as we didn't know who these guys were,' says Robb Huxley. The band had no idea that the two men were the most notorious criminals in Britian at that time, nor that Ronnie Kray had taken a fancy to Roger Holder. 'After the show, when we were in bed at our hotel, the phone rang a few times with somebody inviting us to have a drink at their hotel. We refused, but when the final call came in Dave Watts picked up the phone and told us that we had better get over for the drink as we were invited by the two biggest gangsters in London, the Kray twins: Dave's dad had been a London policeman and he had told Dave about them. I wasn't afraid as it all happened so quickly, and their reputation had not had time to really sink in: Ronnie and Reggie addressed us politely buying us drinks and they gave us each a carton of cigarettes. Ronnie made it clear to us that he wanted to take over the band and send us to America.' The Krays would not have much to gain from managing the group, an act that was enjoying little in the way of tangible success. Record sales were negligible, they had no work coming in from the BBC and outside their live commitments they had little in the way of income. It is possible that the Krays were aware of the thousands of pounds held up in the dispute over the authorship of 'Telstar' and thought that by having a piece of the Tornados they would also be able to get their hands on that windfall, but that money was Meek's, not the current iteration of the band. Certainly, they were looking for ways to make their business interests look more respectable. 'I will never forget his words when we told him that we were contracted to Joe Meek,' Huxley adds. 'He told us, "Don't worry about Joe Meek, we'll take care of him!" Only in later years when we found out more about the Krays did it finally sink in how powerful and potentially dangerous they were.' Sometime later the band's keyboard player was summoned to a private meeting with

Ronnie Kray: 'Dave Watts did go to see Ronnie once at a pub in the East End,' Huxley recalls. 'Once again Ronnie said he would "take care of Joe Meek".'[596]

Ronnie Kray was well-known to London's gay pop promoters, and both brothers had rubbed shoulders with showbiz luminaries. Some have speculated that the Krays, well known for running a protection racket, had been putting the squeeze on Meek, and that when Ronnie Kray turned up unannounced at 304, a furious Meek screamed at the feared gangster to 'fuck off', although Tony Grinham disputes this: 'That's a load of bollocks! Patrick is supposed to have answered the door to Ronnie, but very few people knew what the Krays even looked like then: maybe a few locals if they were involved in their racket. Patrick wouldn't have known who he was.'[597] Norman Fowler, who recorded at RGM Sound as a member of Sammy Browne and the Escorts, adds that 'I understood that the Kray twins were getting protection money off him'.[598] There is unsubstantiated gossip concerning Meek having been beaten up by the twins or their heavies – Geoff Goddard recalled an incident following Meek's arrest, when 'a gang broke into the place and coshed him. After that I always ordered a taxi away from the place; you never knew who was waiting for you between the studio and the underground station'[599] – and Meek had recently been arguing with Maurice King, an associate of the Krays. If Joe had indeed told one of London's most dreaded hoodlums to 'fuck off', or if he owed money to people connected to them, then it is hardly surprising he would have been alert to their threat. Perhaps his request to hang on to the rifle after Heinz moved out was partly motivated by his being a target of the notorious gangsters, but, according to Huxley, no one in the Tornados camp ever revealed that they had been approached by the criminal pair. 'We never ever mentioned anything to Joe about the Krays or how we had met them at Cardiff,' he says. 'We had no idea if Joe even knew who the Krays were. He never ever mentioned anything to us regarding the Krays.'[600]

In October Meek recorded the first of a series of sessions with a local band, the Impac. None of those involved could possibly have known, but the sole release from those sessions, 'Too Far Out' backed with 'Rat Tat Ta Tat', issued by CBS in November, would turn out to be the penultimate record-

It's Hard to Believe It

ing issued from 304 Holloway Road during Meek's lifetime. He also signed Edinburgh band the Blaze (formerly known as the T-Set), with their manager, Douglas McDonald, telling local reporters that the band had 'a standing invitation to go down to London, where Joe Meek will get them into a recording studio and try and work out a hit sound'.[601]

The Impac featured 15-year-old drummer Nigel Silk, who explains that the band came to Meek's attention through their singer, Chas Bond. 'I don't know how he knew him, but he was a bit of a lad!

'Around October 1966 we went to Holloway Road to record with Joe Meek and lay down a few tracks. I remember going up these small narrow stairs to his studio, and the control room had tape everywhere. When I first met Joe Meek I thought how smart he looked, always immaculately dressed in a blue suit, but I also remember thinking, "This isn't a proper recording studio!" I was playing the drums in his front room thinking, "This is all a bit weird."' Silk might have thought the set-up odd, but the results were another thing entirely. 'He said, "Come and listen to the track," and I couldn't believe it was me playing the drums. It was a really amazing sound.'[602]

The Impac sessions were tainted with a sense of foreboding. None of the band were aware of the true state of Meek's health, but they could see that his fixation with being spied on was getting out of control. 'The curtains were always drawn,' Silk recalls, 'but I remember that he kept looking out the window. I thought it was all very odd, I had no idea why.' By this point he was finding it more and more difficult to contain his temper. 'Chas Bond had an old black van with "The Impac" painted all over it, and we broke down,' the drummer remembers. 'We arrived late, and as I went up the stairs Joe was on the first-floor landing looking really unhappy; he was just standing there with his blue suit and shiny black winkle-pickers on, immaculately dressed as always, giving us the look of death.' The session did not go well. 'Chas Bond was a bit of a joker. He was messing about with the microphone and Joe came storming in and went absolutely crazy. At the time I found that really scary. I'd never seen anyone lose their temper like that before. It felt like the guy was going to stab you.'[603]

Ever on the lookout for a way to make some money, at the end of 1966 Meek began to investigate setting up a new company to produce material exclusively for the American market, after being approached by Michigan

Love and Fury: The Life, Death and Legacy of Joe Meek

television presenter, radio DJ and musician Ed Ver Schure. Ver Schure was impressed with Meek's work on the first Blue Rondos single, and Meek still had material from the group in the can, but despite several transatlantic telephone conversations, and the two men meeting after Ver Schure flew into London in January 1967, nothing came of the discussions. Meek made it clear to Ver Schure that he distrusted record companies, and he felt badly bitten by his association with Barrington-Coupe, Major Banks and Tom Shanks; if Meek was going to go into business with another new partner, he wanted a controlling interest in the company. But Meek really was not well, and his fear of people stealing his material or ideas prevented him pursuing a deal. It has been suggested that this new company would be called Gold Disc Productions. Meek had been using the image of a gold disc on letterheads since 1964, but no Meek-related company of that name (or similar) was registered at Companies House. A year after Meek's death, Jewel records (a Melodisc imprint) put out a 7-inch credited to Dave Andrews and the Sugar, the B-side of which was actually Heinz's 1964 track 'The Beating of My Heart'; the publisher credit on the label was Gold Disc.

The final, full Tornados recording session, which took place at 304 over two days in mid-December 1966, was for their next single, which Meek had decided would be a cover of the 'Theme From Lawrence of Arabia'.

'We had already recorded a vocal called 'No More You And Me',' Robb Huxley reveals, 'which we wanted to be our next A-side; 'Lawrence of Arabia' had already been recorded too. Joe wanted 'Lawrence' to be the A-side, but we begged him to make the vocal the A-side as instrumentals were not popular anymore. Eventually, he agreed to go along with our wishes, but I believe if he had lived he would still have made 'Lawrence' the A-side. During our last sessions with Joe, in December 1966, we recorded two of my songs. One has been found and was featured on the Tornados Tea Chest compilation. Unfortunately, they gave it the wrong title. They called it 'You Always Did What You Wanted', when in fact the correct title was 'Signs of You'.

'Joe's demeanour had changed. Instead of being this domineering character calling all the shots and controlling what he thought we should record, he just told us to do whatever we wanted. Joe was pretty much always happy when he was around us as he liked us very much and we were respectful towards him.'[604] Meek and the group agreed to reconvene

It's Hard to Believe It

after the New Year to finish the tracks off – they were booked to play the Regency Club in Widnes from Christmas Day for a week – although the final session, in January 1967, would feature just Dave Watts and Roger Holder, plus female vocal duo the Diamond Twins and guitarist Ritchie Blackmore.

Meek may have been distracted during the Tornados session, but he had recovered sufficiently before the Christmas holiday, which he was due to spend in Newent with his family. Seeing his family always boosted his spirits, and he was clearly in a good mood when, shortly before he took off for his mother's home, he gave the Shentons a Christmas gift: a tape recorder and several pre-recorded tapes. Meek often gave lavish gifts to his friends and those who he felt had supported his work: DJ Barry Alldis, who regularly gave Meek's productions airtime, was rewarded with extravagant Christmas presents and a writing credit on the Tornados' 'Night Rider' as a thank-you, and in spite of his ongoing financial woes, a recent row with Patrick was papered over after Meek turned up on his doorstep with a £50 cash bonus. He seemed to be in relatively good spirits and had talked about the possibility of taking a holiday in Egypt. During the 1950s and 60s the North African countries of Egypt and Morocco were popular destinations for gay male tourists: sex was readily available, male prostitutes were inexpensive and the authorities either turned a blind eye to homosexual visitors or could be bought off cheaply. Meek also saw it as an ideal opportunity to feed his increasing interest in ancient Egyptian culture and beliefs. Harvey Richards, Joe's new musical director, was also going to visit family in Gloucester, and Meek offered him a lift back to London before the New Year.

Meek may have been happy in the days before his break, yet Christmas itself was a different matter. His family were struggling; his mother's home was in dire need of repairs to the leaking roof, and where before Joe had always helped out financially, he was in no position to do so this time. It was a stressed and tearful Joe Meek who took a telephone call from Bob Evans, saxophone player with the Riot Squad, on Christmas Eve and sobbed that Evans was the only member of one of his acts to have thought to have called him that day. On what would turn out to be his last visit home, his family could see that he was not coping. 'We never knew he was on drugs,' his brother Eric would later say. 'We knew he wasn't very well just before the end, and we pleaded with him to come home.'[605] Perhaps if Joe had listened to his brother, things might have turned out differently, but by the end of his visit he had cheered up sufficiently to invite his mother back to London to spend the New Year with him. Eric, Biddy, Joe and his niece Sandra left Newent for London in Sandra's father's Mercedes, stopping off in Gloucester to pick up Harvey Richards. The fivesome had a pleasant journey. It was Sandra's first trip to London, and she was mesmerised by the lights. 'We went up to the flat,' she recalled, 'and Joe took great pride in showing me all around, but most of all it was his [control] room. "Look at all my equipment! I made all this", but I was so worried because the floor was just covered with wires... I felt as though I could be swallowed up by them!'[606] He then took his 13-year-old niece into his office and showed her three tape recorders, telling her that she could take one of them home. 'I chose the littlest one, took that home and put it on the breakfast table. The next morning my brother picked it up and dropped it!'[607] She had been fascinated with her uncle's desk diary, and several weeks later she received a similar one in the post, with the handwritten dedication 'All good girls get what they want, with love from your uncle Joe xx'.

For the next week Meek enjoyed fussing over his mother, while business continued as normal. 'She was lovely; I really liked her,' singer Kim Roberts recalled. 'She was very proud of him... She was really sweet. He thought a lot about her.'[608] Shortly after Biddy Meek returned to Newent, in early January 1967 Joe plucked up the courage to attend a party at EMI's head office, in London's Manchester Square, rubbing shoulders with various members of the board including managing director L. G. 'Len' Wood and chairman Sir Joseph Lockwood. Photos taken that night show Meek looking robust and healthy, but within a few days all that would change. Richards recalls that Meek was soon back to fixating on the subjects that vexed him the most: the lack of settlement in the 'Telstar' affair, despite Meek's recent trip to Paris to testify on his own behalf in the French court, and Robert Stigwood, whose star was once again in the ascendant having signed the rock trio Cream (who he also managed) and The Who to his new record label, Reaction. New acts came to 304 to audition, but Meek's temper was fraying: one band of teenagers, the Syne from Bury St Edmunds, were almost reduced to tears after a frustrated Meek flew into a rage and demanded they pack up and get out. Luckily for them, he soon

It's Hard to Believe It

calmed down and allowed them to continue recording, finally offering them a proper session to take place in early February.

On 16 January, ten days after the release of their latest single, 'Gotta Be a First Time', the members of the Riot Squad met with their producer to discuss ideas for promoting the record, as well as to set future recording dates. Not only would 'Gotta Be a First Time' be the last Meek production issued during his lifetime, it would also be the last time that any of the band would see Meek alive, something that the members – several of whom were keen on spiritualism, séances, tasseography (reading tea leaves) and fortune telling – had singularly failed to foresee. On the very same day a farm worker, Fred Burrgy, discovered two abandoned suitcases in a field in Tattingstone, a few miles south of Ipswich. On opening the cases he made a grisly discovery: inside was the body of a young man, carved into eight pieces, with his torso in one case and his limbs in the other. There is a reasonable chance that Bernard Oliver had been known to Joe; it was later revealed that the young man may have visited 304 in search of work, or possibly more. However, when the suitcases were discovered the identity of the victim was unknown, and police took the unusual step of releasing a photograph of the young man's head to the media. His family – who had no idea what had happened to him – only contacted the police after his brother-in-law saw the photograph in an evening paper.

A post-mortem showed that Bernard Oliver had been sexually assaulted and strangled before his body was dismembered. A lonely, shy boy who worked as a washer-up in a branch of the Wimpy burger chain, it did not take long before police started to investigate the possibility that his death may have been at the hands of a sadistic homosexual. They announced that they were looking into any connections between Bernard and the regulars who haunted the gay bars of North London, and as their inquiries progressed with no resolution the sixty detectives working on the case were 'ordered to investigate the movements of known homosexuals in London and Ipswich' over the time between Bernard going missing and the discovery of his dismembered corpse. Meek became increasingly concerned that he might be questioned, yet although some 2,045 statements were taken following the discovery, he was not interviewed. That may be because there was no credible link between Oliver and Meek, or simply because the police had

313

Love and Fury: The Life, Death and Legacy of Joe Meek

not yet got around to talking to him. The police investigation went on for months, and to this day no one has been charged with Bernard's murder.

Joe had his final meeting with Sir Joseph Lockwood, at EMI, the following day; 17 January 1967. It did not go well. Lockwood had been willing to overlook his eccentricities in the past, but by now his behaviour was becoming so erratic and worrying that there was no way he could countenance offering Meek a position at EMI. The vacant production role was awarded to Mark Wirtz. A few nights later Meek sent Lockwood a six-page letter, accusing EMI of planting bugging devices around 304. The letter was long and rambling and laced with obscenities, expletives and sexual references. Lockwood had been a good friend to Meek, one of the few to even consider employing him at this point in his career, but that letter was the last straw. The following day, after sharing the contents of the letter with Len Wood, a furious Lockwood destroyed it and swore – as he had once done with Robert Stigwood – that he would never work with Meek again. It was a move that would have disastrous consequences.

Yet within days of that meeting, an upbeat-sounding Meek was telling friends that he was due to sign a contract with EMI worth a quarter of a million pounds a year. No one at EMI, not even Lockwood, earned that kind of money; Meek also boasted that his long-held plans to expand his business stateside were about to come to fruition. Both statements were untrue. Meek's braggadocio was either an endeavour to bolster his standing in his friends' eyes or simply an attempt to boost his own, fast-crumbling confidence. This good mood would not last long. Songwriter Mike Batory came to see Meek at 304 during the last week of January. Meek had recorded a couple of Batory's songs, but neither had done much business, and Batory had the distinct feeling that he was getting the brush-off. Needing to find paid work elsewhere, Batory wanted to extract himself from his contractual obligations to Meek, but he was unprepared for what happened. 'He was not in a happy mood,' he explained, 'and he took great exception to my questions. I could see him getting white with anger and he started to shake. "I've got artistes on my books more famous than you'll ever be and they never query anything about their contracts," he said… He made it very clear that I was not welcome there any longer. "Get out," he said. "Get fucking out before I fucking kill you!" I left quickly.'[609]

314

It's Hard to Believe It

Meek needed to get away, and on 30 January he had photographs taken for a new passport, ahead of his planned trip to Egypt. In the photos Meek looks pale, drawn and haunted, and considerably thinner than the man photographed just a few weeks earlier partying with EMI's executives. Arthur Meek was worried about the change in his brother, noting that the last time he saw him alive Joe had lost weight and did not look well. The trip to Egypt would not transpire. Three days later, on 2 February, Meek wrote a letter to Harvey Richards, apologising for his inability to work with him on their latest project. The letter to Richards (who would go on to record for library music specialists Studio G) was almost certainly the last he wrote, apart from the scribbled notes Patrick Pink recalled Meek handing to him the following day. It was written hurriedly on old RGM stationery, and was littered with spelling mistakes and idiosyncratic punctuation. 'Dear Harvey,' he wrote, 'I am not at all well, so if you ring today, I or someone, here will, till [sic] you if the recordings can be made today, as I sujested [sic] you were to confirm it last night, but was to [sic] unwell to answer the problem of if it was worth recording as planned or not.'

The letter, and Meek's admission that he was 'not at all well' was penned on the same day that he had a bad-tempered call with EMI's Roy Pitt. Pitt was formerly at Filmusic (Rank's music publishing arm) but was now in charge of EMI's independent producer liaison, and therefore Meek's first port of call with the company. Meek knew Pitt well: they were old friends, and even after his bruising bust-up with Sir Joseph, Meek had kept plugging away at EMI, desperately trying to get them to accept one of his recordings for release. He no doubt felt that he could call on Pitt to take up the crusade on his behalf. Sadly, Pitt was not receptive. Vic Keary, the independent producer who began his career as an engineer at Lansdowne, had arranged a meeting with Pitt that day and later recalled that 'while I was there, sitting in his office, a phone call came through. It was Joe Meek. I heard Roy say, "I'm sorry, Joe, but we're not going to release that recording." After a few moments of silence, Roy pulled the telephone receiver away from his ear and placed it on my ear. I could hear Joe crying at the other end of the line. Roy then quietly hung up the receiver and ended the call.

'Of course, we were both a bit unsettled by what we'd heard, so Roy played me Joe's recording that he'd just rejected and I had to agree that it did seem a bit dated and out of step with the pop market of 1967. The next day, when Roy heard about Joe's suicide, he must've felt in some way responsible. He went out at lunchtime, got drunk and returned to his office and went berserk, smashing the place up. He walked out, never to return and left the music business for good.'[610] Pitt's name would appear on just one more release, the Migil Five single 'Together'. Keary, who died in late 2022, never revealed the name of the song Pitt played for him, but the day before Meek had sent an acetate by Bobby Ross, bass player with the Off-Beats, to the London offices of Radio London. Meek had great hopes for the disc and had Ross record a promotional interview, specifically for Meek's sometime boyfriend Tony Windsor, to help publicise it. The song was a cover of Meek's own composition 'Lips Are Redder on You', recorded by Gene Pitney in 1964; it sounds terribly old hat for early 1967, but Pitney had recently had a string of Top 10 hits in the UK, so it is possible that Meek saw Ross – who has a voice not dissimilar to the US hitmaker – as his own Gene Pitney, in the same way that Heinz had been his Eddie Cochran and Mike Berry had been his Buddy Holly. However, Ross and Meek had a tempestuous relationship, with Patrick Pink insisting that they once came to blows: 'Joe gave him a black eye on one occasion,' he revealed. Apparently, when Meek realised what he had done, he tried to reduce the swelling by placing a piece of steak over the singer's eye. 'It was for Joe's dinner the next day!'[611] Ross stormed out of the studio saying that he was going to have Meek arrested but came back several hours later and apologised to Meek for upsetting him. Meek had also recently sent Roy Pitt the master for 'Be Yourself', a recording he had produced at 304 in the spring of 1966 for a band called Barry Pender and the Force but had been unable to place. An acetate featuring 'Be Yourself', backed with another Meek production, the Riot Squad's 'Take It or Leave It' (the working title for their mid-1966 single 'I Take It We're Through'), was also given to Dave Adams.

Earlier that same day Meek's mother, Biddy, sent a long letter to her son, a letter that that he would not get to read. That morning she had received two letters from him, clearly sent in quick succession, in which he opened up to her about the state of his health and about the doctor he was seeing. Biddy urged her 'dearest Joe' to 'get on to him at once and tell him it is urgent, because I am sure with a bit of medicinal care you would feel more able to deal with the other problems.' Her letter is full of concern, telling Meek that she would return to London to look after him, but that she was

It's Hard to Believe It

needed at home. She wrote that she was glad that Joe had Patrick there as 'he is a nice boy, and is nice company for you, but I do think you need to be friendly as well with someone older with a bit of business knowledge'. Revealingly, in her letter Biddy referred to the *NME*'s Alley Cat gossip column, which had recently asked: 'Is Joe Meek joining EMI?'. Biddy wrote that she was surprised to read this as '[you] did not tell me anything about it in your letter'.[612] Meek had not told his mother for the simple reason that the door to EMI had already been closed.

CHAPTER 25

Nobody Waved Goodbye

At some point during the day, Joe spoke to Tornado Pete Holder. Holder was convinced that Meek was about to take on a prestigious role at EMI but would later report that, during the phone conversation, Meek 'really didn't make sense'. 'Personally, I was unaware that Joe was under great stress,' says Robb Huxley. 'Pete was the only one who mentioned anything about Joe's state of mind. It was on the last conversation by phone that Pete had with Joe. Pete said that Joe sounded very down and depressed.'[613]

Meek had a busy weekend ahead, with Irish singer Chad Carson (who he had first worked with in 1963)* due in the following morning (Friday, 3 February) and the Impac, the young group whose Meeksville debut, 'Too Far Out', had been issued by CBS the previous November, coming on Saturday to complete work on a recording that had been started the previous week. The Millionaires, the north London group featuring Cliff Cooper and his brother, were also booked to record a follow-up to their Decca single, 'Wishing Well'.

Meek had also recently signed Tommy Bishop, a barber from Brentwood in Middlesex who had previously fronted a band called the Ricochets and had recorded one single for Decca in 1965: 'Meek… agreed to sign me as a solo artist and give me the big build-up,'[614] he later revealed. Bishop, who shared Meek's interest in mediums and clairvoyancy, was not the only singer Meek was intent on grooming for solo stardom. He had also

---

* Carson's next release would be the 1969 single 'I Wanna Be a Country Star' for the Belfast label Outlet.

Nobody Waved Goodbye

been discussing the possibility of recording Robb Shenton as a solo singer, having used him so many times on sessions in the past, and had mentioned trying him out on a cover of the Platters' hit 'Only You'. Singer and guitar player Gerry Scales, from south-east London had been to 304 recently to record his own song, 'Wind of Change'. Scales remembers working with some of the Tornados (it is possible that one of the sessions took place on the same day that Dave Watts and Roger Holder had been in to work on overdubs for an earlier Tornados recording), and forging his parents' signatures on the contract with Meeksville Sound. He last saw Meek just a few days before his death.

And then there was Patrick Pink, who had recently returned to working for Meek after the pair fell out before Christmas. Meek had promised him that he would get his chance to audition, and during the evening of 2 February, and seemingly having recovered from his phone conversation with Roy Pitt earlier that day, Meek finally relented and invited his assistant into the studio to record. Finding a tape containing the backing track to 'True to You', the B-side of the second Jason Eddie and the Centremen single 'Singing the Blues', he positioned Patrick in front of the microphone and, barely speaking a word, had him run through several takes of the song, as well as several takes of Meek's composition 'Cry My Heart'. These would be the last recordings Meek ever worked on. Over the course of the next few hours Joe became more and more distant, at one point barely communicating. Convinced, perhaps, that the studio or control room were bugged, he began to pass hastily scribbled notes containing instructions for his assistant, rather than speak with him.

Patrick – who spent the night curled up on the sofa in the room next to Meek's ofice – would later recall that when he saw him at around eight o'clock on the morning of Friday, 3 February, an agitated Joe was burning papers in a metal bin in his office. 'I thought at the time he was going out of his head,' he told Jim Blake and Chris Knight. 'He took a painting off the wall, one that he had painted himself, and put it next to the electric fire and let it burn. He said, "They're not fucking well getting this!"'[615] Meek's brothers would later confirm this story and claim that the painting he destroyed was the best Meek had ever created. A notebook, containing many of Joe's own compositions, also vanished that day, possibly a further victim of the wastebin fire. 'He had a book

Love and Fury: The Life, Death and Legacy of Joe Meek

with about 150 to 200 songs he'd wrote, and we've never found that,' Eric Meek mused.

Troubled, Pink asked Meek if he wanted him to call his doctor;* after a mouthful of abuse he decided that the best thing he could do would be to get on with his day. Meek had been making toast in the kitchen for breakfast and had left it burning. Pink threw the burnt toast out and made fresh for his boss's breakfast: two slices, as he usually had. While Pink was busy in the kitchen, Margit Blackmore, Ritchie's wife, is supposed to have called at the front door. She lived close by with the couple's 3-year-old son, Jurgen, in the same flat that the Tornados had used. Margit would later state that Meek had answered the door to her, and that he sent her off to buy a pint of milk. Pink claimed he never saw her and was not aware that she had stopped by, although singer Kim Roberts would later corroborate her story, telling Jim Blake and Chris Knight that Margit had indeed been there that fateful day.

At around the same time the Shentons arrived at the door of their shop. The couple lived in East Finchley, in a house they shared with their married daughter, Pauline. Violet Shenton had some washing to do, which she intended to drop off at the laundromat (the same one where Joe's artists had gone to keep warm between wintertime sessions at 304) while her husband opened up the shop. Albert Shenton had an appointment that morning with an estate agent. The couple, now in their fifties, were considering retiring: the lease on the whole building would be up for renewal soon, and they were looking into their options. At some time between 9 and 9.30 a.m. Violet Shenton called in at the local grocer, Graham's Stores, to buy some soap powder. It was just another ordinary day.

'Then he gave me the final note. "I'm leaving now" or "I'm going now" it said, "Goodbye",' Pink recalled. 'Then he went straight upstairs, and the next thing I can hear music again.' Someone else called at the front door; Joe called down to Patrick to tell whoever it was to 'fuck off' – most likely

---

* In interviews, Robbie Duke (Patrick Pink) referred to a Dr Crisp, or Crispe, who had an office in Harley Street. No GP of that name was practising in London in 1967; however, a Doctor Arthur Hamilton Crisp – who specialised in mental health and eating disorders – worked at King's College and the Middlesex Hospital during the 1960s and was appointed Professor of Psychiatry at St George's Hospital medical school, at the University of London, in 1967.

Nobody Waved Goodbye

it was Tom McNamara, another of Joe's tape stackers who lived nearby in Rowstock Gardens, Holloway. McNamara was not present at the time of the shooting, but he was due in that morning, probably to help out with the singer Chad Carson's pre-booked session. The report in the *Evening Standard* that day has Tom McNamara arriving for work at about 10:15 am, just minutes before the fatal shootings took place. Apparently it was McNamara who called in on the Shentons and told Violet that Joe wanted to see her.

Shortly afterwards Pink heard Violet Shenton coming up the stairs. Having deposited her laundry, the shop was now open for business, and she asked her husband to mind the store while she went to find out what Meek wanted. She asked how Meek was doing and enquired about his temper. Pink explained that his boss was in a foul mood, but Mrs Shenton assured him that she would be able to lift his spirits. She handed him her cigarette, as she knew Meek did not like people smoking in his studio, and went up to the next floor. It was approximately 10.15 a.m. Within moments, Patrick heard raised voices, with Meek and Mrs Shenton arguing over what he believed to be the rent book: 'I heard him say to her, in a loud voice, "Have you got the book?"'[616] The rent on the flat was up to date, but payment for the month ahead would have been due that day, and Joe had already let the Shentons know that he intended to renew his lease when it came up that June. 'I was in the studio and I could hear him talking to Mrs Shenton on the stairs,' he told police. Violet was trying to calm Joe, to persuade the clearly agitated man to come down stairs and join her in a cup of tea. 'Suddenly, I heard a bang and thought the lights had fused,' Pink said. 'I went outside and saw Mrs Shenton tumbling down the stairs. I knew she was hurt badly so I rushed for the phone and dialled 999. Then I heard another bang and I knew it was gunfire. I went upstairs and I found Joe on the landing with his head blown off. A shotgun was beside him.'[617]

'About twenty minutes [after she left the shop] I heard two bangs and a bump,' Mr Shenton told reporters. 'I did not know what was going on. I still did not know what had happened until after the police and ambulance men arrived.'[618] The bump was his wife falling back down the stairs with a gunshot wound in her back; apparently she had been turning away from Meek when the gun – the single-barrel 12-bore shotgun that Heinz had purchased in Plymouth – went off. As she fell down the stairs, smoke

321

Love and Fury: The Life, Death and Legacy of Joe Meek

was still coming from the wound. Patrick Pink would later state that the mortally wounded landlady had fallen down the flight of stairs and into his arms, and that he shouted, 'She's dead!', a natural reaction; however, at that point Mrs Shenton was still breathing. The second bang that Albert Shenton had heard was Meek blowing his own head off after reloading the gun. No one at the time realised that the tragedy took place on the eighth anniversary of the death of Meek's idol, Buddy Holly.

Had he intended to shoot himself and Mrs Shenton sadly got in the way? Was it simply a case of Mrs Shenton being in the wrong place at the wrong time, a tragic accident in that he was messing around with the gun and it went off, blasting Mrs Shenton in the back as she turned away from him? Violet Shenton was several feet away from Meek when she was shot, and it appears that she was leaving the room when the gun went off. Meek taking his own life while in the pit of despair is at least understandable; the death of Mrs Shenton is impossible to comprehend as anything apart from a tragic accident or as an act that took place during a fleeting moment of madness. '[Joe] and Mrs Shenton were the best of friends,' Heinz insisted. 'She used to come up, "Do you want some shopping, Joe?" They used to laugh and joke, so what brought this on?'[619]

It would have taken time for him to realise what he had done, reload the single-barrel rifle and then shoot himself. Was his own death a reaction to the horrific event that had just taken place? 'Joe heard Patrick shout, "She's dead, Joe," and that was it. He put the gun in his mouth and that was it,' says Tony Grinham.[620] Dave 'Screaming Lord' Sutch agreed: 'He realised what he had done, and the horror of it hit him hard and he shot himself. He was so sorry for what he'd done… He had a lot of worries, and worry killed him… It tied him up in knots, inside and out, and he couldn't see a way out of it.'[621] The Homicide Act of 1957 states: 'Where a person kills or is party to a killing of another, he shall not be convicted of murder if he was suffering from an abnormality of mental functioning which arose from a medical condition.' Meek had been discussing his mental health with his doctor at this stage, and no doubt a medical expert would have been able to argue that the murder of Violet Shenton happened while Meek was suffering from diminished responsibility, but Meek was in no state to think that clearly.

It's unlikely that he had chosen to end his life that day. Why would a man intent on suicide be signing new acts and booking sessions with

Nobody Waved Goodbye

others? Why would a man with an expensive foreign holiday ahead and the promise of staggering amounts of money to come from the resolution of the 'Telstar' case have planned suicide, especially using a rifle, when – according to his family – he detested guns and had refused, in his youth, to join his brothers who used similar guns to scare the birds from their father's fruit orchards? Eric Meek would always question what occurred that morning: 'It just didn't add up.' A much reported incident in which Meek had reportedly aimed a gun at session drummer Mitch Mitchell, screaming, 'Play it properly or I'll blow your fucking head off,' was later refuted by Mitchell himself, but this was the same man who had pulled a gun – albeit a starting pistol – on Tom Jones, and who had waved around a twin-barrel shotgun in publicity photos for Houston Wells.

Had that final conversation with Roy Pitt tipped him over the edge, pushing his already fragile state of mind to the point of no return? Although Meek would never be diagnosed with a mental health condition, as Dennis D'Ell stated, 'There was obviously something mentally wrong with Joe, you know? I used to feel very sorry for him at times. He wanted treatment, but he wouldn't have any, you see. ...Nobody dared say anything to Joe or discuss it.'[622] As far as the police were concerned, there was one obvious scenario. They believed that the gun had discharged while Mrs Shenton was heading towards the stairs, possibly to fetch her husband, and Albert Shenton seemed to agree: 'I think she must have gone into the studio – he called it the Bathroom – and found him about to shoot himself. Joe may have panicked as she came downstairs to get help.'[623]

For many years people have speculated about the involvement of a third person, who somehow dispatched both Meek and Mrs Shenton, probably because she walked into the studio as this person was threatening Meek, and that a representative of the Krays, or even one of the brothers themselves, pulled the trigger that day. 'I don't believe Joe committed suicide,' says his friend Paul Burns. 'I've been told by someone who interviewed Ronnie Kray that he confessed to killing Joe Meek, but whether that's true or not, I don't know. When you think about it, if they [the Krays] had threatened him, said, "If you don't keep your mouth shut then it's you," you don't know what he might have done in that situation. I believe he was murdered: he was a happy bloke, obviously he had his moments, everyone does, but I never saw him lose his temper or raise his voice. I never saw him shout, and I was there enough times. It's quite strange, really.'[624]

'He was very highly strung,' Chas Hodges would later remark. 'But I never thought that he would end up shooting himself. He was a great, nice quiet bloke, but when he lost his temper he had a voice that could go right through your head... he could really shout when he wanted to, yet he was really quietly spoken.'[625]

While it is true that the Krays had showed interest in using Joe's acts to help legitimise their business, it makes little sense for them to kill him: the Tornados were a spent force, with no hits for years and a limited shelf life remaining. Not only that, but a dead Joe Meek was hardly going to provide the Kray's organisation with a hit record. If a Kray was involved, how would he have known that Meek had Heinz's gun on the premises? Even if he did, would Ronnie Kray or anyone have known where the gun and any spare ammunition was kept? Legend has it that Meek kept the gun in his bedroom; however, Heinz insisted that it was locked in a cupboard in Meek's office. Only two sets of fingerprints were found on the weapon (and those belonged to Heinz and Joe) and the fatal wounds were fully consistent with their having come from Heinz's gun. Still, people close to Meek have questions: 'I don't think that the mystery of Joe's death and its alleged connection with the Krays will ever be proved,' says Robb Huxley. 'There have been countless rumours and allegations that have cropped up over the years which have all been word of mouth but with no physical evidence as proof. For the most part anybody who may have been involved in an alleged murder is probably no longer alive. If I had to make a guess one way or the other, I would side with the theory that the Krays were involved with Joe's death. How can I ever forget Ronnie Kray's words, "Don't worry about Joe Meek, we'll take care of him"? I don't believe that it was because Ronnie wanted the Tornados: I believe that it was something else, something far more serious.'[626] Former Meek recording artist Danny Rivers believed that it was all down to money: 'He used to get his drugs from a gang connected with the Krays and he wasn't paying their bill.'[627]

Several newspapers carried a quote from an unnamed neighbour, who reported that he had 'heard a shot. I saw this young man running into the street. He said there had been accident.'[628] Was he running from the scene of a crime he had committed? The running man was most likely

Nobody Waved Goodbye

the same man who had a pre-arranged appointment with Albert Shenton that morning, to discuss the lease on their property. Later identified as Jim Wilson, Mr Shenton does not mention him in his testimony, and he told police that he knew nothing about what had happened upstairs until the police and ambulance arrived, although this was contradicted by Pink, who says that Mr Shenton came to the door while he was waiting for the police to turn up and, in shock, he shut the door in his face.

In one press article, printed the day after his death, Albert Shenton talked about how Meek was 'always handing out cash to people. They only had to ask and he would give them a cheque for £100. That's why he didn't have much money.'[629] Tony Dangerfield remembered that Meek 'was always handing out money to people. I remember getting behind with maintenance payments and asking for £60 to get the police off my back. He didn't even want to know what it was for, and he would never ask for it back.'[630] Had Mr Shenton witnessed this kind of largesse, or had he seen Meek paying off one or more of his blackmailers? In the days following the shooting, Meek's on-off boyfriend Tony Windsor was also interviewed by police, who boarded the MV *Galaxy*, the ship from which Radio London broadcast. The *Galaxy* was moored off the coast near Frinton-on-Sea, around a dozen miles away from Tattingstone, where Bernard Oliver's remains had been found. It is unclear whether they wanted to speak to Windsor about his relationship with Meek or if they were quizzing him about the Bernard Oliver case, but the DJ was dismissed from Radio London not long afterwards, with his departure blamed on his long-standing alcohol issues.

Police Constable Robert Betty, from the nearby Holloway Police Station, was first on the scene. Patrick recalled that one unnamed policeman surveyed the carnage, began laughing and called to a colleague, 'Come and see what a 12-bore shotgun can do!'[631] After being forced to listen to the police joking about the events, a traumatised Patrick Pink was arrested. As he was the only witness to what had happened, he was taken into police custody where he was questioned for a further five hours. By the time he was led from the scene a small crowd had gathered outside; several of the people there shouted 'murderer' at the startled young man as he was bundled into a police car and whisked away. At first the police seemed convinced that Pink had been involved in the shooting, had possibly pulled the trigger,

325

Love and Fury: The Life, Death and Legacy of Joe Meek

as his story did not quite add up. It was reported in the press that he had arrived at 304 at the same time as Tom McNamara, yet he told police that, following their recording session, he had stayed with Meek overnight and had even made his breakfast that morning. In hindsight it is not surprising that Pink would have tried to fudge the facts: he still lived at home with his parents and sister, and would not want the media to report that he had spent the night, albeit innocently, in the home of a known homosexual with a criminal record. He was cleaved in two by his loyalty to Meek – a man he considered to be his friend and who he cared deeply about – and his wish to avoid any salacious gossip for the sake of his family.

Violet Shenton was taken away by ambulance, her face still visible above the blanket covering her badly injured body. She was pronounced dead on arrival at the Royal Northern Hospital, half a mile away along the Holloway Road. Meek's body was taken to the mortuary, where he was officially identified by Detective Constable John Corner, presumably because his family were in Newent and Pink was in custody. Police also questioned Tom McNamara and Albert Shenton. While this was happening the Shentons' son, John, arrived to close up the shop and look after his father. It did not take long for the police to tell press reporters that they were not looking for anyone else to help with their inquiries. All the while, the telephone in Meek's office rang continually. Several of those unanswered calls came from the songwriter Mike Batory, attempting to reconcile with Meek a week after their explosive last meeting. Margit Blackmore claimed to have returned after the shots took place, stepping over the body of Mrs Shenton on the stairs and running home in shock before anyone saw her and before the ambulance or police arrived. If she was there, it is not surprising that the German-born Margit, whose husband had effectively abandoned her in a strange country where anti-German feeling was still rife, would want to avoid any involvement with the authorities.

Joe's mother and his elder brother Arthur were at home in Newent when the local police came: Biddy Meek fainted on hearing the awful news. Heinz was taken into police custody and questioned about how Joe had managed to get possession of his shotgun. It certainly seemed suspicious, and the singer's fingerprints were all over it. He later told the inquest into Meek's death that 'in the pop business one's nerves tend to get on edge so I used to go shooting on farms and in the country when I had a day

Nobody Waved Goodbye

off'.[632] Heinz claimed that he had intended to sell the gun, which he had owned for around four years, and that Joe asked if he could have it 'because a lot of people would try the strong-arm stuff on him'.[633] Tony Grinham would later recall an incident, at the end of August 1965, when Meek had discovered an intruder at 304: 'This bloke had broken a window to try and get in. Joe rushed down there and he slung a bottle at him, but he said that if he'd had his gun with him he'd have shot his fucking leg off!'[634]

Whatever difficulties the two men had, Heinz clearly still cared for Joe, telling reporters afterwards that 'Joe Meek made me. He found me working in a shop and made me a star.'[635] Steve Howe, then playing guitar with the In Crowd, was stunned at the news. 'We knew [Mrs Shenton], we'd see her as we were in and out of there quite a bit. One is always shocked to see a murder in London, and also then a suicide coupled together. It was a real shock. If Joe had just shot her, he would have been in big trouble, he would have gone to jail, but to then realise that he'd shot himself, that he was so deranged, so disorientated with the world. But when you look at the struggles that he had, they were enormous. Obviously some of it he couldn't help; [his sexuality] was totally natural but it was such a worrying time to be gay, but he struggled, and some of the trouble he got into was self-made.

'He was extremely intense, but we had respect for this guy; he'd had hit records and that was a big thing then. There were only so many people you'd meet who had hit records, and they were revered, you know? Joe had a likeable side. He had style, and he brought that to you, and that's what a producer is supposed to do.'[636]

Meek's diary was as full as ever, with bookings as far ahead as the coming summer including a visit, accompanied by the Tornados, planned for mid-June to officiate at a church fête in Newent – the same church in which he himself would shortly be interred. 'This news is a terrible shock,' Richie Routledge of the Cryin' Shames told the *Liverpool Echo*.[637] 'We were all going down to London on Monday for a recording session with Mr Meek.' (Probably for what would have been the fourth single from the act, the Billy Kinsley co-write 'She's Gone', although they had been recording tracks for a potential album.) Years later Routledge would comment on the time he spent working with Meek, revealing that 'the man was a workaholic... Yes, he was taking speed, but so were we then! He never took drugs in front of us... But Joe was a bit of a mess towards the end. I think the speed had caught up with him.'[638] Engineer and producer Alan Wilson: 'The sheer volume of the work that went through that studio. You're not talking about a very long period of time, and it's no wonder that the guy had mental health problems, because he must have been working around the clock, seven days a week. That's OK in one respect if you're working on your own, but it must have been chaos. It wasn't a serene environment, and it's a big surprise to me that he lasted as long as he did, because I think I would have had a nervous breakdown. I work in that industry, and I know how tough it is, dealing with people, dealing with bands, dealing with egos, and he was dealing with all the other pressures as well, like, "Why is that record not in the charts?" Joe had the added pressure of "This has got to be a hit".'[639]

'I was booked that very next week to go back and make another record, which I was quite excited about,' says Jess Conrad. 'And then he shot himself... or whatever happened.'[640] In spite of the stories of animosity between them, it seems that Jess and Joe were on good terms, especially in the last two or three years of Meek's life. 'I never saw him throw a tantrum; he never lost his temper with me,' Conrad recalls. 'There probably was another side to him, but I never saw that. The sad thing is that we were all lined up to do another record when what happened happened. It was a terrible thing to lose Joe, but one moves on.' Conrad was shocked to learn of Meek's prodigious drug intake. 'If there were any drugs there, we would have known,' he adds. 'I was part of the in crowd. I was never aware of that there... we drank lots of bloody cups of tea, and we had a good laugh, and if you sat there all day, you'd see nearly every pop star in England, because it was quite a fun place to be.'[641]

Nigel Silk, whose band, the Impac, had been booked to work at 304 on the day following Meek's death, reckons that what happened was the result of his explosive temper. 'In my opinion, he was a brilliant record producer but very troubled and [he] had a really bad temper so I can believe that in a rage and out of control Joe shot his landlady and then himself. I don't know but I think it's unlikely anyone else was involved.'[642]

'Having worked closely with him for three years we were shocked, but I can't say altogether surprised, to learn of his tragic death, and the murder of his landlady Mrs Shenton,' Alan Blaikley would recall. 'His behaviour could

Nobody Waved Goodbye

be erratic in the extreme, and groups might find themselves summarily ejected from the studio by his assistant with a minimal explanation that "Mr Meek is unwell".[643]

'I was shocked when I heard,' recalled former Honeycombs singer Dennis D'Ell, 'but I wasn't surprised, really… I think it was a thing that could have happened at any time. When he had one of his moods he was completely irrational, and you could be sure that anybody in the way would have come under fire. I don't think, necessarily, he had anything against the woman downstairs, it could have been anybody.'[644]

Charles Blackwell, Joe's former songwriting associate, musical arranger and occasional co-publisher was in Cannes, at the inaugural MIDEM international music industry conference when he heard the news that Meek was dead. 'I think he drove himself into the ground, working twenty-four hours a day… it was more than flesh and blood could stand. He had a great ability to spot talent, and a great ability to record that talent,' his former collaborator would later say.[645]

On the evening of Friday, 3 February, Jim Blake, a local teenager who had become fascinated with Meek's work, got together with a few friends to mark his death by playing some of his records; before the night was out they had formed the genesis of the Robert George Meek Appreciation Society (RGMAS).

CHAPTER 26

Guess That's the Way It Goes

The inquest into the deaths of Robert George Meek and Violet Ethel Shenton opened on 8 February 1967 and was immediately adjourned until 9 March by deputy coroner Dr John Burton, to give time for 'a considerable amount of analysis and inquiries to be made'.[646] At that later hearing, Albert Shenton could give no reason as to what made Joe snap. The shocked widower confessed that he knew of 'no rational explanation for the shooting', and that despite Meek's reported financial issues, 'Mr Meek's rent was completely up to date and [Joe and Violet] were quite friendly'.[647]

Meek's death certificate stated that death was the result of 'shock and haemorrhage due to gunshot wound of head. Took his own life,'[648] and the murder-suicide was assumed by some involved in the inquest to have been the result of Meek's prodigious drug use. At that time no one considered that his erratic behaviour may have been connected to the state of his own mental health. In fact, although Albert Shenton told the inquest that Joe was 'a man of variable moods' who 'was in difficulties with his company',[649] any financial or mental health issues were ignored. Although there were reports that Meek's business had collapsed, with debts of £30,000, his friend and solicitor, John Ginnett* said that although his client was indeed 'in a financial muddle of the first order', he thought that he 'could have got him out of it. There was no question of distress in his finances, however. Nothing

---

*   Ginnett was married to pianist and radio announcer Patricia Hughes, who Meek had
      worked with in the 1950s. As Pat Hughes, she composed a number of instrumental
      pieces, and Meek is supposed to have helped her find a publisher, although her best-
      known work, 'It Happened in a Dream', was published and recorded in 1968, after
      Meek's death.

Guess That's the Way It Goes

struck me as abnormal about him. He could be moody and difficult, but could be quite reasonable.'[650]

Detective Chief Inspector Brian Kelly told the court that he 'found twenty-four bottles, some empty, which contained amphetamine drugs, barbiturates, a few purple hearts and Dexedrine'[651] on the premises, and Professor Francis Camps, pathologist, surmised that the amphetamines present in Joe's system 'could cause symptoms of delusion', explaining that 'someone who has taken them may get the impression that somebody is against them', [652] and that 'people who had taken an overdose suddenly got an impression that someone was following them, that they may be assaulted or were being attacked'[653] – symptoms that anyone who knew Meek would attest to witnessing. 'As a therapist, I wonder what came first, the psychoactive substance misuse or the anger and paranoia?' asks psychotherapist and writer Tamsin Embleton. 'I say that because regular amphetamine use can lead to increased anger and irritability and paranoia. It may be that the effects of the drugs heightened a pre-existing tendency towards these states, or it may be that the psychoactive substances he relied on for one problem had unwanted side effects like increased anger. Substance misuse often presents alongside diagnosable mental health conditions like anxiety disorders, clinical depression, bipolar I and II and PTSD. Some mental health conditions like PTSD can also present with trust issues and anger problems, alongside other symptoms.'[654]

At the same inquest, held in St Pancras, Patrick Pink told those assembled that Meek believed that his studio 'was "bugged" with electrical devices so that people could listen to his new recordings'.[655] He did not, however, tell the court that he himself had 'found a walkie-talkie set up, in the "on" position, in the living room'. Meek's absolute belief that he was being spied on caused him to buy a remote listening device. His former assistant later claimed that 'he planted it on me and sent me to the shops to buy some bread, and he taped it all from his living room. I was about three or four hundred yards down the road.'[656] John Ginnett backed this up: 'He used to imagine that people were spying on him to get ideas for another recording.'[657] Meek had, apparently, thought that someone using the electrical goods shop next door may have been listening to his conversations, and that perhaps he thought Mrs Shenton was guilty of spying, but as Pink said, 'I just thought it was imagination. I don't see who could have been listening. He always spoke highly of his landlady and never suggested that it was her.'[658] Pink talked about Meek's 'somewhat ungoverned temper', and explained that his former boss 'often threw cups at walls and slammed doors',[659] but Detective Chief Inspector Kelly reckoned that the relationship between Joe and Violet had been good, and that there was no reason for him to have shot her: 'My inquiries show that Mrs Shenton was extremely kind to this young man and acted as a mother.'[660]

The authorities were at a loss to explain Meek's motive for killing Mrs Shenton, and Kelly insisted that 'there was no evidence of insanity in Meek'.[661] It is true that Meek was never diagnosed with any kind of mental health issue, but had the investigating authorities bothered to interview any of the regular visitors to his studio, they would have quickly learned of his unpredictable behaviour and mood swings. Years later Meek's former right-hand man Geoff Goddard would ruminate on his old friend's psyche: 'He literally drove himself into the ground. He was suffering from mental illness anyway, I'm sure. He once told me, without joking, that he thought something was growing inside his head.'[662]

Professor Camps described the shotgun wounds to the inquest, one in Mrs Shenton's back, the other 'near [Meek's] right ear surrounded by scorching which had caused extensive shattering of the skull'.[663] Meek shot Mrs Shenton, the jury concluded, and then turned the gun on himself. Despite the pathologist's expert testimony and his assertion that 'I don't think the risk of this particular drug is fully appreciated',[664] the coroner's final conclusion made no allowance for the amphetamines present in his bloodstream. 'It appears Mr Meek knew what he was doing, shot Mrs Shenton and then he had to reload the gun to shoot himself,' the coroner surmised. 'Why he did this we just do not know.'[665] When asked what he would like to do with the gun, Heinz told police to 'smash it to a thousand pieces. I never want to see it again. It has caused a terrible tragedy – the death of my friend and of an innocent woman. I am heartbroken.'[666]

'I had a great respect for Joe,' says Ted Fletcher. 'He was a great experimenter. He was no musician, but he had an understanding of what would catch the public imagination at the time and he ignored any criticism. He produced some dreadful records, but he also produced some world hits.'[667]

Guess That's the Way It Goes

Recordings that Meek had been working on and which had already been scheduled for release were shelved.

Meek left behind him a huge mess, and no record company wanted to be involved in it. Casualties included a new single by the Tornados, 'No More You and Me', as well as the next Honeycombs release, '(I Can Tell) Something's Up'. 'Joe Meek was like a father to us,' the Honeycombs' bassist, John Lantree, confessed. 'Although he was a moody person and did not get on well with everybody we always found him very helpful and he spared no effort to assist us in any way he could. Now we can't get into the studio to search for the tape, we will be months behind with our schedule.' Lantree dismissed the idea of finding another producer to re-record the last song: 'We just don't want anybody. He might be the most technical man available, but if he doesn't fit into our way of thinking and get on well with us he is no good.'[668] With no end to the legal situation in sight, drummer Honey Lantree decided to leave the group and strike out on a solo career, only to discover that she was still bound by the same contract that was forcing the group to take a hiatus: 'It's terrible,' she told the *Daily Mirror*'s Don Short. 'I can't sing a song until Joe's estate is sorted out.' 'I feel desperately sorry for Honey and all the groups put in this position,' John Ginnett added. 'It's hell for them. They can do nothing until the company's affairs are settled – and I can't say what will happen in the end.'[669] The next five decades would see countless iterations of the Honeycombs surface, some with Honey, most with Martin Murray. Later versions included Meek's session guitarist Roger J. Simmonds and former Meek singer Bobby Rio as a replacement for Dennis D'Ell.

The situation was similar for many of his other acts. The Riot Squad, who first learned about Meek's death when they saw a poster for the *Evening Standard* announcing the horrific events that took place that day, were now without a producer. They struggled on, playing the night of Meek's death at the Shakespeare Hotel in Woolwich, but without Meek to guide them they imploded at the beginning of March. With a further series of live dates lined up, the band's mainstay Bob Evans approached a friend of his to see if he would be interested in taking over as lead vocalist. The man he selected was a young singer he had first met at the Marquee, David Bowie.

An album Meek had planned with the group backing singer Glenda Collins would languish amongst the piles of tapes he left behind him for

333

Love and Fury: The Life, Death and Legacy of Joe Meek

more than half a century, before finally being released in 2023. Glenda was, naturally, shattered by her friend's death. 'Maybe if he had got himself some help and been able to form proper relationships he may have even been alive today,' she said. 'I think, unfortunately, that he was a little bit disturbed and he probably could have done with some help. I only wish that I had been mature enough at the time to realise it, because I was fond of him and I might have spoken to him…' Meek was lonely, she surmised, because he wanted it that way: 'One never really got that close to him, because I don't think he wanted [people to be].'[670] Joy Adams tended to agree: 'I remember feeling a deep sadness and shock, but it did not surprise me in the least to hear of his end. Joe was emotionally or mentally ill, but it was in a time when nobody talked about such things. I think it would have been different if he had somebody of his own. He was always a lonely, lonely man. He wanted a permanent relationship, but in those days you couldn't reveal who you really were, so he kept it hidden. And that was very sad. I thought Joe was an unhappy man. A very sad man. But he was always interested in others, and always interested in the music, and always interested in developing it. As corny as some of it was, I think that if he had lived long enough he would have become a much better known person, much more respected musically.'[671]

Following Meek's death, Robb Shenton auditioned for Brian Epstein, but, like Meek, the Beatles' manager was also battling his demons and despite Shenton making a favourable impression, no contract would be signed. On the afternoon of 27 August, Epstein would be found dead in his bed, having accidentally overdosed.

On Friday 10 February more than 200 people packed into St Mary's Church in Newent for Joe's funeral, although his grave would not be given a headstone until 1974. Patrick Pink, Terry O'Neil and Lional Howard went together, driving down from London to say goodbye to the man who had meant so much to them. Glenda Collins attended. The members of the current Tornados line-up, including Robb Huxley and the Holder brothers, were also there, having travelled to Newent overnight from a gig. The band would struggle on for another year, but following Meek's death the Tornados were left rudderless. 'After Joe's death we were still represented by the George Cooper Organization,' Huxley explains. 'They continued to

334

book us into various cabaret venues. When we tried to negotiate for more money when they wanted us to back the whole show at the Windmill Theatre summer season with Freddie and the Dreamers at Great Yarmouth, they threatened us and implied that they had the rights to the Tornados' name and could stop us using it, so we ended up taking the gig anyway.'[672]

They stumbled on, filling the few bookings they already had; then, when almost everyone else had turned their back on the musicians, they were presented with a lifeline by Meek's former business partner Larry Parnes, who offered the band the opportunity to back Billy Fury for some dates in the autumn, an entirely different version of the Tornados to the one that had backed Fury in 1962 and 1963. A short tour followed, but with fewer and fewer decent-paying dates on the horizon they finally called it a day on the first anniversary of Meek's death, after a gig in Tel Aviv.

Several weeks after his death, Meek's friend and fellow ghost hunter Tony Grinham was taking part in a séance, using Meek's preferred method of a Ouija board and an upturned glass. 'This was in North Kensington, and Joe came through. After a few minutes of unintelligible messages, the glass spelled out that the message was for T-O-N-Y and was from J-O-E M-E-E-K.' Grinham, naturally, asked some questions that might prove the spirit was indeed Joe. 'I asked, "What should I do?" because I had all these songs, and it spelled out D-E-C-C-A...'[673]

As Meek had died intestate, on 23 March the High Court ruled that his mother, Evelyn (Biddy), was legally the sole beneficiary to his estate, but administration was awarded to his siblings, Arthur, Eric and Pamela, who would also get to benefit from an equal portion in any future income raised by the estate should that arrive after their mother's demise (Biddy Meek passed away on 30 December 1971). However, in the months following her son's death Biddy saw nothing. With so many confusing and complicated arrangements surrounding Joe's business affairs, his companies, including RGM Sound and Meeksville Sound Ltd, would continue to generate income – and legal headaches – for decades to come, although most of the money that should have gone to the family was spent on legal fees by the liquidators charged with unpicking Meek's tangled web of companies, contracts and copyrights. In desperation, months after Joe's death, his mother wrote to John Ginnett to try and get some money from the estate to cover the cost of her roof repairs, the same repairs Joe had promised to pay for just weeks

Love and Fury: The Life, Death and Legacy of Joe Meek

before he shot himself. 'Joe had arranged to have it repaired for me,' she explained. 'But when this tragedy occurred we cancelled it. Now it is very much worse. The rain comes in all over the place, even in my bedroom.' In the same letter she expressed her incredulity at Mr Shenton making a claim against the estate, and begged Ginnett to try and help Joe's artists, especially Glenda Collins, get their tapes back: 'I have told her that there is nothing I can do, but that I would appeal to you again to see if there is any possibility.'[674]

Meek's death devastated his family: Arthur Meek had a nervous breakdown and was never the same again, and Joe's mother and his sister Pamela would both pass away before either of them saw any major financial remuneration from Meek's estate. 'Joe's family loved him deeply and he was always extremely close to them,' says Howard S. Berger, co-producer of the documentary film *A Life in the Death of Joe Meek*. 'He loved his mother and involved his brother Eric as much as he could. Arthur carried deep pride for Joe and his songs, all of which he could accurately catalogue in his mind, and he frequently defended Joe against any public aspersions. Joe was never ashamed of his family, but with the terrible tragic turn of his last few years of life, and a parade of scandal and media betrayals, the family became rightly soured by the media.'[675]

All the while the 'Telstar' case, which had tied up so much of Joe's potential income and contributed so significantly to his own failing mental health, continued to rumble on. It has become accepted knowledge that the copyright claim was resolved shortly after Joe's death, and had he been able to hold on for another few weeks the whole course of history would have been altered, with both Joe and Violet Shenton living to a ripe old age, but the case carried on for more than a year. The long-running dispute was settled on 7 February 1968. Jean Ledrut conceded that Meek's composition 'was original and did not infringe the copyright'[676] of his own composition, 'La Marche d'Austerlitz', and the Performing Rights Society, which at that time collected any royalties due to composers and performers whose work is broadcast on TV or radio, performed live or played in public, were able to release the more than £8,200 (worth approximately £182,000 in 2024) they had been holding onto, and paving the way for other similar agencies around the world to release their funds.

A little under two months later, at 2 p.m. on Thursday, 4 April 1968, from the sales rooms of Frank G. Bowen auctioneers on London's Greek

Guess That's the Way It Goes

Street, the contents of Meek's studio and living quarters at 304 Holloway Road were auctioned off. The Meek siblings had taken a few personal items – such as the guitar-shaped clock that had been a gift from his sister Pamela, some papers and photographs, Meek's personal effects including several of his paintings and the Poor Joe print that had hung on the wall of the sitting room – but the rest was sold to pay off his debts. The sale – eighty lots in total – included his studio equipment, his Ampex portable recorder, the Clavioline used on 'Telstar' and other Meek-produced tracks, the famous 'honky tonk' piano with its drawing pins pushed into the hammers (lot 349, which went for a fiver), Joe's disc cutter, plus speakers, amplifiers, microphones and the like. Most of the electrical items up for grabs – the amplifiers and mixers and tape decks he had created his life's work with – had their power cables cut. The people clearing out Meek's studio could not be bothered to untangle the miles of wires snaking around the upper three floors of 304 Holloway Road and simply sawed through them.

What were not included were the hundreds of reels of tape that had been bundled up into sixty-seven tea chests when Joe's studio and living quarters were gutted. 'After his death we had a lot of letters come [from artists] saying could they have their master tapes back that Joe had made,' Eric Meek later revealed. 'I tried my hardest to go through the tapes and give them back, but the legal advisers would not allow it. Unfortunately, there was nothing I could do. I would have liked to have given them all their tapes back... I just couldn't do anything about it.'[677] The Meek family hired a storage unit, keeping them for two years until, as Eric recalled, 'they were sold, as they were, to one man'. That one man was Cliff Cooper, founder member of Meek recording act the Millionaires, and they were sold (according to Cooper for 'three or four hundred pounds, which was a lot of money then') by Meek's solicitor John Ginnett on the understanding that they could only be used if they were wiped clean. Ginnett had been handed the task of erasing the tapes and selling the reels for a few shillings each but he couldn't bring himself to betray his old friend, and it is entirely thanks to his loyalty that they still exist today.

CHAPTER 27

Don't You Know

Two families were blown apart on 3 February 1967, and the relatives of Violet Shenton and Robert George Meek have spent almost six decades trying to put their lives back together since then. It is impossible to ignore how one moment of madness took the life of an innocent woman, but if Violet Shenton was a victim of one man's inner demons, then Joe Meek was a victim of his time, as Tamsin Embleton, clinical lead of the Music Industry Therapist Collective, explains: 'It's likely that his mental health wasn't addressed in the way we might do now, [but] thankfully, things have changed, particularly over the last ten years. Several charities have been established, or have become more prominent in the 2010s, and our knowledge has expanded greatly thanks to a number of high-profile research studies. Joe would hopefully be able to find his way to one of the main service providers the British Association for Performing Arts Medicine or the Music Industry Therapist Collective using a simple Google search. If he needed financial support for hardship, rehabilitation or psychotherapy, he'd be able to contact Music Minds Matter, Royal Society of Musicians of GB, Backup Tech or Stagehand... Many managers and labels are more aware of the help that's out there now too, which is good, though outreach is still needed.'[678] Had he been working after homosexuality had been at least partly decriminalised, or perhaps now, when mental health issues are better understood, he might have fared better.

During the 1970s, partly due to the lobbying of the Robert George Meek Appreciation Society (RGMAS), interest in Joe's career steadily increased. In May 1976 BBC Radio 1 broadcast an hour-long audio documentary presented by Brian Matthew, based on research by Chris Knight of the

Don't You Know

RGMAS, and not long afterwards Decca issued the first Tornados 'best of' collection, *Remembering the Tornados*. The following spring Decca delved into their archives to produce a double album, *The Joe Meek Story*, which was promoted with a tribute concert at the Archway Tavern in Holloway, starring Screaming Lord Sutch, Heinz, Michael Cox, the Tornados and Dennis D'Ell of the Honeycombs. *The Joe Meek Story* was swiftly followed by a third compilation, *Remembering Heinz*. Not to be outdone, EMI launched a series of 'best of' albums with a Meek connection, including collections from Cliff Bennett and the Rebel Rousers and from John Leyton. The release of these retrospectives gave reviewers ample opportunity to reflect on Meek's career, with journalists labelling him 'brilliant', 'sadly missed',[679] 'legendary'[680] and 'totally original'.[681] A decade after his ignoble demise, Meek's rehabilitation was underway.

Further public interest in Meek's life and career followed the publication of John Repsch's biography *The Legendary Joe Meek: The Telstar Man*. Then, on 8 February 1991, the BBC's arts series *Arena* broadcast an hour-long documentary, *The Very Strange Story of the Legendary Joe Meek*, featuring contributions from Meek's brothers Arthur (who, sadly, passed away before the programme aired) and Eric, plus musicians including Heinz, John Leyton, Jess Conrad, Screaming Lord Sutch and Humphrey Lyttelton, and friends such as Tony Grinham and Adrian Kerridge. In September 1992 Radio 2 broadcast their own audio documentary, *The Telstar Man*.

Following his departure from the Tornados in 1965, Clem Cattini had enjoyed a fantastically varied and successful career. One of the most prolific drummers in British recording history, he appeared on hundreds of records over his six-decade career playing on dozens of number 1 singles, including chart toppers from Mike Sarne, Tom Jones ('The Green, Green Grass of Home'), Tony Christie and the Love Affair. In the early 1970s he was asked to overdub drums onto several tracks by Champion Jack Dupree, from a session engineered by Meek for Denis Preston at Lansdowne studios more than a decade earlier. However, he spent years fighting to obtain control of the Tornados' name. Although he left the band several years before they finally called it a day, during the 1970s he had been involved in a number of attempts to relaunch them as a live act and recording entity, often with one or more other former members in tow and usually accompanied by a

Love and Fury: The Life, Death and Legacy of Joe Meek

reissue or re-recording of their biggest hit. Other acts appeared, with varying claims to the name: Alan Caddy formed his own version of the band in 1972 to back Billy Fury, before Cattini launched his own band, known variously as the Tornados or Clem Cattini's Tornados. In 1995, with the backing of the rest of the original band, he issued an injunction against former Tornado Brian Irwin who had been performing with his own band as the Tornados: Irwin, a member of the Tornados between 1963 and 1965, had previously joined former bandmates Ray Randall and Stuart Taylor as Ray Randall's Tornados, for a limited edition tribute CD EP. When Cattini finally decided to retire from the touring circuit, another former member, keyboard player Dave Watts, took over the mantel and kept a version of the Tornados on the road for a further decade.

Cattini's career may have blossomed, but with Meek's death, Heinz's time as a star was over. Beyond a handful of re-recordings of his old hits (including a brief Tornados reformation, where the band – minus Caddy – re-recorded their sole number 1 for George Bellamy's SRT label), there would be no new singles. He married, had two sons and found a job with Ford in Dagenham, before taking a position in sales at the *Basildon Echo*. He was later promoted to advertising manager at the *Echo*'s sister paper, the *Thurrock Gazette*.

An attempted comeback at the end of 1971 brought a few college gigs but little else. He occasionally appeared at rock 'n' roll festivals and 60s revival concerts, notably the London Rock and Roll Show at Wembley in 1972 (with Billy Fury, Screaming Lord Sutch and others) and at Joe Meek tribute shows. In the mid-1970s he made a brief attempt to relaunch his acting career, appearing on stage in the David Hare play *Teeth 'n' Smiles*; a performance at the Royal Court theatre in 1975 was interrupted by a drunk Keith Moon, whose attempt to join the cast onstage was thwarted by theatre staff.

In the 1990s, failing health and the breakdown of his marriage took him back to the south coast, to be near his family. He flirted briefly with politics, was given the honorific 'minister for rock 'n' roll' in Screaming Lord Sutch's Monster Raving Loony Party and spent his last years living in a rented flat in Southampton. Heinz gave his final performance at the Hulse Road Social Club in Southampton on 24 March 2000. Using a wheelchair and looking frail, he struggled through three songs – including, naturally,

Don't You Know

'Just Like Eddie' – for a small but appreciative audience. 'Heinz was great,' Peter Jay recalls. 'But he had a problem with drink.'[682] He died a fortnight later, on 7 April, from a stroke, exacerbated by years of alcoholism and the more recent onset of motor neurone disease. He was cremated at Eastleigh Crematorium, dressed in his stage clothes, to the strains of 'Telstar'. Like Joe, Heinz has a road named after him in his home town. In a cruelly ironic twist, Heinz Burt Close is a dead end street.

Exactly one month after Heinz's funeral took place, on 15 May Geoff Goddard died of a heart attack, aged 62. After leaving the music industry he had lived a quiet life away, looking after his mother and working in the catering department of Reading University, but in recent years he had become increasingly happy about embracing his past successes. Described by colleagues as 'an amiable, introspective man', he played piano occasionally at parties and events organised by the university. Years of bitterness towards Meek over the 'Have I the Right?' court case had made Goddard avoid the spotlight, but as interest in his achievements grew he mellowed. In 1985 he was shocked to discover that a cover of 'Johnny Remember Me', by Bronski Beat and Marc Almond, had reached number 3 in the charts. A hefty royalty cheque soon followed, and this was bolstered further when 'Just Like Eddie' was adapted for a TV commercial for breakfast cereal, as 'Just Like Shreddies': 'I got a nice lump sum for that,' he admitted.[683] Goddard undertook the occasional interview, appeared in the *Arena* documentary in 1991, and modestly admitted that he was happy 'to have written songs that millions of people have enjoyed. My fault was probably not enough self-discipline, ambition. I'm the sort of person who needs to be driven along, which Meek did with people.'[684]

In May 2013, the university celebrated Goddard's life and achievements with a special evening, hosted by former Radio 1 presenter and Meek aficionado Mike Read, *Celebrating the Sounds of the 60s – A Tribute to Geoff Goddard.*[*] A plaque in his honour was unveiled outside the university's Park House building, and John Leyton performed live. Leyton had retired from live performance in the mid-1960s to concentrate on his film and television career; his stage comeback, appropriately, had occurred in October 1992

---

[*]   In 1991, Read announced that he had plans for a new musical, based on Meek's life, entitled *Blessed Are the Meek*. It would not reach the stage.

in Newent, following the unveiling of a plaque outside Meek's place of birth in Market Square, where he was backed by Clem Cattini's Tornados. His successful return led to regular appearances on the nostalgia circuit, and even to talk of a reunion with Geoff Goddard, although that did not come off as Leyton's new record company felt the quality of Goddard's material was somewhat lacking. 'Geoff Goddard was a hugely talented songwriter,' Leyton said. 'His unusual lyrics, a galloping rhythm and tempo, combined with the sound Joe Meek created from his first-floor flat studio, meant Geoff's songs were immensely likeable and popular. He was also a wonderful musician, and played classical and pop music brilliantly, effortlessly switching between the two which is a rare gift... I owe an enormous amount to Geoff. He was a lovely man and I have very fond memories of our time together. He wrote all my hits and was a massive influence on my music career.' [685]

That same year a full-length documentary film, *A Life in the Death of Joe Meek*, from US filmmakers Howard S. Berger and Susan Stahman was screened for the first time. Featuring interviews with more than sixty of Meek's artists, friends, relations and fans, the film was a labour of love from Berger and Stahman, who had spent years piecing it together: rough cuts of the film had been shown at film festivals as early as 2008, and the pair had been on a fundraising mission ever since then to get the film completed and distributed. 'We first consciously encountered Joe Meek sometime in 1994,' Berger recalls, 'when we read a review of *It's Hard to Believe It: The Amazing World of Joe Meek*, the CD that Dennis Diken of the Smithereens curated. His story – and the tragedy of it – instantly haunted us: Joe was such an unexpectedly unique character – a tone-deaf, self-trained electronics boffin who had a knack for catchy tunes and an instinctive, unorthodox production ethic fighting the commercial politics of the music industry and actually making himself into an adversary to the major recording labels. And aside from him being unique, he was also sympathetic – gay at an extremely hostile time for that to be in England – and there was so much inter-relational drama between his private and public life that the mystery surrounding his death was yet more bait on the hook catching our interest. And then, of course, we listened to the music and that experience was profound, to say the least. Diverse, bold, catchy, perverse and unorthodox.' The pair did not originally envisage a documentary,

Don't You Know

Berger explains: 'Originally, we had considered just using Joe as a starting point for a screenplay for an indie film, with a fictional character that would resemble aspects of Joe and a storyline that would get crazier and crazier by the climax: my grandfather was a business partner with Ben Spector, Phil Spector's father, and I was going to blend some of the outrageous stories my own father had related to me about him. As it turned out, the more we factually discovered about Joe, the sooner we realized you couldn't top his actual life for eccentricity.'[686]

In the first week of June 1990, after years of protracted legal wrangling, Clem Cattini received his first royalty cheque for 'Telstar', for the princely sum of £2,900. 'I feel cheated,' the drummer said at the time. 'What I do not understand is where all the money has gone… Who has got it?'[687] Cattini had been part of an organised attempt by around eighty musicians who had worked with Meek – including Cliff Bennett and members of the Honeycombs – to claim at least some of the royalties they had been due, or to win ownership of their recordings from the Official Receiver. The action had been spearheaded by Graham Cole, once the guitarist for the Dorset-based band the Soundsmen, who had recorded for Meek in 1966, but now a lawyer. Cattini and the surviving Tornados won the rights to the music they had recorded with Meek and licensed the tracks to Trojan, who set about compiling the group's first 'best of' of the CD era, *Telstar: The Original Sixties Hits of the Tornados*. Naturally, it did not end there: Decca insisted that they owned – or at least part-owned – the copyright in the same material and issued an almost identical collection that same year, *Telstar: The Complete Deram UK/US Singles*, despite the fact that no Tornados single had ever appeared on the Deram label.

The drummer was not prepared to go back to court to argue about it. 'After 27 years of litigation there is no way I'm going through it again; as far as I'm concerned all the rights are there. It's between Trojan and Decca.'[688] In the mid-1990s, guitarist Steve Howe, who had recorded at RGM Sound in the mid-1960s as a member of the Syndicats, before going on to worldwide stardom as a member of Yes and Asia, was working with RPM Records on a series of archival releases. While discussing the licensing and reissue of some of his early recordings made for EMI, he was shocked to be presented with what the company claimed were the original masters

Love and Fury: The Life, Death and Legacy of Joe Meek

for the Syndicats singles, issued by Columbia in 1964–65. 'They told me that I was getting them as I was the only member of the group they could find, and they said that "Joe never paid you; he never paid anybody, so we're giving you the tapes"!'[689]

In the years following Meek's death, Screaming Lord Sutch – the only one of Meek's artists to walk away from 304 Holloway Road with his tapes tucked under his arm – became something of a national celebrity, known more for his political aspirations than for his singing, but he continued to gig regularly and maintained a loyal fan base. A poll conducted for the 1998 book *All Time Top 1000 Albums*, declared his 1970 LP *Lord Sutch and Heavy Friends* – featuring such rock 'n' roll superstars as Jimmy Page, Jeff Beck, John Bonham and former Savages drummer Carlo Little – the worst album of all time. Nine months later, on 16 June 1999, David 'Screaming Lord' Sutch committed suicide, hanging himself with a skipping rope in the hallway of his late mother's home. His body was discovered by his fiancée, Yvonne Elwood, who at first thought that the Monster Raving Loony was pulling a prank. At the inquest, Yvonne revealed that he had been suffering from manic depression, now known as bipolar disorder: the last entry on his calendar read 'depression depression depression is too much'.[690]

In 2008, Sutch was resurrected for the big screen by singer Justin Hawkins in the film *Telstar: The Joe Meek Story*. The directorial debut from actor Nick Moran, the film was adapted from the 2005 stage play of the same name, written by Moran and James Hicks. Starring Con O'Neill as Meek (who had also starred in the stage version), and Kevin Spacey as Meek's business partner, Major Banks, the film was a great success, but not everyone was happy with the result. Author John Repsch sued Moran and others involved with the film for copyright infringement, alleging that large chunks of the dialogue had been lifted from his book *The Legendary Joe Meek: The Telstar Man*. Patrick Pink, who in 1974 had changed his name by deed poll to Robbie Duke, and who had a cameo appearance in the film, hated the way he was portrayed, and Heinz's family took umbrage with the film's depiction of him as Joe's lover. His former wife, Della Burke, stated that any inference that Meek had a sexual relationship with Heinz was 'completely and utterly untrue. Heinz was definitely heterosexual.'[691] In interviews Heinz always denied that the two of them were involved although he accepted that Meek was infatuated with him, but people who knew both men and witnessed

344

Don't You Know

life at 304 have stated otherwise. Norman Fowler, who recorded at RGM Sound in 1961, felt that Heinz exploited Meek's obsession and 'led him a dance I think, cruelly. It seems to me that somebody who would do that to somebody else who was vulnerable, which Joe was, obviously, would be heartless and it's unforgivable to do that to people.'[692]

Robbie Duke penned an open letter to Moran and producer Simon Jordan, detailing his disgust with the way he, and Meek, were portrayed in the film. Duke was particularly hurt by the way the film implied that he and Meek may have been lovers: 'I do not take kindly to your insinuations that I had a sexual relationship with Joe Meek. To me he was my employer and my friend only. I have stated this unequivocally many times and in many ways. Contrary to what you may believe, homosexual men are capable of forming platonic friendships. This is not "artistic license", this is character assassination. To you, the Joe Meek story is a cash cow. To me, Joe Meek is my life and I relive what happened every day of my life. What you have done has made it worse for me. The way you have portrayed me is beyond hurtful, it is unforgivable… This cheapens the relationship I had with Joe. He was like a father figure to me, a mentor, how could you portray it like this?

'I was upset with the scene of my character holding a gun to Heinz's head. This implied that I knew the gun was there when Joe was acting manically. This also means I could have "stopped him" if I wanted to. As I have said many times, I did not know of the gun's existence. If I had, maybe history would have been very different… Joe Meek was a wonderful person, capable of extraordinary kindnesses. You got his character totally wrong. He appears to be a bastard from beginning to end. Unfortunately, history will now quote your film as the benchmark for Joe Meek. In my opinion you have destroyed the reputation of one of music history's most gifted record producers.'[693] Duke died on 15 May 2018, eighteen years to the day after Geoff Goddard.

Pauline Petchey, the Shentons' daughter, was upset about the film too, feeling that it glorified the man who had robbed their family of its matriarch: 'My mother was my best friend and it was like having half of my life cut away when she was murdered. My father was devastated. You hear about Meek people making him out to be a glamorous hero… You never hear anybody say he was a murderer.'[694] Others thought better of

Love and Fury: The Life, Death and Legacy of Joe Meek

the movie. Clem Cattini – who appeared as a chauffeur in the film – was impressed, especially with O'Neill's performance, and with James Cordon, who played Cattini in the film. Chas Hodges appeared as a fictionalised version of one of Meek's neighbours, always complaining about the noise coming out of 304, while Chas's wife Joan played Joe's mother, Biddy, and *Royal Family* star Ralf Little played Chas during his Outlaws heyday. Both John Leyton and Jess Conrad appeared in the film, Leyton as Decca chairman Sir Edward Lewis and Conrad as Meek's former business partner Larry Parnes.

Hodges, who also passed away in 2018, remained fond of Joe: 'I remember him as being, basically, a nice person... I would class him as a genius, but he was also on the verge of being insane.'[695] 'He was an innovator, and changed pop music forever,' says guitarist Roy Phillips today. 'The schooling at RGM Sound was a great help in our careers, as it was for many of the others that had the Joe Meek experience. He was quite brilliant in his own way as a producer. I wish I had a chance to thank him for giving me a chance.'[696] Norman Fowler, singer with York's Sammy Browne and the Escorts, adds: 'He was incredibly talented and his story is tragic, really. I'm proud to have recorded for Joe Meek. If there was anything that I thought was shaming, then I wouldn't be. I'm very pleased that we recorded with him; he's an icon in the recording business.'[697]

While all this was happening, Meek's now legendary Tea Chest tapes lay in a storeroom, gathering dust. In 1983 Cooper had tasked Alan Blackburn of the RGMAS with cataloguing the tapes as best he could. It would take eighteen months to listen to all 1,856 reels. Then this treasure trove of material went from the tea chests into thick cardboard boxes and back onto the shelves in Cooper's storeroom. Cooper had no idea what to do with the haul. Many of the tapes were unmarked, the contents of the spools unknown to anyone but Meek himself, and others were in the wrong boxes, with track listings which bore no relation to their contents. Even after Blackburn had done his job, hundreds of tracks remained unidentified. 'He was so secretive, so slow in getting anything out, so God knows what other stuff is in there,' Peter Jay laughs. 'The trouble we found with Joe was that we'd record it, finish it, get in the van and drive away and then three months later Decca would be on to us asking us why

Don't You Know

isn't the single out, as we're on tour? And it was because they hadn't got the master from Joe.'[698]

At one point Cooper had considered wiping them and using the blank tapes for his own studio, but as fate would have it Meek's masters were all two-track and he had recently upgraded to four-track. Occasionally, word would come out that the tapes were about to appear or that some of the material would be released, but outside a handful of unauthorised releases featuring second-generation (or worse) copies of some of the tracks, nothing official surfaced. Frustrated by what they saw as a string of broken promises to make the tapes available, or to donate them to an archive where they would at least be preserved, on the thirty-second anniversary of Meek's death, members of the Joe Meek Society (which had formed in the early 1990s after the original RGMAS fizzled out) held a demonstration outside Cooper's business premises, hoping to persuade him to release the precious material.

Slowly, some of the material began to leak out. Cooper had trusted people to help document the tapes only to have that trust exploited: sub-par copies of some tracks were made without Cooper's knowledge and, frustratingly, some of the tapes that Blackburn had catalogued had vanished, only to turn up in the hands of private collectors. Then, in September 2008, Cooper decided to put the remaining tapes up for auction. Purported highlights of the collection included the much rumoured debut recording of David Bowie, as a member of the Konrads, with Bowie – then using his given name, David Jones – playing saxophone on a cover of the Charlie and Inez Foxx hit 'Mockingbird' (despite Bowie's own denial that he ever recorded for Meek) and the missing seventh master from Tommy Scott and the Senators, 'It's You That Needs Me Now'. For years there had been rumours that the tapes also contained early recordings from Marc Bolan (as Marc Feld), members of Status Quo and Ray Davies (of the Kinks) among the hundreds of other unreleased performances, outtakes from the *I Hear a New World* sessions and unissued masters from Joe's chief acts John Leyton, the Tornados, the Honeycombs, Heinz, Screaming Lord Sutch, Glenda Collins and Mike Berry. Although not mentioned, fans and Meek obsessives were aware that the Tea Chest stash included recordings of unreleased material from Meek's personal assistants Terry O'Neil and Patrick Pink, Cornish group Danny's Passion, as well as such off-the-wall recordings as talks given by spiritual healer Harry Edwards at the healing sanctuary he established in Guildford, Surrey, and Meek's version of the infamous talking cat tape. On the day of the auction the tapes were sold for £170,000; however, the sale was cancelled, and Cooper retained ownership of them until, in 2020, after years of negotiations, they were purchased for an undisclosed sum by Cherry Red Records.

Iain McNay, the Chairman of Cherry Red, knew that the company had a daunting task ahead but insisted that they were up to it: 'The work that lies ahead is massive. Baking, then cleaning up, then digitalisation, then clearing rights, then deciding how best to release the tracks. But, as always, we relish the challenge.'[699] McNay asked musician and producer Alan Wilson for his assistance. The lifelong Meek fan was surprised to hear that Cherry Red were buying the tapes but urged caution. 'I said, "But what are you buying? Have they been looked after?" Analogue tape is a very unstable format, so I told him that my worry would be that he was buying a pile of dust.'[700]

At McNay's urging, Wilson went to visit Cooper, who agreed to let him inspect some of the tapes. 'He took me into this warehouse and there were six pallets, chest high, with boxes of tape. It was like the Holy Grail for me.' Wilson had worked with a number of Meek's acts in recent years, including Mike Berry, John Leyton, Chas Hodges, Clem Cattini and Bobby Rio, and his own Somerset studio used a number of Ted Fletcher's Joemeek brand components. 'I had to try and persuade him that I wasn't some rogue who was going to run off with these tapes,' he adds. 'I was very aware that Cliff's trust had been abused in the past, and I didn't want him to think that I was about to do the same thing.'[701]

'Cliff had been a good custodian to these tapes because he knew what he was doing. It could have been a totally different story if someone else had them and had not stored them well.' Wilson, Martin Nichols and their small team's dedication in cleaning, repairing and preserving the haul soon bore fruit: in 2022 the first of a number of archive releases appeared, a 10-inch album *The Telstar Story* which immediately sold out. Since then Cherry Red have continued to mine gold, with collections from Glenda Collins, the Cryin' Shames, Heinz, David John and the Mood, the Tornados, John Leyton and others. Wilson's Western Star label has also issued 10-inch vinyl albums from the tea chests, featuring John Leyton, Screaming Lord Sutch and the first-ever release of the soundtrack from *Live It Up!*

Don't You Know

The sudden availability of Meek's tapes was a godsend to musician and filmmaker Russell Caligari. 'I was working in a studio on the Holloway Road,' he explains. 'I had seen the black plaque outside 304 Holloway Road, but I knew nothing really about him at all. The penny dropped about the importance of this man when I was invited to a screening of *Telstar*. Alan Wilson had been asked to come along and give a talk about the Tea Chest tapes. Alan started telling the story of Joe Meek and how he got the Tea Chest tapes, and then we watched the film, and that was the big moment. I thought, "This is incredible," and that the world needs to know about this guy. I knew that I had to make a film about this.

'My mission is to bring Joe Meek to a younger audience; that's what gave me the USP of the film, which was to invite contemporary artists that I know are still using, every day, techniques that Joe Meek pioneered, and get them to write lyrics to his instrumental tracks.'[702] Caligari's film, *The Unexpected Return of Mr Meek*, has already spun off in a number of directions, with plans for stand-alone mini-documentaries focusing on different aspects of Meek's life and career, a soundtrack album, a concert featuring the artists involved in the movie's soundtrack and an interactive museum exhibition: 'We're still working out what, but there will definitely be something that you can go and touch and experience, and become immersed in the world of Joe Meek,' Caligari adds. The director has also spearheaded the relaunch of RGM Sound Ltd; he and his right-hand woman Pauline Wheeler-Reid helped the Meek family navigate the bureaucracy surrounding the Tea Chest tapes and re-establish the family's rights to Meek's work. 'No one had been managing the estate for a good twenty years,' he explains. 'All we wanted to do was tidy it up for them, make sure that everything is registered properly. All of the material in the Tea Chest tapes that was unreleased – which is the majority of the material – had no publisher assigned. So it's only right and proper that the Meek estate and any of the artists that performed on that music get paid properly. Cherry Red are doing a marvellous job in repackaging everything, and getting it out there, and we're ensuring that those royalties go to the right people.'

In the decades since his death, the musical landscape in which Joe created his best work has evolved. Several of the artists and session musicians he worked with would go on to have bigger, more exciting careers in the 1970s

Love and Fury: The Life, Death and Legacy of Joe Meek

and beyond. Some would become globe-straddling superstars, others huge names in light entertainment. At least one would become a politician – of sorts – and for over three decades provide some much needed comedy relief during both local and general elections.

Meek's impact is everywhere, so much so that, in 2009, the Music Producers Guild created the Joe Meek Award for Innovation in Production: the first recipient of the award was Brian Eno. Generations of musicians, producers and engineers have been influenced by his groundbreaking work and today, almost sixty years after his death, people are still in awe of what Meek achieved over such a short period. Pixies frontman Black Francis (aka Frank Black) has referenced Meek in his solo work, and songwriter and XTC legend Andy Partridge employs Meek-esque techniques: 'The mellotron [on the 1984 single "All You Pretty Girls"] was sent through a palm-sized speaker: we put it at the bottom of a metal waste bin and put a kitchen roll tube over the microphone. I think Joe Meek would've approved.'[703] As an engineer and producer he was a true innovator, and as an independent in an industry dominated by the major labels he was a trailblazer. His influence on the British pop music scene cannot be overstated, yet because of the way he met his demise – and the violent death of Violet Shenton at his hands – for many decades his influence was often overlooked.

'He's the gift that keeps on giving,' says Alan Wilson. 'His life story is incredible, and I'm always learning something new about him. What Joe Meek did at Holloway Road still reverberates through me. I don't try and copy Joe, but the influence is there. Things that he did, the thinking outside the box for want of a corny phrase... I've only got a small studio, and when we get a session going sometimes there are wires everywhere, and I used to be a little embarrassed about that, but then one day Chas Hodges said to me, "I like that, Al. It's just like Joe Meek's studio!" I've embraced that now; Joe has inadvertently helped me. Sixty years later, I'm still feeling the ripples from the pebble he dropped in the pond.'[704]

Bibliography

Beacom, Brian, *The Real Stanley Baxter* (Luath Press, Edinburgh, 2021).

Bloom, Jerry, *Black Knight: Ritchie Blackmore* (Omnibus Press, London, 2006).

Bullock, Darryl W., *The Velvet Mafia: The Gay Men Who Ran the Swinging Sixties* (Omnibus Press, London, 2021).

Clayson, Alan, *The Rolling Stones: The Origin of the Species* (Chrome Dreams, New Malden, 2007).

Dawson, Jim and Spencer Leigh, *Memories of Buddy Holly* (Big Nickel Publications, Milford, New Hampshire, 1996).

Ellis, Lucy and Bryony Sutherland, *Tom Jones: Close Up* (Omnibus Press, London, 2009).

Embleton, Tamsin, *Touring and Mental Health: The Music Industry Manual* (Omnibus Press, London, 2023).

Fry, Colin, *The Krays: A Violent Business* (Mainstream Publishing, Edinburgh, 2011).

Hildred, Stafford and Tom Gritten, *Tom Jones: A Biography* (Sidgwick and Jackson, London, 1990).

Hodges, Chas, *Chas & Dave: All About Us* (John Blake, London, 2008).

Hopkins, Vernon, *Just Help Yourself: Tom Jones, The Squires and the Road to Stardom* (Seren Books, Bridgend, 2018).

Howe, Steve, *All My Yesterdays* (Omnibus Press, London, 2020).

Huxley, Robb, *Do You Come Here Often? The Meeksville Connection* (Silver Tabbies Publishing, Milton Keynes, 2015).

Jones, Tom, *Over the Top and Back* (Michael Joseph, London, 2015).

Kerridge, Adrian, *Tape's Rolling, Take One!: The Recording Life of Adrian Kerridge* (M-Y Books, Hertford, 2016).

Love and Fury: The Life, Death and Legacy of Joe Meek

Massey, Howard, *The Great British Recording Studios* (Hal Leonard Books, Milwaukee, 2015).

Patterson, R. Gary, *Take a Walk on the Dark Side: Rock and Roll Myths, Legends and Curses* (Simon & Schuster, New York, 2004).

Savona, Anthony (ed.), *Console Confessions: The Great Music Producers in their Own Words* (Backbeat Books, London, 2005).

Sharpe, Graham, *The Man Who Was Screaming Lord Sutch* (Aurum Press, London, 2005).

Simmonds, Roger J., *Standing on the Sidelines* (Candy Jar Books, Cardiff, 2016).

Stafford, David and Caroline Stafford, *Halfway to Paradise: The Life of Billy Fury* (Omnibus Press, London, 2018).

Starr, Freddie, with Alan Wightman, *Freddie Starr Unwrapped* (Virgin Books, London, 2002).

Thompson, Dave, *Better to Burn Out: The Cult of Death in Rock 'n' roll* (Thunder's Mouth Press, New York, 1999).

Touzeau, Jeff, *Making Tracks: Unique Recording Studio Environments* (Schiffer Publishing, Atglen, PA, 2006).

Watts, Derek, *Country Boy: A Biography of Albert Lee* (McFarland, Jefferson, NC, 2008).

Acknowledgements

First and foremost, my enormous thanks to Meek fan extraordinaire John Pickford: your help and encouragement throughout this project, and your kindness in sharing rare and exclusive material from your own collection, has helped make this book what it is. Massive thanks to Jim Blake, co-founder of the original Robert George Meek Appreciation Society (and co-compiler of the first Meek retrospective, the 1977 collection *The Joe Meek Story*), who generously allowed me to use the interviews conducted by Chris Knight and himself with a number of Joe's friends, colleagues, artists and family members circa 1974. Thanks too to Pete Wilson, former presenter at BBC Radio Gloucestershire, for allowing me to raid his own archives, and to Craig Newton and the team at the Joe Meek Society for their generous help.

Thanks to Joy Adams (Joy and Dave), Howard S. Berger and Susan Stahman (*A Life in the Death of Joe Meek*), Mike Berry, Samantha Blake (BBC Written Archives, Reading), Paul Burns, Paul Burns (Chris Barnes), Malcolm Cawley, Meghan Cervantes, Russell Caligari, Pauline Wheeler-Reid and the team from Ginger and Pickles Productions (*The Unexpected Return of Mr Meek*), Jess Conrad, Rob Cumner (the Chicanes/the Money Spiders), Mos Day (on behalf of the late Des O'Reilly, the Puppets), Tamsin Embleton, Ted Fletcher (the Cameos/the Fletchers), Norman Fowler (Steve Cassidy), Dean and Andrew Griffith(s), Tony Grinham, Pete Holder (the Saxons/the Tornados), Vernon Hopkins (Tommy Scott and the Senators), the late Ken Howard, Steve Howe (the Syndicats), Robb Huxley (the Saxons/the Tornados), Robin Ince, Peter Jay (Peter Jay and the Jaywalkers), Barry Kingsbeer (the Chicanes), Stephen Komlosy, the Milligan family, Jimmy

Love and Fury: The Life, Death and Legacy of Joe Meek

Page, Andy Partridge and Erica Wexler, Roy Philips (the Saints), Paul Reves, Mike Roberts (Tommy Scott and the Senators), John Stapleton (Wanted Records, Bristol), the late Robb Shenton, Nigel Silk (the Impac), Peter Stockton, Kingsley Ward (the Thunderbolts/the Charles Kingsley Creation), Lisa Ward, Sandra Meek-Williams, Alan Wilson (Western Star Studios), Pip Witcher (the Sorrows), Simon Withington, to the entire team at Omnibus/Wise Music including David Barraclough, Fabrice Couillerot, Claire Browne, Debra Geddes, Greg Morton, Neal Price, Alison Rae, Giulia Senesi and David Stock, and, as always, to Niall and the kids, for keeping me sane for almost two decades.

Notes

Introduction

1 Press release, Fire Records, 28 March 2024.
2 Author interview with Russell Caligari, July 2024.
3 Ian Harrison, 'August 1962: the Tornados Launch Telstar', *Mojo*, October 2022.
4 Author interview with Tony Grinham, July 2024.
5 Author interview with Howard S. Berger, August 2024.

1. Country Boy

6 Heinz Burt, interviewed by Jim Blake and Chris Knight, c. 1974.
7 'Joe Remembers', audio biography recorded by Meek c. 1962, issued on the CD box set *Joe Meek: Portrait of a Genius*, 2005.
8 Arthur and Eric Meek, unaired interview, *The Very Strange Story of the Legendary Joe Meek*, *Arena* documentary, BBC TV, 1991.
9 Arthur and Eric Meek, interviewed by Jim Blake and Chris Knight, c. 1974.
10 'Ten Little Forest Boys', *Gloucester Journal*, 21 July 1945.
11 Arthur and Eric Meek, interviewed by Jim Blake and Chris Knight, c. 1974.
12 Ibid.
13 Ibid.
14 Sandra Meek-Williams, talking to Pete Wilson, *Joe Meek Special*, BBC Radio Gloucestershire, 12 February 2017.
15 'Men Behind the Stars No. 1: Joe Meek', unknown publication, c. 1962.
16 'Joe Remembers', *Joe Meek: Portrait of a Genius*, 2005.
17 Arthur and Eric Meek, interviewed by Jim Blake and Chris Knight, c. 1974.

2. Hobbies

18 Arthur and Eric Meek, interviewed by Jim Blake and Chris Knight, c. 1974.
19 Newent Town Council Newsletter, April 2022.
20 Arthur and Eric Meek, unaired interview, *The Very Strange Story of the Legendary Joe Meek*, *Arena* documentary, BBC TV, 1991.

21 Mike Hellicar, 'Joe Meek's Front Room is Where Hit Discs are Turned Out on a Shoestring', *NME Annual 1963*.

22 'Joe Remembers', *Joe Meek: Portrait of a Genius*, 2005.

23 'Newent Legion Fete', *Gloucester Citizen*, 20 July 1950.

24 Mike Hellicar, 'Joe Meek's Front Room is Where Hit Discs are Turned Out on a Shoestring', *NME Annual 1963*.

25 Derek Davis talking to Pete Wilson, *Joe Meek Special*, BBC Radio Gloucestershire, 12 February 2017.

26 Ibid.

27 Ibid.

3. Keep Moving

28 'Joe Remembers', *Joe Meek: Portrait of a Genius*, 2005.

29 Ibid.

30 Author interview with Joy Adams, May 2024.

31 Press release for *A Life in the Death of Joe Meek*, reprinted in *Thunderbolt 47*, June 2006.

32 Author interview with Roy Phillips, April 2023.

33 Eric Meek interviewed for the film *A Life in the Death of Joe Meek*, Palm Door Films.

34 'Joe Meek Speaks', c. 1957, issued on the CD box set *Joe Meek: Portrait of a Genius*, 2005.

35 Adrian Kerridge, *Tape's Rolling, Take One!*, M-Y Books, 2016, p. 67.

36 Ibid., p. 55.

37 John McCreedy, 'Joe Meek', http://mccready.cwc.net/meek.html, February 2002.

38 'Joe Meek Speaks', *Joe Meek: Portrait of a Genius*, 2005.

39 Adrian Kerridge, unaired interview, *The Very Strange Story of the Legendary Joe Meek*, *Arena* documentary, BBC TV, 1991.

40 Ibid.

41 Neal Arden, 'Discs', *The People*, 24 November 1957.

42 *Sunday Times*, 1979.

43 Author interview with Steve Howe, April 2024.

44 Humphrey Lyttelton, *The Very Strange Story of the Legendary Joe Meek*, *Arena* documentary, BBC TV, 1991.

45 'Record Roundup', *Newmarket Journal*, 9 August 1956.

46 Tom Jones, interview in the documentary film *Red, White and Blues*, 2003.

47 Howard Massey, *The Great British Recording Studios*, Hal Leonard Books, 2015.

48 Author interview with Mike Berry, June 2023.

49 Patrick Doncaster, 'On the Record', *Daily Mirror*, 30 August 1956.

50 A. J. McWhinnie, 'Troops Told Shun!', *Daily Herald*, 29 August 1956.

4. Please Let It Happen to Me

51 'Joe Meek Speaks', *Joe Meek: Portrait of a Genius*, 2005.

52 A. Kahan and Ann G. Mullins, 'Dangers of "Preludin"', letter in the *British Medical Journal*, 7 June 1958.

53 Adrian Kerridge, *Tape's Rolling, Take One!*, M-Y Books, 2016, p. 121.

Notes

54 Lional Howard, interviewed by Jim Blake and Chris Knight, c. 1974.
55 Chas Hodges, interviewed by Jim Blake and Chris Knight, c. 1974.
56 Ibid.
57 Patrick Stapley, 'The Chiswick Tube', *Studio Sound*, October 1993.
58 'Britain's Independent Producers', *Cash Box*, 26 December 1964.
59 Bill Halden, 'Is This Attack on Managers Fair?', *Picturegoer*, 1 March 1958.
60 Arthur and Eric Meek, interviewed by Jim Blake and Chris Knight, c. 1974.
61 Lional Howard, interviewed by Jim Blake and Chris Knight, c. 1974.
62 Ibid.
63 Neal Arden, 'Discs', *The People*, 6 October 1957.
64 'Star Maker's Barbecue', *Record Mirror*, 5 October 1957.
65 Merry Nolan, 'Musical Merry Go Round', *Record Mirror*, 5 October 1957.
66 Lional Howard, interviewed by Jim Blake and Chris Knight, c. 1974.
67 'Girls Will Add Glamour to Skiffle Group', *West London Observer*, 11 October 1957.
68 Neal Arden, 'Discs', *The People*, 8 December 1957.

5. You've Got to Have a Gimmick Today

69 'Meet the New Triumph Recording Stars #3', Triumph Records press release, 1960.
70 Author interview with Joy Adams, May 2024.
71 Ibid.
72 Ibid.
73 Dave Adams, 'The First Meeting', extract from his unpublished biography, *After All these Bloody Years*, 1992.
74 Author interview with Joy Adams, May 2024.
75 R. Gary Patterson, *Take a Walk on the Dark Side: Rock and Roll Myths, Legends and Curses*, Simon & Schuster, 2004, pp. 20–21.
76 'Record Review by Joe Meek', *The Tatler*, 26 May 1966.
77 Letter from Joe Meek to his mother, postmarked 13 May 1958.
78 Neal Arden, 'Discs', *The People*, 22 June 1958.
79 Patrick Doncaster, 'On the Record', *Daily Mirror*, 18 September 1958.
80 Author interview with Joy Adams, May 2024.
81 'They Just Love to Entertain', *Gloucester Citizen*, 18 September 1958.
82 Patrick Doncaster, 'Lone Wolf', *Daily Mirror*, 19 June 1958.
83 Author interview with Tamsin Embleton, July 2024.
84 Record Review, *Disc*, 12 September 1959.
85 Adrian Kerridge, 'Tape's Rolling, Take One!', M-Y Books, 2016, p. 123.
86 'Disctator Joe Meek', *The Sun*, 15 October 1965.
87 Larry Parnes taking about Joe Meek, *Sounds of the Sixties*, BBC Radio 2, 6 October 1990.
88 Jay Martin, 'Joe Meek – the Pop "Star" at the Control Panel', c. 1964.

6. I Hear a New World

89 Patrick Doncaster, 'Lone Wolf', *Daily Mirror*, 19 June 1958.
90 'Teen Page', *Daily Mirror*, 26 February 1960.

91 Disker, 'Off the Record', *Liverpool Echo*, 5 March 1960.
92 Author interview with Joy Adams, May 2024.
93 'Charles Blackwell – Our Youngest MD!', *Record Mail*, June 1962.
94 Neal Arden, 'Discs', *The People*, 6 March 1960.
95 Keith Fordyce, 'Keith Fordyce Forecasts', *New Musical Express*, 25 March 1960.
96 'New Label Is to Be Entirely Pop', *Disc*, 5 March 1960.
97 Don Nicholl, 'Disc Date', *Disc*, 12 March 1960.
98 'Ricky Wayne on the Pye Label', Pye Records Group press release, September 1960.
99 Neal Arden, 'Discs', *The People*, 10 April 1960.
100 Teddy Johnson, '20th Century Greensleeves', *Disc*, 16 April 1960.
101 Nigel Hunter, 'Along the Alley', *Disc*, 23 April 1960.
102 Jack Good, 'Tailored for the Teenager', *Disc*, 15 May 1960.
103 Ibid.
104 Lional Howard, interviewed by Jim Blake and Chris Knight, c. 1974.
105 John Rolls, 'Life in the Mirror', 26 February 1960.
106 Neal Arden, 'Discs', *The People*, 20 March 1960.
107 Ken Graham, 'EPs', *Disc*, 11 June 1960.
108 Spinner, 'Records Roundabout', *Portsmouth Evening News*, 11 June 1960.
109 'Having Fun With Sound', publication unknown, June 1960.
110 'Joe Meek talks about "I Hear A New World"', undated audio excerpt, https://www.youtube.com/watch?v=yIam5Nc4AtA.
111 'Who Buys All the Records?', *Bristol Evening Post*, 17 March 1960.
112 Disker, 'Chance For Michael', *Liverpool Echo*, 3 October 1959.
113 'They All Want Young Mike', *Disc*, 25 June 1960.
114 Jack Good, 'Tailored for the Teenager', *Disc*, 15 May 1960.
115 'They All Want Young Mike', *Disc*, 25 June 1960.
116 Richard Adams, 'Angela, Caroline, Who'll be Next?', *Disc*, 24 September 1960.
117 Author interview with Stephen Komlosy, February 2019.
118 'A Fan Club For Leyton', *The Stage*, 23 June 1960.
119 Ken Simmons (ed.), 'John Leyton', *Top Pop Stars 1963*, Purnell & Sons, 1962.
120 John Leyton interviewed by Mike Quinn, Blast radio, 11 December 2007.
121 Joe Meek interviewed for *World in Action: The Flip Side*, broadcast 22 September 1964.

7. I'm Waiting For Tomorrow

122 David Hughes, 'A Personal History of the British Record Business – Jeffrey Kruger', https://vinylmemories.wordpress.com, 14 October 2017.
123 'England', *Cash Box*, 13 August 1960.
124 Don Wedge, 'British Newsnotes', *Billboard*, 8 August 1960.
125 Author interview with Jess Conrad, November 2023.
126 'Search for a "Golden" Voice', *Cheshire Observer*, 17 September 1960.
127 Tony Kent, interviewed by Jim Blake and Chris Knight, c. 1974.
128 'TV Fans Make a Singer of "Ginger"', *Leicester Evening Mail*, 12 August 1960.
129 Roger Watkins, 'British Indies Disk Jackpot', *Variety*, 25 September 1963.
130 Author interview with Russell Caligari, July 2024.
131 Tony Kent, interviewed by Jim Blake and Chris Knight, c. 1974.

Notes

132 Keith Fordyce, 'Pop Reviews', *New Musical Express*, 23 September 1960.

133 'England', *Cash Box*, 5 November 1960.

134 Don Nicholl, 'Your Weekly Disc Date', *Disc*, 22 October 1960.

8. Dreams Do Come True

135 Lional Howard, interviewed by Jim Blake and Chris Knight, c. 1974.

136 Ibid.

137 Author interview with Roy Phillips, April 2023.

138 Author interview with Joy Adams, May 2024.

139 Author interview with Peter Jay, February 2023.

140 Howard Massey, *The Great British Recording Studios*, Hal Leonard Books, 2015.

141 Screaming Lord Sutch, interviewed by Jim Blake and Chris Knight, c. 1974.

142 Author interview with Alan Wilson, July 2024.

143 Author interview with Mike Berry, June 2023.

144 Cliff Bennett, interviewed by Jim Blake and Chris Knight, August 1974.

145 Sandra Meek-Williams, interviewed by Pete Wilson, BBC Radio Gloucestershire, 2017.

146 John Wells, 'Joe Meek Slammed the Door on John Leyton', *Disc*, 16 September 1961.

147 Patrick Doncaster, 'It's Hitsville!', *Daily Mirror*, 18 October 1962.

148 'He Records in This Front Room', *Record Mirror*, 16 September 1961.

149 Author interview with Mike Berry, May 2019.

150 James Craig, 'The Holly Man', *Record Mirror*, 4 November 1961.

151 Author interview with Mike Berry, May 2019.

152 Author interview with Mike Berry, June 2023.

153 Ibid.

154 Author interview with Mike Berry, May 2019.

155 Chas Hodges, interviewed by Jim Blake and Chris Knight, c. 1974.

156 Author interview with Mike Berry, April 2019.

157 Don Nicholl, 'Your Weekly Disc Date', *Disc*, 4 February 1961.

158 June Harris, 'All or Nothing for Schoolboy Gerry', *Disc*, 14 January 1961.

159 'For the Record: the Laurie Jay Combo', EMI press release, c. November 1963.

9. Time Will Tell

160 Heinz Burt, interviewed by Jim Blake and Chris Knight, c. 1974.

161 Chas Hodges, interviewed by Jim Blake and Chris Knight, c. 1974.

162 John Wells, 'Joe Meek Slammed the Door on John Leyton', *Disc*, 16 September 1961.

163 'The Story of Pop. Part Six: Made in Britain', BBC Radio 1, 3 November 1973.

164 Heinz Burt, interviewed by Jim Blake and Chris Knight, c. 1974.

165 Screaming Lord Sutch, interviewed by Jim Blake and Chris Knight, c. 1974.

166 Patrick Doncaster, 'It's Hitsville!', *Daily Mirror*, 18 October 1962.

167 Cliff Bennett, interviewed by Jim Blake and Chris Knight, August 1974.

168 John Wells, 'Joe Meek Slammed the Door on John Leyton', *Disc*, 16 September 1961.

169 'Disctator Joe Meek', *The Sun*, 15 October 1965.

170 'Chas Hodges Get His First Editing Lesson', www.rockhistory.co.uk, 9 May 2015.

171 Author interview with Joy Adams, May 2024.

Love and Fury: The Life, Death and Legacy of Joe Meek

172 Ibid.
173 Andy Carmichael, 'Spin a Disc', *Alderley & Wilmslow Advertiser*, 18 August 1961.
174 Jack Good, 'This Could Mean a New Pop TV Show', *Disc*, 7 October 1961.
175 Charles Blackwell, interviewed by Jim Blake and Chris Knight, c. 1974.
176 Brian Mulligan, 'For the Record: Geoff Goddard', EMI press release, October 1961.
177 June Harris, 'Buddy Holly Spoke to Me', *Disc*, 28 October 1961.
178 Author interview with Joy Adams, May 2024.
179 Author interview with Mike Berry, April 2019.
180 Geoff Goddard, interviewed by Jim Blake and Chris Knight, c. 1974.
181 Geoff Goddard, interviewed by Mike Quinn, Radio 210, 14 February 1983.
182 Alan Clayson, *The Rolling Stones: The Origin of the Species*, Chrome Dreams, New Malden, 2007. P155-6.
183 Geoff Goddard, interviewed by Jim Blake and Chris Knight, c. 1974.
184 Glenda Collins, interviewed by Jim Blake and Chris Knight, August 1974.
185 Jim Dawson and Spencer Leigh, 'Memories of Buddy Holly', Big Nickel Publications, Milford, New Hampshire, 1996. P99.
186 Cliff Bennett, interviewed by Jim Blake and Chris Knight, August 1974.
187 Maureen Cleave, 'Singing Through Crystal Glass', *Evening Standard*, 20 May 1961.

10. Johnny Remember Me

188 Letter to Joe Meek from Roland Rennie, 10 March 1961.
189 'Life From Behind the Shop Counter', *Nottingham Evening News*, 26 June 1961.
190 James Craig, 'The Holly Man', *Record Mirror*, 14 November 1961.
191 Letter to Roland Rennie from Joe Meek, June 1961. Referenced at www.vinylmemories.wordpress.com/2014/10/26/a-little-john-leyton-story/.
192 Lissa Grey, interviewed by Mike Guy, Radio Link (Lymington Hospital Radio), 13 October 1991.
193 Arthur and Eric Meek, interviewed by Jim Blake and Chris Knight, c. 1974.
194 John Leyton, *The Very Strange Story of the Legendary Joe Meek*, *Arena* documentary, BBC TV, 1991.
195 'The Story of Pop. Part Six: Made in Britain', BBC Radio 1, 3 November 1973.
196 Author interview with Mike Berry, 22 June 2023.
197 Russell Newmark, 'Johnny – Remember Me?', *Record Collector*, October 2007.
198 Brian Mulligan, 'For The Record: Geoff Goddard', *EMI Press Release*, October 1961.
199 James Craig, 'The Holly Man', *Record Mirror*, 4 November 1961.
200 Author interview with Mike Berry, May 2019.
201 Peter Robertson, 'Don't Idolise Joe Meek, He was a Killer, Says Pop Star', *Sunday Express*, 27 March 2022.
202 Author interview with Mike Berry, May 2019.
203 John Reading, '"Pop" Tunes Preferred', *Reading Standard*, 21 July 1961.
204 Martin Slavin, *Record Mirror*, 13 January 1962.
205 'The Voice Docters, Part Three', *New Record Mirror*, 27 January 1962.
206 'Pop Singer Denies Gimmick Charges', *Melody Maker*, 6 January 1962.
207 Ibid.
208 Jack Good, 'Dramatising Pop on TV Pays Off', *Disc*, 26 August 1961.

Notes

209 Charles Blackwell, interviewed by Jim Blake and Chris Knight, c. 1974.

210 Chas Hodges, interviewed by Jim Blake and Chris Knight, c. 1974.

211 Arthur and Eric Meek, interview by Jim Blake and Chris Knight, c. 1974.

212 David Gell, 'I Would Not Have Voted it a Hit', *Record Mirror*, 12 August 1961.

213 Cliff Bennett, interviewed by Jim Blake and Chris Knight, c. 1974.

214 *Melody Maker*, 9 February 1961.

215 Jim Dawson and Spencer Leigh, 'Memories of Buddy Holly', Big Nickel Publications, Milford, New Hampshire, 1996. P99.

216 Geoff Goddard, interview by Jim Blake and Chris Knight, c. 1974.

217 Author interview with Mike Berry, May 2019.

218 James Craig, 'The Holly Man', *Record Mirror*, 4 November 1961.

219 Author interview with Mike Berry, May 2019.

220 Disker, 'Off the Record'. *Liverpool Echo*, 9 September 1961.

221 Mike Nevard, 'Just Like Buddy', *Daily Herald*, 5 September 1961.

222 Author interview with Mike Berry, June 2023.

223 Brian Mulligan, 'For The Record: Geoff Goddard', EMI press release, October 1961.

224 Kieron Tyler, 'Bobby Graham: Career', www.bobbygraham.co.uk/bobbygraham/career.htm

225 Peter Jones, 'Holly's Fans Insult Me', *Record Mirror*, 15 December 1962.

226 Ian Dove, 'Norman Petty talks All About Buddy', *New Record Mirror*, 4 August 1962.

227 Jack Good, 'This is Just One Christmas Disc I Shall Buy', *Disc*, 25 November 1961.

228 Author interview with Mike Berry, June 2023.

229 Author interview with Peter Jay, February 2023.

230 Author interview with Jess Conrad, 2023.

231 Matt Mueller, 'Sympathy For the Devil', *Wonderland*, November 2008.

232 Rod Stewart, *The Autobiography*, Arrow Books, London, 2013, pp. 43–4.

11. Can't You Hear the Beat

233 I. Moulden-Gray, 'Two Sides of John Leyton' CD sleeve notes, Demon-Westside, 2000.

234 'They Seemed to Find Him Funny', *Hertfordshire Mercury*, 11 November 1960.

235 Con Walsh, 'He's the Daftest Yet', *Sunday Pictorial*, 25 September 1960.

236 Advertising poster for Screaming Lord Sutch at the Locarno, Swindon, 26 June 1960.

237 The Foresters interviewed by Pete Wilson, BBC Radio Gloucestershire, 2003.

238 Author interview with Norman Fowler, 25 June 2024.

239 Spencer Leigh, 'Obituary: Don Charles', *The Independent*, 9 December 2005.

240 David and Caroline Stafford, *Halfway to Paradise: The Life of Billy Fury*, Omnibus Press, 2018, p. 144.

241 'Leyton Songwriter Turns Singer', *Record Mirror*, 14 October 1961.

242 John Wells, 'TV Should Boost Iain', *Disc*, 25 November 1961.

243 Ray Coleman, 'It's Cheek to Cheek Meek! Joe Meek Owns Up', *Melody Maker*, 27 April 1963.

244 Chas Hodges and Dave Peacock, *Chas and Dave: All About Us*, John Blake, London, 2008, p. 52.

245 Author interview with Nigel Silk, February 2024.

Love and Fury: The Life, Death and Legacy of Joe Meek

246 Tony Kent, interviewed by Jim Blake and Chris Knight, c. 1974.
247 Author interview with Tony Grinham, July 2024.
248 Author interview with Mike Berry, June 2023.
249 Heinz Burt, interviewed by Jim Blake and Chris Knight, c. 1974.
250 Author interview with Peter Jay, February 2023.
251 Tony Kent, interviewed by Jim Blake and Chris Knight, c. 1974.
252 Author interview with Peter Jay, February 2023.
253 Kieron Tyler, 'Bobby Graham: Career', http://www.bobbygraham.co.uk/bobbygraham/career.htm.
254 Screaming Lord Sutch, interviewed by Jim Blake and Chris Knight, c. 1974.
255 Author interview with Mike Berry, June 2023.
256 Chas Hodges, interviewed by Jim Blake and Chris Knight, c. 1974.
257 Author interview with Peter Jay, February 2023.
258 Cliff Bennett, interviewed by Jim Blake and Chris Knight, August 1974.
259 Glenda Collins, interviewed by Jim Blake and Chris Knight, August 1974.
260 Chas Hodges, interviewed by Jim Blake and Chris Knight, c. 1974.
261 Peter Jones, 'Faith Plus Enthusiasm', *New Record Mirror*, 17 August 1963.
262 Heinz Burt, interviewed by Jim Blake and Chris Knight, c. 1974.
263 Chas Hodges interviewed by John Pickford for *The Joe Meek Story*, BBC Radio Bristol, 2009.
264 Tony Kent, interviewed by Jim Blake and Chris Knight, c. 1974.
265 Author interview with Mike Berry, June 2023.
266 Peter Jones, 'Faith Plus Enthusiasm', *New Record Mirror*, 17 August 1963.
267 Jane Gaskell, 'It Always Comes on Sunday for Mr Telstar!', *Daily Express*, 21 December 1962.

12. Something Better Beginning

268 Author interview with Roy Phillips, April 2023.
269 Author interview with Mike Berry, June 2023.
270 'Fantastic Orders for Leyton's "Wild Wind"', *Disc*, 30 September 1961.
271 Author interview with Mike Berry, June 2023.
272 'Ban Costs Leyton 100,000 Discs', *Disc*, 16 December 1961.
273 Clem Cattini, interviewed by Jim Blake and Chris Knight, c. 1974.
274 Ibid.
275 Ibid.
276 *Mersey Beat*, 23 May 1963.
277 'Topics for Teenagers', *Staffordshire Sentinel*, 23 October 1964.
278 'Scorpions Reunion', *Horley and Gatwick Mirror*, 16 January 1992.
279 Mike Sarne, quoted in the sleeve notes to *Come Outside with Mike Sarne*, RPM, 2002.
280 Author interview with Mike Berry, May 2019.
281 Peter Jones, 'Heinz – Is He Right?', *Record Mirror*, 9 March 1963.
282 'This is Much Better', *Luton News*, 1 March 1962.
283 'Outlaws New Waxing', *Pop Weekly*, 20 October 1962.
284 Chas Hodges, interviewed by Jim Blake and Chris Knight, c. 1974.
285 Ibid.

Notes

13. Telstar

286 'Record Rack', *Bucks Examiner*, 4 May 1962.

287 'Andy Cavell – a Singer by Chance!', *Record Mail*, June 1962.

288 'More Broadcasts via Telstar', *Liverpool Echo*, 24 July 1962.

289 Roderick Random, 'Disc Date – Then Back to His Toys', *Manchester Evening News*, 24 August 1962.

290 James Lee, 'Foggy Screen produces Clearcut "Telstar" Hit', *Washington Evening Star*, 23 November 1962.

291 'Acker's Away With Strings', *New Record Mirror*, 22 September 1962.

292 Mike Hellicar, 'Joe Meek, the Man Behind "Telstar" and Other Hits', *New Musical Express*, 23 November 1962.

293 'The Meek Magician', *Valentine*, 16 March 1963.

294 Jay McDowell, '5 Fascinating Facts About "Telstar" Producer Joe Meek', *American Songwriter*, 11 February 2024.

295 Geoff Goddard interview, BBC Radio Reading, 14 February 1983.

296 Mike Hellicar, 'Joe Meek, the Man Behind "Telstar" and Other Hits', *New Musical Express*, 23 November 1962.

297 Alan Goddard, 'Joe Has It All Taped', *Leicester Evening Mail*, 28 September 1962.

298 John Wells, 'We Still Can't Believe It', *Disc*, 15 December 1962.

299 'Discs', *Sunday Mirror*, 19 August 1962.

300 'New Singles', *Melody Maker*, 18 August 1962.

301 Author interview with Peter Jay, February 2023.

302 Author interview with Jess Conrad, November 2023.

303 Geoff Goddard, interviewed by Jim Blake and Chris Knight, c. 1974.

304 Peter Jones, 'Blackwell's Big 5', *New Record Mirror*, 16 September 1961.

305 Author interview with Stephen Komlosy, February 2019.

306 Author interview with Steve Howe, April 2024.

307 John Wells, 'Joe Meek Slammed the Door on John Leyton', *Disc*, 16 September 1961.

308 Tony Kaye, interviewed by Jim Blake and Chris Knight, c. 1974.

309 Author interview with Roy Phillips, April 2023.

310 Ian Dove, '£5,000 "Telstar" – and the Rumours Start', *New Record Mirror*, 13 October 1962.

14. There's Lots More Where This Came From

311 Author interview with Peter Jay, February 2023.

312 Ibid.

313 Ibid.

314 Wesley Laine, 'Britain's C&W Star - Houston Wells', *Record Mirror*, 12 January 1963.

315 Mike Hellicar, 'Joe Meek, the Man Behind "Telstar" and Other Hits', *New Musical Express*, 23 November 1962.

316 Tim Broun, 'Interview: Andrew Loog Oldham', *Perfect Sound Forever*, February 2013.

317 Alan Clayson, *The Rolling Stones: The Origin of the Species*, Chrome Dreams, New Malden, 2007, p. 156.

318 Peter Jones, 'The Odds Are Against You', *New Record Mirror*, 16 March 1963.

Love and Fury: The Life, Death and Legacy of Joe Meek

319 'Do It, Said Joe Meek', *Disc*, 8 December 1962.
320 'Guitar Greats: Ritchie Blackmore', BBC Radio 1, 1 March 1983.
321 Peter Jones, 'Heinz – Is He Right?', *Record Mirror*, 9 March 1963.
322 Jerry Bloom and Alan Whitman, 'The Ritchie Blackmore Interview', *Record Collector*, issue 228, August 1998.
323 Peter Jones, 'Heinz – Is He Right?', *Record Mirror*, 9 March 1963.
324 'New to You, the Puppets', *Pop Weekly*, 14 September 1963.
325 Norman Jopling, 'A Strange Story', *Record Mirror*, 21 September 1963.
326 'New to You, the Puppets', *Pop Weekly*, 14 September 1963.
327 Owen Adams, 'Joe Meek – Part 2 The Freakbeat Years', *Record Collector*, March 2007.
328 Jerry Bloom, *Black Knight: Ritchie Blackmore*, Omnibus Press, 2006, p. 33.
329 Jane Gaskell, 'It Always Comes on Sunday for Mr Telstar!', *Daily Express*, 21 December 1962.
330 Ibid.

15. Globetrotter

331 'The Voice of Pat Riley', *Newcastle Evening Chronicle*, 9 February 1963.
332 Thomas Alstone, 'A Tribute to Hank', *Bristol Evening Post*, 24 January 1963.
333 Ian Dove, '£5,000 "Telstar" – and the Rumours Start', *New Record Mirror*, 13 October 1962.
334 Geoff Goddard, interviewed by Mike Quinn, Radio 210, 14 February 1983.
335 Author interview with Mike Berry, June 2023.
336 Author interview with Mike Berry, May 2019.
337 Syd Gillingham, 'Going Up… Mike's New TV Career', *Sandwell Evening Mail*, 9 April 1981.
338 David Nicolson, 'The New Discs', *Gloucester Citizen*, 22 March 1963.
339 Author interview with Mike Berry, June 2023.
340 Author interview with Mike Berry, May 2019.
341 'New to You: The Carter, Lewis Boys', *Pop Weekly*, 1 December 1962.
342 Chas Hodges, interviewed by Jim Blake and Chris Knight, c. 1974.
343 Disker, 'Off the Record', *Liverpool Echo*, 8 June 1963.
344 Author interview with Peter Jay, February 2023.
345 Patrick Doncaster, 'Tornados on Test', *Daily Mirror*, 3 January 1963.
346 Screaming Lord Sutch, interviewed by Jim Blake and Chris Knight, c. 1974.
347 Larry Parnes taking about Joe Meek, *Sounds of the Sixties*, BBC Radio 2, 6 October 1990.
348 John Wells, 'The Rush Is On For That Tornados Job!', *Disc*, 5 January 1963.
349 Peter Jones, 'Faith Plus Enthusiasm', *New Record Mirror*, 17 August 1963.
350 Ray Coleman, 'It's Cheek to Cheek Meek! Joe Meek Owns Up', *Melody Maker*, 27 April 1963.
351 Cliff Bennett, interviewed by Jim Blake and Chris Knight, August 1974.
352 Mark Newson, 'The Ray Dexter Story', *Thunderbolt 47*, June 2006.
353 'Don't Kill the Beat Boom', unknown publication, 1963.
354 'Biography', www.mickunderwood.com (accessed January 2021).
355 Peter Jones, 'Starr's Midnighters', *Record Mirror*, 15 June 1963.

Notes

356 Richard Adams, 'Joe Meek Drops a Bombshell', May 1963.

16. Chills and Fever

357 Author interview with Mike Roberts, August 2023.
358 Stafford Hildred and Tom Gritten, *Tom Jones: A Biography*, Sidgwick & Jackson, London, 1990, pp. 29–31.
359 Author interview with Vernon Hopkins, August 2023.
360 Advertisement, *Pontypridd Observer, Leader and Free Press*, 26 October 1963.
361 Gerry G., 'News About the Senators', *Pontypridd Observer, Leader and Free Press*, 18 January 1964.
362 Author interview with Mike Roberts, August 2023.
363 Stafford Hildred and Tom Gritten, *Tom Jones: A Biography*, Sidgwick & Jackson, London, 1990, pp. 29–31.
364 Tom Jones, interview in the documentary film *Red, White and Blues*, 2003.
365 Joe Meek, 'Talking Point: That Controversial Record', unknown publication, 1965.
366 Tony Kent, interview, by Jim Blake and Chris Knight, c. 1974.
367 Author interview with Vernon Hopkins, August 2023.
368 Tom Jones, interview in the documentary film *Red, White and Blues*, 2003.
369 Tom Jones, *Over the Top and Back*, Michael Joseph, London, 2015, p. 115.
370 Author interview with Mike Roberts, August 2023.
371 Author interview with Pip Witcher, 6 October 2023.
372 Ibid.
373 Peter Jones, 'Heinz – Is He Right?', *Record Mirror*, 9 March 1963.
374 Eric Woodward, 'Heinz Does Exactly What He Did in the Film', *Birmingham Mail*, 1 May 1963.
375 Heinz Burt, interviewed by Jim Blake and Chris Knight, c. 1974.
376 Disker, 'On the Record', *Liverpool Echo*, 4 May 1963.
377 'Protest', Letters Page, *New Record Mirror*, 18 May 1963.
378 'Tornados', *Beat Monthly*, issue 1, May 1963.
379 Dick Tatham, 'The Night I Nearly Wept', *Rave*, December 1964.
380 Screaming Lord Sutch, interviewed by Jim Blake and Chris Knight, c. 1974.
381 Author interview with Roy Philips, April 2023.
382 Arthur and Eric Meek, interviewed by Jim Blake and Chris Knight, c. 1974.
383 Tony Kent, interviewed by Jim Blake and Chris Knight, c. 1974.
384 Author interview with Peter Jay, February 2023.
385 Author interview with Graham Sharp, January 2019.
386 Peter Blackmore, 'Ton Up Boy in Top Gear', *Gloucester Citizen*, 3 October 1963.

17. Just Like Eddie

387 Author interview with Roy Philips, April 2023.
388 John McCready, 'The Joe Meek Story', *Electronic Sounds*, February 2020.
389 ibid.
390 Leslie Thomas, 'My Lucky Star', *Evening News and Star*, 26 January 1963.
391 Peter Jones, 'Glenda's Fortune Told', *New Record Mirror*, 25 May 1963.

Love and Fury: The Life, Death and Legacy of Joe Meek

392 Glenda Collins, interviewed by Jim Blake and Chris Knight, c. 1974.

393 Mike Nevard, 'Spinning Disc', *Daily Herald*, 16 May 1963.

394 Disker, 'Off the Record', *Liverpool Echo*, 11 May 1963.

395 Ray Coleman, 'It's Cheek to Cheek Meek! Joe Meek Owns Up', *Melody Maker*, 27 April 1963.

396 Ibid.

397 Author interview with Peter Jay, February 2023.

398 'Threw Flour at Bus Queue', *Birmingham Daily Post*, 10 September 1963.

399 https://forgottenbands.blogspot.com/2010/10/mike-berry-outlaws.html

400 Freddie Starr with Alan Wightman, *Freddie Starr Unwrapped*, Virgin Books, 2002, p. 118.

401 Julian Holland, 'It's Gotta Have Soul', *Daily Mail*, 1964.

402 Author interview with Peter Jay, February 2023.

403 Ibid.

404 Paul Hazell, 'Biography: Houston Wells', www.soundclick.com

405 Ibid.

406 Author interview with Steve Howe, April 2024.

407 'Best Bets', *Cash Box*, 29 June 1963.

408 Jeff Touzeau, *Making Tracks: Unique Recording Studio Environments*, Schiffer Publishing, 2006, p. 163.

409 'Meek Collection Sells for £170,000, But No DB', 4 September 2008.

410 Author interview with Tony Grinham, July 2024.

411 Ibid.

412 Patrick Pink, interviewed by Jim Blake and Chris Knight, c. 1974.

413 Ibid.

414 John Wells, 'We'll Make it One Day, say Joy and Dave', *Disc*, 3 February 1962.

415 Singles reviews, *Record Mirror*, 7 December 1963.

416 Patrick Pink, interviewed by Jim Blake and Chris Knight, c. 1974.

18. Boy Trouble

417 'Comedian Remanded on Bail', *Aberdeen Evening Express*, 1 March 1962.

418 Brian Beacom, *The Real Stanley Baxter*, Luath Press, 2021.

419 Adrian Kerridge, *Tape's Rolling, Take One!,* M-Y Books, 2016, p 63.

420 Author interview with Graham Sharp, January 2019.

421 Chas Hodges, interviewed by Jim Blake and Chris Knight, c. 1974.

422 Adrian Kerridge, *Tape's Rolling, Take One!*, M-Y Books, 2016, p. 64.

423 Author interview with Mike Berry, June 2023.

424 Mark Newson, 'The Don Charles Story', *Thunderbolt 46*, Spring 2006.

425 Geoff Goddard interview, *The Very Strange Story of the Legendary Joe Meek*, *Arena* documentary, BBC TV, 1991

426 Arthur and Eric Meek, interviewed by Jim Blake and Chris Knight, c. 1974.

427 Heinz Burt, interviewed by Jim Blake and Chris Knight, c. 1974.

428 Dennis D'Ell, interviewed by Jim Blake and Chris Knight, July 1974.

429 Guy Fletcher, interviewed by Jim Blake and Chris Knight, c. 1974.

430 Screaming Lord Sutch, interviewed by Jim Blake and Chris Knight, c. 1974.

Notes

431 Kim Roberts, interviewed by Jim Blake and Chris Knight, c. 1974.

432 Chas Hodges, interviewed by Jim Blake and Chris Knight, c. 1974.

433 Jan Olofsson, 'Gunilla Thorne' [sic], *Thunderbolt* issue 7, October 1992.

434 'And It's Nice, I'n't It?', unknown publication, c. November 1963.

435 Andy Smart, 'Meek in Name, Wild in Nature', *Nottingham Evening Post*, 12 August 1997.

436 Brian Gibson, 'Sound Maker Meek On the Ball', *Disc*, 30 November 1963.

437 Maureen Cleave, 'Disc Date', *Evening Standard*, 28 September 1963.

438 Eric and Arthur Meek, interviewed by Jim Blake and Chris Knight, c. 1974.

439 Disker, 'Ding Dong Merrily on Disc', *Liverpool Echo*, 16 November 1963.

440 Author interview with Stephen Komlosy, February 2019.

441 Ibid.

442 Author interview with Ted Fletcher, May 2024.

443 Guy Fletcher, interviewed by Jim Blake and Chris Knight, c. 1974.

444 Author interview with Ted Fletcher, May 2024.

445 'Probable Hit for Mark', *New Record Mirror*, 10 October 1963.

446 Paul Nichols, 'Guy Fletcher: Man of Music', *M Magazine*. 29 December 2016.

447 Author interview with Ted Fletcher, May 2024.

448 Ibid.

449 'Record Review by Joe Meek', unknown publication, 1965.

450 Heinz Burt, interviewed by Jim Blake and Chris Knight, c. 1974.

451 Author interview with Robb Huxley, August 2024.

452 Letter from Joe Meek to Mr and Mrs Holder, February 1965.

453 Author interview with Robb Huxley, August 2024.

454 Ibid.

455 'Deke Arlon Jumped From Lionel Bart to Joe Meek', www.rockhistory.co.uk via YouTube.

19. Have I the Right?

455 Cliff Bennett interviewed by Jim Blake and Chris Knight, c. 1974

456 'Deke Arlon Jumped From Lionel Bart to Joe Meek', www.rockhistory.co.uk via YouTube.

457 'A Personal History of the British Records Business: Wayne Bickerton', www.vinylmemories.wordpress.com

458 Author interview with Steve Howe, April 2024.

459 Ibid.

460 'Indie British Disk Producers Spin to Golden heights as Majors Dig 'Em', *Variety*, 5 February 1964.

461 Pete Goodman, 'Instrument Fair', *Beat Instrumental*, October 1964.

462 http://www.watkinsguitars.co.uk/othersolids.htm

463 Larry Parnes taking about Joe Meek, *Sounds of the Sixties*, BBC Radio 2, 6 October 1990.

464 Author interview with Ken Howard and Alan Blaikley, October 2018.

465 Author interview with Ken Howard, 8 August 2023.

466 Author interview with Ken Howard and Alan Blaikley, October 2018.

467 Ibid.

468 Author interview with Ken Howard, 8 August 2023.

469 Ibid.

470 Ibid.

471 Author interview with Ken Howard and Alan Blaikley, October 2018.

472 Author interview with Ted Fletcher, May 2024.

473 Ray Coleman, 'Honey Hits Back!', *Melody Maker*, 5 September 1964.

474 Peter Jones, 'Of Course Honey Played on our Disc', *Record Mirror*, 17 October 1964.

475 Peter Wills, 'Ready…Go!', *Kentish Express*, 30 October 1964.

476 Jay Martin, 'Joe Meek – the Pop "Star" at the Control Panel', c. 1964.

477 Ibid.

478 Peter Murray, 'Spin a Disc', *Skelmersdale Reporter*, 11 June 1964.

479 Patrick Doncaster, 'Discs', *Daily Mirror*, 28 May 1964.

480 Ritchie Blackmore interviewed by Alexis Korner for 'Guitar Greats', BBC Radio 1, 6 March 1983.

20. Questions I Can't Answer

481 Alan Clayson, 'Geoff Goddard', *Record Collector,* June 1992.

482 Alistair Revie, 'Too Old at 30?', *Sunday Mail*, 23 August 1964.

483 Peter Aldersley, 'Discussion', *Pop Weekly*, 10 October 1964.

484 Author interview with Jess Conrad, November 2023.

485 Richard Green, 'Why Pick on Me? Asks Heinz', *New Musical Express*, 27 March 1964.

486 Author interview with Jess Conrad, November 2023.

487 'Honeycombs Tour', *Record Mirror*, 29 August 1964.

488 'British Hit Makers', *Cash Box*, 7 March 1964.

489 Author interview with Ken Howard, August 2023.

490 'Reflections on Our Pop Poll', *Pop Weekly*, 13 February 1965.

491 Rob Farmer, 'Honeycombs Hoping for Better Things', *Lincolnshire Echo*, 14 April 1965.

492 Dennis D'Ell, interviewed by Jim Blake and Chris Knight, 1974.

493 'Britain's Independent Producers', *Cash Box*, 26 December 1964.

494 Bill Neish, 'Spotlight Searches for Scots Talent', *Aberdeen Press and Journal*, 7 February 1964.

495 Ringo Starr, 'Blind Date', *Melody Maker*, 26 December 1964.

496 Author interview with Ken Howard and Alan Blaikley, October 2018.

497 Dave Dee, 'Where Are They Now', https://www.bbc.co.uk/totp2, 24 September 2014.

498 Patrick Doncaster, 'Discs', *Daily Mirror*, 1 November 1964.

499 Author interview with Graham Sharp, January 2019.

500 https://barnsburyboys.weebly.com/music---bill-pitt-jones.html.

501 Author interview with Steve Howe, April 2023.

502 Author interview with Pip Witcher, October 2023.

503 'Music Matters', *Coventry Observer*, 7 April 2022.

504 Author interview with Barry Kingsbeer, September 2023.

505 Author interview with Rob Cumner, September 2023.

Notes

506 Ibid.
507 Author interview with Barry Kingsbeer, September 2023.
508 Author interview with Rob Cumner, September 2023.
509 Author interview with Pip Witcher, October 2023.
510 Author interview with Rob Cumner, September 2023.

21. Nice While It Lasted

511 Single review, *Record Mirror*, 16 January 1965.
512 Jack Bentley, 'Discs', *Sunday Mirror*, 7 February 1965.
513 Author interview with Tony Grinham, July 2024.
514 Ibid.
515 Andy Smart, 'Meek in Name, Wild in Nature', *Nottingham Evening Post*, 12 August 1997.
516 Klemen Breznikar, 'David John and the Mood', *It's Psychedelic, Baby*, 9 December 2022.
517 Dennis D'Ell, interviewed by Jim Blake and Chris Knight, c. 1974.
518 Author interview with Tony Grinham, July 2024.
519 Author interview with Tamsin Embleton, July 2024.
520 'Talking Point', *Music Echo*, 15 May 1965.
521 'Discorner', *Buckinghamshire Examiner*, 21 May 1965.
522 Bob Farmer, 'In the Groove', *Gloucester Citizen*, 3 June 1965.
523 Joe Meek, 'Talking Point: That Controversial Record', 1965.
524 Author interview with Mike Roberts, 1 August 2023.
525 'Disctator Joe Meek', *The Sun*, 15 October 1965.
526 Letter from Tucker, Turner and Co. to W. A. Banks, Esq., dated 8 February 1979.
527 Author interview with Jess Conrad, November 2023.
528 Ibid.
529 Author interview with Jess Conrad, November 2023.
530 Ibid.
531 Ibid.
532 Michael Cox, interviewed by Jim Blake and Chris Knight, c. 1974.
533 Stan Reed, 'Joe's Our Top Pop Boffin', unknown publication, 1965.
534 Ray Coleman, 'It's Cheek to Cheek Meek! Joe Meek Owns Up', *Melody Maker*, 27 April 1963.
535 'Record Review', *Wishaw Press*, 4 June 1965.
536 George Harrison, 'More Cash in Industry Than is Pops', *Liverpool Echo*, 2 June 1965.
537 Spencer Leigh, obituary, *The Independent*, 8 September 2011.
538 Author interview with Paul Burns, March 2023.
539 Author interview with Rob Cumner, September 2023.
540 Author interview with Paul Burns, March 2023.
541 Ibid.

22. Wipe Out

542 Author interview with Ken Howard and Alan Blaikley, October 2018.

Love and Fury: The Life, Death and Legacy of Joe Meek

543 Author interview with Ken Howard, August 2023.

544 Patrick Doncaster, 'Tornados Galore', *Daily Mirror*, 27 May 1965.

545 Author interview with Robb Huxley, August 2024.

546 Letter from Joe Meek to Mr and Mrs Holder, February 1965.

547 Ibid.

548 Letter from Joe Meek to the Tornados, undated (c. 1966).

549 Author interview with Ken Howard, August 2023.

550 Ibid.

551 Author interview with Mike Berry, May 2019.

552 Author interview with Mike Berry, June 2023.

553 Heinz Burt, interviewed by Jim Blake and Chris Knight, c. 1974.

554 Samantha Milner, 'Down to Earth Life of Telstar's Hit Writer', *Reading Evening Post*, 27 February, 1991.

555 Author interview with Robb Huxley, August 2024.

556 Author interview with Paul Burns, March 2023.

557 Letter from Joe Meek to Paul Riviera, postmarked 4 January 1966.

558 Michael Housego, 'Telstar Joe Fights For His Royalties After Five Years', *Belfast Telegraph*, 29 January 1966.

559 Author interview with Ted Fletcher, May 2024.

560 Chas Hodges, interviewed by Jim Blake and Chris Knight, c. 1974.

561 Letter from Joe Meek to David Peters, postmarked 12 January 1966.

562 David Peters, *The Original Thunderbolt*, issue 37, Spring 2009.

23. Please Stay

563 Author interview with John Pickford, September 2024.

564 Arthur and Eric Meek, interviewed c. 1974.

565 Author interview with Paul Burns, March 2023.

566 Mark Newson and Rob Bradford, 'The Glenda Collins Story', *Thunderbolt 73*, February 2015.

567 Dennis D'Ell interviewed by Jim Blake and Chris Knight, July 1974.

568 'Tax Trial That Cost £150,000 Ends', *The Guardian*, 18 May 1966.

569 Letter from Joe Meek to Keith Becket, Thank Your Lucky Stars, c. 1966.

570 Roger J. Simmonds, *Standing on the Sidelines*, Candy Jar Books, 2016.

571 John McCready, 'The Joe Meek Story', *Electronic Sounds*, February 2020.

572 Screaming Lord Sutch, interviewed by Jim Blake and Chris Knight, c. 1974.

573 Author interview with Tamsin Embleton, July 2024.

574 Letter from Joe Meek to Roger Bruton, undated, c. September 1966.

575 Letter from Joe Meek to Jonathan King, 23 March 1966.

576 'Joe Meek Finds the Answer For the Beatles' *Melody Maker*, 1966.

577 Ibid.

578 George Robinson, 'From Bumblies to Cryin' Shames', www.triumphpc.com/mersey-beat/a-z/bumblies-cryin'shames4.shtml.

579 Letter from Joe Meek to Derek Cleary, undated, c. 1966. Reproduced in *Thunderbolt 69*, October 2013.

580 Heinz Burt, interviewed by Jim Blake and Chris Knight, c. 1974.

Notes

581 Ibid.

582 Letter from Joe Meek to Heinz Burt, dated 14 April 1965.

583 Letter from Joe Meek to Heinz Burt, undated (c. 1966). From the collection of John Pickford.

584 Heinz Burt, interviewed by Jim Blake and Chris Knight, c. 1974.

585 Author interview with Paul Burns, March 2023.

586 Author interview with Robbie Duke, 2018.

587 https://davidfarrant.org/he-heard-a-new-world

588 Author interview with Tony Grinham, July 2024.

24. It's Hard to Believe It

589 Dennis D'Ell, interviewed by Jim Blake and Chris Knight, July 1974.

590 Letter from Joe Meek to the Tornados, undated, c. August 1966.

591 Ibid.

592 Author interview with Paul Burns, March 2023.

593 'Pick of the Week', *Reading Evening Post*, 6 August 1966.

594 Eric and Arthur Meek, interviewed by Jim Blake and Chris Knight, c. 1974.

595 Ted Fletcher, 'Meek Remembered', *joemeek.com* (archived at https://web.archive.org).

596 Author interview with Robb Huxley, August 2024.

597 Author interview with Tony Grinham, July 2024.

598 Author interview with Norman Fowler, June 2024.

599 Mark Newson, 'The Geoff Goddard Interview', *Thunderbolt 30*, October 2000.

600 Author interview with Robb Huxley, August 2024.

601 Jim Johnstone, 'On the Pop Scene', *Dalkeith Advertiser*, 8 December 1966.

602 Author interview with Nigel Silk, February 2024.

603 Ibid.

604 Author interview with Robb Huxley, August 2024.

605 Ian Watson, 'A Meeting with Eric Meek', *Thunderbolt* issue 11, summer 1994.

606 Sandra Meek-Williams talking to Pete Wilson, *Joe Meek Special*, BBC Radio Gloucestershire, 12 February 2017.

607 Ibid.

608 Kim Roberts, interviewed by Jim Blake and Chris Knight, c. 1974.

609 Michael Batory, 'Memories of Joe', *Thunderbolt 6*, spring 1992.

610 Vic Keary interviewed by Jon Pickering.

611 Patrick Pink, interviewed by Jim Blake and Chris Knight, c. 1974.

612 Letter from Evelyn Meek to Joe Meek, postmarked 2 February 1967. Reprinted in *Thunderbolt 81*, October 2017.

25. Nobody Waved Goodbye

613 Author interview with Robb Huxley, August 2024.

614 Sylvia Knight, 'Success is Forecast for Singing Barber', *Brentwood Gazette*, 1 November 1968.

615 Patrick Pink (aka Robbie Duke), interviewed by Jim Blake and Chris Knight, c. 1974.

Love and Fury: The Life, Death and Legacy of Joe Meek

616 'Pop Tune Man Believed "Spies" Were Stealing His Tunes', *Evening News and Chronicle*, 9 March 1967.

617 'Top of the Pops Composer and a Wife Shot Dead', *Evening Standard*, 3 February 1967.

618 'Pop Tune Man Suspected Spies, Inquest is Told', *Belfast Telegraph*, 9 March 1967.

619 Heinz Burt, interviewed by Jim Blake and Chris Knight, c. 1974.

620 Author interview with Tony Grinham, July 2024.

621 Screaming Lord Sutch, interviewed by Jim Blake and Chris Knight, c. 1974.

622 Dennis D'Ell, interviewed by Jim Blake and Chris Knight, July 1974.

623 Brian Dixon, 'Woman "Dies as She Tried to Save Pop Man"', *Daily Sketch*, 4 February 1967.

624 Author interview with Paul Burns, March 2023.

625 Chas Hodges, interviewed by Jim Blake and Chris Knight, c. 1974.

626 Author interview with Robb Huxley, August 2024.

627 Denis Hoare, 'A Woodie Speaks', *Tales From the Woods*, issue 84, April 2015.

628 'Pop Man, Woman Die in Shooting', *Manchester Evening News*, 3 February 1967.

629 Jack Greenslade, 'Fade Out of a Pop Man', *Daily Mail*, 4 February 1967.

630 John McCready, 'The Joe Meek Story', *Electronic Sounds*, February 2020.

631 Patrick Pink (aka Robbie Duke), interviewed by Jim Blake and Chris Knight, c. 1974.

632 'Pop Tune Man Suspected Spies, Inquest is Told', *Belfast Telegraph*, 9 March 1967.

633 'Drug "May Have Made Man Murder"', *Daily Mirror*, 10 March 1967.

634 Author interview with Tony Grinham, July 2024.

635 Ibid.

636 Author interview with Steve Howe, April 2024.

637 'Pop Writer and Woman Shot', *Liverpool Echo*, 3 February 1967.

638 Richie Routledge at the Chattanooga Film Festival, 3 April 2014.

639 Author interview with Alan Wilson, July 2024.

640 Author interview with Jess Conrad, November 2023.

641 Ibid.

642 Author interview with Nigel Silk, February 2024.

643 Author interview with Ken Howard and Alan Blaikley, 2018.

644 Dennis D'Ell, interviewed by Jim Blake and Chris Knight, July 1974.

645 Charles Blackwell, interviewed by Jim Blake and Chris Knight, c. 1974

26. Guess That's the Way It Goes

646 'Shot Pop Man: Inquest Opens', *Evening News*, 8 February 1967.

647 'Pop Tune Man Suspected Spies, Inquest is Told', *Belfast Telegraph*, 9 March 1967.

648 Joe Meek's death certificate, dated 10 March 1967.

649 Ibid.

650 'Pop Writer Shot Woman then Himself', *Reading Evening Post*, 9 March 1967.

651 'Pop Tune Man Suspected Spies, Inquest is Told', *Belfast Telegraph*, 9 March 1967.

652 'Drug "May Have Made Man Murder"', *Daily Mirror*, 10 March 1967.

653 'Pop Man Believed Spies Were Stealing His Tunes', *Manchester Evening News*, 9 March 1967.

654 Author interview with Tamsin Embleton, July 2024.

Notes

655 'Drug "May Have Made Man Murder"', *Daily Mirror*, 10 March 1967.
656 Robbie Duke (Patrick Pink), interviewed by Jim Blake and Chris Knight, c. 1974.
657 'Pop Man Believed Spies Were Stealing His Tunes', *Manchester Evening News*, 9 March 1967.
658 'Coroner Told of Gun Bought in South Devon', *Herald Express*, 9 March 1967.
659 'Pop Tune Man Suspected Spies, Inquest is Told', *Belfast Telegraph*, 9 March 1967.
660 'Pop Writer Shot Woman then Himself', *Reading Evening Post*, 9 March 1967.
661 Joe Meek "Thought He Was Spied On"', *Evening Standard*, 9 March 1967.
662 John McCready, 'The Joe Meek Story', *Electronic Sounds*, February 2020.
663 Ibid.
664 'Mystery Surrounds Reason For Holloway "Pop" Shootings', *Islington Gazette*, 14 March 1967.
665 'Pop Man Believed Spies Were Stealing His Tunes', *Manchester Evening News*, 9 March 1967.
666 Philip Finn, 'Pop Star's Gun Plea', *Daily Express*, 10 March 1967.
667 Author interview with Ted Fletcher, May 2024.
668 'Shooting Mystery Delays Comeback by Honeycombs', *Walthamstow Guardian*, 9 February 1967.
669 Don Short, 'The Strange Reason for Honey's Silence', *Daily Mirror*, 30 March 1967.
670 Glenda Collins, interviewed by Jim Blake and Chris Knight, c. 1974.
671 Author interview with Joy Adams, May 2024.
672 Author interview with Robb Huxley, August 2024.
673 Author interview with Tony Grinham, July 2024.
674 Letter from Evelyn Meek to John Ginnett, undated, c. 1967. Reproduced in *Thunderbolt 83*, June 2018.
675 Author interview with Howard S. Berger, August 2024.
676 '"Telstar" Dispute Agreement, *The Guardian*, 8 February 1968.
677 Arthur and Eric Meek interviewed by Jim Black and Chris Knight, c. 1974.

27. Don't You Know

678 Author interview with Tamsin Embleton, July 2024.
679 Steve Richards, 'Record Week', *Scunthorpe Evening Telegraph,* 17 November 1979.
680 'Music on the Move', *Runcorn Guardian*, 9 November 1979.
681 James Belsey, 'Pops', *Bristol Evening Post*, 16 April 1977.
682 Author interview with Peter Jay, February 2023.
683 Nigel Fountain, 'The Joe Meeks Shall Not Inherit', *The Guardian*, 2 February 1991.
684 Ibid.
685 Press release, 'University celebrates Music legend Geoff Goddard', 24 May 2013.
686 Author interview with Howard S. Berger, August 2024.
687 'Tornados Profit at Last', *The Stage*, 14 June 1990.
688 'Tornados Head for Legal Whirlwind', *The Stage*, 23 September 1993.
689 Author interview with Steve Howe, April 2024.
690 'Obituary', *The Guardian,* 1 September 1999.
691 Duncan Eaton, 'Family's Anger at Heinz Burt Film's Gay Slur', *Southern Daily Echo*, 19 June 2009.

692 Author interview with Norman Fowler, June 2024.
693 Letter from Robbie Duke to Simon Jordan and Nick Moran, 2008. https://filmboards. com/board/t/Open-letter-from-Patrick-Pink-678520/
694 Alun Palmer, 'Telstar Man', *Daily Mirror*, 25 August 2007.
695 Chas Hodges, interviewed by Jim Black and Chris Knight, c. 1974.
696 Author interview with Roy Phillips, April 2023.
697 Author interview with Norman Fowler, June 2024.
698 Author interview with Peter Jay, February 2023.
699 Robin Murray, 'Cherry Red Acquire Joe Meek Unreleased Archive', *Clash Magazine*, 2 September 2020.
700 Author interview with Alan Wilson, July 2024.
701 Ibid.
702 Author interview with Russell Caligari, July 2024.
703 Huw Thomas, 'Angular Saxons', *Shindig* issue 153, July 2024.
704 Author interview with Alan Wilson, July 2024.

Index

A.H. Shenton Leather Goods 85–6

Adams, Dave 45–7, 53, 50–1, 60–1, 84, 89, 127, 132, 144, 149, 153, 169, 194, 210, 223, 298, 316

Adams, Joy 22, 45–7, 50–1, 60–1, 75, 87, 101, 104, 210, 223, 334

Alan Dean and His Problems 249–50

Angela Jones 68–9, 71–2, 73, 76, 79, 81, 108

Arden, Don 131, 195, 202, 203, 222, 294

Arlon, Deke 229–30

Arnéz, Chico (Jackie Davies) 41, 44, 52, 231

Atlantic Showband, the 190, 254

Bad Penny Blues 30–1

Banks, Wilfred Alonzo (Major) 56–7, 74–5, 78, 85, 96, 99, 149, 195, 233, 257, 264, 275, 304, 310, 344

Barber, Chris 39, 52, 137

Barrington-Coupe, William (Barry) 57–8, 72, 73–5, 78, 264, 289–90, 304, 310

Barry, John 54, 105, 123, 126

Bart, Lionel 101–2, 229

Bassey, Shirley 30

Batory, Mike 284, 314, 326

Beatles, the 31, 35, 40, 141–2, 161, 167, 171, 172, 176–7, 181–3, 184, 204, 205–6, 217, 230, 232, 240, 293, 294–5, 304–5

Bellamy, George 135, 146, 152, 177, 274–5, 340

Benjamin, Louis 237, 246

Bennett, Cliff 89, 93, 99, 132, 138, 143, 182, 263

Berger, Howard S. x, 336, 342

Berry, Chuck 115, 231, 232

Berry, Mike 88–90, 91–3, 99, 104, 111–2, 115, 117–8, 130, 131–2, 134–5, 136–7, 138, 145–6, 153, 172–5, 175–6, 196, 203, 209, 216, 278–9, 284, 316, 347

Best, Pete 230

Blackmore, Margit 320, 326

Blackmore, Ritchie 164–5, 168, 192, 202–3, 209, 240, 264, 266, 283, 298, 311, 320

Blackwell, Charles 40, 44, 54–5, 60, 69, 71, 75, 103, 110–1, 114, 121, 126, 127, 132, 138–9, 145, 146, 151, 156, 196, 220, 221, 230, 265, 278, 284

Blaikley, Alan 234–6, 242–3, 246–7, 249–50, 272, 273, 278, 284, 287, 296, 328–9

Blake, Jim 96, 189, 319, 320, 329

Blue Notes, the 204–5

Blue Rondos, the 252–3, 310

Bolan, Marc ix, 347

Boswell, Eve 74

Bowie, David ix, 208–9, 333, 347

Boy With the Eyes of Blue, the 77–8

Boyd, Colin 288, 305

Brown, Joe 118, 131, 184

Love and Fury: The Life, Death and Legacy of Joe Meek

Bruton, Roger 292–3

Burns, Paul (Christopher Barnes) 269–71, 280–1, 288, 298, 323–4

Burt, Heinz 1, 55, 96, 97, 130, 133–5, 136, 137, 139–140, 144, 152, 158, 174, 178–9, 184, 190, 191–4, 195, 196–7, 198–9, 201–2, 208, 217–8, 220, 224, 227, 230, 232, 239, 243–5, 252, 259–60, 265, 269, 271, 274, 276, 277, 279–80, 281, 296–8, 310, 316, 321, 322, 324, 326–7, 332, 339, 340–1, 344–5, 347

Buzz, the 284–5

Caddy, Alan 67, 133, 135, 153, 179, 211, 274, 302, 340

Caligari, Russell viii, 80–1, 349

Calvert, Reg 133–4, 136, 162, 257, 302–3

Cameos, the (the Fletchers) 223–4

Camps, Professor Francis 331, 332

Can Can '62 131, 159–161, 176

Cannon, Judy 273–4

Carson, Chad 192, 318, 321

Carter-Lewis 144, 256, 291

Cattini, Clem viii–ix, 118, 120, 126, 133, 135, 140–1, 145, 146, 150, 153–5, 157, 172–3, 211, 225–6, 233, 240, 258, 266, 275, 276, 339–40, 346

Cavaliers, the (the Blue Men) 60, 66–67, 142

Cavell, Andy 148–150, 191, 194, 196, 203, 207, 278

Chakiris, George 63–4, 76, 85

Charles Kingsley Combo, the (the Thunderbolts) 207

Charles, Don 126, 216, 274–5, 284, 291, 302

Checkmates, the 54, 106, 180, 223

Chicanes, the (the Money Spiders) 255–6, 257

Chris Williams and his Monsters 61–2, 101

Christian, Chad (Christine Chadwick) 239–40

Christian, Neil 85, 163–4, 258

Clayton, Curly 251, 252, 275

Cleary, Derek 295–6

Cleave, Maureen 107–8, 220

Cliff Bennett and the Rebel Rousers 106–7, 108, 143, 144, 151, 182, 184, 240, 284, 339

Cochran, Eddie 201, 202, 316

Cole, Graham 303, 343

Collins, Glenda 105, 132, 163, 200–1, 202, 225, 287–8, 296, 298, 305, 333–4, 347, 348

Conrad, Jess 76, 118, 167, 208, 244–5, 265–7, 274, 328, 339

Cooper, Cliff 280, 318, 346–8

Cox, Michael 62, 68–9, 71, 73–4, 75, 79, 81, 82, 85, 95, 115, 124, 133, 137, 167, 224–5, 256, 265, 267, 284, 339

Crane, Paul 296, 305

Cryin' Shames 288–9, 293–4, 295–6, 305–6, 327, 348

Cumner, Rob 255–6, 271

Dangerfield, Tony 198, 239, 325

Danny's Passion 285–6, 347

Dave Dee, Dozy, Beaky, Mick and Tich (Dave Dee and the Bostons) 250, 296

David John and the Mood 260–1, 262, 348

Davies, Ray ix, 272, 347

Davis, Billie (Carol Hedges) 137–8, 171, 211

Davis, Derek 15, 16–7

de Rouffignac, Peter 85

de Ville, Gerry 268

Dean, Billy (Billy Gray / Mark Douglas) 93, 162, 192

D'Ell, Dennis 218, 234, 236, 247, 288, 323, 329, 333, 339

Dexter, Ray 182

Diane and the Javelins 272

Do You Come Here Often? 246, 290–1

Doncaster, Patrick 90, 99, 174

Donegan, Lonnie 29, 30, 39, 59, 75, 92

Don't You Think It's Time 105, 172–4

Dowlands, the 136, 158, 222

Dylan, Bob 293, 289, 261

Eddie, Jason (Albie Wytcherley) 268–9, 319

Index

Embelton, Tamsin 53, 262, 292, 331, 348
Epstein, Brian 141–2, 181–3, 184, 185, 194, 203, 214, 217, 229, 259, 261, 293–5, 306, 334
Everett, Kenny 299
Every Little Kiss 172–3, 175–6
Eyes 246–7
Faith, Adam 39, 137, 303
Fame, Georgie (Clive Powell) 101–2, 118
Farewell Performance 179, 191–2, 199
Farrant, David 299–300
Flee-Rekkers, the (the Fabulous Flee-Rakkers) 63, 77, 82, 93, 106, 108, 118, 135, 159, 248, 252, 258, 267
Fletcher, Guy 218, 224–5, 236, 274, 302
Fletcher, Ted 224–5, 236, 282–3, 302, 306, 332
Fletchers, the (vocal trio) 225, 236, 282, 284, 291
Flip and the Dateliners (the Davernettes) 88, 197, 214–5, 251–2
Ford, Emile 54, 59, 106, 180
Fordyce, Keith 61, 82, 105
Foresters, the 122–3
Fortune, Lance 55, 93, 121
Fowler, Norman (Sammy Bowne) 123–6, 308, 345, 346
Freddie Starr and the Midnighters 183, 199, 203–4, 238
Fury, Billy 118, 120, 127, 133, 139–140, 148, 152, 159, 167, 177, 179, 211, 219, 222, 335
Garfield, Johnny 254
Gemini', the 274–5
Gerry and the Pacemakers 141, 171, 181, 249, 295
Ginnett, John 304, 306, 330–2, 335–6
Glastonbury, John 185–7
Globetrotter 172–3, 177, 241
Goddard, Geoff 67, 97, 102–6, 108, 109–112, 114–5, 117, 126–7, 132, 135, 137, 138–9, 145, 151, 154, 156, 158, 162, 171,

172, 173, 199–200, 201, 211, 216, 219, 222, 223, 231, 232, 242–3, 265, 275, 278, 332, 341–2
Godfrey, Raymond 185–8
Good, Jack 63, 68–9, 76, 91–2, 103, 113, 115, 117
Graham, Bobby (Bobbie) 48, 89, 93, 116, 120, 130, 131
Graham, Kenny 38, 54, 57, 112
Gray, Lissa 110
Green Door, the 38
Gregory, Iain 73, 103, 127, 139
Grinham, Tony ix, 129, 209, 210, 216, 259–60, 261–2, 300–1, 308, 322, 327, 339
Hale, Norman 135, 142, 152
Hall, Leslie 296, 298–9
Harvey, Ken 66–67
Have I the Right? 234, 235, 236, 237, 242–3, 246, 247, 278, 341
Hawker, Ken (Carter-Lewis) 106, 175
Hawkins, Reg 89, 93, 94, 132
Hendrix, Jimi 193, 240
Hinsley, Harvey 240, 283
Hodges, Chas 36–37, 89, 93, 94, 96, 100, 114, 128–9, 132–3, 134–5, 137, 146–7, 165, 176, 179, 199, 201–2, 204, 215, 218, 283–4, 324, 346, 350
Holder, Pete 227, 276–8, 318
Holder, Roger 227, 276–8, 307, 311, 319
Holland, Tony 175
Holly, Buddy 47–48, 78, 93, 94, 103–4, 111, 116–7, 134, 137, 209, 260, 299, 301, 316, 322
Hollywood, Kenny 162–3
Honeycombs, the 144, 167, 176, 218, 234–8, 249–50, 257, 272, 273, 281, 285, 288, 333, 339, 347
Hopkins, Vernon 186–9
Howard, Ken 234–6, 242–3, 246–7, 249–50, 272, 273, 278, 284, 287, 296
Howard, Lional 22–4, 35–36, 40–2, 51, 65, 85, 100, 144, 149, 196, 215, 216–7, 334

377

Love and Fury: The Life, Death and Legacy of Joe Meek

Howe, Steve 29, 157, 206–7, 231–2, 252, 253, 268, 327, 343–4

Humperdinck, Engelbert 142

Huxley, Robb 227–8, 276, 278, 307–8, 310, 318, 324, 334–5

I Hear a New World vii, 43, 52, 64–68, 94, 144, 154, 158, 347

I Lost My Heart at the Fairground 200–1

Impac, the 308–9, 318, 328,

International Broadcasting Company (IBC) 21–27, 30–31, 32, 34, 46, 53, 63

Irwin, Bryan 211, 240, 245, 258, 340

Jack the Ripper 184, 302

Jay, Peter (drummer) 87–8, 130–1, 132, 155, 159–161, 175–7, 197, 205–6, 341, 346–7

Jay, Peter (singer, Peter Lynch) 60, 81, 85

Jillette, Doris 175

Johnny Kidd and the Pirates 67, 133

Johnny Leyton Touch, the 127–8, 137, 139

Johnny Remember Me 108, 109–115, 135, 138, 341

Jones, Carol 74, 77

Jones, Tom 31, 40, 142, 185–190, 262–4, 323, 339,

Joy and Dave 49–51, 60, 82–3, 101, 103, 112, 143

Juke Box Jury 100, 105, 113

Just Like Eddie 201–3, 217–8, 341

Kaye, Dave 219, 239, 260

Keary, Vic 27, 315–6

Keating, Johnny 76–7

Kelly, Brian (DCI) 331, 332

Kelly, Clive 261

Kennedy, Terry 106

Kent, Tony 62, 78–9, 101, 129, 130, 134, 157, 197

Kerridge, Adrian 24–6, 27, 30, 32, 34, 35, 36, 54, 214, 216, 243, 339

King, Jonathan 293

King, Maurice 294

Kingsbeer, Barry 255–6

Kingston, Bob 102–3, 224

Klein, Alan 146

Knight, Chris 96, 189, 319, 320, 338–9

Komlosy, Stephen 70, 156–7, 221–2

Kray, Reggie 294, 306–8, 324

Kray, Ronnie 294, 306–8, 323–4

Kruger, Jeff 73, 106, 162

Kuy, Bill 89, 93, 128, 130, 132, 133

Lantree, Anne 'Honey' 234, 237, 247

LaVern, Roger 97, 152, 153, 222, 274–5, 333

Lawrence, Derek 283, 284, 291, 302

Lay Down Your Arms 30, 33

Ledrut, Jean 177–8, 282, 336

Lee, Brenda 203, 252

Lennon, Jimmy 190–1, 223

Lennon, John 107 (footnote), 142, 173, 181–2, 222, 294

Les Paul and Mary Ford 49

Lewis, Jerry Lee 107, 191, 194

Leyton, John 62, 69–71, 73, 74, 75–6, 78, 79–80, 82, 88, 103, 109–112, 113–4, 118, 120, 122, 126, 127, 135, 137–9, 141, 145–6, 158, 174–5, 195, 220–1, 256, 264–5, 278, 284, 339, 341–2, 347, 348

Life in the Death of Joe Meek, A 336, 342–3

Little Richard 92, 240

Live It Up! 192–3, 198, 348

Lockwood, Sir Joseph 110, 111, 175, 259, 264, 306, 312, 314, 315

Lone Rider 105, 106, 108, 145

Loog Oldham, Andrew 162–3, 243

Love and Fury 142–3, 152

Lundgren, Ken 146–7, 165, 195, 203

Lyttelton, Humphrey 30–1, 61, 339

Marriott, Steve 192–3, 273, 284

Martin, George viii, 49–50, 66, 101, 103, 123, 126, 141–2, 207, 249, 295, 306

Martin, Tab 146, 179, 194, 196, 202, 209

Masters, Valerie 257

McCartney, Paul 31, 142, 181–2, 217, 222

McNamara, Tom 320–1, 326

Meek, Alfred George (Joe's father) 1–6, 11–12, 14

Index

Meek, Arthur 2–3, 7, 10, 11, 13, 14, 20, 22, 39, 110, 196, 315, 326, 335, 336, 339

Meek, Eric 2–3, 7–8, 10, 11, 18, 20, 22, 39, 196, 260, 287–8, 304, 311–2, 319–20, 323, 335, 336, 337, 339

Meek, Evelyn 'Biddy' (Joe's mother) 1–4, 6, 14, 312, 316–7, 326, 335–6

Meek, Marlene (Marlene Williams) 18, 24

Meek, Pamela 4, 8, 14, 335, 337

Meek, Robert George 'Joe'

arrest ix, 215–8, 219, 220, 222, 223, 229, 233, 235, 242–3, 259, 274, 308

dance MC and mobile DJ 9, 14–5

drug use 34–35, 54, 219, 235–6, 261–2, 281, 311, 328, 331

early experiments with electronics 7, 8–9, 10, 11

early life 1, 4–10

homosexuality 3, 13, 18–20, 22–4, 46, 60, 82, 104, 125, 128–9, 181, 213–8, 313, 344–5

interest in spiritualism and the occult 14, 47, 92, 99–100, 103–4, 111, 116, 213, 281, 298–9, 300–1

mental health viii, 52, 233, 282, 292, 304, 322, 323

national service 12–13

songwriting 42, 46–7, 48–50, 53, 58, 60–1, 81–2, 94, 98, 120, 143–4, 174, 176, 182, 199, 200, 272

temper 3, 24, 35, 52, 87, 88, 104, 114, 129, 130, 137, 140, 147, 160, 173, 182, 186, 188, 189–90, 194, 217, 219, 225–6, 253, 254, 257, 269, 276, 282, 309, 312, 315, 321, 323–4, 328, 332

work as sound engineer 21–2, 24–7, 28–33, 53–4, 140–1

working in Gloucester 15–20, 21 (footnote)

Meek-Williams, Sandra 1, 8–9, 89, 312

Miller, Gary 28, 29, 33, 48

Miller, Jimmy 40–3, 47, 83

Mitchell, Mitch 193, 323

Moontrekkers, the 29, 119, 142

Morgan, Davy 261

Morley, Julia (Wally Stott) 53–4

Moseley, Len 296, 298–9

Moss, Jenny 175–6, 193, 225

Murray, Martin 234, 237, 247, 333

Newell, Norman 70, 298

Nicholas, Paul 241

Oliver, Bernard 313–4, 325

Olofsson, Jan 211–12

O'Neil, Terry 97, 204, 212, 218, 227, 228, 235, 285, 334, 347

Outlaws, the 68, 93, 99–101, 110, 116, 128, 129–130, 133, 134, 146–7, 148, 150, 151, 164–5, 168, 182, 191, 193, 194, 199, 201, 212, 223, 283, 284

Packabeats, the 165–6, 175

Page, Jimmy 164, 187, 274, 298, 344

Paramor, Norrie 40, 127

Parnes, Larry 40, 49, 55, 76, 82–3, 118, 120, 133, 139–140, 148, 152, 159, 162, 177, 203, 211, 222, 229, 233–4, 335

Partridge, Andy 350

Peter Chris and the Outcasts 274, 291

Peter Jay and the Jaywalkers 118, 141, 152, 155, 159, 176–7, 199, 205–6, 241

Philips, Roy 23, 85, 136, 158, 194, 198, 226

Pink, Patrick (Robbie Duke) 209–10, 212, 252, 260, 299, 306, 308, 315, 316, 317, 319–22, 325–6, 331–2, 334, 344–5, 347

Pitney, Gene 238, 316

Pitt, Kenneth 148

Pitt, Roy 175–6, 315–6, 323

Pitt-Jones, Bill 252–3

Please Stay 288–9

Poor Joe 106, 143–4, 337

Presley, Elvis 35, 76, 91, 98, 137, 171, 177, 191, 192, 219, 229, 260

Preston, Denis 27–8, 29, 31–2, 34, 35, 36, 37–8, 39, 40–2, 43, 47, 48–9, 51–3, 54, 59, 61, 75, 304, 339

Puppets, the 166–7

Put a Ring on Her Finger 49, 52, 55, 144
Ramblers, the 219–20
Randall, Ray 240, 340
Raymond, Peter (Peter Yaquinandi) 91, 93, 100
Raymonde, Ivor 151, 164, 272, 274, 287
Reader, Pat 77–8
Ready Steady Go! 198, 250, 303, 305–6
Richard, Cliff 51, 98, 102, 103, 137, 171, 181
Richards, Harvey 298, 311, 312, 315
Rio, Bobby 273–4, 333
Riot Squad, the 163, 281, 284, 311, 313, 316, 333
Rivers, Danny 76, 107, 108, 144, 175, 298, 324
Robb Gayle and the Whirlwinds 227–8, 276
Roberts, Kim 194, 218, 223, 226, 312, 320
Roberts, Mike 186–190
Robot, the 148 (footnote), 179, 191
Rolling Stones, the 131, 163, 167, 206, 232, 238, 243, 288
Ross, Bobby 230, 316
Routledge, Ritchie 293–4, 296, 305, 327–8
Rowe, Dick 79, 93, 159
Saga Records 56–7, 62, 64, 71–2, 106
Saints, the 194, 198–9, 203, 209, 220, 227, 240
Sands, Wes 163
Sarne, Mike 145, 152, 156, 221, 339
Saxons, the 233, 276–8, 280
Scales, Gerry 319
Shade Joey and the Night Owls 248–9
Shadows, the (the Drifters) 49, 51, 102, 105, 135, 137, 147, 158, 159, 165, 195
Shakespeare, John (Carter-Lewis) 106, 175
Shane Fenton and the Fentones 118, 152–3, 159
Shane Spencer and the Casuals 231, 243
Shanks, Thomas Edwin Southey 195–6, 264, 269, 296–7, 304, 310
Sharades, the 223
Sharp, Graham 197, 214–5, 251–2

Sharpe, Pip 218, 227, 292, 297
Shelton, Anne 30, 33
Shenton, Albert 238, 311, 320, 325, 330, 336
Shenton, Robb (Robb Deka) 166–7, 319, 334
Shenton, Violet 97, 147, 238, 269–70, 311, 320–3, 326, 327, 328, 330, 332, 338, 345, 350
Silk, Nigel 309, 328
Silver, Eddie 49–50, 216
Simmonds, Roger J. 290, 333
Sizzlin' Hot 40–1, 42, 44, 144
Slavin, Martin 112–3
Small Faces, the 131, 193
Smith, Mike 187, 230
Sorrows, the 254–5, 257
Sounds Incorporated 159, 194, 263
Space Walk 274–5
Spector, Phil viii, ix, 130, 157, 225–6, 343
Stagg, Allen 22, 26, 27, 32
Starr, Freddie 183–4
Starr, Ringo 249
Status Quo 208, 347
Steele, Tommy 49, 55, 59, 91, 118, 133
Stewart, Rod 40, 119
Stigwood, Robert 69–71, 73, 82, 103, 109, 111–2, 114, 121, 126–7, 138, 139, 140, 145–6, 155–6, 163, 171, 173–5, 220–2, 229, 264–5, 275, 279, 312, 314
Sutch, David 'Screaming Lord' 98, 119, 121–2, 146, 164, 177, 184, 193, 206, 215, 218, 239, 241, 261, 292, 299, 302–3, 322, 339, 340, 344, 347, 348
Sutton, Lee 215
Swingin' Low 100–1
Syndicats, the 231–2, 253, 268, 343
Taylor, Stuart 240, 258, 340
Taylor, Vince 121
Tea Chest tapes vii, ix, 78, 87, 280, 310, 346–9
Tell Laura I Love Her 74, 76, 78, 79–80, 82

Index

Telstar 150–2, 153–5, 157, 158, 162, 168, 169, 172, 174, 179, 180, 199, 216–7, 232, 275, 281, 282, 303, 312, 323, 336, 337, 339, 343

Telstar: The Joe Meek Story 344–6, 349

Temple, Gerry (Keith De Groot) 94–5, 171–2, 175

Temptation Baby 194–5, 221

Thorn, Gunilla 67, 211–12, 219

Tommy Scott and the Senators 185–90, 262, 347

Top Rank 75–6, 78, 79, 80, 81, 93,112, 135

Tornados, the viii, 1, 137–8, 139–140, 142–3, 148, 152–155, 158, 159, 168, 174, 175, 177–9, 180, 191, 193, 196, 200, 207, 219, 224, 231, 240–1, 244, 245–6, 252, 258, 266, 267–8, 274, 283, 290–1, 299, 303–4, 306–8, 310–11, 319, 320, 324, 327, 334–5, 339, 343, 347, 348

formation 127–8, 133–5

line-up changes 152, 178–9, 211, 222, 240, 258, 267, 276, 279–280

recording 'Telstar' 153–4

Tribute to Buddy Holly 115–8, 138, 172, 174

Triumph Records 57–8, 59–72, 73–9, 81, 82, 83, 95, 101, 106, 127, 158

Underwood, Mick 164–5

Vaughan, Frankie 38, 59, 95

Ventura, Toby 171–2, 175

Venus in Blue Jeans 173

Ver Schure, Ed 309–10

Victor, Tony 148–9

Vincent, Gene 129 (footnote), 137, 167, 191, 193–5, 198–9, 202, 203, 221, 224

Ward, Kingsley 207

Watts, Dave 307–8, 311, 319

Wayne, Ricky 62, 74, 76, 79, 82, 95, 230

Weedon, Bert 105, 306

Wells, Houston 161–2, 206, 243, 323

What Do You Want to Make Those Eyes at Me For? 53–4

Wild Boys, the (the Wild Ones) 196, 240, 243, 277

Wild Wind 117, 135, 137

Wilde, Marty 55, 59, 68–9, 115, 118, 126, 211

Wilson, Alan 328, 348, 350

Windsor, Tony 298–9, 325

Witcher, Philip 'Pip' 190–1, 254–5, 256–7

Yolanda (Yolande Bavan) 38, 58, 62, 73